Health Labor Market Analyses in Low- and Middle-Income Countries

DIRECTIONS IN DEVELOPMENT
Human Development

Health Labor Market Analyses in Low- and Middle-Income Countries

An Evidence-Based Approach

Richard M. Scheffler, Christopher H. Herbst, Christophe Lemiere, and Jim Campbell, Editors

WORLD BANK GROUP

Contents

Boxes

Figures

Tables

Foreword

The Sustainable Development Goals (SDGs) set out an agenda of unprecedented ambition, not just with respect to the health goal of ensuring healthy lives for all at all ages but also in relation to the Goals on poverty, nutrition, education, gender, and employment, to which the health system and health workers also contribute.

The related health workforce needs are enormous. A collaboration among the World Bank, the World Health Organization (WHO), and research partners estimates that the health workforce requirement to accelerate progress toward universal health coverage must overcome a potential deficit of 15 million health workers by 2030, the majority of these in low- and middle-income countries (LMICs). At the same time population growth, demographic and epidemiological transitions, and economic growth are creating additional demand for social and health care. Both the population need and the economic demand for health workers will be equally challenged by the existing constraints on the technical and financial resources available to educational institutions to produce the future health workforce of the necessary quantity, quality, and relevance. This mismatch poses a threat to the stability of health systems and global health security and may be further exacerbated due to increasing trends in the migration of health personnel.

Fortunately, a more sophisticated understanding of the root causes of these imbalances is emerging. The chronic underinvestment in education and training of health workers and the mismatch between education strategies in relation to health systems and population needs are resulting in continuous and alarming shortages and periodic swings between over- and undersupply, in countries at all levels of socioeconomic development. These are compounded by difficulties in deploying domestic-trained health workers to rural, remote, and underserved areas. Moreover, distribution and retention challenges contribute to labor mobility across countries. But the phenomenon of labor mobility is not only international: internal and intersectoral mobility, and loss of health workers to other sectors, continue to affect equitable access to health services within countries.

Steering an effective response by health systems to navigate the complexity of increasingly interconnected national and global health labor markets requires that countries build data management, analytical, and planning capacity to develop human resources for health (HRH) policy and strategies that quantify and match health workforce needs, demands, and supply under different future scenarios.

This extensive collation of tools and data needs for health labor market analyses in low- and middle-income countries provides pragmatic guidance and concrete examples to address many of the challenges. It offers planners and policy makers practical approaches to how they can assess the labor market capacity to recruit, deploy, and retain health workers; explore health worker preferences and motivation drivers; and develop the most appropriate workforce deployment, remuneration, and retention strategies through financial and nonfinancial interventions.

Devising and implementing effective strategies to optimize health labor markets is key to improved health workforce availability, accessibility, and performance—a prerequisite for the attainment of universal health coverage and health goals more broadly. In addition, there is potential to link this work to employment, fiscal, and education policies that can unlock economic growth potential through the creation of employment opportunities and decent jobs, making the health sector a key contributor to economic growth and socioeconomic development at large.

Tim Evans
Senior Director
HNP Global Practice
World Bank Group

Foreword

Health care is essentially about people and has memorably been described by Sir Muir Gray as being a "human contact sport." The great ambitions of the SDGs, and especially universal health coverage, can simply not be achieved without an adequate workforce and everything that goes with it: from education and training to conditions of employment and the working environment.

The health workforce is a complex and difficult area that exemplifies the fact that we need always to think about health and health care in systems terms—any change anywhere affects everything else. Tweak job descriptions or salaries for one group of staff or increase the numbers being trained and there will be knock-on effects everywhere else in the system. Moreover, as we know from migratory flows of health workers from poorer to richer countries, we are not simply talking about national systems here but about global ones. Actions by planners in countries anywhere in the world may impact on anywhere else. Decisions about workforce issues are subtle and sophisticated, and the potential for costly mistakes is enormous.

Much recent innovation in the health workforce has come from low- and middle-income countries (LMICs), which, without the resources of the richer countries, have innovated and adapted. Many countries have found new ways of educating their health workforce; created community health workers, clinical officers, and other "mid-level" workers; and created new ways to engage people in their own health care. Some of these approaches have found their way to high-income countries and are informing the development of new cadres and approaches worldwide. Biological and information and communications technologies and advances will accelerate these changes.

Health policy makers and planners can draw on this rich tradition and these more recent developments as they plan for the future. This timely and cutting-edge book will be useful in guiding them on the types of data and tools needed to develop health workforce interventions that are based on evidence for maximum impact. Written by people with vast experience at the local, national, and global level, the book discusses and presents in an accessible way the different methodologies and strategies that can be applied to carry out both comprehensive and more targeted health labor market assessments.

Such assessments are critical in generating a better understanding of health workforce issues and informing the development and implementation of evidence-based solutions toward meeting the SDGs.

Lord Nigel Crisp

Member of House of Lords

Chair of the All Party Parliamentary Group on Global Health

Acknowledgments

This book was developed jointly by the World Bank, the World Health Organization (WHO), and the University of California, Berkeley. The process was led by Christopher H. Herbst (senior health specialist) from the World Bank, with collaborative input from Richard M. Scheffler (professor), University of California, Berkeley; Christophe Lemiere (program leader), World Bank; and Jim Campbell (director), WHO. The editors are grateful to Carmen Carpio (senior health specialist), Akiko Maeda (lead health specialist), Son Nam Nguyen (lead health specialist), and Tamer Sabah Rabie (lead health specialist) from the World Bank for providing constructive comments on the final version of the book. The team also thanks Olusoji Adeji (director), Mickey Chopra (lead health specialist), Tim Evans (senior director), Trina Haque (practice manager), and Ernest Massiah (practice manager) from the World Bank, as well as Agnes Soucat (director) from WHO, for their overall guidance and support. Last but not least, a special thank you goes to Rumit Pancholi, who led the production management from the World Bank side; Hope Steele (consultant at Steele Communications) for her editing support; Daniel Arnold, Grayson Dimick, and Angela Kline from the Nicholas C. Petris Center at the University of California, Berkeley, who were also instrumental in editing chapters; and program manager Kati Phillips, who assisted with coordinating multiple rounds of drafts of this final version.

About the Contributors

About the Editors

Jim Campbell is the director of the Health Workforce Department at WHO and the executive director of the Global Health Workforce Alliance, a hosted partnership established at WHO in 2006 with a 10-year mandate to support actions on the health workforce crisis in LMICs. His role at WHO has included the development of and a global consultation on the *Global Strategy on Human Resources for Health: Workforce 2030* for submission to the 69th World Health Assembly and support to the High-Level Commission on Health Employment and Economic Growth, an initiative to inform multisectoral engagement on the Global Strategy. Before joining WHO and the Global Health Workforce Alliance, he spent eight years as the founder/director of a nonprofit research institute. He authored *A Universal Truth: No Health Without a Workforce* (2013) and two *State of the World's Midwifery* reports (2011 and 2014).

Christopher H. Herbst is a senior health specialist at the World Bank's Health, Nutrition, and Population Global Practice. He has worked in more than 25 low- and middle-income countries in Africa, Asia, and the Middle East. On an operational level, he manages grant and lending operations covering both health and education sectors. His research focuses primarily on health systems in low- and middle-income countries, in particular health workforce issues as they relate to health labor market dynamics, health professional education, community-based service delivery, and the assessment of health workforce performance. His research has been widely published and presented, and he has served on expert panels including at the World Health Organization and the African Development Bank. Prior to joining the Bank, he worked as a researcher for the U.K. government and the Washington, DC Department of Health. Herbst received a BA from King's College London, an MSc from the London School of Economics and he pursued a PhD, with a focus on health labor markets, at Lancaster University (U.K.).

Christophe Lemiere is a World Bank program leader for Health, Social Protection, and Education in West Africa. Before this, he was a senior health specialist at the World Bank, having spent more than a decade working on and in developing country contexts, mostly Sub-Saharan Africa. Before his time at the Bank,

Lemiere worked as a hospital manager for several years in France, as well as an international consultant focusing on issues related to health services management (including hospital reforms) and human resources issues, his two specific areas of expertise. Lemiere holds an MS in health economics from Paris University and an MBA from Harvard University.

Richard M. Scheffler is a distinguished professor of health economics and public policy at the School of Public Health and the Goldman School of Public Policy at the University of California, Berkeley, and holds the endowed chair in healthcare markets and consumer welfare. In 2003, Scheffler served as the elected president of the International Health Economics Association. He has been a visiting professor at a number of universities, including the London School of Economics and Charles University in Prague, and at the Departments of Economics at the University of Pompeu Fabra in Barcelona and Carlos III University of Madrid, Spain. Scheffler has been a visiting scholar at the World Bank, the Rockefeller Foundation in Bellagio, and the Institute of Medicine at the National Academy of Sciences. He has been a consultant for the World Bank, WHO, and the Organisation for Economic Co-operation and Development. Scheffler has been a Fulbright Scholar at Pontificia Universidad Católica de Chile in Santiago and at Charles University. He was awarded the Chair of Excellence Award at the Carlos III University of Madrid in 2013. In 2015, Scheffler was awarded the Gold Medal at the Charles University for his long-standing and continued support of international scientific and educational collaboration. In 2016, he was awarded the Astor Visiting Lectureship at Oxford University. He earned his PhD in economics with honors at New York University.

About the Foreword Authors

Tim Evans is the senior director of the Health, Nutrition, and Population Global Practice at the World Bank. From 2010 to 2013, Evans was the dean of the James P. Grant School of Public Health at BRAC University in Dhaka, Bangladesh, and a senior advisor to the BRAC Health Program. From 2003 to 2010, he was the assistant director-general at the WHO. Before that, he served as the director of the Health Equity Theme at the Rockefeller Foundation. Earlier in his career, he was an attending physician of internal medicine at Brigham and Women's Hospital in Boston and was an assistant professor of international health economics at the Harvard School of Public Health. He is a board member of a number of international health alliances. Evans has been at the forefront of advancing global health equity and strengthening health systems delivery for more than 20 years. At the WHO, he led the Commission on Social Determinants of Health and oversaw the production of the annual *World Health Report*. He has been a cofounder of many partnerships, including the Global Alliance on Vaccines and Immunization, and has contributed to efforts to increase access to HIV treatment for mothers and innovative approaches to training community-based midwives in Bangladesh.

Evans received his MD from McMaster University in Canada and was a research and internal medicine resident at Brigham and Women's Hospital. He earned a DPhil in agricultural economics from the University of Oxford, where he was a Rhodes Scholar.

Lord Nigel Crisp is an independent member of the House of Lords, where he cochairs the All Party Parliamentary Group on Global Health. He was the chief executive of the National Health Service in England—the largest health organization in the world—and the permanent secretary of the U.K. Department of Health between 2000 and 2006. Crisp chairs Kings Partners Global Health Advisory Board, the Zambia U.K. Health Workforce Alliance, and the Uganda U.K. Health Alliance. He is a senior fellow at the Institute for Healthcare Improvement, an honorary professor at the London School of Hygiene and Tropical Medicine, and a foreign associate of the National Academy of Medicine. He was formerly a distinguished visiting fellow at the Harvard School of Public Health and regents' lecturer at the University of California, Berkeley. His books include *Turning the World Upside Down*, *African Health Leaders* (edited with Francis Omaswa), and *One World Health*.

About the Authors

Edson C. Araújo is a senior economist at the World Bank's Health, Nutrition, and Population Global Practice. At the World Bank he works primarily on health workforce issues. His work includes the analysis of health labor markets and the synergies between health workforce compensation and health financing policies, the assessment of health workforce performance and incentives, and the application of stated preference methods to elicit health workers' employment preferences. Over the past few years he has provided technical assistance and policy advice to governments in low- and middle-income countries in Africa, Latin America, and Asia. Before joining the World Bank he worked as a health economist at University College London, the Brazilian Ministry of Health, and the Federal University of Bahia (Brazil). He graduated with a degree in economics from the Federal University of Bahia and specialized in health economics at the University of York (United Kingdom) and Queen Margaret University (United Kingdom).

Tim Bruckner is a professor of public health in the Department of Planning, Policy, and Design at the University of California, Irvine. He has been a professor since 2009. He earned an MPH in epidemiology and biostatistics and a PhD in epidemiology, both at the University of California, Berkeley. Bruckner is a population health scholar who examines how communities respond to ambient changes in the environment, including policy changes. His scholarly activities related to the health care workforce involve the application of epidemiologic methods to estimate the population's need for health care. He has collaborated with international and state health agencies to conduct research at the intersection of epidemiology and health policy.

Health Labor Market Analyses in Low- and Middle-Income Countries
http://dx.doi.org/10.1596/978-1-4648-0931-6

Jean Damascène Butera is a country project director at the Health Finance and Governance Project, with 16 years of experience in health system strengthening. He has focused on human resources for health, community-based health insurance schemes, malaria control issues, and governance. In his technical role as human resources for health advisor, he supported and provided strategic guidance for the establishment of state-specific human resources for health policies, structures, and systems. As community-based health insurance advisor, he assisted developing countries with developing schemes and scale-up strategies. Butera holds a master's degree in public health from the National University of Rwanda. His country experience includes Benin, Ethiopia, Guinea, Ivory Coast, Kenya, Nigeria, Rwanda, Tanzania, and Uganda. He has more than 10 years of administration, finance, and management experience in different settings.

Robert Cohen is a preventive medicine physician at the U.S. Army Public Health Command. His work for the Army focuses on primary prevention and tropical medicine, including HIV and Ebola, as well as health economics and cost-effectiveness analyses. He also works as a consultant to the WHO, conducting statistical analyses of determinants of maternal and child mortality in developing countries. He received an MD from Columbia University and an MPH from Johns Hopkins University.

Atef El Maghraby is currently leading WHO's health systems strengthening portfolio in Iraq. Before that, he was chief health analyst at the African Development Bank. Maghraby is an expert in global health with an emphasis on human resources for health, service delivery, and health systems strengthening. His focus is on promoting greater value for money through investments in medical education, institutional capacity, and health policy development. He has a strong profile in designing and managing health programs and technical assistance on a large scale in more than 25 countries in Africa, the Middle East, and South Asia. Before joining the African Development Bank, Maghraby worked for the United Populations Fund, WHO, and the European Commission. He holds an MD and an MA.

Wanda Jaskiewicz is a program director at IntraHealth International; with 20 years of experience in global health and development. She has focused on human resources for health, HIV/AIDS, family planning, and reproductive health. In her technical role as a senior health workforce advisor, she supports national stakeholders in strengthening human resource management systems to effectively develop, recruit, retain, and support the health workforce for increased access to quality health services. She has developed evidence-based tools to build organizational capacity in developing costed rural recruitment and retention strategies, as well as improving health workforce productivity and performance. She holds an MPH in international health and development from the Tulane University School of Public Health and Tropical Medicine and has field experience in more than 25 countries.

Eric Keuffel is a specialist in health finance and policy with more than 18 years of experience in industry, policy, and academic roles in health economics, finance, and operations. An expert on international health systems and pharmaceutical policy, he has served as an assistant professor and instructor at both the Wharton School at the University of Pennsylvania and at the Fox School of Business at Temple University. He has published in health policy and health economic journals and books and has presented his research at numerous international and domestic conferences. Keuffel has served as a consultant to the World Bank/International Finance Corporation and has extensive commercial consulting experience advising pharmaceutical industry clients on strategy, policy, and economic issues. He has taught graduate and undergraduate courses in health finance, health policy, and international health systems. Recent consulting engagements include work for multinational pharmaceutical clients, the U.S. Agency for International Development, the World Bank, WHO, the Gates Foundation, and the Rockefeller Foundation. He earned a bachelor's degree in economics from Princeton University, an MPH from the Johns Hopkins Bloomberg School of Public Health, and a doctorate in applied health economics and finance from the Wharton School at the University of Pennsylvania. Prior funding sources include the U.S. National Institutes of Health and the National Bureau of Economic Research.

Kenneth Leonard is an applied development economist with expertise in Africa and a focus on human capital services in the rural economies of developing countries. His research deals primarily with the delivery of health care in Africa, particularly the role of institutions in mitigating the adverse consequences of asymmetric information. This has led him to research in peer effects and social networks as well as the role of nongovernmental organizations in the provision of public services—particularly services characterized as credence goods. He usually collects his own data, choosing field sites and research teams and designing his own surveys and experiments. He lived in Tanzania from 2001 to 2002 and collected data through 2003. In 2005 and 2010 he returned to Tanzania to collect more data on health workers. In 2010 he spent time in Malawi implementing a study on competitiveness on another National Science Foundation–funded project, using specifically designed laboratory experiments. Most recently he spent his sabbatical leave in Tanzania, working with researchers and policy makers in Dar es Salaam.

Tomas Lievens (Oxford Policy Management) is an experienced health economist with expertise in quantitative research, health financing, health labor markets, and health insurance. He carried out several health expenditure reviews, tracking surveys, and costing studies, often to inform health financing strategies. Currently he works on sustainable financing for health and HIV services and researches health worker motivation and behavior to improve health labor market outcomes. Previously he was an International Labour Organization regional advisor in Africa and advisor to the Belgian minister for international development, and he consulted with Philippe Naert. He holds a master's degree in engineering from the Catholic University of Leuven (Belgium) and a master's degree in economics from the University of Nottingham (United Kingdom).

Jenny Liu is an assistant professor of health economics, specializing in global health. Her research lies in the intersection of health economics, economic development, and population health with the overarching aim of improving the delivery and utilization of reproductive, maternal, neonatal, child, and adolescent health services in developing counties. She conducts programmatic and policy-relevant research in four focal areas: (1) designing and evaluating of interventions aimed at encouraging behavior change, including applications of behavioral economics theories; (2) assessing the introduction of new health devices and technologies designed for underserved populations in new markets and populations; (3) generating evidence to support global and local workforce policy, with a particular focus on deepening the health workforce cadre diversity and understanding how lower-skilled (both formal and informal) providers can effectively deliver basic services in underserved communities; and (4) examining the human capital investments needed to ensure long-run health and well-being among adolescents and young adults during the transition to adulthood. To achieve these goals, she uses a multitude of methods, including conducting rigorous experimental and quasi-experimental analyses of primary and secondary data, and executing integrated qualitative-quantitative mixed-methods studies to answer complex social and behavioral problems. She also consults for international nongovernmental organizations and multilateral organizations on global health policy, data systems to support monitoring and evaluation, and program design and implementation.

Ottar Mæstad is an economist with a research focus on global health, human resources for health, quality of health care, health systems, health policy, governance in the health sector, the ethics of priority setting, and health and economic development. He has also worked on climate policy and energy issues, and on international trade and development. He has wide experience in research, research management, and policy analysis. He has led a number of research projects for clients such as the OECD, the Norwegian Ministry of Foreign Affairs, the Norwegian Agency for Development Cooperation, the World Bank, the Hewlett Foundation, Statoil, the Norwegian Shipowners Association, and the Research Council of Norway.

Genta Menkulasi is a PhD candidate in economics at the University of Delaware. Her fields of specialization are health economics, economic growth, public finance, and applied econometrics. She is currently a principal statistician at Capital One in the Credit Risk Management Department. Before joining Capital One, she worked as a consultant for the World Bank and Aga Khan Foundation.

Health Labor Market Analyses in Low- and Middle-Income Countries
http://dx.doi.org/10.1596/978-1-4648-0931-6

Çağlar Özden is a lead economist in the Development Research Group's Trade and Integration team. He received his undergraduate degrees in economics and industrial engineering from Cornell University and his PhD in economics from Stanford University. Before joining the World Bank six years ago, he was on the faculty of the Economics Department at Emory University. His research explores the nexus of globalization of product and labor markets, government policies, and economic development. He has published numerous papers in leading academic journals that have explored the dynamics of protectionist trade policies, the adverse consequences of unilateral trade preferences, and the placement of highly educated migrants in unskilled jobs in the U.S. labor market—the "brain waste" effect. His most current research explores the role of diasporas and social networks on migration flows and patterns; the performance of migrants in the destination labor markets; links between migration, trade, and foreign direct investment flows; and causes of the migration decisions of physicians from Sub-Saharan Africa. He has edited three books on migration, remittances, brain drain, and their impact on economic development. The latest, *International Migration, Economic Development, and Policy*, was published in 2007 by the World Bank and Palgrave Macmillan.

David Phillips is a research assistant professor for the Wilson Sheehan Lab for Economic Opportunities in the Department of Economics at the University of Notre Dame. His research focuses on poverty, particularly as it relates to low-wage labor markets, crime, and health care staffing. His research has been published in high-quality economics field journals, and he has presented his work widely, including at the Michigan Sentencing Policy Commission, the World Bank, and the Ghana Ministry of Health. He joined the Lab for Economic Opportunities in July 2016. Before coming to Notre Dame, Phillips received a bachelor's degree from Butler University and a PhD in economics from Georgetown University and worked for four years at Hope College in Holland, Michigan.

Alex S. Preker is the president and CEO of the Health Investment & Financing Corporation in New York. He is an active investor and member of the board of several health care companies. Preker also serves as one of the commissioners for the Global Commission on Pollution, Health, and Development and as the chair of the External Advisory Committee of the International Hospital Federation's *World Hospital and Health Services Journal*. From 2007 to 2012, Preker was head of the Health Industry Group and Investment Policy for the IFC. Previously, he was chief economist for the health sector at the World Bank. Preker has published extensively, having written many scientific articles and authored more than 15 books. He is an executive scholar and adjunct associate professor at the Icahn School of Medicine at Mount Sinai, New York; an adjunct associate professor of public policy at New York University's Robert F. Wagner Graduate School of Public Policy; and an adjunct associate professor for health care management at the Mailman School of Public Health at Columbia University. His training includes a PhD in economics from the London School of Economics and Political

Science; a fellowship in medicine from University College London; a diploma in medical law and ethics from King's College, London; and an MD from the University of British Columbia.

Anthony Scott leads the Health Economics Research Program at the Melbourne Institute of Applied Economic and Social Research at the University of Melbourne, and jointly coordinates the University of Melbourne Health Economics Group. He has a PhD in economics from the University of Aberdeen. Scott is a National Health and Medical Research Council principal research fellow. He is an associate editor of the *Journal of Health Economics* and of *Health Economics*. He leads the Centre of Research Excellence in Medical Workforce Dynamics. Funded by the National Health and Medical Research Council, the Centre runs a large nationally representative panel survey of physicians: Medicine in Australia: Balancing Employment and Life. Scott's research interests focus on the behavior of physicians, the health workforce, incentives and performance, and primary care.

Pieter Serneels is an associate professor and reader in economics at the University of East Anglia. His research focuses on development, behavioral, and labor economics. He codirects the Centre for Behavioural and Experimental Social Sciences at the University of East Anglia. Serneels obtained his PhD from the University of Oxford, and worked at the University of Oxford, the University of Copenhagen, the World Bank, and the International Labour Organization. He has given extensive advice to governments and policy makers and has published widely in peer-reviewed journals and books. He is a research fellow at the Institute of Labor (IZA), the Centre for the Study of African Economies, and the Oxford Department of International Development, and he is a full member of the European Development Network and Evidence in Governance and Politics.

Agnes Soucat is the director for Health Systems Financing and Governance at the WHO. Before this, she was the director for human development for the African Development Bank, where she was responsible for health, education, and social protection for Africa, including 53 countries in Sub-Saharan Africa and the Maghreb. Previously she worked at the World Bank, where she variously served as lead economist and advisor to the director for human development for Africa and advisor to the director for health. She has been leading the Health Systems for Outcomes program of the Africa Region, a program focused on health systems strengthening to reach the Millennium Development Goals (MDGs). Soucat has more than 25 years of experience in international health, directly covering more than 30 countries in Africa, Asia, and Europe. She is a public sector and public finance specialist, and has worked extensively on designing and implementing community-based financing programs, poverty reduction strategies, social services decentralization, and performance-based financing. She has been responsible for multisectoral and results-based budget support programs, covering sectors such as agriculture, education, health, water, and energy, and focusing on reaching the MDGs in several countries, particularly Rwanda. Soucat was a coauthor of the *Poverty Reduction Strategy (PRSP) Toolkit* and the *World Development Report 2004: Making Services Work for Poor People*, as well as a main author of the background reports to the High-Level Task Force on Innovative Financing. She was a member of the Global Expert Team on Health Systems of the World Bank. Before joining the Bank she worked for the Joint United Nations Programme on HIV/AIDS, the United Nations Children's Emergency Fund, and the European Commission. She holds an MD and a master's in nutrition from the University of Nancy in France, and an MPH and PhD in health economics from Johns Hopkins University.

Joanne Spetz is a professor at the Institute for Health Policy Studies and in the Department of Family and Community Medicine and the School of Nursing at the University of California, San Francisco (UCSF). She is associate director for research strategy at the UCSF Center for the Health Professions and director of the UCSF Health Workforce Research Center. Her fields of specialty are labor economics, public finance, and econometrics. She has led research on the health care workforce, the organization of the hospital industry, the impact of health information technology, the effect of medical marijuana policy on youth substance use, and the quality of patient care. Spetz's teaching is in the areas of quantitative research methods, health care financial management, and health economics. She is a member of the Institute of Medicine Standing Committee on Credentialing Research in Nursing and was a consultant to the Institute of Medicine Committee on the Future of Nursing. She frequently provides testimony and technical assistance to state and federal agencies and policy makers. Spetz received her PhD in economics from Stanford University after studying economics at the Massachusetts Institute of Technology. She is an honorary fellow of the American Academy of Nursing.

Kate Tulenko has worked at the highest levels of health workforce, health financing, and health policy development with institutions around the world. She has been an advisor to national governments on health policy and reform and served on expert panels for the World Bank, WHO, the Regional Office for Africa (WHO), the American Public Health Association, the Global Health Workforce Alliance, and the American Hospital Association, among others. She has published on a wide array of topics. Her most recent book is *Insourced: How Importing Jobs Impacts the Healthcare Crisis Here and Abroad*, published by Dartmouth College Press. She holds academic appointments at the Johns Hopkins School of Public Health and the George Mason University College of Health and Human Services. Tulenko holds an MD and MPH from Johns Hopkins University, and an MPhil from the University of Cambridge, Emmanuel College.

Yah M. Zolia is the deputy minister for Planning, Research, and Development at the Ministry of Health, Republic of Liberia, and also lectures on a part-time basis at the A. M. Dogliotti College of Medicine, University of Liberia. She holds an MS

Health Labor Market Analyses in Low- and Middle-Income Countries
http://dx.doi.org/10.1596/978-1-4648-0931-6

in parasitology and immunology from the University of Nairobi, Kenya, and has more than 14 years' working experience in areas of research, policy, and strategic planning; human research development; health finance; and monitoring and evaluation in the health sector. She led the development of the 10-year National Health and Social Welfare Plan of the Ministry of Health and Social Welfare (2011–21) and, more recently, had oversight for the development of the post-Ebola Investment Plan for Building a Resilient Health System in Liberia (2015–21).

Abbreviations

2SLS	two-stage least squares
AMA	American Medical Association
ARIMA	autoregressive integrated moving average
CO	clinical officer
DALY	disability-adjusted life year
DCE	discrete choice experiment
DHS	Demographic and Health Surveys
DID	difference in differences
DPT	diphtheria, pertussis, and tetanus
ERF	Economic Research Forum
FAIMER	Foundation for Advancement of International Medical Education and Research
GDP	gross domestic product
GMM	generalized method of moments
GVAP	Global Vaccine Action Plan
HIV/AIDS	human immunodeficiency virus/acquired immune deficiency syndrome
HLM	health labor market
HNP	Health, Nutrition, and Population (sector of the World Bank)
HRH	human resources for health
HWIS	Health Workers Incentive Survey
ICT	information and communication technology; item count technique
IFC	International Finance Corporation
iHRIS	Integrated Human Resources Solutions
ILO	International Labour Organization
IMG	international medical graduate
IPUMS	Integrated Public Use Microdata Series
ISCO	International Standard Classification of Occupations
IV	instrumental variable

LATE	local average treatment effect
LFS	labor force survey
LIC	low-income country
LIS	Luxembourg Income Survey
LMICs	low- and middle-income countries
LSMS	Living Standards Measurement Survey
MABEL	Medicine in Australia: Balancing Employment and Life
MCV	meningococcal vaccine
MDGs	Millennium Development Goals
MENA	Middle East and North Africa
NBER	National Bureau of Economic Research
NGO	nongovernmental organization
NHMRC	National Health and Medical Research Council
NIH	National Institutes of Health
OECD	Organisation for Economic Co-operation and Development
OLS	ordinary least squares
OPD	outpatient department
OWW	Occupational Wages around the World
PETS	Public Expenditure Tracking Survey
PSM	propensity score matching
RCT	randomized control trial
RDD	regression discontinuity design
RRT	randomized response technique
SDGs	Sustainable Development Goals
SEDLAC	Socioeconomic Database for Latin America and the Caribbean
SOPs	standardized operating procedures
STD	sexually transmitted disease
UHC	universal health coverage
UN	United Nations
UN DESA	United Nations Department of Economic and Social Affairs
UNICEF	United Nations Children's Fund
USAID	United States Agency for International Development
WFME	World Federation for Medical Education
WHO	World Health Organization
WHO-AIMS	World Health Organization-Assessment Instrument for Mental Health Systems

All monetary amounts are U.S. dollars unless otherwise indicated.

Tools and Data Needs to Guide Evidence-Based Policy Making on Human Resources for Health

Christopher H. Herbst, Jim Campbell, Richard M. Scheffler, and Christophe Lemiere

Introduction

The health workforce has received major policy attention over the past decade, driven in part by the need to achieve the Millennium Development Goals (MDGs) and more recently the Sustainable Development Goals (SDGs) and universal health coverage (UHC). There is wide acceptance that a health workforce sufficient in numbers, adequately distributed, and well performing is a central health systems input, and critical for the achievements of these goals.

The recently published *Global Strategy on Human Resources for Health: Workforce 2030* offers a vision to accelerate progress toward UHC and the SDGs by ensuring universal access to health workers (WHO 2016). The vision incorporates the ambition of the *2030 Agenda for Sustainable Development*, adopted by the UN General Assembly in September 2015. SDG goal 3 aims to: "Ensure healthy lives and promote wellbeing for all at all ages" by 2030. Closely linked to this is SDG target 3.8, which is directed towards achieving Universal Health Coverage (UHC). The importance of the health workforce in the context of the SDGs sits in goal 3, target 3.c, which aims to: "Substantially increase health financing and the recruitment, development, training and retention of the health workforce in developing countries, especially in least developed countries and small island developing states" (table O.1). The target reflects the global recognition that countries, across all income groups, are facing similar challenges in delivering an evidence-based response to address or strengthen the following:

- Tensions between need, supply, and demand for health workers
- Increasing acceleration of domestic and international migration of health professionals

- Imbalances in the composition, skills, performance, and distribution of health workers
- Leadership, governance, and management weaknesses
- Limited data, evidence, and accountability

Many of these issues can be better understood and addressed through the lens of health labor market analysis. This book aims to be a contribution toward the *how*.

Table O.1 Sustainable Development Goal 3

SDG 3: Ensure healthy lives and promote well-being for all at all ages

Target 3.8: Achieve universal health coverage, including financial risk protection, access to quality essential health care services, medicines, and vaccines for all

MDG unfinished and expanded agenda	New SDG 3 targets	SDG 3 means of implementation targets
3.1 Reduce maternal mortality	3.4 Reduce mortality from NCDs and promote mental health	3.a Strengthen implementation of framework convention on tobacco control
3.2 End preventable newborn and child deaths	3.5 Strengthen prevention and treatment of substance abuse	3.b Provide access to medicines and vaccines for all, support R&D of vaccines and medicines for all
3.3 End the epidemic of HIV, TB, malaria, and NTDs, and combat hepatitis, waterborne, and other communicable diseases	3.6 Halve global deaths and injuries from road traffic accidents	3.c Increase health financing and health workforce (especially in developing countries)
3.7 Ensure universal access to sexual and reproductive health care services	3.9 Reduce deaths from hazardous chemicals and air, water, and soil pollution and contamination	3.d Strengthen capacity for early warning, risk reduction, and management of health risks

Interactions with economic, other social and environmental SDGs and SDG 17 on means of implementation

Source: Adapted from UN 2016.
Notes: HIV = human immunodeficiency virus; NCDs = noncommunicable diseases; NTDs = neglected tropical diseases; R&D = research and development; TB = tuberculosis.

The World Bank has been instrumental in generating new data, evidence, and knowledge in the field of HRH to assist governments in analyzing and finding solutions to their health workforce challenges. Working under the coordinating leadership of ministries of health with national technical working groups on HRH, the Bank has been at the vanguard of using the theory and practice of labor economics to cast new light on the underlying factors that affect policy success or failure in health systems strengthening (see for example Leonard et. al 2015; McPake, Scott, and Edoka 2014; Soucat, Scheffler, and Ghebreyesus 2013; Vujicic and Zurn 2006). Collaboration with international organizations and development partners, including World Health Organization (WHO), the United States Agency for International Development (USAID), and the African Development Bank, has further contributed to an increasing wealth of literature (for example Scheffler, Bruckner, and Spetz 2012; Sousa et al. 2013; WHO 2016).

The *Global Strategy on Human Resources for Health: Workforce 2030* builds on this contemporary evidence and integrates the technical strengths of health labor market analyses as a guiding framework for governments and relevant stakeholders on how they can optimize their present workforce, align new investments with workforce needs, strengthen HRH management, and generate much needed data for evidence-informed policy.

This book, produced by the World Bank in collaboration with the University of California, Berkeley, and WHO, aims to provide decision makers at subnational, national, regional, and global levels with additional insights into how to better understand and address their workforce challenges rather than just describe them. To optimize and align HRH investments and develop targeted policy responses, a thorough understanding of unique, country-specific labor market dynamics and determinants of these dynamics is critical. Policies need to take into account the fact that workers are economic actors, responsive to different levels of compensation and opportunities to generate revenue found in different sublabor markets.

Policies need to take into account not only the behavioral characteristics of the individuals who provide health care but also the individuals who consume health care services and the institutions that employ health personnel. In other words, it is necessary to understand what the determinants are of the supply (numbers of health workers willing to work in the health sector) and the demand for health workers (resources available to hire health workers); how these interact; and how this interaction varies in different contexts. This interaction will determine the *availability* of health personnel, their *distribution*, and their *performance* levels, thus ensuring stronger health systems capable of delivering UHC.

The book, which is structured to be of use to researchers, planners, and economists tasked with analyzing key areas of health labor markets (HLMs), includes examples of overall labor market assessments and more narrow and targeted analyses of demand and supply (including production and migration), performance, and remuneration of health workers. The chapters discuss data sources and empirical tools that can be used to assess HLMs across low- and middle-income countries (LMICs) and high-income countries, but draws primarily from examples and case studies in LMICs. Each chapter should be read as a contribution to the field, exploring a particular element of HLMs and reflecting the experience and perspectives of the authors.

Chapter Summaries

The order of the chapters is designed to allow the reader to build from the general, initial concepts; grasp the terminology; and understand its overall application in later chapters. Those already familiar with the concepts in chapters 1 and 2 may wish to read chapters of specific interest in a random order.

While all chapters draw on the principles of HLM economics, specific labor market concepts and terminology are interpreted and applied differently by the authors of each chapter. The differing perspectives, and preferences for certain tools and approaches over others, demonstrate the relative infancy of HLM and the continuing evolution of good practice. Readers should draw from these examples to determine how to apply the concepts and tools introduced in various chapters to their own context.

Chapters 1 and 2 discuss the concepts, tools, and data sources that can be used to assess overall labor market dynamics. Chapter 3 discusses tools to capture demand- and needs-based forecasts of health workers. Chapter 4 discusses the tools to measure and analyze the production of health workers, and chapter 5 discusses the willingness and job choice that health workers have of entering and applying themselves in one labor market over another. Chapter 6 discusses the tools that can be used to assess the migration of health care professionals. Chapters 7 and 8 discuss the conceptual framework and methodologies to assess health worker performance and the determinants of performance, while chapters 9 and 10 discuss assessments of health worker remuneration, including the use of sensitive survey techniques to obtain information often not provided by health workers. The following provides a summary of each chapter in more detail.

Chapter 1: A Labor Market Framework for Human Resources for Health for Low-and Middle-Income Countries
Richard M. Scheffler
All LMICs have health worker labor markets. Some of these countries' markets function better than others and all can be improved. This chapter introduces the terms and tools of labor market analysis for those with little or no formal training in economics. It sets out definitions and explanations on need, supply, and demand concepts, and explores the issues of shortage, underemployment, and market clearing. The author builds from these labor market principles and connects to real-world case studies from four LMICs: Thailand, Kenya, Malawi, and Rwanda. The data needed to examine labor markets are also noted to allow human resource practitioners to begin empirical examinations of health worker labor markets in their own countries. The examples help explain the basics of labor markets and illustrate why understanding labor market concepts can help address the workforce challenges described in the vignettes.

Chapter 2: Data Requirements for the Economic Analysis of Health Labor Markets
Anthony Scott, Edson Araújo, Genta Menkulasi, and Robert Cohen
The application of HLM analysis has potential to provide a deeper understanding of health workforce dynamics and provide additional evidence and insights for solving HRH challenges. The use of an explicit labor economic framework moves the focus away from simplistic policy responses such as "train more nurses and physicians" toward understanding more carefully the role of incentives, productivity, and the distribution of health workers. To date,

however, very few comprehensive and rigorous HLM analyses have been carried out, largely because of the lack of relevant data to conduct them. HRH datasets are often disconnected and suffer from a lack of reliable and consistent data on different dimensions of the health workforce (pay structure, health worker preferences, training choices, productivity, and so on). For example, central to any labor market analysis is an understanding of the absolute and relative levels of health worker remuneration from all sources. Two main types of labor market analysis use an explicit economics framework: descriptive and causal analysis. Descriptive labor market analysis helps establish the nature and extent of labor market disequilibrium. It might provide data about demand, compensation, market structure, supply, interaction of demand and supply, trends, and distribution. Causal labor market analysis aims to identify the effects of changes in labor market conditions or regulation on the behavior of both employers and workers, and on the value of these changes to society. This chapter provides an overview of the suitability of existing HRH data sets for HLM analysis, and proposes strategies to fill the existing data gaps by building upon existing data collections in LMICs.

Chapter 3: Demand-Based and Needs-Based Forecasts for Health Workers
Tim Bruckner, Jenny Liu, and Richard M. Scheffler
Much attention in the HRH field in LMICs focuses on the shortage of skilled health professionals. Researchers, policy makers, and international agencies have issued calls for federal governments to "scale up," or increase, their health workforce. Given the resources and time needed to increase the production of skilled health professionals, policy makers and other stakeholders must understand the magnitude of future workforce needs in order to plan appropriately today. Government officials and health care planners benefit from having the tools to estimate the future number and types of health workers required in response to population needs. This chapter introduces the practitioner to several approaches used to forecast needs for health workers.

The chapter first introduces needs-based forecasts that estimate the epidemiologic need of workers based on their ability to meet specific healthcare delivery thresholds. Second, it provides steps for the economic, demand-based forecasts that predict the population's ability to pay for health workers. Third, it outlines a strategy for forecasting the supply of health workers. The chapter concludes with a comparison of the discussed approaches and provides suggestions for the practitioner in communicating the forecasts.

Chapter 4: Measuring and Analyzing Production Supply
Kate Tulenko, Atef El Maghraby, Agnes Soucat, Alex Preker, and Tim Bruckner
This chapter focuses on preservice education. The preservice education system serves as a crucial component of the HLM. The authors highlight indicators and tools that local and national planners may use to evaluate which education systems produce a cadre of well-trained professionals and which systems may fall below expectations. They consider six domain indicators that could stimulate

more effective policy formation, and recommend more attention to rigorously measure and evaluate preservice education systems so that successful elements of training programs can be identified and disseminated in other schools, regions, and countries.

Chapter 5: Health Worker Labor Supply, Absenteeism, and Job Choice
Pieter Serneels, Tomas Lievens, and Damas Butera
This chapter focuses on microeconomic analysis as a starting point for a better understanding of health worker labor supply. Recent evidence from in-depth studies indicates major challenges related to labor supply at the microeconomic level. For example, health worker presence and on-the-job performance have been identified as primary constraints for the delivery of health care. Because health care is labor intensive, the authors assume that there is a demand for health workers; therefore, they analyze worker labor supply, absenteeism, and occupational choice. They also discuss the appropriate framework for the analysis of labor supply, absenteeism, job choice, and dual work. The authors present the evidence available on each of these topics along with lessons for policy making. Furthermore, they discuss the types of analysis that can be carried out to improve understanding of data and measurements, distinguishing between descriptive and casual analysis.

Chapter 6: Migration of Health Care Professionals from Sub-Saharan Africa: Issues, Data, and Evidence
Çağlar Özden
This chapter provides an overview of health worker migration challenges facing LMICs and presents the need for the proper analysis of determinants and implications of migration for source countries. The chapter then discusses both shortcomings of the existing data and the conclusions that can be drawn from them. The chapter provides two examples of analysis. The first combines different data sets in a variety of ways to identify potential career paths for African doctors in the United States. This analysis tracks their place of birth, training, and professional practice. The second analysis utilizes a detailed survey in which Ghanaian physicians answer career and migration questions.

After focusing on migration in general, the chapter hones in on specific motivators for health workforce migration, the process of measuring these factors, and the data constraints policy makers and researchers face in making evidence-based trade-offs. The goal of this chapter is to remove some of the controversy and emotion from the debate so that facts and analysis gain some ground.

Chapter 7: Measuring the Performance of Health Workers
Kenneth Leonard and Ottar Mæstad
HRH may be the single most important data contribution to the health sector in low-income countries. Shortages of health personnel and poor health worker performance are among the most pressing issues for health systems in these countries. This chapter focuses on the performance of health workers within the system.

The knowledge, experience, skills, and dedication of health workers help translate other key data inputs from hospitals and medicine.

The chapter also presents three measures of health worker performance: presence, quality, and productivity. Although these measures are difficult to assess in the health care setting, the need for streamlined data collection is essential.

Health care is different from most other production processes, which can make measuring performance difficult in the following areas: quantitative measurement in skilled professions, the fact that health workers face varying patient populations (case-mix), and the impact of scrutiny on behavior. To combat this difficulty, the chapter recommends using multiple tools to evaluate performance within the health system.

Chapter 8: Analyzing the Determinants of Health Worker Performance
Kenneth Leonard and Ottar Mæstad

In this chapter, the authors examine common tools that offer insight into the determinants of performance. Data acquired from these tools inform the performance improvement process. The chapter addresses three main variables of health worker aspects to improve quality: competence, capacity, and performance. The chapter begins by developing measures of performance and introduces the three-gap model: know, know-can, and can-do. This specific model combines health workers' training, effort, and equipment. Each of these elements is a variable that could introduce bias in quality worker measurements because the quality of health workers is heavily influenced by the training they have received, the effort they put forth, and the equipment they operate. The authors include an analysis of motivations of health worker productivity in LMICs and present the motivation analysis as an underlying cause of low worker productivity and performance.

Performance improvement is multifaceted, and a thorough assessment of gaps in the organization is needed to better evaluate the quality process of health workers. The chapter ends with a discussion of key indicators that help explain the performance shortfalls observed and provides advice on policy recommendations on how to close the gaps.

Chapter 9: Measuring and Analyzing Salaries and Incentives
Wanda Jaskiewicz, Christophe Lemiere, David Phillips, Joanne Spetz, and Eric Keuffel

This chapter examines the finding that unofficial income as a source of revenue for health workers in low-income countries is increasing. Officially, the main sources of income are (a) base salaries, (b) cash allowances, (c) in-kind benefits, and (d) a share of user fees. However, in public sector employment in many countries the official income may not be adequate, and thus health workers rely on unofficial incomes as important sources of revenue. Four main types of unofficial incomes are described, which include per diem payments, revenue from moonlighting, income from the sale of medical products and drug pilfering, and informal payments asked of patients. Streams of unofficial income are difficult to measure, however, partly because reliable data are difficult to obtain. Regardless of the difficulty, the authors offer various means to measure both official and unofficial income.

Chapter 10: Sensitive Survey Techniques to Capture Sensitive Information from Health Workers: An Example of Their Application in Liberia
David Phillips, Christopher H. Herbst, and Yah Zolia

Health workers commonly generate informal income, which contributes to determining revenue generation and labor market dynamics in many HLMs. However, measuring or capturing the participation of health workers in these activities—selling pilfered drugs, moonlighting, and charging informal payments (when services are officially free of charge) to gain income—can be difficult because health workers may be reluctant to admit to their participation.

This chapter provides an overview of an application of sensitive survey techniques to capture information about informal income generation activity from health workers. The chapter describes application and results of a Liberia Ministry of Health and Social Welfare survey conducted with support from the World Bank in July and August 2012, which aimed to measure the prevalence among health workers in Liberia's public hospitals of selling pilfered drugs, moonlighting during regular business hours, and charging informal payments. This example of a practical application of sensitive survey techniques on health workers is meant to provide a more in-depth understanding of these methods for anyone considering their use.

Although limitations in data quality indicate that the results derived from these techniques should not be the sole basis for policy decisions, when carefully designed and applied, and when combined with other information (including, for example, patient exit surveys), sensitive survey techniques hold the potential to obtain information on illicit income-generation activities otherwise difficult to capture.

Conclusion

The *2030 Agenda for Sustainable Development* introduces a new era for the global community. The 17 goals—and their respective targets—will require intersectoral collaboration to make concerted progress. This is especially relevant to the health sector, which through the lens of health labor market analysis demonstrates a strong convergence of the SDG targets.

The ten chapters in this book should be viewed as contributions to improving knowledge on the application of health labor market analysis. The concepts, tools, data, and examples form a body of evidence that provides some guidance on how to inform evidence-based policy. In parallel, improved application of health labor market analysis lends itself to far more than a research agenda. It offers insights on how to progress toward the achievement of UHC, health and well-being for all and at all ages, and the broader aspirations of the SDGs (e.g., on education, gender, employment, and decent work). We hope the potential to achieve so much will spur readers of this book to apply their learning immediately.

References

Leonard, K. L., M. C. Masatu, C. H. Herbst, and C. Lemiere. 2015. "The Systematic Assessment of Health Worker Performance: A Framework for Analysis and Its Application in Tanzania." Health Nutrition and Population Discussion Paper, World Bank, Washington, DC.

McPake, B., A. Scott, and L. Edoka. 2014. *Analyzing Markets for Health Workers: Insights from Labor and Health Economics.* Directions in Development Series. Washington, DC: World Bank.

Scheffler, R. T. Bruckner, and J. Spetz. 2012. *The Labour Market for Human Resources for Health in Low- and Middle-Income Countries.* Geneva: Department for Health Systems Policies and Workforce, World Health Organization.

Soucat, A., R. M. Scheffler, and T. A. Ghebreyesus, eds. 2013. *The Labor Market for Health Workers in Africa: A New Look at the Crisis.* Directions in Development Series. Washington, DC: World Bank.

Sousa, A. R. M. Scheffler, J. Nyoni, and T. Boerma. 2013. "A Comprehensive Health Labour Market Framework for Universal Health Coverage." *Bulletin of the World Health Organization* 91: 892–94.

UN (United Nations). 2016. "Sustainable Development Goals: 17 Goals to Transform Our World." New York: UN. http://www.un.org/sustainabledevelopment/health/.

Vujicic, M., and P. Zurn. 2006. "The Dynamics of the Health Labour Market." *International Journal of Health Planning and Management.* 21 (2): 101–15. http://www.ncbi.nlm .nih.gov/pubmed/16846103.

WHO (World Health Organization). 2016. *Global Strategy on Human Resources for Health: Workforce 2030.* Geneva: WHO. http://www.who.int/hrh/resources/glob -strat-hrh_workforce2030.pdf.

A Labor Market Framework for Human Resources for Health in Low- and Middle-Income Countries

Richard M. Scheffler

Various sections of this chapter were derived from Scheffler, Bruckner, and Spetz (2012). The chapter was developed in close collaboration with individuals from University of California, Berkeley. Brent D. Fulton, assistant adjunct professor, was invaluable for his advice; Angela Kline, a master of public health student, and Grayson Dimick, an undergraduate student, were instrumental in editing the chapter; Daniel Arnold, a doctoral student in economics, developed vignette 3 and helped with editing the chapter.

Introduction

All low- and middle-income countries (LMICs) have health labor markets (HLMs). Some of these countries' markets function better than others and all can be improved. What does it mean when experts say there is a "shortage" of health workers? Is there more than one definition of a shortage, and if so, how can it be measured? What is the difference between the "need" and the "demand" for a health worker? What factors influence wages paid in the public and private health sectors, and how can it be determined whether the wages are adequate to attract workers in rural areas? Why do some LMICs have "ghost workers" (workers who draw salaries but do not show up to work) in HLMs? This chapter will explore these and other questions using the basic tools of labor market analysis.

The chapter provides an introduction to the terms and tools of labor market analysis for those with little or no formal training in economics. It also connects these labor market principles to real-world case studies from LMICs. The data needed to examine labor markets are also noted so that human resource practitioners can begin their own empirical examination of the HLMs. This information will increase the number of people who understand labor markets in health.

The chapter begins with vignettes from four LMICs: box 1.1, workforce shortage in Thailand; box 1.2, unfilled posts in Kenya; box 1.3, maternal health

Box 1.1 Vignette 1: Workforce Shortage in Thailand

Thailand has experienced a twofold increase in gross national income per capita over the past 10 years, making it one of the fastest-growing economies in Asia (Pagaiya and Noree 2009). Recent estimates indicate that Thailand requires more than 12,000 new health workers to adequately treat the mental, neurological, and substance-abuse disorders of its population (Bruckner et al. 2011). This gap between the need and the supply of workers probably underestimates Thailand's total shortage of workers needed to treat mental and physical disorders. The prevalence of untreated disorders imposes high costs on the health system, resulting in lost worker productivity, impaired functioning of health workers, and caregiver burdens on family members. If the epidemiologic need for health care remains high, why does Thailand have a health workforce shortage?

Box 1.2 Vignette 2: Unfilled Posts in Kenya

Kenya was projected to have 1.44 health care professionals per 1,000 population by 2015, much lower than the World Health Organization's (WHO's) minimum threshold level of 2.28 per 1,000 population (Scheffler et al. 2009). In 2006, Enock Kibunguchy, Kenya's assistant minister for health, said the country should hire 10,000 additional professionals as a matter of urgency to meet the health needs of the population (Ambrose 2006). Despite the Ministry of Health's efforts to hire these workers, many postings in rural areas remained unfilled (Vujicic, Ohiri, and Sparkes 2009). When posts were filled, the recruited health workers often did not arrive to start the job until much later, sometimes up to 18 months after the position had been advertised (Soucat et al. 2013). Why do available jobs remain unfilled and why does it take so long to place health workers after they are recruited?

Box 1.3 Vignette 3: Maternal Health in Malawi

In 2004, Malawi's Ministry of Health assessed the country's health worker situation as "critical and dangerously close to collapse" (Mandeville et al. 2015). Improving the situation faced a number of challenges: doctors migrating to high-income countries (Mandeville et al. 2015); human immunodeficiency virus/acquired immune deficiency syndrome (HIV/AIDS) leading health care providers to exit the medical profession in favor of less risky professions (UNDP 2002); and providers spending less time with patients in order to care for their relatives infected with HIV/AIDS (Chilopora et al. 2007). These challenges contributed to Malawi having a doctor-to-population ratio at the time of 1:91,000, one of the world's lowest ratios (Mandeville et al. 2015). Through all these challenges, Malawi was trying to live up to the Millennium Development Goal of reducing maternal mortality by 75 percent from 1990 to 2015. How did Malawi attempt to accomplish this goal with a limited number of doctors?

in Malawi; and box 1.4, ghost workers in Rwanda. Next it describes the basics of labor markets and illustrates why understanding these concepts can help in addressing the workforce challenges described in the vignettes. The responses are shown in box 1.5 for Thailand workforce shortages, box 1.6 for unfilled posts in Kenya, box 1.7 for maternal health concerns in Malawi, and box 1.8 for ghost workers in Rwanda.

Box 1.4 Vignette 4: Ghost Workers in Rwanda

Before 2004, most doctors in the public sector in Rwanda received a salary for their services. A doctor was typically assigned to a particular clinic. In many of these clinics, patients waited in long lines, sometimes all day, without seeing a doctor; often the doctor did not even show up at the clinic. This type of doctor is known as a "ghost worker"—one who draws a salary from a clinic but is mostly absent (Lievens and Serneels 2006).

When physicians do attend the clinic, patients and staff benefit from the doctor's time and expertise, but the unreliable nature of the doctor's work schedule leads to inadequate health care and resentment from other clinic employees. How did the Rwandan government address its ghost worker problem?

Box 1.5 Vignette 1: Response to Workforce Shortage in Thailand

Figure 1.2 reflects the situation for the health workforce in Thailand. The perceived need for health workers, determined by the assessed morbidity of the population, represents line NE. The minimal number of "needed" workers, however, remains much greater than the number of health workers employed (NB). Why is this so? Despite Thailand's high prevalence of HIV and the recent reemergence of tuberculosis, neither the public nor the private sectors provide sufficient compensation for health professionals to enter the labor market (Pagaiya and Noree 2009). In addition, given other employment options in Thailand's rapidly expanding economy, citizens may choose other careers with higher wages and greater prestige.

Since 2001, Thailand's Ministry of Health has acted to provide universal health care coverage and destigmatize various health conditions, such as HIV and mental disorders.[a] Such initiatives, in conjunction with reallocating federal funds toward training and retaining health workers, have led to an increase in the health workforce over the past decade. Such policies, if sustained into the future, may close the workforce gap between lines NB and E (figure 1.2).

a. See Thailand Ministry of Public Health, Office of Health Care Reform.[1]

Box 1.6 Vignette 2: Response to Unfilled Posts in Kenya

Kenya's experience of unfilled rural posts is mirrored in many LMICs (Scheffler et al. 2009). Despite the political will to hire more health workers, Kenya had insufficient funds to augment the workforce in understaffed rural areas. To address this problem, in 2006 Kenya adopted a multifaceted approach. First, the Ministry of Health used external donor resources (separate from the federal wage budget) to initiate the Emergency Hiring Program (Vujicic, Ohiri, and Sparkes 2009). This separate funding stream provides three-year contracts to health workers, stipulating that they focus on underserved geographic regions (Capacity Project 2009). The Ministry of Health administers these funds and hires the workers. Second, applicants from rural regions can be interviewed in their home region rather than having to travel to the capital, Nairobi (Soucat et al. 2013). This local management process in rural areas appears to reduce time-to-hire and increase retention rates. Third, for workers in rural areas, the Ministry of Health has implemented hardship allowances, housing grants, and two sessions of paid leave. The goal of these incentives is to offset the wage deficit (that is, the difference between W1 in figure 1.4a and W3 in figure 1.4b) of those not working in urban centers.

Box 1.7 Vignette 3: Response to Maternal Health in Malawi

In 1976, Malawi introduced the position of clinical officer (CO) to meet the country's increasing demand for health care (Chilopora et al. 2007). COs are mid-level health care providers who have undergone four years of medical training. Upon completion of their training, COs are licensed to practice independently and perform major emergency and elective surgery.

COs are similar to surgery technicians: they perform procedures typically done by doctors while receiving lower wage than doctors. Hence, figure 1.5 is applicable to COs. As Figure 1.5 predicts, the number of COs employed has increased since the CO position was created. A study conducted in 2005 shows that COs now perform the majority of emergency obstetric operations across all government district hospitals and Christian Health Association of Malawi hospitals in Malawi. Of the 2,131 emergency obstetric operations performed during the timeframe of the study, 1,875 (88 percent) were done by COs while 256 (12 percent) were done by doctors (Chilopora et al. 2007).

Box 1.8 Vignette 4: Response to Ghost Workers in Rwanda

The chronic absence of assigned physicians from clinics in Rwanda is illustrated in figures 1.6 and 1.7. The "ghost worker" physician lies on point A of figure 1.6 because he or she works relatively few hours and sees few patients in the clinic. Additional hours worked in the clinic could improve the physician's output to point C. The ghost worker represents point y in figure 1.7 because the delivery of health services at the clinic falls far below the worker's potential, based on his or her level of training and ability to provide care.

box continues next page

Box 1.8 Vignette 4: Response to Ghost Workers in Rwanda *(continued)*

Ghost workers produce low output, resulting in low productivity, because they draw a salary from the federal government *regardless of their attendance at the clinic* and are rarely fined for absenteeism. They have little fixed motivation, therefore, to see patients at the clinic. The ghost worker, instead, may decide to provide private care outside the clinic while also drawing a clinic-based salary. To rectify the problem of absenteeism, in 2005 the Rwanda government restructured health worker compensation by linking wages to clinic attendance. This pay-for-performance strategy allows administrative districts to reward clinicians for hours worked and quickly terminate the contracts of ghost workers (Soucat et al. 2013). Rigorous evaluation of pay for performance in Rwanda indicates a dramatic reduction in ghost workers and improvements in the quantity and quality of care provided at public clinics (Basinga et al. 2010). Noting this success, other Sub-Saharan countries in Africa have recently implemented pay-for-performance strategies.

Forces Affecting HLM

The HLM in a country is made up of two independent economic forces: the supply of health workers and the demand for health workers (Scheffler 2008). The interplay between the supply of and demand for health workers determines wages and other forms of compensation paid, such as housing allowance and fringe benefits; the number of health workers employed; and the number of hours they work (Dussault and Vujicic 2008). These labor market forces also determine the geographic location of health workers and their employment setting (for example, hospitals or clinics).

A complete picture of the HLM includes the productivity and performance of health workers. Productivity measures the units of care or service that workers provide; the rate of health worker productivity is often measured as services or visits per hour. The performance of health workers is determined primarily by two components: the quality of service provided and the appropriateness of that service for treating the patient. Performance is often measured by examining what the health worker is trained to do. Productivity and performance might be linked also to the health outcomes of the population served; this is discussed later in this chapter. The health worker's potential is then compared with what he or she actually does. The closer the performance is to the potential, the better the health worker's performance.

This chapter discusses each of these labor market concepts in turn to show how it operates in the health care sector. The components of the HLM are then assembled to show how they relate to each other. This synthesis is followed by a more technical discussion of the key concepts of HLMs, illustrating how the labor market determines wages, employment, geographic distribution, task shifting, productivity, and performance. A preliminary list of key labor market indicators and data with which to conduct these studies is presented in annex 1A. Which data are needed will depend on the labor market studied.

Health Workers Labor Market and Health and Medical Services Market

The labor market for health professionals is derived from and directly connected to the market for health and medical services (Global Health Workforce Alliance 2011; Sorkin 1984). The process for delivering health care services requires the input of health workers along with other inputs, such as medicines, equipment, and other health care supplies. Clinics and hospitals have a demand for health workers in order to produce health services, which are demanded by purchasers of health care. This point is often overlooked. The demand for health services is linked to the willingness of the government, patients, health insurers, and other purchasers of health care, such as donors, to fund health services.

The *demand* for health workers can be defined as the willingness and ability of the government, private sector, and/or donors to pay to have health workers placed in clinics, hospitals, or other parts of the health system. The demand for health workers is the sum of the demand from all of these purchasers or funders.

The supply side of the market shows how many health workers are available at any given moment and how many hours they are willing to work. In general, the higher the wage offered, the greater the number of available health workers. *Wage* is defined as a formal payment from the public or private sector to the health worker, via salary, capitation, or fee for service. However, informal payments, housing allowances, and other benefits are also frequently offered to workers for their services. The positive relationship between wage and the number of workers available exists for several reasons. Some may have training as health workers but do not work in the health care sector because wages are too low. Those with training in health care will offer more of their services as the wage increases (that is, they will work more hours). Those working in other sectors of the economy will consider training for jobs in health care as health care wages become more attractive. Others will consider being trained as health workers so that the future supply of health workers will be increased.

The demand for health care training is, therefore, derived from the market for health workers. This demand creates the market for health worker education. The supply side of this market is the number of training slots (seats in the class) available. The supply of training slots (seats) depends on the cost of providing training and the funds available to pay for it. The cost of training includes physical infrastructure and its amortization, faculty salaries, classroom maintenance, and other educational supplies. A substantial portion of the cost of training is often offset by government or private organizations on the premise that health worker education is a "public good" that benefits society broadly and, therefore, the cost should not be borne solely by the student. Some portion of the cost is typically paid by the student through tuition and educational fees. Voluntary bonding schemes, in which students commit to a period of national service in exchange for a reduction in the cost of training, are commonly used to create mutually beneficial arrangements between students and the government. As the total cost of training a health worker declines, the number of training slots (seats) increases. Tuition charges affect the demand for health worker training.

If the tuition charge of education is zero or near zero, there will probably be excess demand for health worker education. This is rarely the case in practice, however, because many health education programs have entry requirements that impose other costs on students. If tuition is too high relative to the wages of health workers, then not enough individuals will apply for the health care training seats available. As the wages for health workers increase, the demand for health worker training will also increase. The link between the market for health care and the market for health workforce training is a crucial part of the HLM dynamic (Buerhaus, Auerbach, and Staiger 2009).

A crucial dimension of the supply of health workers is their geographic distribution, often observed through migration into and out of the country or between rural and urban areas (Global Health Workforce Alliance 2011). Migration is influenced by wage levels and other non-wage aspects of the health-worker position (Jack et al. 2010). These include, but are not limited to, safety; status; access to housing and child education; cultural activities; and the attractiveness of the hospital or clinic given its working conditions and the status of its logistics, diagnostic facilities, and pharmaceutical supplies (WHO 2010).

In summary, the two key components of the HLM are:

- The demand side, which is linked to the demand for health care
- The supply side, which is linked to the market for health worker training

To offer a fuller understanding of the labor market for health workers, these components are next described in an integrated framework.

Integrated Framework for the HLM

Figure 1.1 shows each of the components of the HLM (see Soucat and Scheffler (2013) for a more extensive discussion of this framework). Box A contains the number of seats available to train health workers in, for example, medical schools, nursing schools, or training programs for community health workers. The supply of the seats generally is determined by the cost of training the health worker relative to the funds available to pay those costs, although social priorities or political decisions may also have an influence. The demand for health worker training (box B)—the number of people who apply for available seats—is determined by the cost of the tuition and the wages and rewards of being a health worker. The net outcome of the supply and demand for training is the number of graduates from the training program, who feed into the overall health worker supply (box C) (Scheffler et al. 2011). Health worker supply is also affected by retirement, death, the competitiveness of the health market, temporary movements out of the labor market to engage in childcare or other employment, movements of health workers out of the country, and movements of health workers into the country. The attractiveness of employment in nonhealth sectors will affect the number of people who pursue health worker training, as well as the share of those trained who choose to actually work in the field. The demand for health

Figure 1.1 HLM: An Integrated Framework

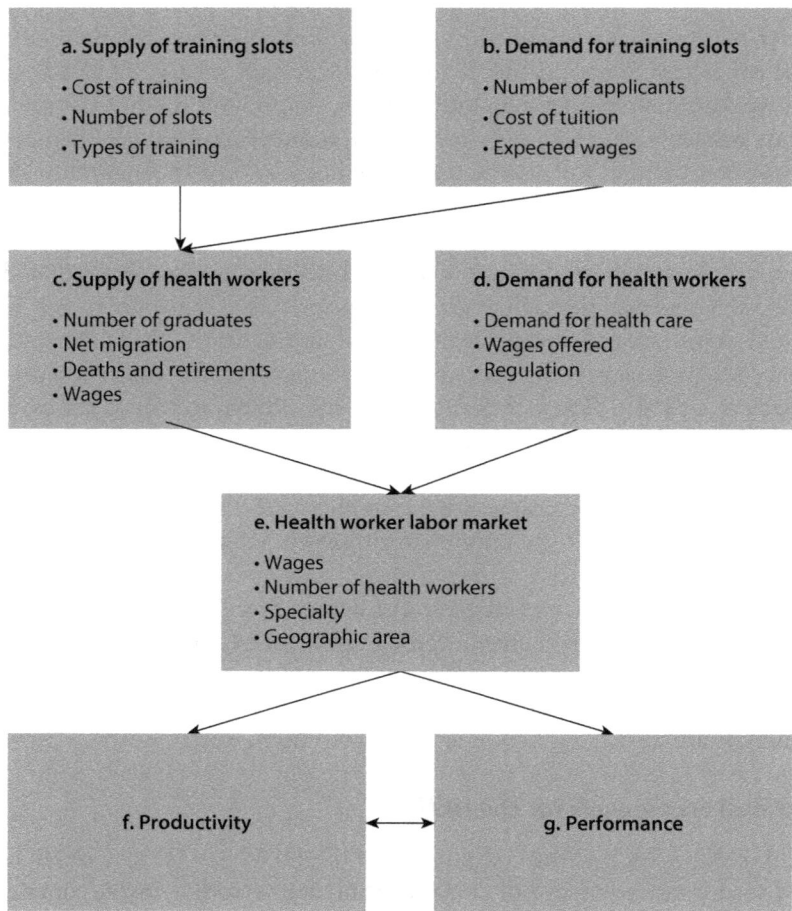

a. Supply of training slots	b. Demand for training slots
• Cost of training • Number of slots • Types of training	• Number of applicants • Cost of tuition • Expected wages

c. Supply of health workers	d. Demand for health workers
• Number of graduates • Net migration • Deaths and retirements • Wages	• Demand for health care • Wages offered • Regulation

e. Health worker labor market

• Wages
• Number of health workers
• Specialty
• Geographic area

f. Productivity	g. Performance

Note: HLM = health labor market.

workers is shown in box D. This demand is derived from the demand for health services. State regulations play a key role in determining the total wage bill and the number of civil servants wanted in the health field. The higher the demand for health services, the higher the wages that will be offered.

Demand and supply (boxes C and D) are the primary components of the HLM (box E). The dynamics of this labor market will determine the wages and other compensation, the number of health workers employed, and the geographic and sectoral (public or private) location of their employment (box E). Shortages and surpluses overall, by institution (hospital or clinics), by geographical location (urban versus rural), and by sector (public versus private) are determined by these dynamics. These are discussed in the following section.

Box F represents the productivity of health workers, which is determined by the setting in which they work and their level of motivation, work organization, and management capacity as well as the division of labor and other resources available. Such resources include equipment, drugs, examination rooms, and other characteristics of the setting. Finally, box G represents the performance of the health workers. Their performance includes the quality of their work, the technical skills they use, the care they deliver, and the impact of their work on health outcomes. Interactions between productivity and performance often occur, so that when performance improves, so too does productivity. It is possible, however, that an increase in productivity—such as a rise in the number of patients seen—could reduce performance (more mistakes made, for example).

Technical Structure and Dynamics of the Impact of the HLM

Consider first a labor market framework with only one health worker type and one employer, such as nurses being demanded by one hospital that is government funded in an LMIC as defined by the World Bank.

Figure 1.2 shows the demand (D) and supply (S) of nurses discussed in the previous section. The demand and supply of nurses will be matched when wage level WB is offered. When this happens, the market wage equals WB and nurses are employed (NB). If the wage is lower than WB (WA), there will be a shortage of nurses in the labor market (C minus B). The supply of nurses willing to work

Figure 1.2 Demand and Supply of Nurses

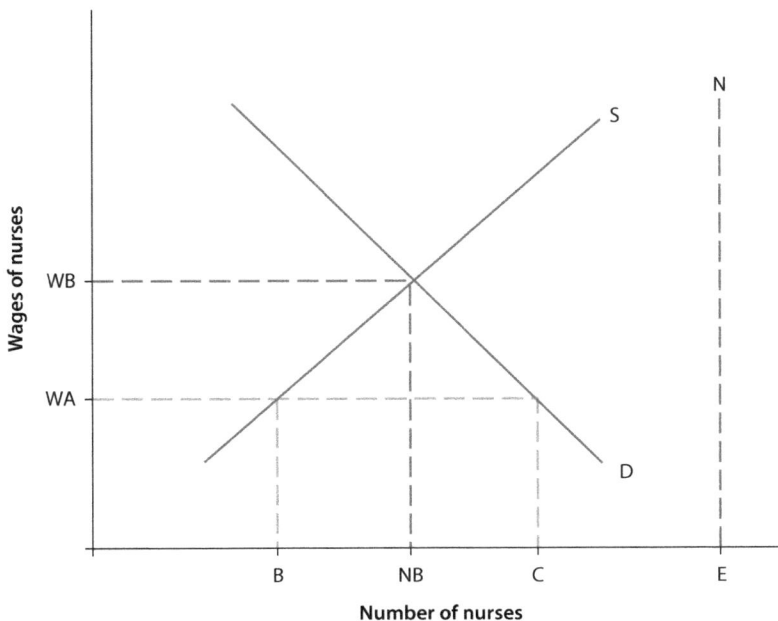

Note: The diagram depicts the labor market for nurses. WB is the equilibrium wage that matches the demand (D) and supply (S) of nurses. As the wage falls to WA, demand will exceed supply and there will be a shortage of workers equal to C–B. E represents the number of nurses needed, NE measures the healthcare needs; and NB is the number of nurses employed at the equilibrium wage WB.

is B while the demand for nurses is C. If wages are not permitted to rise to WB, the shortage will persist.

The level of employment that arises from this market-based model is different from the perceived need for nurses. How is the market-based model different from the need for nurses? Figure 1.2 shows the need for nurses as the dotted line NE. It is the quantity demanded when wages are zero and is represented by a vertical line, because the needs-based demand does not change with the wage in the market. The number of nurses employed will still be NB but the need is E, so the needs-based shortage is E minus NB.

Note that a labor market may be dominated by a small number of employers, perhaps only one employer, causing it to behave differently than a competitive market. In this scenario, a monopsony, the employer has a great deal of control over the wages offered and will find that increasing wages to attract more workers has a big effect on overall wage costs. Therefore the monopsonistic employer will be reluctant to increase wages to remedy a shortage but might nonetheless report a shortage of workers. This is more likely to be the case in rural regions or other areas where there is one dominant employer.

Figure 1.3 illustrates how a health worker will respond to dual labor markets: both the public sector demand of D1 and the private sector demand of D2.

Figure 1.3 Public and Private Market for Health Workers: One Worker's Hours and Wages

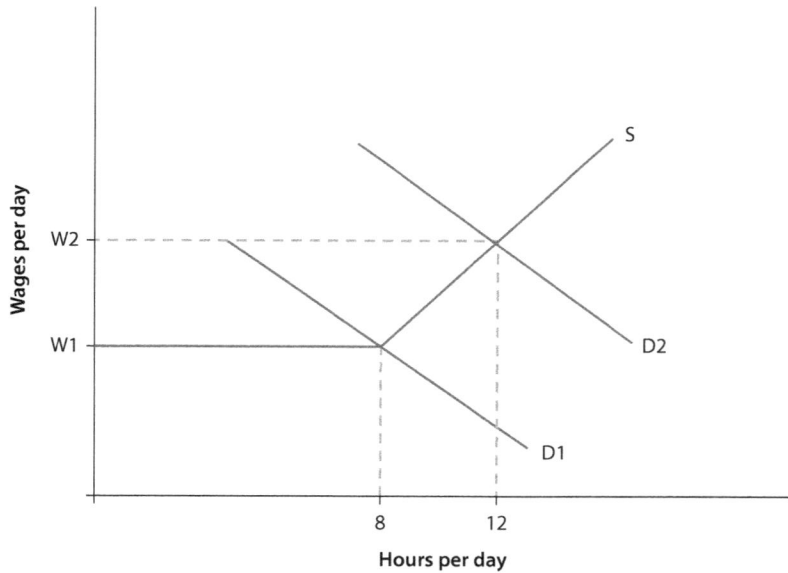

Note: A health worker works eight hours per day in the public sector at W1, and may work beyond eight hours per day in the private sector—for an additional four hours at W2. In this case, health workers meet their maximum eight hours per day at the public sector wage and often work additional hours, but also assist in meeting the demand, where D1 represents public sector demand and D2 represents private sector demand. In an ideal situation, health workers would give the minimum hours possible to the public sector at W1 and maximize their hours in the private sector at W2, given that W2 exceeds W1.

The public sector market wage is W1, which is lower than the private sector market wage (W2). According to the figure, a health worker works eight hours per day in the public sector at W1, and may work beyond eight hours per day in the private sector—for an additional four hours at W2. In this case, health workers meet their maximum eight hours per day at the public sector wage and often work additional hours, but also assist in meeting the demand. In an ideal situation, health workers would give the minimum hours possible to the public sector at W1 and maximize their hours in the private sector at W2, given that W2 exceeds W1.

In the geographic HLM represented in figure 1.4, health worker markets also allocate and distribute work by geographic area. The figure depicts the supply and demand for health workers in both rural and urban areas and shows how these markets are interrelated. In rural markets, the initial equilibrium wage of W1 is lower than the initial equilibrium wage of W3 in urban markets. This wage difference can occur because of the different work conditions and different worker preferences in the two markets. An example illustrates how the markets are interrelated. If urban incomes increase, demand for health workers in urban areas will also increase. This boosts the urban equilibrium wage to W4. Because some rural health workers will be willing to move to urban areas as a result of this wage increase, the supply of workers in urban markets will increase to S2, reducing the equilibrium wage to W5, while causing the supply of rural workers

Figure 1.4 Rural and Urban HLMs

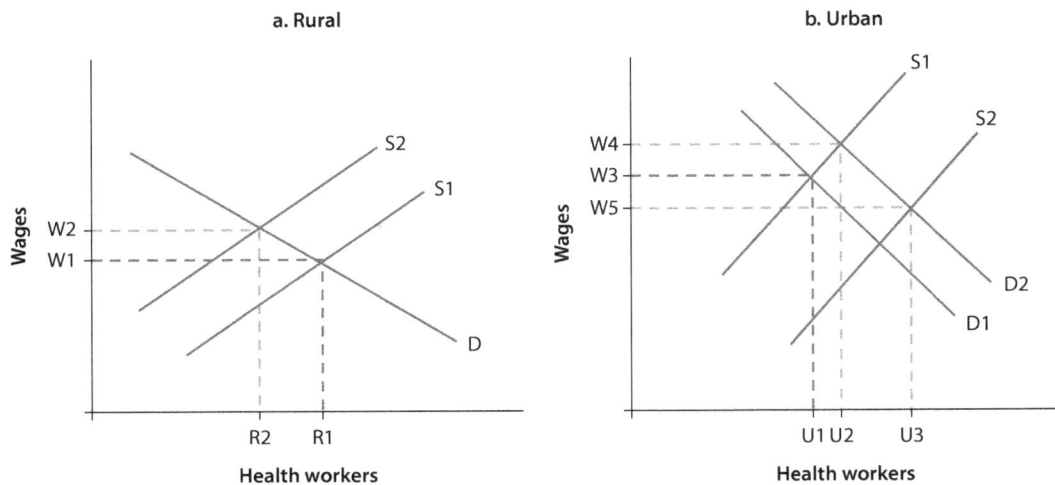

Note: The figure depicts the supply and demand for health workers in both rural and urban areas and shows how these markets are interrelated. In rural markets, the initial equilibrium wage of W1 is lower than the initial equilibrium wage of W3 in urban markets. This wage difference can occur because of the different work conditions and different worker preferences in the two markets. An example illustrates how the markets are interrelated. If urban incomes increase, demand for health workers in urban areas will also increase (from D1 to D2). This boosts the urban equilibrium wage to W4. Because some rural health workers will be willing to move to urban areas as a result of this wage increase, the supply of workers in urban markets will increase to S2, reducing the equilibrium wage to W5, while causing the supply of rural workers to decrease to S2, increasing that market's equilibrium wage to W2. Both markets will then settle at new equilibrium conditions, but the urban wage will still be higher than the rural wage. HLM = health labor market.

to decrease to S2, increasing that market's equilibrium wage to W2. Both markets will then settle at new equilibrium conditions, but the urban wage will still be higher than the rural wage.

In theory, this fluctuation should continue until the urban wage equals the rural wage. However, this is not the case. Why not? Wage is not the only factor that influences worker migration (Lemiere et al. 2010). The cost of living, living conditions, safety, and the quality of life in each area matter. Health workers typically prefer to live and work in larger cities that offer better job opportunities, career growth opportunities, and infrastructure (Buchan and Calman 2004). The intrinsic preference of the worker for an area also matters, as does proximity to family and friends. The pressure on wages does exist, however, because workers migrate from rural to urban areas or choose these locations after graduation. Furthermore, the relatively low wages of preventive medicine positions in LMICs means there is less incentive for workers in these countries to choose this field (Lievens, Serneels, and Butera 2010). Instead, workers tend to "move" to training in clinical specialties and locations that promise higher wages (Jack et al. 2010).

Consistent with WHO guidelines to increase the rural workforce, Kenya also decentralized and computerized several clinical education programs so that workers could train in rural areas without having to move (WHO 2010). For example, the African Medical and Research Foundation offers computer-based distance education to 4,500 nurses (Righetti et al. 2013; Riley et al. 2007). Kenya also developed a national electronic nursing workforce database so that it could better match nurses to underserved regions (Riley et al. 2007; Scheffler et al. 2009; Spetz 2011). This multifaceted approach resulted in fewer rural posts and a faster time-to-hire.

Task Shifting in the HLM

Task shifting is another important dynamic of the labor market for health workers (Ferrinho et al. 2011; Fulton and Scheffler 2009; Fulton et al. 2011). One example is where tasks normally performed by a surgeon are shifted to a surgery technician. Since surgery technicians are paid less than surgeons, this task shifting increases the demand for surgery technicians, increasing their wages and the number of technicians employed (see figure 1.5).

Task shifting (figure 1.5) increases the demand for surgery technicians from D1 to D2 and increases their wages from W1 to W2. At the same time, the number of surgery technicians employed increases from E1 to E2. The wages of surgeons would fall unless there is an excess demand for their labor, which is often the case in LMICs.

These market dynamics assume the market is allowed to function freely and adjust to movements in supply and demand. However, HLMs are often regulated by the government or lack transparency, so wages either do not adjust or they take a long time to adjust. For example, the market for doctors often does not allow market adjustment (task shifting) to follow labor market forces.

Figure 1.5 Task Shifting of Surgery Technicians

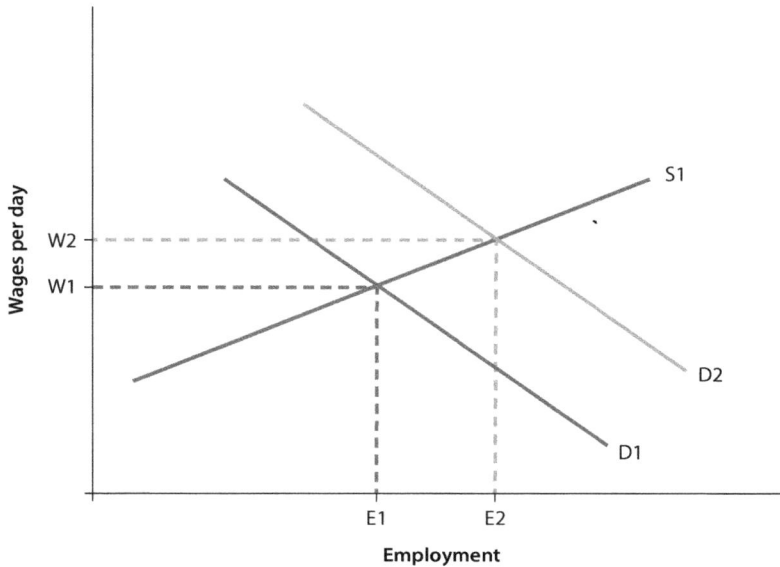

Note: An increase in the demand for surgery technicians from D1 to D2 increases their wages from W1 to W2. At the same time, the number of surgery technicians employed increases from E1 to E2. The wages of surgeons would fall unless there is an excess demand for their labor, which is often the case in LMICs.

This circumstance is often described as a "market failure" because the labor market does not produce the optimal number of health workers employed in the most appropriate jobs.

Health Worker Productivity

Health worker productivity can be described as the relationship between the input of health workers, such as the number of hours they work, and the health service output.

These outputs can be measured by the number of patient visits, the number of days spent in the hospital per patient, or the number of medical procedures and other encounters. A typical measure of output would be the visits per hour per health worker over a period of a week or a month. Productivity is also influenced by other factors, such as the number of tasks assigned, management practices, modes of remuneration, the motivation of workers, the way work is organized, the regulation of the division of labor, and the other labor and nonlabor resources available.

In the productivity function shown in figure 1.6, worker productivity is represented by the curve ACEF. As health workers increase their hours from A to B, the output increases by BC. When hours increase from C to D, the increase in output as measured by visits is DE. This shows an output increase but the rate

Figure 1.6 Function of a Health Worker

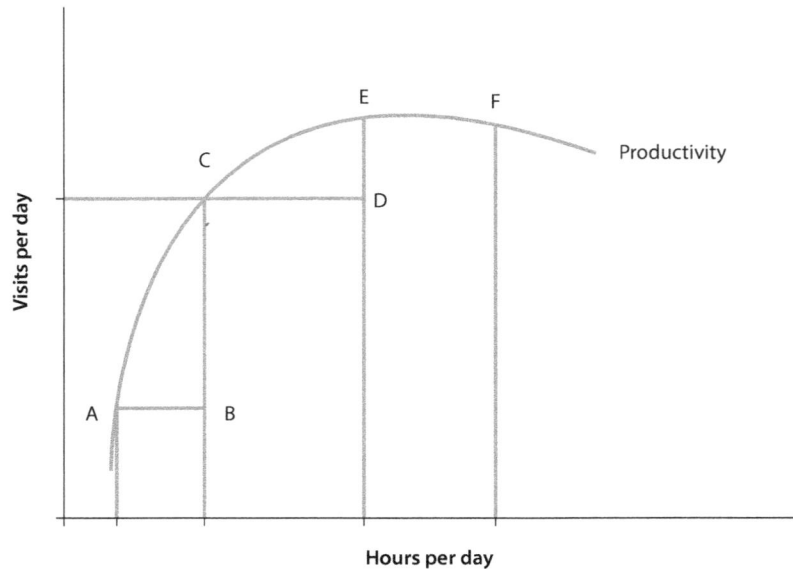

Note: Worker productivity is represented by the curve ACEF. As health workers increase their hours from A to B, the output increases by BC. When hours increase from C to D, the increase in output is measured by visits is DE. This shows an output increase but the rate of the increase is decreasing.

of the increase is decreasing. This pattern of "diminishing returns" to hours of work per day is considered by economists to be widespread throughout all occupations, with workers functioning somewhat less efficiently as they spend more time at work. Point E shows the near-maximum level of output; point F shows that output can decrease at some point because of inefficiencies.

Health Worker Performance

The performance of health workers can be assessed by comparing what they are trained to do with what they actually do. When workers perform at their "best," they are producing health services at a level and rate that matches their training and ability (see line AB in figure 1.7). The quality of training can vary substantially between institutions in LMICs. In general, as the quality of training improves, so does the potential quality of health service delivery.

Another way to measure performance is to compare a health worker's services with standardized operating procedures (SOPs). Adherence to SOPs might help workers meet minimum job expectations in accordance with their training. SOPs often have not yet been established, however, and the quality of services provided may vary between workers even if SOPs are strictly followed.

When workers deliver services at a level that matches their training and ability, their work would fall on the 45-degree line, AB (figure 1.7). Point y represents the service a worker produces. It is below the 45-degree line, which means this

Figure 1.7 Health Worker Performance

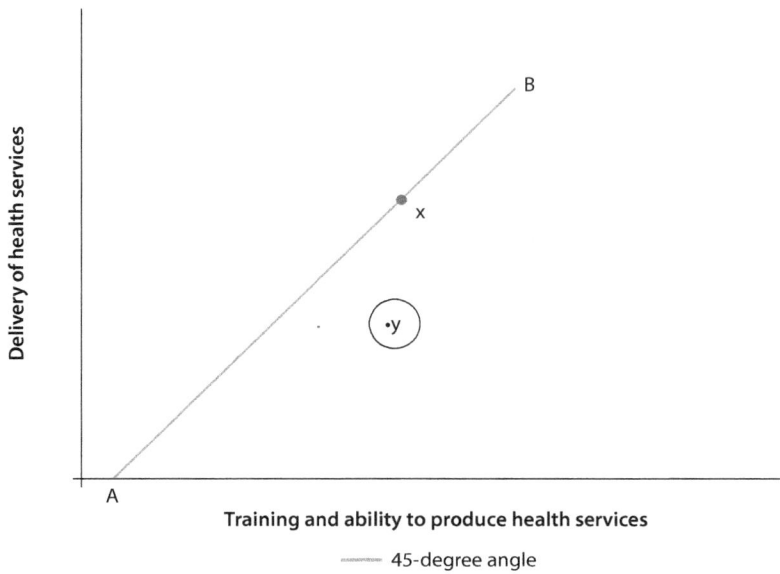

Note: The performance of health workers can be assessed by comparing what they are trained to do with what they actually do. When workers perform at their "best," they are producing health services at a level and rate that matches their training and ability (i.e., they are on the 45-degree line).

worker is not performing at his or her potential, which is represented by point x on the 45-degree line.

This shortfall in performance, perhaps the consequence of a lack of facilities or equipment, can be substantial. Low salaries can also affect performance, resulting in workers being less motivated to deliver services. Policies need to be devised, therefore, that increase health worker performance and effectiveness.

HLM Indicators

Should the market determine the level of employment for health workers and would such a level meet the health needs of the population? To determine whether this is feasible, a needs-based analysis using different measures of health needs is performed (Scheffler et al. 2010). Then, using a labor market approach as described in the previous section, the numbers of workers who are employed and at what wage level are observed. If the need for health workers exceeds the number employed, how much a wage should increase to generate the necessary movement of health workers into the market—from other countries, from urban to rural areas, or from the private to the public sector—to satisfy need can be calculated. The key indicator in this context is the wage elasticity of health worker supply, as seen in equation 1.1. It shows how much a wage must increase to boost health worker supply by a certain percentage.

Health Labor Market Analyses in Low- and Middle-Income Countries
http://dx.doi.org/10.1596/978-1-4648-0931-6

Wage elasticity of health worker supply (E)

$$E = \frac{Percentage\ change\ in\ supply}{Percentage\ change\ in\ wages} \qquad (1.1)$$

For example, when wages increase by 10 percent and supply increases by 10 percent, $E = 1$. If a 10 percent wage increase increases employment by less than 10 percent, the elasticity is less than 1. This elasticity is an overall measure of the responsiveness of the labor market to changes in wages.

Another indicator of a shortage is the vacancy rate in the HLM (Tulenko, Dussault, and Mercer 2009). A large number of vacancies often indicates a shortage. However, if wages are not permitted to increase to remove shortages, then the vacancies may be the result of low wages, which causes a shortage of labor in the health sector.

Development of a Future Health Workforce

Nearly all LMICs face shortages of health workers, either in general or in specific professions or geographical regions. To achieve the new ambitions of the Sustainable Development Goals (SDGs), such as in child and maternal health, a sufficient supply of health workers is needed to ensure access to reproductive health services, attendance by a skilled health worker during birth, and the delivery of vaccinations and medications. As another example, for the SDG relating to HIV prevention, it is recommended that strategies to increase the supply of health workers align with HLMs.

Health care decision makers must determine whether shortages arise from insufficient educational capacity, wages that are inadequate to attract people into health work, low funding in health facilities resulting in demand that is too low, or other market imbalances. By understanding the dynamics of labor markets and how they apply to global health workforce challenges, policy makers and administrators can develop successful and sustainable strategies to achieve population health goals.

Annex 1A: Preliminary List of Data Needed to Analyze the HLM

WHO recently published the Assessment Instrument for Mental Health Systems (WHO-AIMS),[2] which provides estimates of health workforce data in more than 60 LMICs. WHO-AIMS data can be used with the collection and analysis of other data at the national and regional level (Gupta et al. 2003; Vujicic and Zurn 2006).

To perform an HLM analysis, these data components can be used:

I. Number of health workers prepared to work (potential supply)
    a. By health occupation
    b. By gender
    c. By location (urban versus rural)
    d. Graduates of a training program
    e. Immigration and emigration of workers

   II. Hours worked by qualified health workers
      a. By health occupation
      b. By facility
      c. By sector (public or private)
      d. By gender
      e. By location (urban or rural)
  III. Wages paid
      a. By government, private sector
      b. For full- and part-time work
      c. In urban or rural areas
      d. By facility
  IV. Other nonwage compensation
      a. Health benefits
      b. Housing
      c. Moving expenses
      d. Pension
      e. Job security
   V. Vacancy data by the categories in II above
      a. Unfilled positions
      b. Turnover
      c. Time-to-hire
  VI. Unemployment data by the categories in I above
 VII. Productivity of health workers in all categories in I above
      a. Visits per hour
      b. Hours worked per week
      c. Number of health workers per hospital patient day, or per patient day in other types of facilities
VIII. Performance of health workers
      a. Training level of each health worker
      b. Quality of service health workers deliver, as measured by medical guidelines
      c. Ability of workers to perform as measured by the equipment and drugs they need

Notes

1. See Thailand Ministry of Public Health, Office of Health Care Reform, www.phdb .moph.go.th.
2. See WHO-AIMS Country Reports 2015, available at http://www.who.int/mental _health/who_aims_country_reports/en/index.html.

References

Ambrose, S. 2006. *Preserving Disorder: IMF Policies*. New York, NY: Global Policy Forum. http://www.globalpolicy.org/socecon/bwi-wto/imf/2006/0601imfhealth.htm.

Basinga, P., P. J. Gertler, A. Binagwaho, A. L. B. Soucat, J. R. Sturdy, and C. M. J. Vermeersch. 2010. "Paying Primary Health Care Centers for Performance in Rwanda." Policy Research Working Paper 5190, World Bank, Washington, DC.

Bruckner, T. A., R. M. Scheffler, G. Shen, J. Yoon, D. Chisholm, J. Morris, B. D. Fulton, M. R. Dal Poz, and S. Saxena. 2011. "The Mental Health Workforce Gap in Low- and Middle-Income Countries: A Needs-Based Approach." *Bulletin of the World Health Organization* 89: 184–94.

Buchan, J., and L. Calman. 2004. *The Global Shortage of Registered Nurses: An Overview of Issues and Actions*. Geneva: International Council of Nurses. http://www.icn.ch/images /stories/documents/publications/GNRI/Global_shortage_Overview.pdf.

Buerhaus, P., D. Auerbach, and D. Staiger. 2009. "The Recent Surge in Nurse Employment: Causes and Implications." *Health Affairs* 28: 657–68.

Capacity Project. 2009. *Planning, Developing and Supporting the Health Workforce: Results and Lessons Learned from the Capacity Project, 2004–2009*. Washington, DC: USAID; Chapel Hill, NC: Capacity Project. http://www.intrahealth.org/files/media/planning -developing-and-supporting-the-health-workforce-results-and-lessons-learned-from -the-capacity-project-2004-2009/capacity_project_final_report.pdf.

Chilopora, G., C. Pereira, F. Kamwendo, A. Chimbiri, E. Malunga, and S. Bergstrom. 2007. "Postoperative Outcome of Caesarean Sections and Other Major Emergency Obstetric Surgery by Clinical Officers and Medical Officers in Malawi." *Human Resources for Health* 5: 17. doi:10.1186/1478-4491-5-17.

Dussault, G., and M. Vujicic. 2008. "Demand and Supply of Human Resources for Health." In Vol. 2 of *International Encyclopaedia of Public Health*, edited by K. Heggenhougen and S. Quah, 77–84. San Diego, CA: Academic Press.

Ferrinho, P., S. Siziya, F. Goma, and G. Dussault. 2011. "The Human Resource for Health Situation in Zambia: Deficit and Maldistribution." *Human Resources for Health* 9: 30. doi:10.1186/1478-4491-9-30.

Fulton, B. D., and R. M. Scheffler. 2009. "Health Care Professional Shortages and Skill-Mix Options Using Community Health Workers: New Estimates for 2015." Working Paper, Global Center for Health Economics and Policy Research, Berkeley, CA.

Fulton, B. D., R. M. Scheffler, S. P. Sparkes, E. Y. Auh, M. Vujicic, and A. Soucat. 2011. "Health Workforce Skill Mix and Task Shifting in Low Income Countries: A Review of Recent Evidence." *Human Resources for Health* 9: 1. doi:10.1186/1478-4491-9-1.

Global Health Workforce Alliance. 2011. "Outcome Statement of the Second Global Forum on Human Resources for Health." Bangkok, January 27–29. http://www.who .int/workforcealliance/forum/2011/en/.

Gupta, N., K. Diallo, P. Zurn, and M. R. Dal Poz. 2003. "Assessing Human Resources for Health: What Can Be Learned from Labour Force Surveys?" *Human Resources for Health* 1: 5. doi: 10.1186/1478-4491-1-5.

Jack, W., J. De Laat, K. Hanson, and A. Soucat. 2010. "Incentives and Dynamics in the Ethiopian Health Worker Labor Market." World Bank Working Paper 192, World Bank, Washington, DC. https://openknowledge.worldbank.org/handle/10986/5951.

Lemiere, C., C. H. Herbst, N. Jahanshahi, E. Smith, and A. Soucat. 2010. "Reducing Geographical Imbalances of Health Workers in Sub-Saharan Africa: A Labor Market Perspective on What Works, What Does Not, and Why." World Bank Working Paper 209, Africa Human Development Series. World Bank, Washington, DC. http://elibrary .worldbank.org/doi/abs/10.1596/978-0-8213-8599-9.

Lievens, T., and P. Serneels. 2006. *Synthesis of Focus Group Discussions with Health Workers in Rwanda*. Washington, DC: World Bank.

Lievens T., P. Serneels, and J. D. Butera. 2010. "Diversity in Career Preferences of Future Health Workers in Rwanda." World Bank Working Paper 189, Africa Human Development Series. World Bank, Washington, DC. doi: 10.1596/978-0-8213-8339-1.

Mandeville, Kate L., G. Ulaya, M. Lagarde, L. Gwesele, T. Dzowela, K. Hanson, and A. S. Muula. 2015. "Early Career Retention of Malawian Medical Graduates: A Retrospective Cohort Study." *Tropical Medicine & International Health* 20: 106–14. doi: 10.1111/tmi.12408.

Pagaiya, N., and T. Noree. 2009. "Thailand's Health Workforce: A Review of Challenges and Experiences." NHP Discussion Paper, World Bank, Washington, DC. http://siteresources.worldbank.org/HEALTHNUTRITIONANDPOPULATION/Resources/281627-1095698140167/THLHealthWorkforce.pdf.

Righetti, P., R. Strasser, P. Materu, and C. H. Herbst. 2013. "Becoming a Health Worker Student." In *The Labor Market for Health Workers in Africa: A New Look at the Crisis*, edited by A. Soucat, R. M. Scheffler, and T. A. Ghebreyesus, 319–33. Directions in Development Series. Washington, DC: World Bank.

Riley, P. L., S. M. Vindigni, J. Arudo, A. N. Waudo, A. Kamenju, J. Ngoya, E. O. Oywer, C. P. Pakuom, M. E. Salmon, M. Kelley, M. Rogers, M. E. St. Louis, and L. H. Marum. 2007. "Developing a Nursing Database System in Kenya." *Health Services Research* 42 (3 Pt. 2): 1389–405.

Scheffler, R. M. 2008. *Is There a Doctor in the House? Market Signals and Tomorrow's Supply of Doctors*. Stanford, CA: Stanford University Press.

Scheffler, R. M., T. A. Bruckner, B. D. Fulton, J. Yoon, G. Shen, D. Chisholm, J. Morris, M. R. Dal Poz, and S. Saxena. 2011. "Human Resources for Mental Health: Workforce Shortages in Low- and Middle-Income Countries." *Human Resources for Health Observer* 8. Geneva: World Health Organization. http://apps.who.int/iris/bitstream/10665/44508/1/9789241501019_eng.pdf.

Scheffler, R., T. Bruckner, and J. Spetz. 2012. "The Labour Market for Human Resources for Health in Low- and Middle-Income Countries." *Human Resources for Health Observer* 11.

Scheffler, R. M., J. X. Liu, Y. Kinfu, and M. R. Dal Poz. 2010. "Forecasting the Global Shortage of Physicians: An Economic- and Needs-Based Approach." *Bulletin of the World Health Organization* 86: 516–23.

Scheffler, R. M., C. B. Mahoney, B. D. Fulton, M. R. Dal Poz, and A. S. Preker. 2009. "Estimates of Health Care Professional Shortages in Sub-Saharan Africa by 2015." *Health Affairs* 28 (5): 849–62.

Sorkin, A. L. 1984. *Health Economics: An Introduction*. 3rd ed. Lexington, MA: Lexington Books.

Soucat, A., R. Scheffler. 2013. "Labor Market Analysis of Human Resources for Health." In *The Labor Market for Health Workers in Africa: A New Look at the Crisis*, edited by A. Soucat, R. M. Scheffler, and T. A. Ghebreyesus, 93–108. Directions in Development Series. Washington, DC: World Bank.

Soucat, A., M. Vujicic, A. Sy, and C. Sekabaraga. 2013. "Fiscal Issues in Scaling Up the Health Workforce." In *The Labor Market for Health Workers in Africa: A New Look at the Crisis*, edited by A. Soucat, R. M. Scheffler, and T. A. Ghebreyesus, 93–108. Directions in Development Series. Washington, DC: World Bank.

Spetz, J. 2011. *Unemployed and Underemployed Nurses.* Geneva: International Council of Nurses. https://www.nurse.or.jp/nursing/international/icn/report/pdf/2012/02-04 -2.pdf.

Tulenko K., G. Dussault, and H. Mercer. 2009. "Framework and Measurement Issues for Monitoring Entry into the Health Workforce." In *Handbook on Monitoring and Evaluation of Human Resources for Health with Special Applications for Low- and Middle-Income Countries,* edited by M. R. Dal Poz, N. Gupta, E. Quain, and A. L. B. Soucat. 37–47. Geneva: World Health Organization. http://apps.who.int /iris/bitstream/10665/44097/1/9789241547703_eng.pdf.

UNDP (United Nations Development Program). 2002. *The Impact of HIV-AIDS on Human Resources in the Malawi Public Sector.* New York: UNDP. http://www.undp.org/content /undp/en/home/librarypage/hiv-aids/the-impact-of-hiv-aids-on-human-resources-in -the-malawi-public-sector.html.

Vujicic, M., K. Ohiri, and S. Sparkes 2009. *Working in Health: Financing and Managing the Public Sector Health Workforce.* Washington, DC: World Bank. http://www.who.int /workforcealliance/knowledge/resources/wb_workinginhealth/en/.

Vujicic, M., and P. Zurn. 2006. "The Dynamics of the Health Labour Market." *International Journal for Health Planning and Management* 21: 101–15.

WHO (World Health Organization). 2010. *Increasing Access to Health Workers in Remote and Rural Areas through Improved Retention: Global Policy Recommendations.* Geneva: WHO. http://www.who.int/hrh/retention/guidelines/en/index.html.

CHAPTER 2

Data Requirements for the Economic Analysis of Health Labor Markets

Anthony Scott, Edson C. Araújo, Genta Menkulasi, and Robert Cohen

Introduction

Applying (labor) economic frameworks to analyze the labor market for health workers helps to understand the diverse and interrelated constraints affecting human resources for health (HRH), the impact of health policies on these resources, and the employment dynamics in the health sector. Although employment in the health care industry exhibits a consistently upward trend (even during recession periods) in most countries, there are dynamics within the industry that are important to note. For instance, in the United States, hospital jobs are countercyclical—that is, when general unemployment rises, hospital employment shows a greater rate of growth (Wood 2011). Technology change is also a major factor in changes in health care employment patterns. The evidence suggests that technological change has increased the demand for more highly skilled and specialized workers, resulting in higher returns to schooling for these categories of health workers and producing a skilled-bias movement in health care sector employment (McPake et al. 2013; Schumacher 2002). This is problematic for most countries, particularly low- and middle-income countries (LMICs), because these categories of health workers cost more to produce and to employ and are less flexible in the application of their skills. These issues show that decisions about the health workforce should not be made in isolation from the rest of the health care system or from the broader economic and employment cycles.

To identify where the problem areas lie and to design effective policy to solve them requires evidence that, in turn, requires comprehensive and up-to-date data. Generally, these data can serve two objectives:

- *Descriptive.* They describe, monitor, and track trends and variation in the characteristics of HRH. This category of data can influence policy generally by highlighting areas where there may be problems (for example, shortages), and where further investigation, research, and policy development work can be undertaken to understand them.

- *Policy design and evaluation.* Research focuses on understanding how a specific policy can solve the problems identified for a specific workforce. Policy design uses research from existing studies or conducts new research to examine the nature of specific HRH problems to help inform the design of new policies intended to address those problems. Policy evaluation uses data to examine the impact of changes in HRH policy on a range of outcomes.

McPake, Scott, and Edoka (2014) highlight the importance of conducting economic analysis of health labor markets (HLMs) in addressing key policy issues. Their report argues that any analysis of issues surrounding the demand and supply of health workers should use an economic framework to help understand the complexities of labor markets. This is especially necessary where there is significant market failure and strong concern for equity in the allocation of resources.

One key reason that economics has not been used extensively to date is the poor quality of the available data. It is essential to develop HRH data sets that move beyond simply counting the number of health workers and their basic characteristics to improved (comprehensive) data that help in understanding the determinants and solutions to labor market disequilibrium. In this way, improved data can be used to generate better quality evidence to develop and design evidence-based HRH policies built on HLM analysis. Improvements in data would enable more rigorous and comprehensive HLM analysis, and would also attract more economists to conduct research in the HRH area. This chapter explores different strategies for consistently collecting comprehensive data for HLM analysis. Specifically, it does the following:

- Provides an overview of the available data for the health workforce by reviewing existing labor force surveys, household surveys, census data, and administrative data from LMICs
- Makes recommendations for systematically improving data collection that will enable more rigorous economic analysis of health worker labor markets

The next section reiterates the broad data requirements for HLM analysis. This is followed by the methods used to identify and critically appraise existing HRH data sets in LMICs. The results of this review are then presented and followed by recommendations for improvements in HRH data collection for HLM analysis.

Data Requirements for HLM Analysis

Data requirements depend on the research questions being asked, and data sets should be developed so they can address these questions and broader sets of issues.

Types of Research Questions That Can Be Addressed

Relevant for HLM analysis are the issues of demand and supply of HRH. The demand for health workers involves issues surrounding how pay and remuneration levels are determined, how many health workers to employ, and what mix of different types of health workers to employ. Issues concerning the supply of health workers are more likely to be addressed using data on or from health workers. These issues include occupational choice, education and training, compensation, specialty choice, and career pathways. Workforce participation and labor supply are also important matters that focus on the impact of changes in earnings on hours worked through the estimation of labor supply elasticities.[1] Migration and retention—including other forms of exit such as retirements—are also central to the labor supply of health workers both within (for example, rural versus urban) and between countries (for example, international migration and global labor markets).

One of the largest challenges faced by health policy makers in LMICs, where new research can yield actionable policy advice, is the issue of "dual practice." Dual practice is the common pattern in LMICs whereby health workers supplement their income from public hospitals by taking time off to working in private hospitals, thereby significantly undersupplying labor to public health care facilities. From a labor market standpoint, the debate touches on the extent to which health workers can supply their labor across a number of jobs and between the private and public sectors, and it raises issues about the consequences of such behavior in terms of access and quality of care.[2] Finally, the productivity and performance of health workers are key lines of inquiry that can be influenced by the type of remuneration (for example, the use of pay for performance) and incentives built into career structures. The economic approach also incorporates the fact that earnings and remuneration are but one of many factors influencing the above decisions, and that the intrinsic motivation of health workers and working conditions also play important roles. McPake, Scott, and Edoka (2014) provide more detail on these topics. Though no single data set can examine them all, there is considerable scope for improving existing data to capture key dimensions of these HRH challenges.

Each of the issues noted previously can be examined using two main types of labor market analysis that use an explicit economics framework: *descriptive analysis* and *causal analysis*. Descriptive labor market analysis helps establish the nature and extent of mismatches between demand and supply (labor market disequilibrium), which in turn help to inform the identification of key issues, research questions, and further analysis and policies that aim to improve the efficient operation of the labor market (Angrist and Krueger 1999; McPake, Scott, and Edoka 2014). Descriptive analysis might provide data about demand, compensation, market structure, supply, interaction of demand and supply, trends, and distribution.

Causal analysis aims to identify the causes of labor market behavior by examining the effects of changes in labor market policies, conditions, or regulation on the behavior of both employers and workers, and on the value of these changes to society. Causal approaches include evaluating changes in policies on labor markets by using a range of study designs that attempt to identify the effects of a policy change by comparing them with a control group as similar as possible to the group experiencing the policy. Experimental, quasi-experimental, and nonexperimental approaches are used to make these comparisons.[3] Causal analysis is essential to understand how to change labor market behavior and design effective policies to do this. Without such analysis, policy design is based on weaker evidence and so may have more limited impact or unintended consequences.

A significant limitation is the lack of data on the earnings of health workers, which is central to HLM analysis. The price of labor (wage rate) is a key variable that provides incentives to health workers. Wage rates determine the choice to be a health worker; the specialty (nursing, medicine, or another occupation); the number of hours to work; the worker's productivity, performance, and quality of care; the geographic location (whether to migrate or to move from an urban to a rural area); and sector of work (including dual practice). Wage rates also provide incentives to employers that determine how many and what mix of health professionals to hire, and can provide signals to patients about the quality of health care workers. Furthermore, the flexibility of wage rates determines the speed at which HLMs can adjust to imbalances in demand and supply as well as affecting the policy interventions required to assist markets to move back to equilibrium.

The price of labor is not usually measured in many health workforce datasets; this is a major barrier to undertaking an economic analysis of the sector. It is also a difficult variable to measure because health workers often hold multiple jobs and their remuneration, especially in LMICs, consists of multiple elements that include salaries, informal payments, and bonuses and allowances that can vary considerably among individual health workers.

Key Characteristics of HRH Data

To conduct economic analysis of HRH data, a number of characteristics of the data need to be present (McPake, Scott, and Edoka 2014). These include not only the range of fields and types of variables collected but also the structure of the data—these structural elements include the level of aggregation or unit of observation (for example, the individual worker or country) and whether the unit of observation is linked over time. Often the data requirements for causal analysis are more stringent than they are for descriptive analysis. For example, a wider range of variables needs to be collected and controlled for to identify the causal impact of a specific variable. Data sets also have to be longitudinal in nature, preferably panel data in which data on individual health workers are linked over time. An ideal data set needs to be able to address a range of policy-relevant research questions. In addition, data sets need to accurately describe and define health workers, and they require a sufficient sample size if focusing on specific groups of health workers. For example, limited data may indicate that a correlation exists between rural-urban pay disparities and labor supply distribution, but without controlling for individual factors using longitudinal data, or other variables such as concentration of job satisfaction, causal inference cannot be drawn.

A variety of sources contain data on the health workforce. Some data sets are from administrative sources, which include personnel records of employers, registration and accreditation databases, tax records, and health insurance records used to pay providers. These data usually have good definitions of health workers, include the whole population of health workers (so sample size is not an issue), yet can be of variable quality depending on how they are collected and processed. Administrative data sets may also have data on health workers grouped by health care organization (for example, hospitals). The main disadvantage of administrative data is that they usually contain only a limited number of fields, since they are collected for specific administrative purposes. At a minimum, these data sets often include the number of health workers of different types, age, gender, hours worked, specialty, and the geographic location of their work. These fields are sufficient for basic descriptive analysis and are an important basis for more extensive health workforce data collections and for basic policy evaluation. However, they are often insufficient for HLM analysis because they do not usually contain information on earnings or more detailed characteristics of health workers and their jobs.

The other main source of data is from surveys that may incidentally include health workers. Health workers participate in population censuses, household surveys, labor force surveys, and specific surveys of the health workforce. The main advantage of surveys over administrative data sets is that they often contain a much wider range of variables; this enables one to control for other factors when trying to examine the impact of a specific policy variable. HRH survey data can enable the collection of much richer data on the characteristics of health workers, their jobs, their families, and the characteristics of where they live. However, household surveys may not contain sufficient sample sizes of health workers, or the definitions of health workers may be aggregated into larger occupational groupings in such a way that health workers cannot be identified, or can be identified only as an aggregate group.

Since neither administrative nor survey data sets are complete by themselves, it is important to obtain the best of both worlds by attempting to ensure that administrative and survey data can be linked at the unit record level (for example, the unit of the individual health worker). This is rarely seen in practice, but concentrated efforts in this direction will be critical to establishing high-quality data for HLM analysis.

A concrete example of a survey data set that has been explicitly designed for HLM analysis is the Medicine in Australia: Balancing Employment and Life (MABEL) panel survey of doctors (Joyce et al. 2010).[4] Though used in a high-income country setting, MABEL is included here as an example of the characteristics of the data and types of variables that should be collected to address most types of HLM analysis. The type of data it collects on health workers is generic and can be applied to any country. The MABEL data include a number of key characteristics necessary for HLM analysis:

• The data come from a panel survey that follows doctors over time and asks the same questions every year. This provides opportunities to apply panel data econometric methods that are used in causal labor market analysis. In particular, it enables the application of random and fixed effects models that can control for factors that are unobserved but do not change over time.

• The data set was designed to address a range of different questions. There are three research themes that MABEL is used to address: (a) workforce participation (such as labor supply models); (b) career transitions (for example, specialty choice and retirement, retention); and (c) rural workforce supply and distribution. The research also focuses on the role of financial incentives and a range of other factors that influence labor market decisions and outcomes.

• The data encompass a wide range of variables essential in a causal HLM analysis. In addition to collecting data on earnings, the survey collects a range of information on the family circumstances of the health worker, including information about their spouse and children, which can have important effects on hours worked and on choosing whether or not to work in a rural area. The data collected in the survey are summarized in the conceptual framework in figure 2.1. The primary outcomes, on the right-hand side of figure 2.1, are measured by observing changes in respondents' circumstances over time.

Figure 2.1 Conceptual Framework Used to Define the Key Information Collected in the MABEL Survey

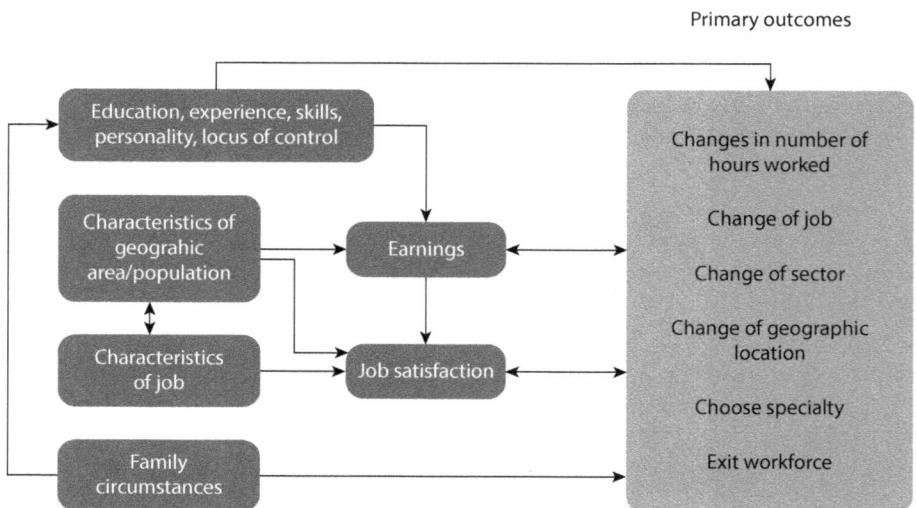

Source: McPake, Scott, and Edoka 2014, 72.
Note: MABEL = Medicine in Australia: Balancing Life and Employment.

Identifying Data Sets for Review

This section outlines the methods used to identify and summarize the HRH data sets. A number of stages were used in this review, including identifying the data sets to be reviewed, summarizing the key features of these data sets, and critically appraising the scope and content of these data sets. Data sets were identified for inclusion using existing knowledge and expertise, contacts in the global HRH field, and literature review.

In the process of identifying data sets, the following organizations were consulted: the World Health Organization (WHO),[5] the International Labour Organization (ILO), the Organisation for Economic Co-operation and Development (OECD), and the World Bank Group Social Protection and Labor and the Development Economics Data Group teams. The process also involved a review of global data sources that include information on health workforce, such as the Integrated Public Use Microdata Series (IPUMS), the Socioeconomic Database for Latin America and the Caribbean (SEDLAC), the Economic Research Forum (ERF), and the Luxembourg Income Survey (LIS).

A literature review was conducted to find publications that identify or describe health workforce data or data initiatives. Searches were undertaken in the following databases: Econlit, Google Scholar, MEDLINE, PubMed, Science Direct, Web of Science, and WHOLIS. Specific HRH and health policy journals were also explored (*Human Resources for Health, Health Policy and Planning*, and the *Bulletin of the World Health Organization*). The following search terms were applied: *human resources for health, health professionals, health workforce, health labor market, health professionals labor market*, and *medical labor market*, which were combined with the following terms using the Boolean operator *(AND)*: *information system, minimum dataset, key variables, household surveys, labor force surveys, salaries and income, wages, international standard classification of occupations, labor statistics, MABEL, employment, registry, database*, and *data strategy*.

The review of existing data is not a systematic review and therefore does not yield a comprehensive understanding of data availability in LMICs. Some good-quality data may not have been included. The review was designed to provide a reasonably representative view of the type and quality of HRH data available that might be suitable for economic analysis. Data that are not publically available, such as governments' administrative data and registration databases, are unlikely to have been identified in this review. Such identification would have required a separate survey of LMIC governments to determine what is collected, which was beyond the scope of this review.

A number of criteria were used to select the data sets to be included. Each data set had to include data from an LMIC and had to be able to identify health occupations. In addition, it was important that the data could be accessed to be reviewed. Data that have already been analyzed and summarized in papers or country reports that rely on other primary sources of data are not included.[6] These are secondary analyses of existing data sets, and so are not in the scope of this review.

For each data set included in the review, key characteristics were extracted and summarized by asking the following questions:

- Are the data microdata or macrodata? Microdata include primary data collected from surveys or contained in administrative data sets, usually from individual health workers or health care providers. Macrodata include summary or aggregate data, usually from a range of different sources (for example, survey data, administrative data, and health facilities data).
- What is the unit of observation and nature of aggregation (for example, individual health worker, hospital or other health facility, geographic area within a country, or entire country)?
- Are the data cross-sectional (a single year), longitudinal (more than one year, but unit of observation are not linked across years), or a panel (more than one year and the unit of observation is linked over time)?
- Which years do the data cover? What is the extent of missing data across years?
- How many health occupations are included? Do the data follow standard classifications (for example, the ILO International Standard Classification of Occupations 2008 [ISCO-08])?
- Do the data include the total count or full-time equivalents of health workers for that country or countries? (Exceptions to this would be sample surveys, including some types of microdata.)
- Which variable fields do the data contain (for example, age, gender, and earnings)?

Results of the Review of Data Sets

Thirteen journal papers were found that used different data sets. Ten data sets were included in the review. Many of the journal papers contain analyses and summaries based on HRH data; only a handful present a thorough review of the state of existing data or a discussion of how to use global databases for HRH monitoring, or both (Boerma and Siyam 2013; Dal Poz et al. 2009; Gupta et al. 2003; Riley et al. 2012; Samwel 2008). Two initiatives on improving health workforce data collection were identified: the WHO HRH Minimum Data Set (Krishnamurthy 2013; WHO 2008) and the United States Agency for International Development (USAID) Capacity *Plus*-iHRIS (Integrated Human Resources Solutions) (see Spero, McQuide, and Matte 2011).[7] These are important initiatives designed to assist countries in collecting better health workforce data.

For example, iHRIS is helping to establish improved infrastructure, reportage, and collection of government and health facility administrative and human resources data. Software to support data collection is now being used in over 19 LMICs. The software provides capacity for countries to collect data for a wide range of variables, including earnings, though it is up to each country to determine which fields to complete and whether to include country-specific fields. Different iHRIS applications have been developed for different human resources support functions: management, regulatory, training, workforce planning, and retention planning.[8] Data from each country are not centrally reported, but the fact that a common software platform exists suggests the potential to centrally collect better quality administrative data across countries. The development of an iHRIS in Uganda is an example of the establishment of basic data collection systems to describe the health workforce and collect data on its basic characteristics (Spero, McQuide, and Matte 2011).

The purpose of the WHO HRH minimum data sets is to create a minimum data set with a set of domains (broad area of required information) and indicators, along with definitions for each indicator, to provide standardization both in the Western Pacific and South-East Asia Region (WHO 2008) and globally (Krishnamurthy 2013). The goal is to encourage countries to adopt the standards of the minimum data set.

The WHO HRH Minimum Data Set and the USAID Capacity *Plus*-iHRIS will eventually yield more data for research, but at the moment they are not collecting actual data—rather, they are assisting countries to collect data in a more structured and standardized way. These are key first steps that seek to establish or make better use of administrative data, which can then be used as sample frames for more detailed surveys. However, there is a long way to go before such data can be collected across many LMICs and used for HLM analysis.

Ten data sets were found and included in the review. These data sets included LMICs and identifiable health occupations (for example, OECD health data were excluded because they do not include any LMICs). Summaries of key characteristics of these data are in table 2A.1 in annex 2A.

Five data sets were macrodata. These data sets do not involve any primary data collection but simply summarize data from a wide range of other sources. These data sets usually provide counts of health workers and a few other variables. Many of these data sets are collated to facilitate cross-country comparisons, so few microdata or data disaggregated within countries are collected. Since these data sets are designed for cross-country comparisons, they are limited in their capacity to address policy and research questions within countries. They are largely designed and used for monitoring and providing descriptive analysis of trends rather than for causal labor market analysis. Earnings data are generally not available in WHO or World Bank data sets, but are available in the other macrodata sets.

The second broad type of data identified come from microhousehold or labor force surveys, which contain much more detailed information than macrodata sets, and so enable both descriptive and causal analysis. However, because these are often general population surveys, the number of health workers in them is often very small. For example, the Integrated Public Use Microdata Series (IPUMS) is a collection of population census data from many countries, but each survey includes only between 50 and 100 health workers. One study from India used the population census and other household survey data to describe the size and characteristics of the health workforce (Rao, Bhatnagar, and Berman 2012). Similarly, country-specific labor force surveys (for example, the South African Quarterly Labour Force Survey) contain rich data but often on only a small number of health workers. HLM analysis has been conducted on similar data in high-income countries (see Hanel, Kalb, and Scott 2014); this analysis has also obtained larger sample sizes by pooling data across different time periods.

It was not possible to identify general health workforce surveys conducted in LMICs. There are examples of cross-section surveys conducted in a few countries; an example is the World Bank's Cambodia Medical Workers Professional Development Survey (World Bank 2013). Although many topic-specific surveys—such as discrete choice experiment surveys and one-off cross-sectional surveys—have been conducted to answer specific research questions,[9] these are of limited general use. No examples of administrative data being generally available or used were identified.

A key issue, particularly when conducting international comparisons, is the use of the ILO ISCO-08 to define the different types of health workers. This classification provides consistent definitions of health workers across countries. The two-digit code of 22 types of health professionals comprises 6 three-digit codes divided into 15 four-digit codes (annex 2B shows the ISCO-08 codes for health professionals). These codes are designed to help define and compare health workers across countries.[10] However, substantial heterogeneity in the types of health workers often exists between countries, which means that these types of descriptions are not comparable, especially in LMICs where there is more variation in licensing, registration, educational requirements, and skills for each type of health worker. For example, nurses in some countries may have only basic school qualifications and undertake a very limited range of tasks, whereas in other countries nurses may be registered and have a bachelor's degree. The ISCO codes are relevant only where the purpose of the economic analysis is to make cross-country comparisons, which is often less relevant if the purpose is to examine the policy issues within a specific country. The scope of this review has meant that many country-specific administrative data sets and surveys have been omitted. Among these are health professional registration databases and personnel records.

Recommendations for Collecting Health Workforce Data for HLM Analysis

Based on the analysis of existing data sets, the literature review, and consultations with key partners, a number of lessons can be learned and recommendations made in the systematic collection of comprehensive health workforce data that can be used for HLM analysis.

Current macrodata collections, where they exist, are not suited for the economic analysis of HLMs. At best they can be used to provide a very basic description of the health workforce and enable cross-country comparisons of trends, but they do not enable any causal analysis to be conducted:

- More analysis should be conducted of those macrosurveys that collect earnings data from health professionals within and across countries.
- Macrodata designed for cross-country analysis and country profiles need to include data on earnings.

Microdata collected from surveys usually contain a much richer set of variables but have a smaller sample size of health workers. These data sets are usually more suited to causal HLM analysis if the sample size is sufficient:

- Microsurvey data sets that identify health workers should be pooled over time to produce sample sizes sufficient for meaningful descriptive and causal HLM analyses. An example is seen in Tijdens, De Vries, and Steinmetz (2013), who use data from the Wage Indicator Foundation. Furthermore, greater use of these data for analysis should be encouraged and access to these data sets should be made easier.

International bodies seem to have emphasized collecting data for cross-country comparisons (Dal Poz et al. 2009). Although this is necessary for analyzing trends and highlighting issues, such data are less useful for the purposes of HLM analysis or for addressing within-country policy issues in either a descriptive or causal way.

- A recommended course of action is to increase investment and support to countries for collecting data that can be used to address within-country policy issues, including the conduct of general health workforce surveys.

Generally, resources invested in data collection seem to be focused on refining and compiling more macrodata sets rather than on strategically investing in new global or within-country HRH surveys. Though the latter would require additional resources, it remains to be determined whether the value of such surveys would outweigh the value of the current continuing investments being made in macrodata collections. For example, the MABEL panel survey of 10,000 doctors costs on average $40 per doctor, though this relies on a high-quality sampling frame and high contact rates. The costs of conducting such surveys are likely to be higher in LMICs. New data sets for HLM analysis need to be strategically defined, developed, and collected. A number of options are available:

- *New approach to HRH surveys.* Consideration should be given to the funding and establishment of more regular HRH surveys that sample a proportion of health professionals in selected LMICs with a core set of common questions plus questions specific to each country. Such surveys should be able to be linked, where possible, to within-country administrative data sets (see the last bullet below) so that health professionals can be tracked over time and linked to other data. These surveys should be repeated every five years. The administration of these surveys could involve building capacity within countries to assist them with questionnaire development and providing funds for questionnaire administration.

- *Supplemental surveys.* New surveys can be added every few years as supplements or modules to existing labor force or household surveys that oversample those working in health occupations. This practice may be cost-effective where the infrastructure for data collection already exists, or where modules can be added at a low marginal cost and repeated every few years. A small number of countries could be approached first and the feasibility of extra modules examined.

- *Compulsory HRH employee surveys.* In addition to developing management information systems for HRH, health professional registration bodies and employers in LMICs should be supported and encouraged to administer compulsory surveys at regular intervals to health workers as part of registration and employment. It is crucial that these data include information on earnings and are able to be linked over time, so that panels of health professionals can be formed and followed up. These databases can then be used as sampling frames for more detailed and less frequent surveys.

In an example of strategic investment in obtaining better data sets, Australia moved from a state-based to a national registration scheme for 10 health professions in 2010. As part of registration, health workers are encouraged to complete a short survey, which is then used for health workforce planning. Though the survey is not mandatory, the online completion of the survey comes before the webpages where the registration is paid, increasing response rates. Although this survey does not contain data on earnings and cannot be used for causal labor market analysis, it is a useful example of how registration data can be built upon and linked over time.

- *Addition of specific health workforce surveys.* More specific surveys of the health workforce, which address one or two policy questions, need to be conducted. A good example of this is the recent growth in the application of discrete choice experiments in LMICs to examine issues surrounding recruitment into rural areas.
- *ISCO as standard for data collection.* The ISCO should be implemented more widely as a standard definition for all health workforce data, recognizing that countries may wish to develop their own more detailed classifications that can be mapped into ISCO-08.

Conclusions

Given the key role of HRH across the world in improving global health, it is imperative that a better understanding of how HRH labor markets work be used to generate a stronger evidence base to inform health workforce policy within and among countries. Such evidence needs to be gathered through the use of high-quality and comprehensive HRH data.

Existing data collections have been useful in highlighting problems by describing trends and monitoring, and these data are essential building blocks for the development of broad policy directions. However, they are less useful for HLM analysis. Additional data collection can be costly but should be considered in the context of existing investment in HRH data. Given the cost of new data collection, it is important to extend, augment, and build on existing data where

Annex 2A: Data Sets Included in This Review

Table 2A.1 Characteristics of Data Sets

Data set	Type of data	Unit of observation	Cross-section, longitudinal, or panel	Time period	Health occupations	Total count of health workers	Variables	Comments
Cambodia Medical Workers Professional Development Survey	Micro	Individual health workers; public and private health facilities	Cross-section	2013	Responses from 1,168 health professionals and 208 facilities; specialist and medical doctors, nurses, midwives, others	No	From individuals: economic profile, training, recruitment, performance management, hours and duties of work, perceptions on other sectors, job satisfaction, government salary, government incentives, dual-practice income; from facilities: facility needs, management challenges, management perception, census count, salaries and characteristics of all health workers	Example of a recent country-specific survey with a focus on HLM analysis
ILOSTAT	Macro	34 countries	Panel	2009–12	Health professionals, health associate professionals, nursing	No	Age, gender, earnings, working hours, occupational injuries	Data prior to 2009 were migrated from LABORSTA (see below)
IPUMS, https://international.ipums.org/international/	Micro	Individuals, year	Longitudinal (multiple cross-sections)	1970–2010, but only 1–2 years for each country	Each survey contains only 50–100 health workers 42 surveys covering 30 countries that use 3-digit ISCO-08, with 1–4 years available per data set. Other surveys (> 250) use ISCO-08 1-digit system	No	Age, gender, earnings, hours, work settings, job characteristics, household characteristics, geographic characteristics	None

table continues next page

Table 2A.1 Characteristics of Data Sets *(continued)*

Data set	Type of data	Unit of observation	Cross-section, longitudinal, or panel	Time period	Health occupations	Total count of health workers	Variables	Comments
LABORSTA (ILO)	Macro	180 countries	Panel	1969–2008 for some variables, 1983–2008 for earnings; 34 countries from 2009–11; substantial missing data	One health professionals and health associate professionals category for earnings data; other variables have different classifications	Yes	Age, gender, earnings, working hours, occupational injuries	Difficult to use Not being updated and will be replaced by ILOSTAT; LABORSTA is very similar to OWW, with a few more indicators such as working hours
OWW Database (NBER), http://www.nber.org/oww/	Macro	Occupation, 150 countries, annual	Panel	1983–2008 Missing data for different countries in different years; best year is 1995, with 57 countries with health worker wages	ISCO-08 Six health occupations: general physician, dentist, nurse, auxiliary nurse, physiotherapist, medical x-ray technician	No	Earnings	None
South Africa—Quarterly Labour Force Surveys, https://www.datafirst.uct.ac.za/dataportal/index.php	Micro	Individual, quarter	Longitudinal (multiple cross-sections)	Quarterly 2008–13, semiannually 2000–2007	ISCO-08 1–2 digit	No	Earnings, age, gender, experience, employment status	None

table continues next page

Table 2A.1 Characteristics of Data Sets (continued)

Data set	Type of data	Unit of observation	Cross-section, longitudinal, or panel	Time period	Health occupations	Total count of health workers	Variables	Comments
Wage Indicator Foundation	Micro	Individuals, annual, 65 countries	Longitudinal (multiple cross-sections)	2000 onward, annual LMICs from around 2008; missing values for some variables and for some countries	ISCO-08; unclear how many health workers because this will differ by country and sample size of each country's data	—	Earnings, benefits, working conditions, employment contracts and training; questions about education, occupation, industry, household characteristics	Sampling strategy differs across countries, but mostly volunteers
WHO Global Health Repository	Macro	All countries	Panel	1981–2010	10 different types of health worker	Yes	Only number of health workers per capita	None
World Bank Databank	Macro	214 countries	Panel	1960–2012; more complete data for physicians than other types of health worker	Physicians, nurses, community health workers	Yes	Only number of health workers per capita	More complete than WHO Global Data Repository
World Bank Microdata Library	Micro	Individual data from 1,570 unharmonized household and business surveys from >180 countries	Cross-section	1970–2012	Very few surveys cover occupation	Yes	Few surveys contain occupation data	Many surveys link to country websites or IPUMS, and most surveys are not relevant to health

Note: HLM = health labor market; ILO = International Labour Organization; IPUMS = Integrated Public Use Microdata Series; ISCO = International Standard Classification of Occupations. LMICs = low- and middle-income countries; NBER = National Bureau of Economic Research; OWW = Occupational Wages around the World; WHO = World Health Organization; — = not available.

possible, as well as consider ways to establish new data collections and surveys of health workers that are integrated into health professional registration databases and administrative data collected by governments. This would provide the building blocks to ensure high-quality research into the role of HRH in improving global health.

Annex 2B: International Standard Classification of Occupations: ISCO-08 22 Health Professionals

221   Medical doctors
    2211   Generalist medical practitioners
    2212   Specialist medical practitioners
222   Nursing and midwifery professionals
    2221   Nursing professionals
    2222   Midwifery professionals
223   Traditional and complementary medicine professionals
    2230   Traditional and complementary medicine professionals
224   Paramedical practitioners
    2240   Paramedical practitioners
225   Veterinarians
    2250   Veterinarians
226   Other health professionals
    2261   Dentists
    2262   Pharmacists
    2263   Environmental and occupational health and hygiene professionals
    2264   Physiotherapists
    2265   Dieticians and nutritionists
    2266   Audiologists and speech therapists
    2267   Optometrists and ophthalmic opticians
    2268   Health professionals not elsewhere classified

Source: ILO 2016.

Notes

1. For examples of studies focusing on labor supply elasticities, see Antonazzo et al. (2003); and Hanel, Kalb, and Scott (2014).

2. For an overview of the policy issues around dual practice, see Araújo, Mahat, and Lemiere (2013).

3. For more technical information on impact evaluations in health care conducted by the World Bank Group, see http://www.worldbank.org/health/impactevaluationtoolkit.

4. See http://mabel.org.au for more information.

5. Geneva office and regional offices databases of WHO are available online.

6. Summaries of data from the WHO Regional Observatories are therefore not considered. For example, the East Mediterranean Regional Observatory, http://rho.emro.who.int /rhodata/?vid=2623; the Africa Health Workforce Observatory, http://www.hrh -observatory.afro.who.int/en/data-and-statistics/online-hrh-database.html; the WHO South East Asian Regional Office, http://www.searo.who.int/entity/human_resources /data/en/; and the Asia Pacific Action Alliance, http://www.aaahrh.org/, which produce country profiles based on analysis and summaries of primary data, were omitted.

7. These initiatives can be accessed at http://www.who.int/hrh/statistics/en/ and http:// www.ihris.org/. The countries participating in iHRIS are Botswana, Chad, Democratic Republic of Congo, Ghana, Guatemala, India, Kenya, Lesotho, Liberia, Namibia, Nigeria, Malawi, Mali, Rwanda, Senegal, Sierra Leone, Tanzania, Togo, and Uganda.

8. See http://www.ihris.org/ihris-suite/ihris-demos/ for more details about iHRIS applications. The countries using iHRIS are Guatemala, Senegal, Mali, Sierra Leone, Liberia, Togo, Nigeria, Chad, Democratic Republic of Congo, Uganda, Rwanda, Kenya, Tanzania, Malawi, Namibia, Botswana, Lesotho, and India.

9. See McPake, Scott, and Edoka (2014) for a review of topic-specific surveys.

10. For more information on ISCO-08, see http://www.who.int/hrh/statistics/workforce _statistics/en/ and http://www.ilo.org/public/english/bureau/stat/isco/isco08/.

References

Angrist, J. D. and A. B. Krueger. 1999. "Empirical Strategies in Labor Economics." In *Handbook of Labor Economics*, edited by O. C. Ashenfelter and D. Card, chapter 23, 1277–366. New York: Elsevier.

Antonazzo, E., A. Scott, D. Skatun, and R. E. Elliott. 2003. "The Labour Market for Nursing: A Review of the Labour Supply Literature." *Health Economics* 12 (6): 465–78.

Araújo, E., A. Mahat, and C. Lemiere. 2013. "Managing Dual Job Holding among Health Workers: A Guidance Note." World Bank, Health, Nutrition, and Population Global Practice, Manuscript, Washington, DC.

Boerma, T., and A. Siyam. 2013. "Health Workforce Indicators: Let's Get Real." *Bulletin of the World Health Organization* 91: 886.

Dal Poz, M. R., N. Gupta, E. Quain, and A. Soucat. 2009. *Handbook on Monitoring and Evaluation of Human Resources for Health: With Special Applications for Low- and Middle-Income Countries.* Geneva: World Health Organization.

Gupta, N., K. Diallo, P. Zurn, and M. R. Dal Poz. 2003. "Assessing Human Resources for Health: What Can Be Learned from Labour Force Surveys?" *Human Resources for Health* 1 (5): 1–16.

Hanel, B., G. Kalb, and A. Scott. 2014. "Nurses' Labour Supply Elasticities: The Importance of Accounting for Extensive Margins." *Journal of Health Economics* 33: 94–112.

ILO (International Labour Organization). 2016. ISCO: International Standard Classification of Occupations, Geneva. http://www.who.int/hrh/statistics/workforce_statistics/en/.

Joyce, C. M., A. Scott, S. Jeon, J. S. Humphreys, G. Kalb, J. Witt, and A. Leahy. 2010. "The 'Medicine in Australia: Balancing Employment and Life (MABEL)' Longitudinal Survey: Protocol and Baseline Data for a Prospective Cohort Study of Australian Doctors' Workforce Participation." *BMC Health Services Research* 10 (50): 1–10.

Krishnamurthy, R. S. 2013. "Minimum Data Set for Health Workforce Registry." Paper presented at the 3rd Global Forum on HRH, Recife, Brazil, November 10–13.

McPake, B., A. Maeda, E. A. Araújo, C. Lemiere, A. El Maghraby, and G. Cometto. 2013. "Why Do Health Labor Market Forces Matter?" *Bulletin of the World Health Organization* 91: 841–46. doi: http://dx.doi.org/10.2471/BLT.13.118794.

McPake, B., A. Scott, and I. Edoka. 2014. *Analyzing Markets for Health Workers: Insights from Labor and Health Economics.* Washington, DC: World Bank. doi: 10.1596 /978-1-4648-0224-9.

Rao, K. D., A. Bhatnagar, and P. Berman. 2012. "So Many, Yet Few: Human Resources for Health in India." *Human Resources for Health* 13 (10): 19.

Riley, P. L., A. Zuber, S. M. Vindigni, N. Gupta, A. R. Verani, N. L. Sunderland, M. Friedman, P. Zurn, C. Okoro, H. Patrick, and J. Campbell. 2012. "Information Systems on Human Resources for Health: A Global Review." *Human Resources for Health* 10: 7.

Samwel, W. 2008. *Data Quality Considerations in Human Resources Information Systems (HRIS) Strengthening.* Capacity Project Knowledge Sharing, Technical Brief 10. Chapel Hill, NC: USAID.

Schumacher, E. J. 2002. "Technology, Skills and Health Care Labor Markets." *Journal of Labor Research* 23 (3): 397–415.

Spero, J. C., P. A. McQuide, and R. Matte. 2011. "Tracking and Monitoring the Health Workforce: A New Human Resources Information System (HRIS) in Uganda." *Human Resources for Health* 9: 8.

Tijdens, K., D. H. De Vries, and S. Steinmetz. 2013. "Health Workforce Remuneration: Comparing Wage Levels, Ranking, and Dispersion of 16 Occupational Groups in 20 Countries." *Human Resources for Health* 28 (11): 11.

WHO (World Health Organization). 2008. *WHO Human Resources for Health Minimum Data Set.* Geneva: WHO.

Wood, C. A. 2011. "Employment in Health Care: Crutch for the Ailing Economy During the 2007–09 Recession." *Monthly Labor Review* (April). http://www.bls.gov/opub /mlr/2011/04/art2full.pdf.

World Bank. 2013. "Cambodia Medical Workers Professional Development Survey: A Review of Cambodian Public Health Professionals' Earnings Composition, Motivation and Human Resource Practices." Unpublished manuscript, World Bank, AUSAID, DFID, HR, Cambodia, Washington, DC.

CHAPTER 3

Demand-Based and Needs-Based Forecasts for Health Workers

Tim Bruckner, Jenny Liu, and Richard M. Scheffler

Introduction

Much attention in the human resources for health field focuses on the shortage of health workers in low- and middle-income countries (LMICs). In its *World Health Report 2006: Working Together for Health*, the World Health Organization (WHO) estimated that 57 countries had an absolute shortage of 2.3 million physicians, nurses, and midwives (WHO 2006). This widely read report stimulated much research and policy discussion about whether the estimated shortages could be expected to improve or worsen over time. Increasingly, researchers, policy makers, and international agencies have issued calls for federal governments to "scale up," or increase, their health workforce.

Given the resources and time needed to increase the training of health workers, it is crucial to understand the magnitude of future workforce needs in order to plan appropriately today. Government officials and health care planners may benefit from tools that can estimate these future quantities of health workers. This chapter introduces the analyst (that is, the development economist or development practitioner) to several approaches used to forecast health workers. Each forecasting method has a distinct goal, set of assumptions, and interpretation. Even with the authors' extensive experience with forecasting, predicting the future is inherently uncertain. Despite this uncertainty, however, policy makers must allocate resources and set priorities today based on expectations of future need and capacity of health workers. The chapter aims, therefore, not to give the "right" answer about the expected workforce in, say, 2030, but instead to equip analysts with methods that enable their own forecasts. Guidance regarding how to clearly communicate the forecasts—with appropriate caveats—to a broad audience is also provided.

The chapter first introduces needs-based forecasts that estimate the epidemiologic need of workers based on their ability to meet specific health care delivery thresholds. Second, it provides steps for the economic, demand-based forecasts

Health Labor Market Analyses in Low- and Middle-Income Countries
http://dx.doi.org/10.1596/978-1-4648-0931-6

that predict a population's ability to pay for health workers; it then outlines a strategy for forecasting the supply of health workers. The chapter concludes by comparing these three approaches and providing suggestions for communicating the forecasts.

Needs-Based Forecasts of Health Workers

A needs-based forecast involves estimating the number of health workers that could provide a minimum desirable level of services to the population in need. Ideally, *need* would be defined by using the prevalence of specific illnesses that are a priority for that country's health care system. With these prevalence figures, a specific number of health workers (or number of work days) per patient in need could be calculated to yield the overall workers required to deliver care for that set of illnesses (Bruckner et al. 2011). In practice, however, reliable prevalence estimates of priority conditions are not widely available in LMICs. The use of previously established health worker thresholds that would meet specific health care delivery targets is therefore recommended. These worker thresholds are calculated from statistical models that assess the relation between the number of health workers needed and their attainment of key health system targets. Because desired needs-based targets depend on the set of conditions that the LMIC deems to be a priority, several approaches are described here.

Needs-Based Approach 1: Skilled Birth Attendant Benchmark

The reduction of infant and maternal mortality is central to the United Nations (UN) Millennium Development Goals (MDGs) and remains a top health priority for most LMICs. Much research demonstrates that the presence of a skilled birth attendant during labor and delivery substantially lowers the risk of neonatal mortality as well as maternal mortality relating to childbirth (Adam et al. 2005). Because the presence of health workers effectively reduces this mortality burden, WHO calculated in 2006 that 2.28 workers per 1,000 population are needed to meet a minimum desired coverage level of 80 percent of all births with a skilled birth attendant (WHO 2006). WHO arrived at this worker threshold after fitting a curve to existing countries, similar to information shown in figure 3.1.

The curve in figure 3.1 is consistent with diminishing returns of additional health workers, especially as the workforce becomes large. The analyst could update this calculation using more recent workforce and skilled birth attendant data from the World Bank's Health, Nutrition, and Population (HNP) statistics database[1] (see also Berman and Bitran 2011). This data set contains information on several aspects of a country's health systems, collected from a variety of sources, including WHO, the United Nations Children's Fund (UNICEF), and other international organizations (World Bank HNP 2014).

The chapter recommends using the HNP database's survey information for a country's percentage of births with a skilled birth attendant as the outcome

Figure 3.1 World Health Organization Skilled Birth Attendant Benchmark, 2006

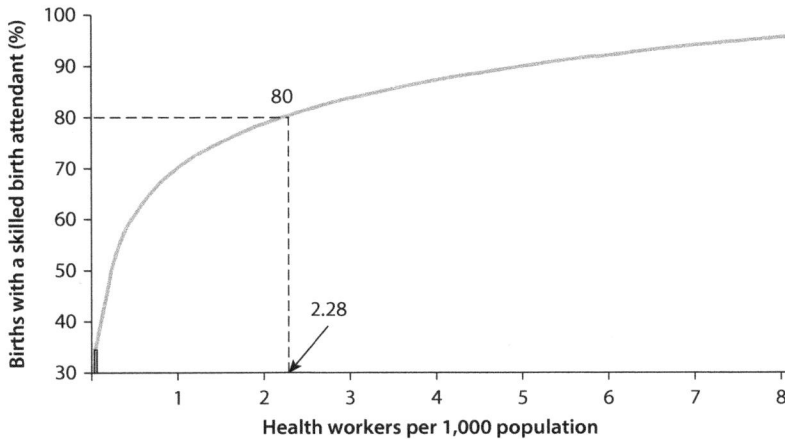

Source: WHO 2006.
Note: The target number is calculated as the number of health workers required to meet the 80 percent threshold of births attended by a skilled health worker. The orange curve represents a best-fitting regression curve of the association between health workers and the skilled birth attendant benchmark, based on empirical data from countries assessed in the *Global Atlas Report* (WHO 2006).

variable; it proposes using a regression model that includes as many countries as possible with workforce density data in the HNP database. In this model, the natural logarithm of health workers per 1,000 population is the explanatory variable. The suggested equation (3.1) appears below:

$$\%BirthsCovered_i = \beta_0 + \beta_1 \ln(HW_i) + \varepsilon_i, \tag{3.1}$$

where $\%BirthsCovered_i$ is the percent of births with a skilled birth attendant for country i, β_0 is a constant, $\ln(HW_i)$ is the natural log of health workers for country i, and ε_i is a normally distributed error term. The coefficient β_1 is the slope of the health worker variable. Using the most recent data available is recommended (the example uses 2012 data). Once all coefficients are estimated, the analyst would insert the desired skilled birth attendant threshold (for example, 80 percent) and solve for HW_i to arrive at the level of health workers needed.

The current needs-based estimate of health workers to attain the skilled birth attendant threshold (80 percent births covered) is anticipated to lie close to WHO's 2.28 workers per 1,000 population estimate using 2005 data. For illustrative purposes, assume that the current (that is, 2012) estimate is 2.30 workers per 1,000 population. As an example, the HNP database for Pakistan is used to forecast that country's needs-based shortage in health workers in 2020. Pakistan currently has 1.40 health workers per 1,000 population, which places it at a current needs-based shortage of 0.90 workers per 1,000 population (that is, 2.30–1.40). Based on supply forecasts, in 2020 (using equation 3.1) Pakistan is estimated to have 4.26 health workers per 1,000 population, and thus would exceed the minimum threshold as defined by coverage of skilled birth attendants and would no longer have a worker shortage. Assuming no gain or loss in productivity of health workers, the 2.30 worker threshold is employed as a minimum goal to meet the health needs of pregnant mothers and children.

The analyst could build on the preceding model and take into account the possibility that geographic factors also influence the country's need for health workers. Sparsely populated rural areas might benefit relatively more from additional health workers than urban areas would because of the numerous barriers to treating patients that exist in rural areas. Urban and rural composition may also drive health care access (Scheffler and Fulton 2013). For this reason, the regression model (equation 3.1) could be augmented with two more explanatory variables: the percent of population living in an urban area and population per square kilometer.

The HNP database contains data on both population variables. After including these independent variables in the regression for as many countries as possible, the analyst could solve the equation for HW_i to arrive at the level of needs-based health workers required. In solving for HW_i, the mean observed value of urbanization and population density across all countries would be assumed. To forecast the influence of urbanization trends on needs-based workers, UN forecasts into 2020 and 2030 of population density and urbanization for all countries in the augmented regression model would be used (UN DESA 2012).

Needs-Based Approach 2: Disability-Adjusted Life Year Weight

In 2013 WHO issued a Global Vaccine Action Plan (GVAP) report, which includes input from 290 organizations and individuals representing more than 140 countries (WHO Global Health Observatory 2013). WHO established a 90 percent minimum threshold for nationwide vaccination coverage by the year 2020. This threshold relates to established vaccine programs that, in particular, reduce infant and child mortality. For this needs-based approach to estimating health workers, these vaccine coverage thresholds and the skilled birth attendant threshold are incorporated into a summary measure. This method, termed *DALY weight*, builds upon the cause-specific disability-adjusted life year (DALY) burden that is unique for each country. The DALY weight method arrives at the need for health workers based on a weighted average of various health system outcomes—each with designated target coverage rates.

Three vaccine programs, with information from a sufficient number of countries contained in the HNP database, permit needs-based health worker estimates: these programs are for diphtheria, pertussis, and tetanus (DPT); measles; and tetanus toxoid vaccine. The GVAP encourages countries to attain this 90 percent target level as early as 2015. The use of this threshold is therefore recommended as the coverage goal. Figure 3.2 shows the relation between health

Figure 3.2 Hypothetical Fitted Health System Values as a Function of Health Workers

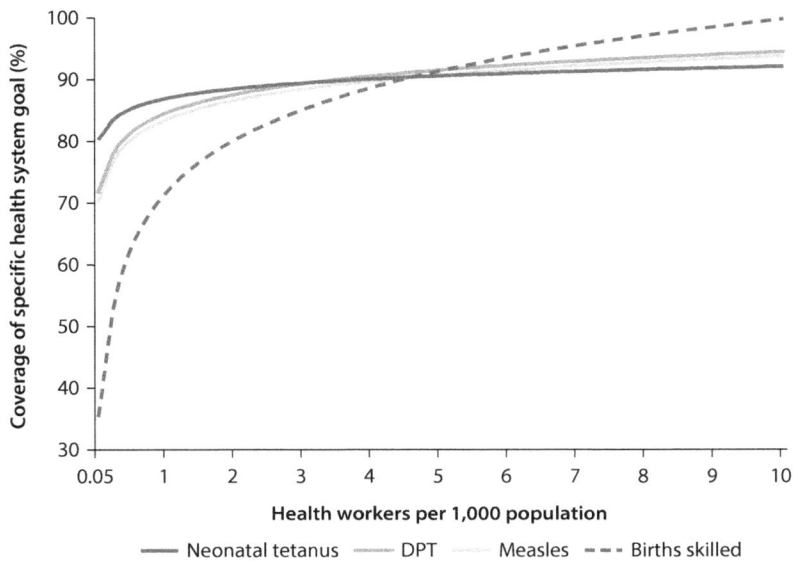

Source: Data from the World Bank HNP database, accessed October 21, 2014.
Note: The four health systems outcomes were selected based on Millennium Development Goals and World Health Organization Global Vaccine Action Plan coverage targets. DPT = diphtheria, pertussis, and tetanus.

workers and these coverage goals. Publicly available data from the HNP database are used to generate these curves.

As with figure 3.1, a curvilinear relation is assumed such that additional workers have diminishing returns especially at high workforce levels. Note that more health workers are needed to attain the 90 percent vaccine coverage level than are required for the 80 percent skilled birth attendant level.

To produce the fitted curves above, the DALY weight method begins with a regression model to estimate the relation between health workers and each of the four health system measures: births in the presence of a skilled birth attendant, vaccine coverage for DPT, vaccine coverage for measles, and vaccine coverage for tetanus toxoid. Each regression fits a separate outcome. Using the most recent data from as many countries as possible, the analyst would estimate the number of health workers needed to attain coverage thresholds using each of the following four equations (3.2–3.5):

$$\%BirthsCovered_i = \beta_0 + \beta_1 \ln(HW_i) + \varepsilon_i \tag{3.2}$$

$$\%DPTCoverage_i = \beta_0 + \beta_1 \ln(HW_i) + \varepsilon_i \tag{3.3}$$

$$\%MeaslesCoverage_i = \beta_0 + \beta_1 \ln(HW_i) + \varepsilon_i \tag{3.4}$$

$$\%TToxoidCoverage_i = \beta_0 + \beta_1 \ln(HW_i) + \varepsilon_i \qquad (3.5)$$

Inserting the desired coverage threshold (that is, 80 percent for births and 90 percent for all vaccines) and solving for HW_i produce the level of health workers needed under these criteria. The fitted curves would be expected to look similar to the hypothetical curves shown in figure 3.2.

Each of the four health outcomes is expected to yield a different needs-based estimate of health workers. To generate a summary of worker need for each country, a weighted average of these four estimates could be calculated. WHO provides data on each country's DALY burden of disease by cause of death, which allows weighting of each of the four health outcomes by the relative burden it imposes on that country (WHO 2014). For example, in Pakistan, the DALYs lost as a result of diphtheria, pertussis, and childhood tetanus are 104.1 (in 1,000s), whereas the DALYs lost as a result of measles are 42.2 (in 1,000s). Therefore, the DPT vaccine coverage intends to address a 2.47-fold greater DALY burden than the measles vaccination program (that is, 97.0/66.9). For this reason, the health worker estimate from the DPT threshold would receive a greater weight in Pakistan's calculation than the estimate from the measles threshold. Through this process, a weighted average of health workers could be derived by assigning each of the four health system outcomes to the specific DALY weights each intends to address. DALYs lost because of not having a skilled birth attendant typically account for 75–90 percent of the country's DALY burden across these four health outcomes. For this reason, the skilled birth attendant worker estimate (that is, 2.30 workers per 1,000 population at the 80 percent coverage threshold) would receive the largest weight in all countries.

Once the DALY weight health worker estimate is calculated for the current year, various assumptions could be made when forecasting needs-based shortages into the future. The analyst could assume that any DALY reduction that resulted from general health improvements occurs evenly across the four health domains (that is, skilled birth attendants, DPT, measles, and tetanus toxoid). In this circumstance of even health improvements across health domains, DALY-weighted health worker needs for 2012 could be applied directly to future years. Multiplying the health worker need per 1,000 population by the forecasted population size in 2020, for example, would yield the needs-based number of health workers. Alternatively, analysts who know the country's circumstance regarding progress on vaccination and skilled birth attendant coverage, or who wish to simulate a specific scenario, might alter DALY burdens for future years based on expected progress. WHO provides forecasts of DALY burden by disease type for each of the six regions in the world. These data could serve as a starting point for more complex needs-based forecasts (Mathers and Loncar 2006).

To give the analyst a sense of how these needs-based approaches may map onto high-need countries, forecasted worker shortages per 1,000 population in 2020 are provided in figure 3.3. The figure shows the 20 countries hypothesized to have the greatest per capita shortage. Note, however, that this figure is not based on the most recent HNP database and therefore should be viewed only as

Figure 3.3 Hypothetical Health Worker Shortage per 1,000 Population, 2020: The 20 Countries with the Greatest Per Capita Shortage

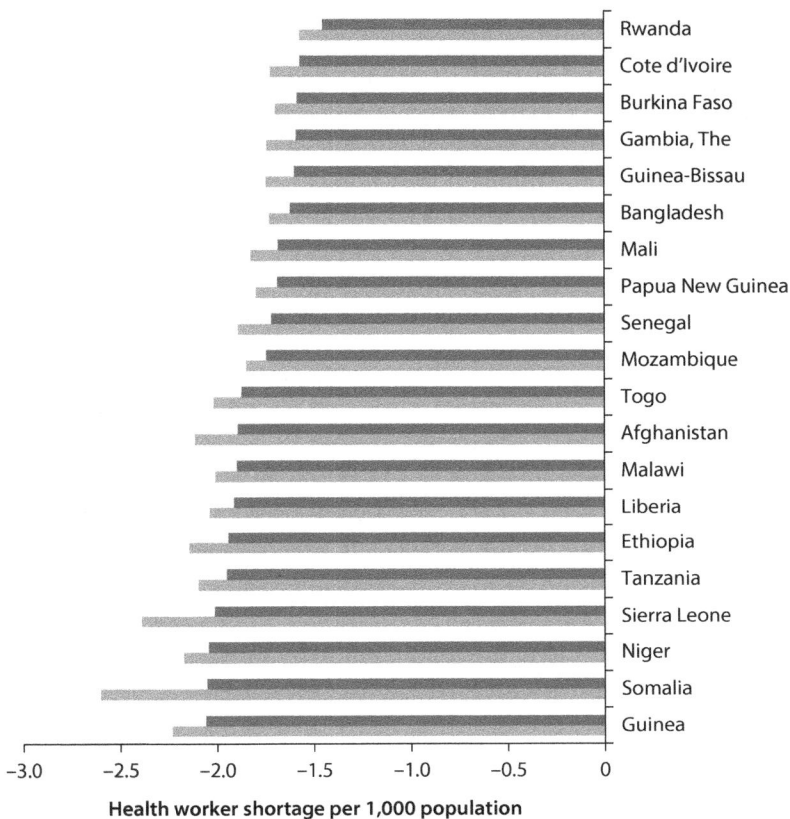

Health worker shortage per 1,000 population

Note: Red bars indicate shortage based on the hypothetical WHO benchmark of 2.30 workers per 1,000 (approach 1); blue bars indicate shortage based on the disability-adjusted life year (DALY) weight approach (approach 2).

an illustration of the needs-based method. In addition, calculation of the needs-based shortages requires forecasted supply, described in a later section. Overall, the DALY weight method provides a greater estimated shortage than does the WHO skilled birth attendant benchmark.

Needs-Based Approach 3: SDG Composite Index

A third needs-based approach, called the SDG composite index, represents a hybrid of the two previous methods, but with a key additional premise: all countries should strive to attain workforce goals that permit universal health coverage (UHC). UHC indicates the ability of all people who need health services to receive them without incurring financial hardship. With UHC as the standard, WHO specifies 12 tracer indicators listed in the Sustainable Development Goals (SDG) framework for which countries should achieve 80 percent coverage: family planning, antenatal care, skilled birth attendance, diphtheria, tetanus, and

Health Labor Market Analyses in Low- and Middle-Income Countries
http://dx.doi.org/10.1596/978-1-4648-0931-6

pertussis (DTP3) immunization, tobacco smoking, potable water, sanitation, antiretroviral therapy, tuberculosis treatment, cataract surgery, diabetes, and hypertension treatment.

The SDG composite index approach includes the term *composite* because each country can score a maximum of 12 points—one point for each SDG tracer in which coverage of greater than 80 percent occurs. Given that each of the 12 tracer indicators corresponds with a different global burden of disease (as measured by DALYs), we recommend differentially weighting the importance of attaining 80 percent coverage for each of these conditions. For instance, diabetes treatment and tobacco prevention efforts reportedly reduce the global burden of disease much more than does, for example, cataract surgery (WHO 2014).

Given data availability on treatment coverage for 12 SDG tracer indicators, the analyst could score each country on this weighted 12-point scale and then regress this outcome as a function of the health workforce concentrations of the analyzed country. The point at which the median level of SDG tracer indicator attainment intersects with the best-fitting regression curve could then be used to identify a target of health workers per 1,000 population (see figure 3.4 as an example). In a recent WHO report, researchers used this method to identify a target of between 4 and 5 health workers per 1,000 population needed to attain

Figure 3.4 Illustration of SDG Composite Index Method

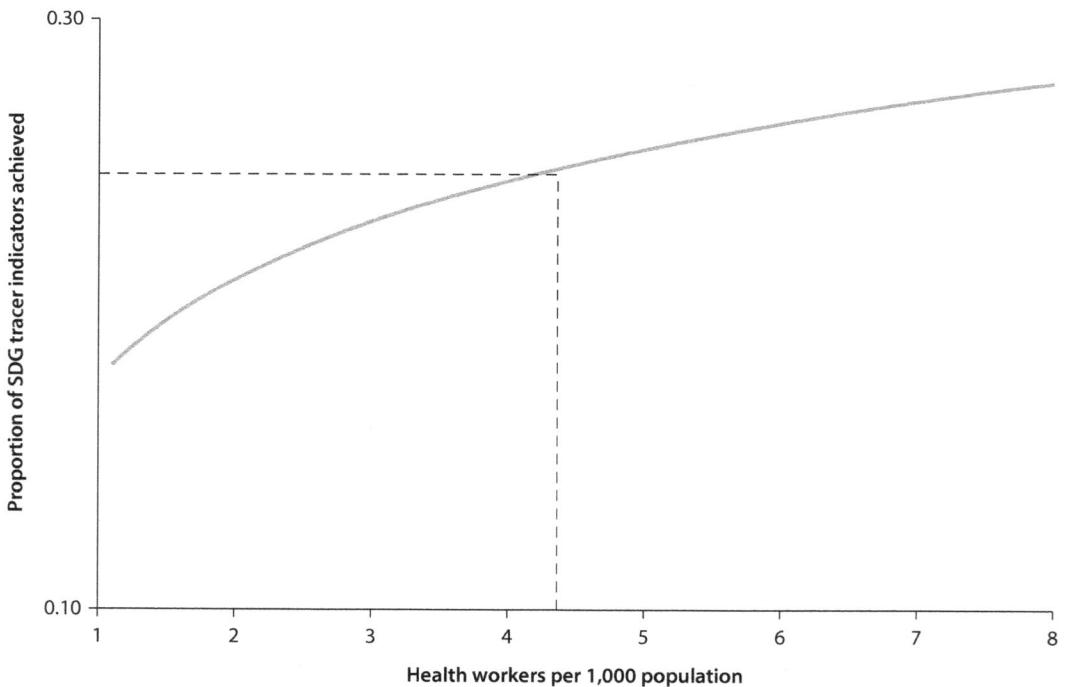

Note: The researcher must select and defend a goal, or a range, of the proportions of selected SDG tracer indicators being met. One goal could involve the median level of the SDG index attainment for the countries analyzed. Implicit in the "median" goal is that countries below the median should strive to attain at least the median level of SDG tracer indicator coverage. SDG = Sustainable Development Goal.

UHC (Scheffler et al. 2016). Analysts, however, may want to use a subset of countries in their relevant region or income level to hone the precision of the SDG composite index method to their particular circumstance. We also note that WHO's calculated target of 4 to 5 health workers per 1,000 population appears much higher than that of the other two needs-based approaches, given that the SDG composite index sets an aspirational standard of UHC across the globe to determine health workforce needs.

Strengths and Limitations of Needs-Based Forecasts

The skilled birth attendant benchmark and the DALY weight approach allow the analyst to arrive at country-level estimates of the need for health workers given epidemiological conditions. Key strengths of these two approaches include the requirement of only few data variable inputs to yield country-level findings and the computational ease of all linear regression approaches. In addition, both the skilled birth attendant benchmark and the DALY weight method hold intuitive appeal in their straightforward interpretation of the log-linear regression coefficient of health workers. By contrast, the SDG composite index method covers many other health domains (e.g., diabetes) but requires much more data on 12 distinct SDG tracer indicators. The analyst, therefore, will want to consider trade-offs of data availability and feasibility when choosing among these needs-based approaches.

Each method requires several simplifying assumptions that often cannot be verified with current health worker data. For instance, the skilled birth attendant coverage approach assumes that confounding variables that may drive birth coverage, but that are not directly caused by the supply of health workers, are not included in the linear regression equation. The DALY weight method assumes that health workers that contribute to birth coverage do not influence other important services, such as DPT vaccination. Whereas more advanced approaches (for example, simultaneous equation methods) can address this cross-equation dependency, they require additional resources and expertise.

Another limitation of the needs-based forecasts is that they assume that attaining worker concentrations would meet not only desired health care coverage thresholds but also delivery of a basic standard of care across all health domains. For instance, attaining 2.30 health workers per 1,000 population to meet the 80 percent skilled birth attendant threshold assumes that these health workers will also provide care to *other* patients with health needs. In addition, the forecasts make strong assumptions of no migration as well as no change in worker productivity and no improvements in efficiency (for example, increasing efficiency through technology) (Fulton et al. 2011).

All three needs-based approaches focus at the country level. Analysts interested in assessing health worker needs at subnational (that is, regional or state) levels would require detailed epidemiologic and health worker data at these finer geographic levels. The application of these approaches to the subnational level could substantially assist planning for future health worker needs should the minimal data inputs be prospectively collected.

Demand-Based Forecasts of Health Workers

A country's ability to pay for health workers is reflected in the demand-based forecasting approach. Unlike the needs-based approach, a demand-based forecast does not take into account the country's burden of disease or its desired attainment of public health goals. Instead, a demand-based forecast estimates the joint interest of the government and the private market in purchasing health care, including the cost of health worker wages. The logic underlying this approach is that countries will not spend more than they can afford on health care even if their health or level of health utilization is suboptimal relative to an internationally established benchmark.

Previous research finds that gross domestic product (GDP) or national income best predicts health expenditures, of which labor is the principle component (Cooper, Getzen, and Laud 2003; Getzen 1990; Newhouse 1977; Pfaff 1990). A demand-based forecast that uses indicators of overall economic growth or specific health sector indicators that represent spending within the health care sector—including per capita GDP, total national health expenditures, public or private health expenditures, and out-of-pocket health expenditures—as the main predictors of the demand for health workers is therefore recommended.

The following regression model, which represents the relationship between selected economic indicators and the number of health workers that an economy can support, is presented here for illustrative purposes (equation 3.6):

For all countries i at time t,

$$\ln(workers\ per\ 1{,}000\ population_{it}) = \beta_0 + \beta_1{}^*\ln(GDP\ per\ capita_{it-1})$$
$$+ \beta_2{}^*\ln(HealthExpd\ per\ capita_{it-1})$$
$$+ \beta_3{}^*\ln(Out\text{-}of\text{-}Pocket\ HealthExpd\ per\ capita_{it-1}) + \mu_i + \xi_{it},$$

(3.6)

where μ_i represents a vector of country fixed effects (for example, individual dummy indicators for each country), ξ_{it} is the disturbance term, and the β coefficients are unknown parameters to be estimated from the model.

Country fixed effects are included to account for time-invariant unobservable heterogeneity across countries (that is, differences in baseline characteristics between countries). The economic indicators included in this illustrative model are GDP, total health expenditures, and out-of-pocket health expenditures, all in per capita terms to account for differences in population sizes across countries.

Overall economic growth is expected to drive demand for health care with a positive elasticity as a normal good, in accordance with findings from Cooper, Getzen, and Laud (2003). The number of health workers employed is also a function of total expenditures on health as a primary indicator of spending in the health care sector. Out-of-pocket spending is included as an indicator of the extent of social protection for private household spending on health care. Based on theory, out-of-pocket payments per capita are expected to lower the derived demand for health workers per capita (that is, $\beta_3 < 0$).

All three economic indicators and the outcome are logged because the transformation facilitates an interpretation of the estimated coefficients as a demand elasticity. For example, an estimated coefficient of 0.177 on logged per capita GDP can be interpreted as a 10 percent increase in per capita GDP and is related to a 1.77 percent increase in the per capita number of health workers. In addition, economic indicators are lagged by several years to allow economic investments to impact health worker numbers. Cooper, Getzen, and Laud (2003) find optimal lags within the 5- to 10-year time frame for the United States and other developed countries. No recommended standard exists for LMICs, although a 5-year lag for GDP has been utilized in previous global forecasting exercises (Scheffler et al. 2008). In choosing a specific lag structure, the analyst may either choose a length of time according to *a priori* assumptions or allow the structure to be empirically derived. In the latter case, choosing a lag structure that fits the data optimally may result in different lengths of time for different economic indicators (for example, 5 years for GDP, 3 years for health expenditures).[2]

The resulting model's estimated coefficients can be used to predict the future logged numbers of workers per capita. The inclusion of country fixed effects allows a separate estimate to be generated for each country. Multiplying the per capita physicians by the forecasted population size (from the UN's Probabilistic Population Projections based on UN DESA 2014) would yield the total number of physicians the population will demand, based on willingness to pay. Using indicators that account for changing population demographics (for example, population age structure, urban proportion) may also be desired.

The specification of the demand model may be partially driven by the amount of available data with which to estimate the model. Note that in order to generate estimates of the future demand, future values of the indicators included as independent variables in the model are needed to generate workforce forecasts. In other words, future values of GDP, total health expenditures, and out-of-pocket health expenditures are needed to predict future values of workers per capita. In addition, to maximize the amount of information used to generate the demand-based forecasts and generate more accurate predictions, utilizing information on health workers for as many countries and years as possible is recommended.

Because global data on physicians are more widely available across more countries and years than data for other health worker cadres (for example, nurses or midwives, laboratory technicians, and administrators), an approach that focuses, first, on forecasting the demand for physicians is proposed. The database on physicians appears in the WHO Global Health Observatory. The data for other health cadres are less plentiful; indeed, obtaining these data represents a challenge for estimating the demand model. An alternative approach for estimating the demand for other cadres of health workers applies a "bootstrap" method to physician estimates. To obtain the projected demand of nurses or midwives, the projected physician demand for each country can be multiplied by the ratio of nurses or midwives to doctors. The ratio can be country-specific or chosen based on similar region- or income-group classifications, or even chosen based on a desired simulation of health worker skills mix. For example, if the ratio of nurses to physicians is 2 to 1, then 4.6 nurses per 1,000 population will be demanded given an estimated 2.3 physicians per 1,000 population. If this ratio is held constant, then it assumes that the production function for health workers stays constant; choosing different ratios over time would allow simulation of different mixtures of health worker cadres.

A hypothetical set of results from this illustrative demand-based model is provided here. Assume that, based on the results of the regression model, the estimated coefficients for Pakistan are as follows (equation 3.7):

$$\ln(workers\ per\ 1{,}000\ population_i) = -3.013 + 0.177 * \ln(GDP\ per\ capita_{it-3})$$

$$+\ 0.243 * \ln(HealthExpd\ per\ capita_{it-5}) \hfill (3.7)$$

$$-\ 0.157 * \ln(Out\text{-}of\text{-}Pocket\ HealthExpd\ per\ capita_{it-5}) + 1.246_i.$$

This model reflects an optimal lag of 3 years for GDP per capita and 5 years for per capita total health expenditures and out-of-pocket health expenditures. To obtain estimates for logged physicians per 1,000 in 2030, we can substitute in the future values of our economic indicators ($GDP\ per\ capita_{\text{Pakistan},2027}$ = 1,223, $HealthExpd\ per\ capita_{\text{Pakistan},2025}$ = 29, $Out\text{-}of\text{-}Pocket\ HealthExpd_{\text{Pakistan},2025}$ = 20— all in terms of standardized US$2005) into equation 3.7 to obtain 0.85 logged per capita physicians per 1,000. Per capita physicians per 1,000 can then be calculated as $e^{0.85} * e^{\sigma^2/2}$, where σ^2 is the mean squared error for the estimated regression model.[3] Thus the final forecasted number of physicians per 1,000 population demanded for Pakistan in 2030 is 0.87. Applying a nurse or midwife-to-physician ratio of 2.31 to 1, we can estimate that 2.0 nurses or midwives per 1,000 population will be demanded for Pakistan in 2030. Multiplying these estimates by the population size of Pakistan in 2030 gives a demand-based forecast of 201,840 physicians and 466,250 nurses or midwives.

Supply of Health Workers

Any forecast of a future shortage or surplus of health workers requires a baseline measurement of supply. *Health workers* are defined as the sum of physicians, nurses, and midwives because, for forecasting purposes, more data are readily available on these professions than for other cadres. The WHO Global Health Observatory (2013) provides health worker counts per 1,000 population for 193 countries.[4] Ideally, the analysis of a specific country would have worker counts for each year over as many time points as possible. With this series, the analyst could use the shape of the pattern of growth (or decline) in the workforce in that country to project worker counts into, for example, 2020 or 2030.

Various econometric approaches, each with advantages and disadvantages, can be used to project supply numbers: these include exponential growth rate, moving average or distributed lag, and autoregressive integrated moving average (ARIMA). Of these three types of econometric approach, the exponential growth rate is the simplest and most straightforward, and requires the least amount of data, but it may be less accurate given its relatively stronger functional form assumption. Other methods rely less on the functional form assumption but they require more data points. A moving average or distributed lag model, which gives more weight to more recent data, requires that data be available for a continuous number of years; an ARIMA model requires that a long time series be available and that it have very few missing data points.

Unfortunately, most countries have a large number of missing data. An exponential growth model, which has the least stringent data requirements, is therefore recommended. This model essentially pools workforce data *across countries* to estimate a general growth rate in health workers. For each country for time $t = \{1990,..., 2013\}$, the following regression can be estimated (equation 3.8):

$$\ln(physicians\ per\ 1,000\ population_t) = \alpha_0 + \alpha_1{}^*year_t + \varepsilon_t \qquad (3.8)$$

where ε_t is the random disturbance term and α_0 and α_1 are unknown parameters to be estimated from the model. The growth rate for each country can then be calculated as $exp(\alpha_1)-1$. This model assumes that the historical growth rate of physicians per capita for each country will continue into the future at the same rate of growth. See box 3.1 for an example.

The supply forecasts make several simplifying assumptions. First, they assume no increase in the growth rate of health workers above a historical growth rate.

Box 3.1 Calculation of Workforce Supply in Pakistan, 2020

Assume that Pakistan has a supply in 2010 of 0.80 physicians per 1,000 population and the estimated a_1 = .035. Exponentiating a_1 and subtracting 1 yields 0.0356. Projecting forward 10 years to 2020 yields 0.8 + (8*.0356) = 1.16 physicians per 1,000 population. To find an absolute number of physicians in 2020, the analyst would multiply 1.16 physicians per 1,000 population by Pakistan's 2020 forecasted population size. The United Nations Population Division provides easily accessible country-level population forecasts by target year.[a] For Pakistan, the forecasted population size in 2020 is 1,480,000, which leads to an estimated 1,711 physicians in that year.

Absent detailed annual data on nurses and midwives in most countries from 1990 through 2013, the use of the most recent data available on the country's ratio of nurses or midwives to physicians is recommended as a starting point (that is, the "bootstrap" approach). With this ratio taken from more recent years (for example, from 2008 to 2013), to forecast the supply of nurses and midwives, the forecasted physician supply would be multiplied by that ratio. For example, if the ratio of nurses and midwives to physicians is 2.31 to 1 for Pakistan, a supply of 2.67 nurses or midwives per 1,000 population is estimated for 2020 (that is, 1.16 times 2.31). If the country of interest does not have sufficient workforce information to generate a ratio of nurses and midwives to physicians, ratios in other countries in that region with a similar income level can be used.

a. See the United Nations Population Division at http://esa.un.org/unpd/wpp/unpp/panel_population.htm.

Second, they assume that past trends will describe workforce growth in the future. Third, the application of the nurse or midwife to physician ratio asserts that the production of each of these cadres will remain constant into the future. If the analyst views these assumptions as unrealistic, they can be modified with advanced forecasting and modeling techniques.

Needs-Based and Demand-Based Forecast Comparisons and Shortage Calculations

If equipped with forecasts of needs-based and demand-based worker volume along with health worker supply, the analyst can calculate projected worker shortages or surpluses. At a conceptual level, a shortage of workers results when the demand or need exceeds the supply. See figure 3.5 (reproduced from chapter 1, figure 1.2), which is a static depiction of a health worker market.

In this market, shortage results according to a demand-based model when the wage rate is equal to WA and the quantity demand (C) exceeds the quantity supplied (B). Additionally, the estimated number of workers needed (E) exceeds any amount of workers supplied; hence a needs-based shortage results. Subtracting supply from needs-based worker volume yields the needs-based shortage. Similarly, subtracting supply from demand-based worker volume yields the demand-based shortage.

Figure 3.5 Demand and Supply of Nurses

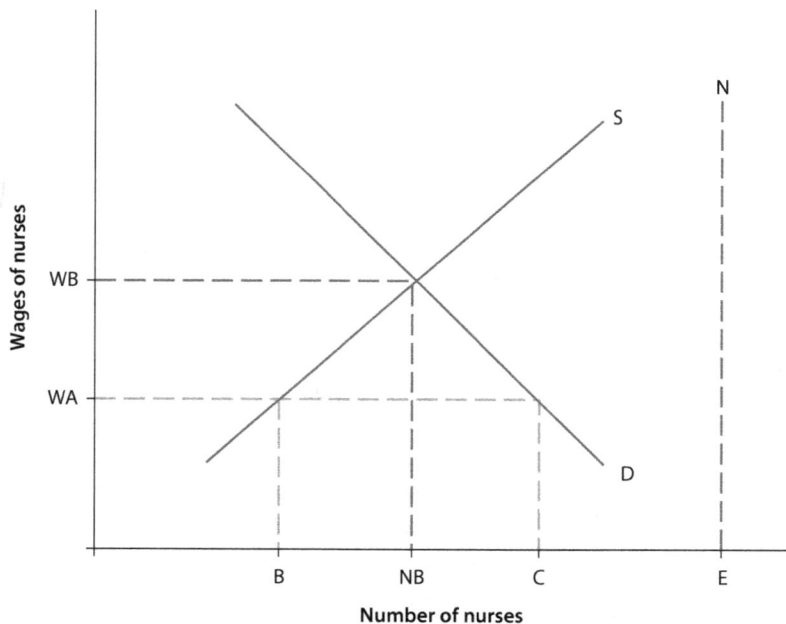

Note: The diagram depicts the labor market for nurses. WB is the equilibrium wage that matches the demand (D) and supply (S) of nurses. As the wage falls to WA, demand will exceed supply and there will be a shortage of workers equal to C–B. N represents the number of nurses needed, NE measures the healthcare needs; and NB is the number of nurses employed at the equilibrium wage WB.

Plotting the numbers of demand, supply, and need over time illustrates the trends of shortages or surpluses. Figure 3.6 provides an overview of this concept.

In the example illustrated in figure 3.6, by 2030, 4.1 physicians per 1,000 population will be needed to deliver health care services according to a needs-based estimate (N), but only 3.4 physicians per 1,000 population that will likely be supplied (S). This corresponds to a shortage of physicians compared to what is needed. Alternatively, the nation's rate of economic and health spending growth may demand only 2.3 physicians per 1,000 population by 2030, represented by scenario D1, which would indicate an excess number of physicians compared to the number that could be supplied by then. In a different scenario, if income growth and health care spending are strong, future shortages of physicians may occur. The scenario represented by D2 indicates that 2.4 physicians per 1,000 will be demanded in 2015, increasing to 4.8 physicians per 1,000 in 2030. This translates into a shortage of 0.45 physicians per 1,000 in 2015; this shortage will increase to 1.4 physicians per 1,000 if nothing is done to actively augment worker supply. This estimated shortage or surplus can be multiplied by projected population numbers to calculate the absolute deficit or excess numbers of physicians.

Table 3.1 provides an example of a specific LMIC, Pakistan, for which forecasted shortages have been previously calculated. Taking the estimated shortage ratios of workers per 1,000 population displayed in the table and multiplying by Pakistan's forecasted population size in 2020 (from UN DESA 2012 estimates) yields a needs-based shortage of 484,148 health workers (155,838 physicians and 328,310 nurses and midwives), but a demand-based shortage of 300,874

Figure 3.6 Assessing Shortages and Surpluses of Workers: Conceptual Forecasting Framework

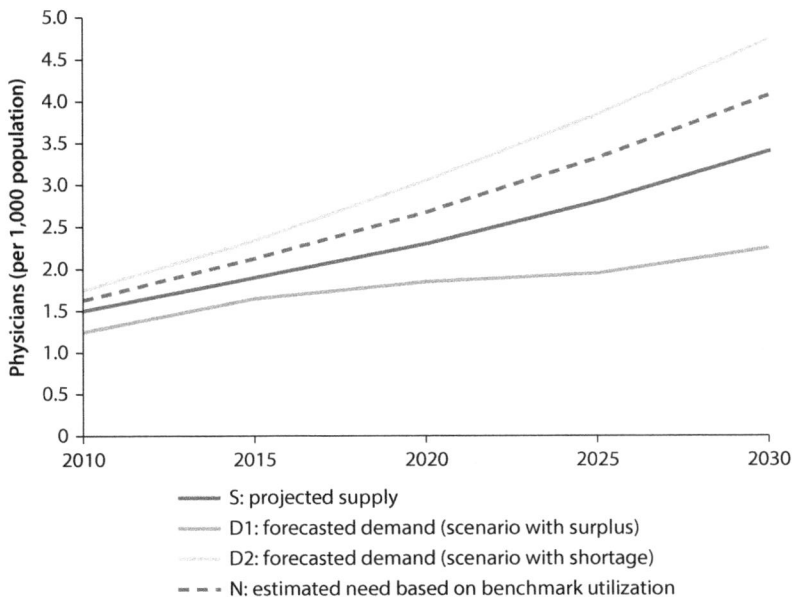

S: projected supply
D1: forecasted demand (scenario with surplus)
D2: forecasted demand (scenario with shortage)
N: estimated need based on benchmark utilization

Table 3.1 Hypothetical Forecasts of Demand-Based and Needs-Based Health Worker Shortages per 1,000 Population: Pakistan

Year	Demand-based shortage: physicians	Demand-based shortage: nurses and midwives	Needs-based shortage: skilled birth attendant method, physicians	Needs-based shortage: skilled birth attendant method, nurses and midwives
2012	0.166	0.384	0.450	0.883
2020	0.447	1.035	0.768	1.617
2030	0.973	2.251	1.315	2.882

health workers (90,841 physicians and 210,038 nurses and midwives). In the case of Pakistan, worker shortages result from both need and demand forecasts.

The results of table 3.1 suggest that, assuming the historical growth in the supply of health workers continues into the future, Pakistan will probably not have enough physicians and nurses or midwives to meet service utilization targets (per the need forecast) in 2020. Further, given the expected growth in spending on health care supported by anticipated economic growth, more health workers to provide services will be demanded than will be supplied in 2020 if no changes to health worker production are instituted. Even if the future economy were to fully employ all the health workers it could afford, the number of workers needed exceeds the number demanded, still yielding an insufficient level of staffing to deliver on service utilization targets. Thus, the relative shortages between the demand- and needs-based forecasts provide health policy makers with an indication of the degree of ameliorative measures needed to close staffing gaps.

Conclusions

The needs-based and demand-based forecasts of health workers serve as complementary approaches to describing workforce scenarios. The needs-based forecasts provide a visioning exercise in that they attempt to address how many workers it would take to achieve a desired level of health care coverage for all members of society. For this reason, estimates of needs-based shortages depend strongly on how need is defined (Campbell et al. 2013). Analysts should note this important caveat when communicating needs-based shortage forecasts to the lay public and to nontechnical audiences. Needs-based forecasts promote agendas, shed light on epidemiologic need, and alert policy makers in countries with shortages to the population health consequences of doing nothing.

By contrast, economic and market approaches to the health workforce rely heavily on demand-based forecasts of workers. The intuitive appeal of demand-based forecasts involves the ability to incorporate a practical limit of the capacity of health workers that the economy can reasonably support. Demand-based forecasts of worker shortages are able to account for macroeconomic factors (and potentially for demographic factors), which strongly determine the size of the health labor market. These forecasts, however, do not take into account likely dynamic changes in worker productivity and they do not consider worker redistribution—whether caused by policy changes or migration—which may offset the need for more workers. Demand-based forecasts are also data-intensive and should be employed only when there is sufficient information on worker numbers and economic indicators to support forecasting procedures.

When comparing demand- and needs-based forecasts, several different scenarios may arise, each with different policy implications. Because the demand for health workers typically increases over time in tandem with economic growth, trends in the labor market will probably enable many countries to employ more health workers. For countries with fewer workers than are needed to deliver health service utilization targets, these economic forces will help to close the needs-based deficits. However, in other situations, robust demand may present additional dilemmas for workforce policy. Demand for health workers for relatively higher-income countries, especially among upper-middle-income countries where robust economic growth is predicted, will add considerable pressure to employ a larger workforce. These countries will need to produce more health workers of acceptable quality or otherwise attract health workers from other countries. While transnational migration of workers from lower-income countries to higher-income countries will close the gap in receiving countries, it will probably exacerbate health worker deficits in sending countries.

Furthermore, in many low-income countries, forecasts of the needs-based and demand-based worker shortages will diverge significantly. This discrepancy can arise because low-income countries may not afford a robust level of health workers. The same countries, moreover, may have substantial preventable morbidity coupled with an inability to meet desired vaccination and birth attendant coverage thresholds. Taken together, the "shortage" picture for these countries would suggest low willingness to pay but a strong epidemiological need for health workers. Whereas several strategies to optimize labor market efficiency could better align workforce volume with population health need, many governments will likely require a comprehensive approach to alleviate forecasted health worker shortages.

The examples and steps outlined in this chapter are presented for cross-national comparisons and to provide national health worker targets. Provided sufficient data were available at lower levels of government, analysts could employ similar forecasting methods for deriving subnational targets across geopolitical units. Although such data may be more readily available among higher-income countries, these data often do not exist in countries where the largest health worker shortages exist (Scheffler et al. 2008). As national health information systems are further developed and standardized, policy makers may want to consider incorporating the minimal reporting requirements for the data parameter inputs—selected epidemiological and economic indicators as well as health worker numbers—needed to apply these methods.

Notes

1. See World Bank HNP at http://datatopics.worldbank.org/hnp/.

2. There are a number of ways to empirically derive the optimal lag structure, but they all depend on the number of time data points used for each country and the estimator chosen. For longer time series, moving averages and autoregressive methods may provide a better fit and are preferred for forecasting procedures. However, because of the limited time-series data available for health workforce numbers, simpler methods, such as linear regression, may be more feasible.

3. The correction factor is required to account for the skewness in the logged transformation of the dependent variable.

4. See the WHO Global Health Observatory database at http://www.who.int/hrh/statistics/hwfstats/.

References

Adam, T., S. S. Lim, S. Mehta, Z. A. Bhutta, H. Fogstad, M. Mathai, J. Zupan, and G. L. Darmstadt. 2005. "Cost Effectiveness Analysis of Strategies for Maternal and Neonatal Health in Developing Countries." *BMJ* 331 (November): 1107.

Berman, P., and R. Bitran. 2011. "Health Systems Analysis for Better Health System Strengthening." World Bank HNP Discussion Paper Series, World Bank, Washington, DC. http://siteresources.worldbank.org/HEALTHNUTRITIONANDPOPULATION/Resources/281627-1095698140167/HealthSystemsAnalysisForBetterHealthSysStrengthening.pdf.

Bruckner, T. A., R. M. Scheffler, G. Shen, J. Yoon, D. Chisholm, J. Morris, B. D. Fulton, M. R. Dal Poz, and S. Saxena. 2011. "The Mental Health Workforce Gap in Low- and Middle-Income Countries: A Needs-Based Approach." *Bulletin of the World Health Organization* 89 (3): 184–94.

Campbell, J., G. Dussault, J. Buchan, F. Pozo-Martin, M. Guerra Arias, C. Leone, A. Siyam, and G. Cometto. 2013. *A Universal Truth: No Health without a Workforce*. Forum Report, Third Global Forum on Human Resources for Health, Recife, Brazil, November 10–13. Geneva, Global Health Workforce Alliance and World Health Organization.

Cooper, R. A., T. E. Getzen, and P. Laud. 2003. "Economic Expansion Is a Major Determinant of Physician Supply and Utilization." *Health Services Research* 38 (2): 675–96.

Fulton, B. D., R. M. Scheffler, S. P. Sparkes, E. Y. Auh, M. Vujicic, and A. Soucat. 2011. "Health Workforce Skill Mix and Task Shifting in Low Income Countries: A Review of Recent Evidence." *Human Resources for Health* 9: 1.

Getzen, T. E. 1990. "Macro Forecasting of National Health Expenditures." In *Advances in Health Economics and Health Services Research*, edited by L. Rossiter and R. M. Scheffler, 27–48. Greenwood, CN: JAI Press.

Mathers, C. D., and D. Loncar. 2006. "Projections of Global Mortality and Burden of Disease from 2002 to 2030." *PLoS Medicine* 3 (11): 442.

Newhouse, J. P. 1977. "Medical-Care Expenditure: A Cross-National Survey." *Journal of Human Resources* 12 (1): 115–25.

Pfaff, M. 1990. "Differences in Health Care Spending across Countries: Statistical Evidence." *Journal of Health Politics, Policy and Law* 15 (1): 1–67.

Scheffler, R. M., G. Cometto, K. Tulenko, T. Bruckner, J. Liu, E. L. Keuffel, A. Preker, B. Stilwell, J. Brasileiro, and J. Campbell. 2016. "Health Workforce Requirements for Universal Health Coverage and the Sustainable Development Goals." Background paper 1 to the WHO *Global Strategy on Human Resources for Health: Workforce 2030*. Geneva: World Health Organization.

Scheffler, R. M., and B. Fulton. 2013. "Needs-Based Estimates for the Health Workforce." In *The Labor Market for Health Workers in Africa: A New Look at the Crisis*, edited by A. Soucat, R. M. Scheffler, and T. A. Ghebreyesus, 15–31. Washington, DC: World Bank. doi: 10.1596/978-0-8213-9555-4.

Scheffler, R. M., J. X. Liu, Y. Kinfu, and M. R. Dal. 2008. "Forecasting the Global Shortages of Physicians: An Economic- and Needs-Based Approach." *Bulletin of the World Health Organization* 86: 516–23.

UN DESA (United Nations, Department of Economic and Social Affairs), Population Division. 2012. *World Urbanization Prospects: The 2011 Revision*. CD-ROM Edition— Data in digital form (POP/ DB/WUP/Rev.2011). New York: UN DESA.

———. 2014. *World Population Prospects: The 2015 Revision*. http://esa.un.org/unpd/ppp/.

WHO (World Health Organization). 2006. *The World Health Report 2006: Working Together for Health*. http://www.who.int/whr/2006/en/ (accessed October 15, 2014). Geneva: WHO.

———. 2013. "Global Vaccine Action Plan 2011–2020." http://www.who.int /immunization/global_vaccine_action_plan/GVAP_doc_2011_2020/en/.

———. 2014. *WHO Global Burden of Disease, 2014: Disease and Injury Country Mortality Estimates, 2000–2012*. Geneva: WHO. http://www.who.int/healthinfo/global _burden_disease/estimates/en/index1.html (accessed August 15, 2014).

WHO Global Health Observatory. 2013. *Global Health Workforce Statistics*. Geneva: World Health Organization. http://www.who.int/hrh/statistics/hwfstats/ (accessed August 15, 2014).

World Bank HNP (World Bank Health, Nutrition, and Population database). 2014. Washington, DC: World Bank. http://data.worldbank.org/data-catalog/health -nutrition-and-population-statistics (accessed August 15, 2014).

CHAPTER 4

Measuring and Analyzing Production Supply

Kate Tulenko, Atef El Maghraby, Agnes Soucat, Alex Preker, and
Tim Bruckner

Introduction

Preservice education has long been neglected by most health systems and donors
(Frenk et al. 2010). The vast majority of countries do not train enough health
workers to meet their needs, and the health labor markets in most countries suffer from an inadequate supply of skilled health workers that is manifested in the
number of vacancies in the health labor market. Even when the overall number
of trained workers is sufficient to match a country's need, health workers often
concentrate in urban areas and in specialty care, which creates a scarcity of
workers in rural areas and in primary care professions.

Both the overall vacancy issue and the maldistribution challenge originate
in part from the preservice education system and the weak management of the
supply chain producing health professionals. Neglect of the health professional education system, however, persists despite the fact that the system is
uniquely responsible for the number of health workers. In addition, over-
whelming evidence indicates that preservice education largely determines
where a health worker practices and what type of care they provide (primary
care versus specialty care) (WHO 2010). The report from the World Health
Organization (WHO) entitled *Increasing Access to Health Workers in Remote
and Rural Areas through Improved Retention: Global Policy Recommendations*
cites preservice education as one of four factors (along with regulatory interventions, financial incentives, and personal and professional support) most
likely to influence practice location (WHO 2010). Some of the strongest evidence involves approaches that begin before students arrive at a school, such
as recruiting students from rural communities to increase the likelihood that
they will practice in rural areas.

Preservice education also significantly affects other attributes of the health
workforce (Jhpiego 2012). For instance, targeted pipeline programs, proactive
recruitment strategies, and low-interest loans for students from underrepresented

ethnicities and rural geographic areas may increase minority enrollment (Atkinson, Spratley, and Simpson 1994). In addition, creating a training environment that minimizes strict gender roles for particular professions may increase recruitment of female health workers. From a financial standpoint, moreover, the cost and length of preservice education shapes students' debt burden as well as affecting their wage expectations and years of deferred income (Kassebaum and Szenas 1993). Health workers' ability to adapt to new information and communication technologies (ICTs) may depend on whether they had any training or exposure to such technologies during their preservice education.

Curriculum, essential infrastructure, training environment, and institutional culture of preservice education also strongly influence health workers' future performance, choice of work setting (hospital versus community), skills, and attitudes. All of these factors, in turn, contribute to the workers' choice of clinical focus and geographic setting, and their decision to continue in their training programs and ultimately serve the community in their professional roles.

The purpose of this chapter is to introduce the main labor market challenges within the health professional education system and related indicators, along with tools and analytical approaches, to help design solutions.

Institutional Dynamics

Given the large potential of preservice education to influence all aspects of the health workforce, ministries of health and ministries of education in low- and middle-income countries (LMICs) should plan such programs more carefully than they do at present. Governments frequently divide the roles and responsibilities of educating and training health professionals between ministries of health and ministries of education, and the lack of effective coordination and collaboration between the two ministries plays a critical role in the outcomes of the health workforce supply line. For example, in Uganda the Ministry of Education and Sports is responsible for the education of physicians while the Ministry of Health is the main employer of physicians.

Strengthening preservice institutions is a complex, multiyear endeavor. Successful models rely on effective partnership, collaboration, and coordination, although the lack of best models to follow presents a major challenge. Shared vision, effective involvement, and consensus among stakeholders are crucial. The dynamic interaction among ministries of health and ministries of education, educational institutions, professional associations, regulatory bodies, donors, partner organizations, local organizations, and communities will shape the performance of the preservice education in the country. The expansion of the preservice education of health professionals can place a significant burden on ministry budgets. Because of concerns over creating recurrent costs, these ministries, as well as donors, are reluctant to invest in preservice education. When they have invested, funds tend to be earmarked for curriculum development and faculty pedagogy rather than for improving school management or reducing high dropout rates.

Medical Education Transformation

Many health professional education systems have remained virtually unchanged for decades and have not been able to respond to epidemiologic changes, economic changes, demographic changes, and the introduction of team care and large shifts in donor priorities that drive service delivery (examples can be seen in the areas of HIV/AIDS and maternal health). Labor market analyses of national health professional education systems are badly needed to increase both the efficiency and the responsiveness of the systems to current health priorities. Preservice education is a central component of the pipeline that must provide the health workforce requirements for the country—the right number, mix, and caliber of health professionals. The health workforce requirements should be defined through a rational performance needs assessment process. Market-oriented country strategic investments plans for preservice education are essential to set country priorities, strategic objectives, budgets required, time frames, and expected outcomes. Other health professional schools are undergoing rapid change. For example, Ethiopia has more than doubled the number of its medical schools in the past decade. Increasing global demand for medical education has led to the founding and rapid expansion of private medical schools in the Caribbean. These schools, which originally focused on training North Americans with North American faculty, are evolving over time and are starting to hire local faculty and reserve slots for local students.

Modernizing preservice education is necessary and critical to respond to the evolving health needs of the population. It is paramount to ensuring that the education and training institutions are designed to be flexible and capable of assessing trends, modifying curricula and methodologies, and pursuing competency-based approaches to produce the right health professionals who are equipped with the levels of knowledge, skills, and practices that the health labor market needs.

Improving educational infrastructure, advancing teaching and learning skills, and strengthening education management and leadership are among the essential components needed for health workforce educational reform. Obviously this improvement comes at a cost that strategists have to factor in and justify to ministries of finance while tapping other innovative funding streams in the meantime.

Competency-based preservice education programs are designed to enable students to acquire a specific range of knowledge, skills, and behaviors and to demonstrate using them effectively to bring about the highest health outcomes for the population served. As such, health labor markets should enhance the supply of these kinds of skilled professionals by using market forces within the right enabling set of health and education policies.

The ICT revolution provides countries with the opportunity to leverage e-learning opportunities to overcome challenges in access, finance, and human resources to deliver high-quality education programs. Furthermore, training health workers in how to use ICT as part of their work can greatly benefit their ability to diagnose and manage patients, provide the health system with data, and respond to various emergencies, including epidemics.

WHO and the World Federation for Medical Education have each identified a set of fundamental domains of the educational process for producing skilled health professionals (table 4.1).

Although this book is the first to approach the measurement and evaluation of preservice education from a labor market point of view, previous publications have addressed the issue more generally. The two most important are WHO's *Handbook on Monitoring and Evaluation of Human Resources for Health* (WHO 2009; hereafter WHO *Handbook*) and CapacityPlus' *Human Resources for Health (HRH) Indicator Compendium* (CapacityPlus 2011). The *Handbook* provides suggested indicators for the health workforce labor market as well as detailed descriptions of these indicators and their collection and use. The *HRH Indicator Compendium* provides tables of indicators along with their definitions and methods of calculation.

Not all monitoring, evaluation, and analysis of preservice education are based on simple labor market indicators, however. Education systems are complex and consist of many different actors, institutions, inputs, processes, and funding sources. Health workforce planners would also benefit from reliable analytical tools to help assess the health professional education system.

Although the health professional domains listed previously focus exclusively on the school level, it is important to look more widely at the entire health professional education system. An analytical framework of the health professional education system includes six components: financing, regulation, stakeholders, health professional schools, health facilities, and employers.

Financing Education Institutions

Financiers vary by country but include ministries of finance, ministries of health, ministries of education, donors, the private sector (both for-profit and not-for-profit), banks, and students and their families. The International Finance Corporation has estimated that, given the public sector's resource constraints,

Table 4.1 Essential Domains of Health Professional Education

World Health Organization	World Federation for Medical Education
• Faculty (academic, clinical, and professional development)	• Mission and objectives
• Admission (policy and selection; student type and intake)	• Governance and administration
	• Academic staff/faculty
• Curriculum (design, core partnerships, student assessment)	• Student body
	• Educational program (academic and clinical curricula, program management)
• Development/revision (government, accreditation, infrastructure)	• Educational resources (physical facilities, clinical training resources, information technology)
• Graduates (outcomes, attributes)	• Assessment of students
	• Program evaluation
	• Continuous renewal

Sources: WFME 2003; WHO 2013.

there is a private investment opportunity of $1.7 billion in medical education in Africa (WHO 2008). In 2005 some 60 percent of the total health expenditure in Africa was financed by private parties (WHO 2008). In some countries, health insurance or patient fees directly or indirectly subsidize health worker education. The Medicare residency payments in the United States, which subsidize graduate medical education, serve as one example of an indirect subsidy of medical student tuition (Rich et al. 2002).

Effective Regulation

Regulators include the institutions that license or accredit health professional education programs and the professional associations or other bodies that license the graduates and therefore determine the skills that schools must teach. In many countries the accreditation role is played by professional councils, such as the nursing or medical council. In other countries this function is performed by the ministry of health or the ministry of education. Some countries additionally require that schools hold business licenses to operate legally. Accreditation ensures that only those schools that deliver a curriculum and training at or above that country's determined standard level are allowed to operate.

Stakeholders

Stakeholders include constituencies that have a formal or informal voice within the health professional education system or that are directly affected by the system. These include student groups, communities in which schools are based, underserved communities that need the service of health professionals, patient groups, health professional associations, and unions.

Health Professional Schools

Schools include all programs that provide preservice education for health workers. These include those traditionally recognized as schools, such as medical, nursing, dental, and pharmacy schools; schools of public health; allied health professional schools; and preservice training programs for community health workers. Training programs may be freestanding, such as many medical schools, or they may be incorporated within a larger university or school of health science.

Health Facilities

The most important training of any health worker is the training received beyond the classroom: hands-on training in the working environment of a health facility. Successful education models ensure the acquisition of essential skills and competences in the classroom and in the workplace where those health professionals are planning to be deployed upon successful completion of their education programs. Adequate exposure to clinical practices is paramount. It is particularly important that health workers be exposed to primary health care settings, since this is the setting in which the majority of health workers will practice after graduation. Facilitating and arranging the clinical sites for students to learn and practice in an environment conducive to learning and gaining experiences are key components of the health professional education and must be closely coordinated with the country's health systems and services delivery.

Some health facilities involved in training health professionals may be owned by health professional schools; others are owned by the ministry of health, a faith-based organization, or a third party that has an agreement with the school to help train their students. In many high disease burden countries there is a dearth of health facilities in which students may professionally train, despite the paradoxically high need of the population for a trained health workforce. This training bottleneck may arise as a result of administrative, cultural, or financial barriers to integrating training into routine care in health facilities.

Employers

Employers are the institutions that directly or indirectly hire the graduates of health professional schools. These include ministries of health; ministries of civil service; local governments; and for-profit, nonprofit, and faith-based health facilities.

Data Needs

Three main uses of information gathered from interventions and evaluations of the health professional education programs have been identified: policy and planning, active management of the education system, and global reporting.

Policy and Planning

Policy and planning permeate almost all aspects of the health professional education system. The specific educational information needed to inform policy depends greatly on which component of the health professional education system is being focused on. For example, from a financing perspective, the ministry of finance and the ministry of health may use data on state revenues, the projected epidemiologic-based demand for health workers, and patients' ability to pay for services to decide how much money to invest in training additional health workers.

Ministries of health and professional councils that intend to match graduating health workers with specific health facilities would ideally retrieve data on the geographic distribution of schools and health facilities and the geographic distribution of open posts.

Active Management of the Education System

Active management of the system includes all the changes made on a regular basis to improve its performance and to meet national health goals. From an individual school's perspective, monitoring and evaluation occurs mainly at the school level to help it run as efficiently as possible and train an appropriate number of qualified health workers as cost-effectively as possible. The ministry of health or the ministry of education, on the other hand, may want to evaluate a scholarship program that targets students from underserved communities to compare their graduation rates with those of other students and to determine whether the former were more likely to be employed in an underserved community upon graduation. From a policy perspective, retrieval of this information in a systematic and standardized fashion—throughout all schools in the country—would serve ministries of health and ministries of education better than if each school gathered their own data in an uncoordinated and ad hoc manner. Such standardized data would permit a countrywide assessment of the geographic distribution of successfully performing schools.

Global Reporting

A variety of functions are served by global reporting. Global reporting results in the standardization of indicators and data so that cross-country comparisons can be made and so that country and regional data can be combined to track progress over time. With this aggregated data, countries may benchmark their progress against other countries in various regions and with various gross domestic product (GDP) levels and health system models. Examples of global reporting of health professional education systems include the World Federation for Medical Education (WFME, the global organization that sets standards for medical schools) and the Foundation for Advancement of International Medical Education and Research (FAIMER, the U.S. organization that qualifies foreign-trained physicians to enter residency in the United States), which copublish the *World Directory of Medical Schools* (WFME/FAIMER 2015), and WHO's *Global Health Workforce Alliance Annual Report* (GHWA 2015). One benefit of global reporting involves the ability to assess the relative merits or drawbacks of particular country strategies relative to those of other countries confronting similar health workforce and education challenges.

Indicators That Measure Progress

Disease-control programs have been able to define input, process, and output indicators to measure program success and return on investment relatively easily. For example, HIV/AIDS programs measure and report the number of people who have received HIV counseling and testing and the number of people receiving antiretroviral treatment. Malaria programs report the percentage of children under five sleeping under a bed net and the percentage decrease in malaria rates. By contrast, experts cannot agree on a set of similar measures to gauge the quality of health sciences education.

A strong measure for evaluation purposes would have the following four characteristics:

- The measure would be collected in a relatively low-cost, straightforward fashion.
- The measure would be reproducible, such that the same construct in a different school, which undergoes similar improvements, would show a similar result.

Health Labor Market Analyses in Low- and Middle-Income Countries
http://dx.doi.org/10.1596/978-1-4648-0931-6

- The indicator would reflect a true improvement in the health system.
- The measure would assist with decision making regarding health system planning, financing, and management decisions.

Financing

This section looks at the tools and analytical methods to assist with decisions of financing preservice education. Neither the WHO *Handbook* nor the Capacity*Plus HRH Indicator Compendium* proposes indicators to determine how to measure or track the financing of preservice education. The "Health Professionals for a New Century" report provides a tool to estimate the total amount spent on health professional preservice education at the national and regional levels and the cost per graduate (Frenk et al. 2010) (table 4.2). This methodology helps reveal variations in investments per worker between countries. Although the estimates are crude, they nevertheless provide an initial approximation that can help planning and estimating budgets for scaling up medical education (Frenk et al. 2010). Capacity*Plus* also developed a methodology for calculating the cost of training health workers at the school level.[1]

Table 4.3 presents proposed financing indicators needed for adequate policy and planning—as well as school management—on both local and national levels.

Fund flows are an important element of financing. As demonstrated by Vujicic, Kelechi, and Sparkes (2009), health workforce funding can be more efficiently allocated if it flows in a lump sum from the ministry of finance to the ministry of health. If preservice education funding goes instead to the ministry of education or directly to schools, this impairs the ability of the ministry of health to flexibly invest in preservice education to meet changing needs.

Table 4.2 Cost of Medical Education in Different Countries

Country	Study	Metric	Year	Cost estimate
United States	Rein et al. 1997	Cost per graduate	1994–95	US$357,000
Vietnam	Bickell 2012	Cost per graduate	1997	VND 111,426,989
Thailand	Vimolket, Kamol-Ratanakul, and Indaratna 2003	Cost per graduate	2003	THB 2,174,091
Sweden	Karolinska Institutet 2009	Cost per graduate	2006	SKr 1.32 M
United States	Goodwin, Gleason, and Kontos 1997	Annual cost per student	1994–95	US$69,992[a]
United States	Franzini, Low, and Proll 1997	Annual cost per student	1994–95	US$57,370[a]
Ghana	Beciu, Ayettey, and Amponsah 2010	Annual cost per student	2009	US$8,975
Canada	Valberg et al. 1994	Annual cost per student	1993	Can$48,330

Source: Frenk et al. 2010.
Note: Because of the severe lack of data, the metrics for the costs are not strictly comparable.
a. Studies are for different schools.

Table 4.3 Proposed Indicators of Health Professional Education Financing and Their Purpose

Indicator	Purpose
Preservice education fund flows: Preservice education funding is part of general ministry of health funding rather than earmarked or in another ministry (such as the ministry of education)	To measure the flexibility the ministry of health has to adjust investment in preservice education
Percentage of preservice education investment: Total amount spent from all sources on preservice education annually as percentage of total health spending	To indicate the level of investment in training new workers relative to the size of the health system
Average student debt burden	To allow the comparison of individual graduate debt burden to average salaries for that profession or to GDP per capita
Total cost to train a health worker of a particular cadre (includes the school's budget plus students' costs)	To measure the efficiency of schools
	To provide an input in determining the cost-effectiveness of different cadres—for example, physicians versus clinical officers
Fraction of funding devoted to recruitment and retention of students from underserved communities	To identify the extent to which the institution invests in redressing uneven, inefficient geographic distribution of health care workers
Fraction of funding devoted to faculty development (pedagogy and technical knowledge)	To identify the extent to which the institution invests in ensuring that its faculty have current teaching skills and technical knowledge in their field of expertise

Effective Regulation

Regulation is the process of setting rules and guidelines to protect the public and students. As such, regulating health professional education is a complex process that entails setting an organizing framework of guiding principles, binding rules, and instruments that together ensure the effective and efficient management of education that delivers the desired outcomes in a fair and just environment. The widely known regulatory mechanisms and tools used are the accreditation of education institutions and the licensing or certification of graduates.

The Capacity*Plus HRH Indicator Compendium* contains two indicators of health professional education system regulation. The existence of an accrediting agency measures the extent to which the government values one of the most basic steps in the quality control of health professional and higher education. The number and percentage of schools meeting accreditation standards is a more complex indicator. Many countries set their accreditation standards too high given the resources they have available for education and given the actual practice conditions of graduates. When a large number of schools do not meet accreditation standards, the standards may need to be changed. In many developing countries, access to health workers is a greater barrier to better health than quality of care, and closing down large numbers of schools would dramatically decrease the number of health workers available. Under these circumstances it is also important to look at how effective a school is in graduating health workers who work in underserved communities.

Accreditation standards should be at an appropriate level to balance the availability, accessibility, acceptability, and quality of health workers. No standardized global accreditation standards exist, although some global professional associations—such as the World Federation for Medical Education and the

Box 4.1 Framework for Changing Regulatory Requirements

Proposed changes to health professional school regulatory requirements must do the following:

- Improve or not harm entry of people from underserved communities into the profession
- Improve or not harm communities' access to essential care (defined by number and location of practitioners)
- Be cost-effective or cost-neutral (in both preservice education costs and labor costs of the new professionals)

Table 4.4 Proposed Indicators of Health Professional Education Regulation and Their Purpose

Indicator	Purpose
Existence of an accreditation agency for most cadres	To provide a basic measure of the effort to regulate schools
Number and percentage of training programs meeting accreditation standards	To provide a basic measure of the quality of schools compared to standards
Public health–mindedness: Requirements that accreditation boards need to have either significant representation of institutions responsible for public health or requirements that all regulatory changes must improve access to care by underserved populations	To provide a basic measure of the alignment between accreditation and national public health goals

International Confederation of Midwives—have created general standards for their professions. No current tools for analyzing regulations and accreditation standards are known to be available. Most accreditation standards do not consider the impact that changing the standards (and making education more expensive) would have on access to school for students from underserved communities or on the future practice choice of graduates and the effect this would have on access to care. This lack is an area that needs to be addressed; a framework for changing regulatory requirements is proposed in box 4.1.

Most accreditation board members represent the profession; the boards do not have representatives who represent communities or are responsible for taking national health goals into account. This area warrants more careful research to understand the role accreditation standards have in promoting quality of the preservice education system as well as evaluating access that underserved communities have to health careers and to health workers.

Table 4.4 proposes indicators needed to determine whether there is adequate regulation of health professional education.

Stakeholders

There is a great need for more work analyzing how health professional schools engage their stakeholders. No indicators are available in either the WHO *Handbook* or the Capacity*Plus Compendium* that are relevant to stakeholders.

Table 4.5 Proposed Indicators of Stakeholder Engagement in Health Professional Education and Their Purpose

Indicator	Purpose
Percentage of schools that engage underserved communities in a dialogue about the types of health workers they need and relevant skills	To measure the engagement of schools with the populations that most need the services of the graduates
Feedback collected from health professional students on the quality and relevance of their professors	To measure the quality and relevance of the education
Feedback collected from health professional students on the educational experience more broadly	To measure the quality and relevance of the education
Number of professional associations and unions engaged in a dialogue with the health professional education system	To measure the engagement of the schools with the professional associations that represent their students upon graduation

The CapacityPlus *Bottlenecks and Best Buys Analysis* (Bailey and Tulenko 2015) does include some questions and indicators on the engagement of stakeholders, particularly students and employers. Since stakeholder engagement may lead to improved recruitment and retention of qualified workers, a checklist of measures to analyze stakeholder engagement is needed. Important indicators to collect are included in table 4.5.

Health Professional Schools

Both the WHO *Handbook* and the CapacityPlus *Indicator Compendium* outline more than a dozen school-level indicators. This detailed information is necessary because schools are arguably the most complicated part of the lifelong health professional education system. The topic is too lengthy to address here; the *Handbook* and the *Indicator Compendium* offer details on these indicators.

Health Facilities

Neither the WHO *Handbook* nor the CapacityPlus *Indicator Compendium* provides an indicator to determine the adequacy of the variety or quality of health facilities in which health professionals receive their practical training. The School Management Tool and the Dean's Dashboard both prompt for data collection and analysis of the following indicators.

Table 4.6 proposes indicators needed to determine the adequacy of clinical practicums in health professional education.

Employers

Neither the WHO *Handbook* nor the CapacityPlus *Indicator Compendium* contains indicators on the employers of health professional school graduates. Employers are essential to the health professional education system for a variety

Table 4.6 Proposed Indicators for Clinical Practicums as Part of Health Professional Education and Their Purpose

Indicator	Purpose
Number of students per instructor at clinical facilities	To measure the teaching load of each instructor
Number of students per patient	To measure students' access to patients
Existence of a program to improve the clinical knowledge and case-based teaching skills of relevant staff in health facilities	To measure effort to improve case-based clinical teaching
Percent of clinical practicum time spent in primary care settings	To prevent the exclusive training in "ivory towers" and tertiary centers even though the majority of graduates will work at the community and primary care level, where facilities and resources are quite different from those in the educational environment

of reasons. Employers are often in the best position to provide data on the current and projected need and skill mix for health cadres. They also can provide the most relevant data on the specific skills required for each cadre and the job description under which each cadre will be hired. These data can inform curricula (for example, preparing nurses to administer antiretrovirals) or teaching techniques (for example, shifting to interprofessional education). Employers can also provide data on career advancement and salaries that can help potential students decide which field to enter. In addition, close coordination with employers can facilitate the hiring of students upon graduation and prevent the well-documented loss of large numbers of graduates as a result of hiring delays of a year or more.[2]

In addition, where large numbers of graduates are employed by a single employer—for example, the ministry of health—induction programs can be integrated into preservice education where students are an easily reachable "captive" audience. For example, when medical education was managed by the Ministry of Health in Uganda, induction was integrated into the education. However, when medical education was transferred to the Ministry of Education and Sports, the induction was dropped and the Ministry of Health was unable to coordinate the induction of hundreds of health professionals who were hired at different times in different locations. This lack of induction has had an adverse effect on the performance of the health workers.[3] There are no known tools to evaluate the engagement of employers in the health professional education system.

Information gained from employers about the performance of their workforce could also assist with gauging the ability of particular schools to train and place highly productive students. Chapter 7 in this book provides more detail regarding measurements of worker performance and productivity that, if linked to school information, may highlight specific "high-yield" schools that other institutions may want to emulate.

Indicators that can be used to determine the level of engagement of employers in the health professional education system are proposed in table 4.7.

Table 4.7 Proposed Indicators of Employers' Engagement in the Health Professional Education System and Their Purpose

Indicator	Purpose
Percentage of engagement: Percentage of schools in dialogue with employers (public and private)	To improve the relevance of students' education and to facilitate the timely hiring of graduates May also increase the likelihood that employers will invest in preservice education
Percentage of employment: Percentage of graduates employed in the health sector within six months	To measure the efficiency of the hiring system as well as evaluating the match between skill mix and number of graduates and employers' demand

Conclusions

The preservice education system serves as a crucial component of the health labor market. Planners and policy makers, however, have not adequately evaluated the preservice system performance, especially in LMICs. This chapter highlights indicators and tools that local and national planners may use to evaluate education systems and determine which ones produce a cadre of well-trained professionals and which fall below expectations. Although more indicators of the six domains than those listed previously could stimulate more effective policy formation, the current tools already in place remain severely underutilized. Decision makers should devote more attention to rigorously measuring and evaluating their current preservice education systems so successful elements of training programs can be identified and disseminated in other schools, regions, and countries.

Notes

1. See Capacity*Plus*, http://www.capacityplus.org/preservice-education-costing-tool.

2. V. Oketcho. Personal communication to K. Tulenko. February 27, 2013.

3. P. Okwero. Personal communication to K. Tulenko. September 8, 2009.

References

Atkinson, D. D., E. Spratley, and C. E. Simpson Jr. 1994. "Increasing the Pool of Qualified Minority Medical School Applicants: Premedical Training at Historically Black Colleges and Universities." *Public Health Reports* 109 (1): 77–85.

Bailey, R. J., and K. Tulenko. 2015. *Scaling Up Health Workforce Education and Training: Guide for Applying the Bottlenecks and Best Buys Approach.* Washington, DC: Capacity*Plus* IntraHealth International.

Beciu, H., S. Ayettey, and K. Amponsah. 2010. "Good Governance and the Role of the Hospital in Health Worker Education in Africa." *World Hospitals and Health Services* 46 (3): 24–27.

Bickell, J. 2012. "What Can Be Done to Improve the Retention of Clinical Faculty?" *Journal of Women's Health* 21 (10): 1028–30.

CapacityPlus. 2011. Human Resource for Health (HRH) Indicator Compendium. Washington, DC: CapacityPlus IntraHealth International. http://www.capacityplus.org/hrhic/.

Franzini, L., M. D. Low, and M. A. Proll. 1997. "Using a Cost-Construction Model to Assess the Cost of Educating Undergraduate Medical Students at the University of Texas–Houston Medical School." Academic Medicine 72 (3): 228–37.

Frenk, J., Z. A. Bhutta, L. C. Chen, J. Cohen, N. Crisp, T. Evans, H. V. Fineberg, P. Garcia, Y. Ke, P. Kelley, A. Meleis, D. Naylor, S. Reddy, S. Scrimshaw, J. Sepulveda, D. Serwadda, H. Zurayk, P. B. Kistnasamy, A. Pablos-Mendez. 2010. "Health Professionals for a New Century: Transforming Education to Strengthen Health Systems in an Interdependent World." Lancet 376 (9756): 1923–58. doi:10.1016/S0140-6736(10)61854-5.

GHWA (Global Health Workforce Alliance). 2015. The Global Health Workforce Alliance 2014 Annual Report. Geneva: World Health Organization.

Goodwin, M. C., W. M. Gleason, and H. A. Kontos. 1997. "A Pilot Study of the Cost of Educating Undergraduate Medical Students at Virginia Commonwealth University." Academic Medicine 72 (3): 211–17.

Jhpiego. 2012. The Health Impacts of Pre-Service Education: An Integrative Review and Evidenced-Based Conceptual Model. Baltimore, MD: Jhpiego.

Karolinska Institutet. 2009. Karolinska Institutet Annual Report 2008. Stockholm: Karolinska Institutet.

Kassebaum, D. G., and P. L. Szenas. 1993. "Relationship between Indebtedness and the Specialty Choices of Graduating Medical Students: 1993 Update." Academic Medicine 68 (12): 934–37.

Rein, M. F., W. J. Randolph, J. G. Short, K. G. Coolidge, M. L. Coates, and R. M. Carey. 1997. "Defining the Cost of Educating Undergraduate Medical Students at the University of Virginia." Academic Medicine 72 (3): 218–27.

Rich, E. C., M. Liebow, M. Srinivasan, D. Parish, J. O. Wolliscroft, O. Fein, and R. Blaser. 2002. "Medicare Financing of Graduate Medical Education." Journal of General Internal Medicine 17 (4): 283–92.

Valberg, L. S., M. A. Gonyea, D. G. Sinclair, and J. Wade. 1994. "Planning the Future Academic Medical Centre." Canadian Medical Association Journal 151 (11): 1581–87.

Vimolket, T., P. Kamol-Ratanakul, and K. Indaratna. 2003. "Cost of Producing a Medical Doctor at Chulalongkorn University." Journal of the Medical Association of Thailand 86 (1): 82–92.

Vujicic, M., O. Kelechi, and S. Sparkes. 2009. Working in Health: Financing and Managing the Public Sector Health Workforce. Washington, DC: World Bank.

WFME (World Federation for Medical Education). 2003. Postgraduate Medical Education: WFME Global Standards for Quality Improvement. Copenhagen: WFME. http://wfme .org/standards/pgme/17-quality-improvement-in-postgraduate-medical-education -english/file.

WFME/FAIMER (World Federation for Medical Education/Foundation for Advancement of International Medical Education and Research). 2015. World Directory of Medical Schools. Ferney-Voltaire, France, and Philadelphia, PA: WFME and FAIMER in col- laboration with WHO and the University of Denmark. http://www.wdoms.org/.

WHO (World Health Organization). 2008. "Financing and Economic Aspects of Health Workforce Scale-Up and Improvement: Framework Paper." Alliance Financing Task Force, WHO, Geneva.

————. 2009. *Handbook on Monitoring and Evaluation of Human Resources for Health.* Geneva: WHO. http://whqlibdoc.who.int/publications/2009/9789241547703_eng .pdf.

————. 2010. *Increasing Access to Health Workers in Remote and Rural Areas through Improved Retention: Global Policy Recommendations.* Geneva: WHO.

————. 2013. *Transforming and Scaling Up Health Professionals' Education and Training: World Health Organization Guidelines 2013.* Geneva: WHO. http://apps.who.int/iris /bitstream/10665/93635/1/9789241506502_eng.pdf.

CHAPTER 5

Health Worker Labor Supply, Absenteeism, and Job Choice

Pieter Serneels, Tomas Lievens, and Damas Butera

Introduction

The last decade has seen a vigorous debate about shortages and absenteeism of health workers, especially in low- and middle-income countries (LMICs). To understand the issues at stake better and to inform policy making, recent work aspires to provide further structure to the analysis (Soucat, Scheffler, and Ghebreyesus 2013). Starting from the perspective of classic labor economics, this chapter presents a framework for the analysis of the labor supply of health workers and provides an overview of the evidence available; it also discusses ways forward for applied research in this field.

Reliable data on the labor supply of health workers are scarce. The World Health Organization (WHO) Global Health Atlas database[1] provides the best available source for comparable data across countries, and contains information on four variables: age, gender, geographic distribution, and health worker occupations. But its usefulness is limited for several reasons. First, these data are available for only 52 countries, with those in Sub-Saharan Africa overrepresented (see table 5A.1, annex 5A, for details). The data also suffer from a number of biases. Countries, or areas within countries, that have weak public sector capacity or that are in conflict are largely missing from the data. Second, the data lack information on the private sector because they focus on public sector health professionals. Both types of bias are likely to lead to an underestimation of health professionals in urban areas and in specific occupations; furthermore, although the potential bias for gender and age is unknown, it may be considerable.[2]

Data available at the country level tend to be equally poor, especially in developing countries. Administrative information about the number of health workers trained is often incomplete, and socioeconomic characteristics of students are often unrecorded. Data on employment are also patchy. Obtaining and maintaining comprehensive data are further hampered by the weak reporting requirements for private sector training institutions and for private facilities. Administrative data on health workers are, moreover, scattered across ministries— these typically include the ministry of education (data on educational achieve- ment), the ministry of health (data on the cadre, grade, and career path within the ministry), and the ministry of finance or labor (data on earnings and social security). Since unified data at the country level are rarely available, compiling comparable data across countries would require huge effort. Data available from specific surveys within each country therefore continue to constitute the best source for economic analysis.

This chapter focuses on microeconomic analysis because this offers the best starting point to building a better understanding of health worker labor supply. Recent evidence has identified major challenges for the delivery of micro-level health care, including health worker presence and on-the-job performance. Throughout the chapter, the term *health worker* refers to health professionals in allopathic medicine who work in the health sector as (one of) their professional activities to earn a living, and the demand for their labor is taken as "given"; the chapter refers to other work for its explanation.[3]

The chapter is structured as follows. Part 1 discusses the appropriate frame- work for analysis of labor supply, absenteeism, job choice, and dual work. Part 2 presents the available evidence on each of these topics and lessons to be learned for policy making. Part 3 begins with a discussion of the types of analysis that can be carried out to improve our understanding, distinguishing between descriptive and casual analysis. Next is a section focusing on data and measurement, and the final section presents conclusions.

1. Framework for Analysis

Labor supply, health worker absenteeism, and occupational choice are intricately connected. To provide a framework to analyze these different elements of health worker supply, each is considered in turn below.

Labor Supply

To better understand the labor supply provided by individual health workers, the static labor supply model provides a useful starting point. This framework considers people deciding how much they work to maximize their happiness, or utility, which is a function of leisure (F) or "free time"—that is, time not working—and consumption (C). Following standard assumptions, labor supply (L) can then be written as a function of the wage rate (w); the wage rate of the spouse or partner (w_s); other household income that is independent of labor supply (y), such as transfers or inheritance; and an error term (ε). A more tech- nical presentation of the equation can be found in annex 5B, equations 5B.1 and 5B.2. *Labor supply* can refer to either labor force participation or hours of work. The former is typically proxied by an indicator variable that takes the value 1 if the individual is working or 0 if not. Labor supply is usually measured by hours worked. The error term reflects unobserved variation that results from differences in preferences; this can, to some extent, be approximated by individual characteristics. Tastes for labor supply may, for instance, differ across gender: for example, having young children tends to be associated with a desire to provide less labor supply, especially among women.

From an analytical and policy perspective, the relationship between labor supply and wages is of primary interest. A key question is what effect a rise (or fall) in wages has on labor supply—in other words: what is the *wage elasticity* of labor supply. This effect is traditionally decomposed into an income and a substitution effect, where the first reflects the increased uptake of both consumption and leisure that result from a rise in income, and the latter reflects a substitution away from the more expensive of the two goods (leisure and consumption).[4] Classic theory argues that both consumption and leisure are normal goods, and thus the substitution effect dominates the income effect. As a consequence, a rise in wages will lead to an increase in labor supply, or a positive wage elasticity of labor supply. But alternative outcomes are conceivable. The income effect may, for instance, dominate beyond a certain point, reflecting the fact that people do not always want to work more, thus resulting in a backward-bending labor supply curve beyond a point where workers supply less labor when wages rise more. Ultimately, across what range the elasticity is positive is an empirical question.

Recent advances in behavioral economics question the canonical assumption of the static labor supply model. People may not maximize utility but may instead target specific income levels, adapting their labor supply to reach their target. Reanalyzing data on New York City taxi drivers that was collected and analyzed earlier, Crawford and Meng (2011) conclude that, at least in their setting, there is strong evidence that workers target specific levels of income (see also Camerer et al. 1997; Farber 2008). This finding is supported by emerging evidence from laboratory experiments (Abeler et al. 2010). The next section discusses the existing evidence in more detail.

The static framework can be further extended in a number of directions. The most relevant for our purpose is to consider a dynamic setting, where labor supply is decided—and allowed to vary—over the individual's life cycle.[5] In the context of health professionals, the dynamic setting is especially relevant in the presence of a growing private sector. Although health workers frequently aspire to combine work in the public and private sectors, they are often constrained and unable to do so. Many health workers are attracted by the private sector but do not get access to private employment until later in life. Qualitative research suggests that these workers often start their careers in the public sector and (try to) move to the private sector later. The obligation to work for some time in the public sector in order to repay subsidized training, often called "bonding," is a common reason for this career path, although it is also observed in the absence of a bonding policy. Public sector employment may also provide good access to professional training and specialization, which is most relevant early in a career. As a result, health workers may prefer to start in the public sector in order to build human capital and accumulate savings,

Health Labor Market Analyses in Low- and Middle-Income Countries
http://dx.doi.org/10.1596/978-1-4648-0931-6

and then switch to the private sector, or combine their public sector job with a job in the private sector, or start their own practice. A model reflecting these stylized facts is discussed in more detail later, relying on insights from Ensor, Serneels, and Lievens (2013).[6]

Although the preceding microeconomic framework is widely used to analyze the labor supply in general, its application to the health workforce is limited. It is useful to consider the challenges that have arisen for empirical analysis in other contexts, because even the simple static model set forth earlier requires care when applying it to the data. A first concern in the estimation of labor supply is selection bias. Estimating labor supply only for those who are working and excluding those who are not (that is, the corner solutions) yields biased results since at least some of the factors driving labor supply also drive labor force participation. Female nurses who become mothers may, for instance, decide to stop working because they consider their salaries to be too low to delegate child-care. Selection bias is widely discussed in the early literature on labor supply (Penceval 1986), particularly for female labor supply (Killingworth and Heckman 1986). Labor force participation and labor supply are therefore often considered jointly. The traditional approach is to estimate labor force participation equations as a first step to obtaining a selection correction term that is then included in the labor supply equation. But finding identifying instruments may be a challenge. The early literature proposes family formation variables such as marital status and number of children or dependents, even though more recent evidence questions whether this is appropriate (that is, whether it fulfills the exclusion restriction) in all contexts. Another way of looking at this is to focus on the labor supply that is being censored: working hours are observed only for those participating in the labor force. This data censoring can be addressed by estimating a Tobit regression or variations thereof.[7]

Second, the empirical estimation of labor supply is also related to a number of measurement challenges. Although the primary interest may be to analyze effort, effort remains typically unobserved and empirical analysis characteristically focuses on hours worked, which is observed in the data. A small body of mostly experimental labor economics literature separates effort from hours worked, providing new insights (see Charness and Kuhn 2011 for an overview). This independent consideration of effort and hours worked is also increasingly adopted when studying health workers, where effort is measured directly either through vignettes or observation—as discussed in chapter 7, "Measuring the Performance of Health Workers" (see also Das, Hammer, and Leonard 2008 and Leonard, Masatu, and Serneels 2013 for overviews). Moreover, although it is relatively straightforward to estimate the relationship between hours worked and wages, the key question is whether it reflects a causal relationship. The standard assumption—that wages are set exogenous to the individual worker, and the obtained coefficient can therefore be given a causal interpretation—may hold for some health occupations, where government regulation plays an important role, but it does not hold for all. Specialists, for instance, may negotiate a contract that stipulates wages and hours worked simultaneously, making it impossible to tease out a causal effect of wages on labor supply for this group by simple ordinary least squares (OLS) estimation on observational data. Even if wages are set exogenously, unobserved variables may simultaneously affect both selection into the occupation and wages themselves, rendering the estimated coefficient biased. In both cases more advanced approaches are needed, as discussed in part 3.

Absenteeism

One key assumption underlying the traditional model of labor supply is that contracted hours of work reflect actual hours worked. This is tenable when absenteeism from work is limited. Evidence indicates that absence rates of 25 percent among health workers are no exception across many LMICs. In this context the analysis is more informative when focusing on actual rather than contracted labor supply. This is especially relevant where the public sector—which tends to offer standard contracts with fixed working hours—dominates.[8] Absenteeism is also of interest because it informs policy making (and debate) on health worker shortages. If absenteeism is high and widespread, shortages may be overestimated and there may be less reason for increasing the number of health workers.

A standard way to analyze absenteeism starts from the preceding static labor supply framework. Workers choose to be absent when required working hours exceed the number of hours at which utility is maximized (see Allen 1981; Brown and Sessions 1996). Absenteeism is then explained as a function of wages (w), contracted number of hours (h_c), and the expected cost of detection (C), which in itself is a product of the probability of being detected (π) and the penalty when detected (P) (equation 5B.3 in annex 5B).[9] If absenteeism is mainly related to work in a second job, this can be made more explicit in this framework, as discussed in the section "Dual Jobs." A key message to note from a theoretical perspective is that the effect of a wage increase on absenteeism is ambiguous because income and substitution effects have opposite signs.

The caveats mentioned previously for estimating the static labor supply model apply here as well. When looking at the effects of wages on absenteeism, a key issue remains whether the variation in wages is exogenous, and thus whether the estimated coefficient can be given a causal interpretation. Although most empirical analysis of absenteeism among health workers remains descriptive and considers correlates of absenteeism, some evidence on causality is emerging, as discussed in part 2 below.

Occupational Choice and Job Choice

To analyze the choice between different possible occupations and jobs, a framework similar to the one described previously can be used. Here workers compare utilities across jobs. In a context where markets function relatively well, the choice between jobs will be based primarily on wages, which are believed to reflect differences in valuations fairly well in this setting. Posts that have undesired job attributes will have higher wages attached in order to compensate for the loss in utility. However, when wages are the outcome of political and administrative decisions—as is the case for most of the public sector, and possibly for the entire health sector—they do not necessarily reflect valuations well and other job attributes (O) need to be taken into account more explicitly. A worker will then choose job A above job B if it yields higher utility, given his or her preferences. Job choice is then modeled as a function of wages and job attributes across the respective jobs (see equations 5B.4 and 5B.5 in annex 5B).[10] As in the labor supply models presented previously, the wage of the worker's spouse and other household income can be included as well.

In practice, some key job attributes are used to identify the type of job being considered. The left-hand variable of the equation then reflects whether the job is in the private or public sector, whether it is located in urban or rural areas, whether the setting is hospitals or clinics and health posts, and so on. International migration can be considered a separate choice. The other relevant attributes are then included on the right-hand side of the equation. When considering one job versus all the other jobs, the equation is estimated using a probit model; when considering more than two jobs at once, the equation is estimated using a multinomial logit.

The role of wages for job choice remains the center of attention in the analysis, but interest extends to the role of other attributes as well as individual preferences. Recent qualitative research obtains a useful categorization of relevant job attributes for distinguishing between monetary attributes such as wages, benefits, and allowances, and nonmonetary attributes such as workload, training, availability of equipment, and social recognition.

An individual characteristic now receiving increased consideration is the worker's intrinsic motivation (see Leonard, Serneels, and Brock 2013). This can be incorporated in different ways. Besley and Ghatak (2005), for example, consider motivation as an individual's preference for a mission that is to be matched to the organization's mission. Emerging empirical evidence supports this view (Serra, Serneels, and Barr 2011).

The challenges for empirical estimation are similar to those mentioned for labor supply and absenteeism: some relevant job attributes, such as workplace culture and management style, as well as ability and motivation, may be difficult to observe. Correcting for self-selection by including a selection correction term can be applied in a fashion similar to the way it is applied in labor supply models. Although this procedure is more cumbersome, the application is well developed (Bourguignon, Fournier, and Gurgand 2007).

Dual Jobs

The framework in the previous section assumes that health workers work exclusively in one sector. This may not be the case. Dual work in the public and private sectors occurs across the world and comes in many shapes and forms. One example is that of private clinics, group practices, and even hospitals that are run by out-of-hours public sector staff. Another form of dual work occurs by conducting activities for personal profit during unauthorized absenteeism from a public sector job. Informal or unofficial payment to obtain better and quicker service in public facilities can also be considered dual practice. The first type is legally permitted; the latter two are officially illegal. In both cases the analysis will concentrate on the incidence of dual practice (D), but their different nature requires a distinct approach. When the second job is carried out *outside* the working hours of the first job, the focus lies on factors that determine labor supply and job choice, along the lines of the preceding models (see equation 5B.6 in annex 5B).

When the second job is carried out *during* working hours of the first job, the decision is related to absenteeism that can be seen as the use of public office for private gain (since the first job is often in the public sector), and can be modeled in the spirit of shirking models (Rijckeghem and Weber 1997; Shapiro and Stiglitz 1984). Here, dual practice (D) will also depend on the expected cost of detection (C), which is a function of the probability of being caught (π) and the penalty (P) when caught (see equation 5B.7 in annex 5B).

The possibility of taking up a second job can also be seen as representing an additional job attribute that drives sector choice, as modeled in the previous section. The value of this benefit depends on the expected income from the secondary activity, which in turn depends on the wage in the second sector, the probability of being caught, and the penalty or fine imposed if caught. In most of Sub-Saharan Africa, a health worker in the public sector typically does not run the risk of being fired. If this additional benefit is positive, jobs where dual work is possible may therefore be more attractive.

Note that the policy implications from this theoretical model remain unclear, since a higher wage in the primary activity does not automatically make a worker cease absenteeism because much depends on the probability of being detected and the sanction imposed if detected. The issue is further complicated when the income from the first job (w) is barely sufficient to survive. Merely increasing monitoring and punishment is unlikely to be productive in such circumstances. Policies such as clamping down on the number of hours that are required to be worked in a public sector may then have adverse effects and induce workers to leave the sector entirely (Ensor 2004).

Existing empirical analysis provides evidence for dual work along the lines set out earlier, with increasing real wages apparently having limited impact on unofficial payment and practice (Lievens, Lindelow, and Serneels 2009). This will be discussed more in part 2.

2. Evidence

Although our understanding of labor supply, absenteeism, and the job choice of health workers is currently limited, a number of insights emerge from existing studies. The discussion that follows concerns both what is known for LMICs, with most research from Africa, and what can be learned from high-income countries. Although this chapter focuses on quantitative analysis, it recognizes the value of qualitative research.[11]

Health Labor Market Analyses in Low- and Middle-Income Countries
http://dx.doi.org/10.1596/978-1-4648-0931-6

Labor Supply and Elasticity of Own Wages

Empirical evidence on the labor supply of health professionals in developing countries is scarce. However, insights can be gained from existing work on high-income countries. The present analysis is primarily motivated by a perceived shortage of health workers; it focuses on the effects of wages on labor supply, usually concentrating on one occupation, typically doctors or nurses.

Qin, Li, and Hsieh (2013) study the wage elasticities for both nurses and doctors in China using 2005 census data. Estimating an instrumental variable (IV) model that uses individual migration status as well as local density of health workers and provincial density of hospitals—which are argued to affect wages but not labor supply—as identifying instruments, the study finds a short-run elasticity of 0.58 for self-employed practitioners inelastic labor supply. This finding is presumably the result of the health workers' fixed payment scheme, although the hours worked are related to other factors, such as hospital asset holdings and ownership type. The study concludes that remuneration and hospital ownership may offer potential policy levers to impact labor supply in China. This estimated elasticity exceeds those typically found for high-income countries.

Two overview studies for nurses indicate that the responsiveness of labor supply to a rise in wages may be limited in high-income countries. Shields (2004) summarizes the results of studies on the labor supply of registered nurses, mostly from the United States but also from the United Kingdom and Norway. Based on his overview study, he finds that short-run labor supply, with an average elasticity of around 0.30, is relatively unresponsive to changes in wages. The survey concludes that even large wage increases are unlikely to be successful in tackling current and predicted nurse shortages, at least in the short run, and points to the importance of nonpecuniary job aspects in influencing labor supply. The overview study also recognizes the reviewed studies' theoretical and econometric limitations, including the limited variation in labor supply, the lack of exogenous variation in wages, and the possible bias in estimation results due to unobserved characteristics such as motivation (Shields 2004).

A low elasticity is confirmed by an earlier overview, which finds that estimates of labor supply elasticities are often close to zero, with considerable variation depending on the method used (see Antonazzo et al. 2003). Many of the reviewed studies rely on observational data obtained from surveys where the variation in wages is not necessarily exogenous, and the estimated coefficients cannot be given a causal interpretation. Since many of the data are also cross-sectional, relevant individual characteristics—such as motivation—typically remain unaccounted for. The overview study pleads for more work looking at discontinuities in the labor supply function because the effect of wages on labor supply may not follow a smooth linear path,[12] and also suggests that more effort is needed to analyze the relative importance of pecuniary and nonpecuniary job characteristics, and the application of dynamic and family labor supply models.

A more recent study incorporates some of these suggested improvements. Using a rich long-term panel data for nurses in Australia, it paints a more nuanced picture (Hanel, Kalb, and Scott 2012). Finding labor supply elasticities ranging between 0.21 for irregular shifts and 0.28 for regular night shifts, the study observes figures at the lower end of the range of previously found wage elasticities for nurses, and for women in general (Blundell and Macurdy 1999). Dropping other control variables from the analysis, Hanel, Kalb, and Scott (2012) also find an unconditional elasticity of 0.44, which is larger because former nonemployed nurses now enter the occupation. The study also finds evidence for heterogeneity, with positive elasticities of wages higher for less-qualified, older, and childless nurses. The labor supply elasticity of other household income, which tends to be negative, is higher for nurses with children. The study finds no differences in elasticities by personality trait.

Lower figures are obtained by another study for Norway. Askildsen, Baltagi, and Holmås (2002), using a unique matched panel data set of Norwegian nurses covering the period 1993–98, find an estimated wage elasticity of 0.21 after controlling for individual heterogeneity, sample selection, and possible endogeneity. The study concludes that both individual and institutional characteristics are statistically significant and important for working hours. In line with Hanel, Kalb, and Scott (2012), the paper concludes that contractual arrangements as represented by shift work are also important for hours of work, and that omitting information about this common arrangement is likely to underestimate the wage effect.

Di Tommaso, Strøm, and Sæther (2009) go a step further and extend the static labor supply model, taking into account insights from a job choice model that allows nurses to choose between workplaces and types of jobs based on wages and other job attributes, and focusing on shift versus daytime work. Estimating this model for Norwegian registered nurses in 2000, the study finds an elasticity of labor supply with respect to wages of 0.33. Interjob-type responses are estimated to be larger, and the study finds that Norwegian nurses who are working in shifts (rather than 9 to 5) may be willing to do this shift work for a lower wage than the prevailing one.

Another study, this time in the United States, uses two-stage least squares (2SLS) estimates to derive posterior distributions for short- and long-run own wage elasticities of labor supply by registered nurses (Burkett 2005). The median of the distribution for the short-run elasticity is 0.64 while that for the long-run elasticity is 1.06.[13]

Studies for doctors seem to draw similar conclusions. Sæther (2003), using a discrete choice model to allow for different jobs and contracts, finds a modest response in total hours to a wage increase, and reallocation of hours in favor of the sector with increased wages. Baltagi, Bratberg, and Holmas (2003) estimate the labor supply of physicians employed at hospitals in Norway using personnel register data merged with other public records and applying a dynamic labor supply equation making use of the generalized method of moments (GMM) method. The study rejects the static model in favor of a dynamic model and obtains a long-run wage elasticity of 0.55, which is considerably higher than previously estimated for physicians, in particular for those who are not self-employed.

A creative identification strategy used by Kantarevic, Kralj, and Weinkauf (2008) exploits a reform in doctor remuneration in Ontario, Canada, using a change in the threshold system that taxes practice income to limit increases in physician compensation. The study finds that income effects are small but significant. Only for a minority of services that have relatively low prices and high volumes does the income effect dominate the substitution effect, while the cross effect of fee changes on other services tends to be significant only for services with relatively high prices and low volumes.

One study looks at the *type* of labor supply. Using cohort data for Canadian general practitioners, Crossley, Hurley, and Jeon (2009) observe a downward trend in hours worked in direct patient care for men but not for women, and finds a strong age effect for women but not for men.

A remaining question on the conceptual front is whether there is evidence for a backward-bending labor supply curve or for income targeting. Although many of the existing studies do not allow for a quadratic term, in his overview, Shields (2004) concludes that a number of studies that do allow for a quadratic term have found evidence of a backward-bending labor supply function for nurses. Wage increases thus actually lead to reduced labor supply in some U.S. markets (see Bognanno, Hixson, and Jeffers 1974; Link and Settle 1979). Focusing on physicians in Ontario, Canada, the previously mentioned study by Kantarevic, Kralj, and Weinkauf (2008) finds that a negatively sloped supply curve arises only for a minority of services with relatively lower prices and higher volumes. The same study interprets these results as refuting the target income hypothesis for physicians, arguing that this would imply infinitely large income effects.

Another remaining question is how sensitive the results are to measurement issues. One possible explanation for the low estimates of wage elasticity may be that hours worked, rather than effort, are used to measure labor supply and that health workers substitute on-the-job leisure for off-the-job leisure. A study by Ault and Rutman (1994) investigates this issue and finds that estimated wage effects depend indeed on the measure of labor activity that is being used, comparing results for annual hours worked, hours worked per week, and weeks worked per year.

Even with the growing body of work and the improving identification of exogenous variation, the evidence of high-income countries leans toward positive but limited labor supply elasticity of own wages, even though recent, more advanced estimation techniques tend to yield higher estimates. A methodological shortcoming of most studies is that the underlying model focuses on labor supply alone and does not take into account the demand side of the labor market for health workers, as also argued by Shields (2004). In other words, a low observed own-wage elasticity may also be explained by the rigidities associated with a high degree of market power or monopsony on the demand side for health workers.

This possibility can be investigated in the future by research using matched worker-employer data for both the private and the public sectors.

Unfortunately, as with labor markets in general, very limited work is available for LMICs. The results of the only study on China (Qin, Li, and Hsieh 2013) are reported at the start of this section. This area deserves further study, in particular given the opportunity for expanded labor supply associated with the emergence of a private sector in LMICs. Although hours of work conditional on being present at work are strongly regulated in the public and not-for-profit sectors, they are much more flexible in the for-profit sector.

Absenteeism: Incidence, Causes, and Remedies

This section provides a brief overview and discusses the scope of absenteeism and its consequences, and how it is explained. It also considers ways forward to address absenteeism among health workers and lessons for research and policy making.

Scope and Consequences

Chaudhury et al. (2006) were the first to provide systematic evidence of absenteeism across countries. Enumerators made unannounced visits to primary health clinics in Bangladesh, Ecuador, India, Indonesia, Peru, and Uganda; the study concludes that more than a third of health workers were absent.

Although absence is typically spread across workers and facilities rather than concentrated, there is some heterogeneity. Absence tends to be higher in poorer regions; more prevalent among higher-ranking and more powerful health workers, such as doctors; and higher among men.

Investigating absenteeism correlates, the Chaudhury et al. (2006) study finds that health workers who are absent from public facilities are likely to be providing private health care. Those with opportunities to earn more at private clinics—such as doctors—are also more often absent. In Peru, for instance, 48 percent of doctors reported outside income from private practice, compared with 30 percent of other health workers.

Facility-level characteristics also play a role in absenteeism, with lower absence rates for facilities that had been inspected more recently. The correlation with distance to a ministry of health office and the size of the facility differs across countries. Absenteeism is lower at facilities that have potable water in India, Indonesia, and Uganda, but this is not the case in the other countries, and having a toilet is not correlated with absence anywhere. Absenteeism also tends to be lower in primary health care centers that are close to a paved road in Indonesia, and where employers provide housing—which is typically on the facility premises—in Uganda and Bangladesh.

The data for Peru—the only country with available information on contract employment—show that contract workers are less frequently absent, even though they are paid a salary similar to that of their civil service colleagues. This finding is consistent with previous results (Alcázar and Andrade 2001).[14]

A number of follow-up papers to this cross-country comparison provide more detailed information. Muralidharan and Venkatesh (2011) present results from the nationally representative survey conducted in India in 2003 in over 1,400 public health centers across 19 states. Close to 40 percent of these health workers were found to be absent from work; absenteeism ranged from 30 percent in Madhya Pradesh to over 67 percent in Bihar. Absence was not concentrated among a particular cadre of health workers, although those at facilities in remote locations, with long commutes, or with poor infrastructure and equipment attended least. Pharmacists and lab technicians also had high absence rates. Doctors were more absent than others, and there seem to be knock-on effects because staff are also more absent when doctors are not around.

Banerjee, Deaton, and Duflo (2004) provide further evidence from an in-depth study with primary health care facilities in rural Udaipur District in Rajasthan, India, measuring absence more intensively through weekly unannounced visits on random days for one year by a locally hired person, complemented by monthly visits by an enumerator. In cases of absence, the monitors also looked for the nurse in any of the villages where she was supposed to be working. The average absence rate was 36 percent, and 45 percent in rural subcenters. Again, absence rates were widespread and not systematic, making it unlikely that villagers could know when health care would be available. The study provides scarce suggestive evidence of a link with health outcomes, reporting that outcomes seem to be negatively correlated with low-quality public facilities, while much of the health care was provided by private providers, who were often unqualified. Nevertheless, satisfaction levels were high, indicating that quality of care does not necessarily affect user perceptions. The later section on addressing absenteeism further discusses its consequences.

A more recent combined survey of health workers and communities of primary health centers in Rajasthan, India, observes absenteeism of 27 percent in general and 36 percent among doctors using permanent observation (Cheriyan, Arya, and Singh 2010). Only 35 percent of users report having access to service at night. The study confirms that nonavailability and quality of equipment and infrastructure are often related to absenteeism.

Chaudhury and Hammer (2003) provide background information for the earlier quoted Bangladesh results, and report an average absenteeism of 26 percent, 40 percent for doctors at large clinics, and 75 percent at smaller subcenters with a single doctor.[15] Their main findings are that health worker absenteeism during the day is correlated with distance from the workplace and access to roads.

There is some work on this topic for Sub-Saharan Africa. Bjorkman and Svensson (2009), in their randomized control trial (RCT) study on community monitoring of health facilities in rural Uganda, observe an absence rate of 47 percent (in the control group that did not receive treatment). A recent report for a study with 104 health facilities in Bushenyi District in Uganda using unannounced visits observes a very similar figure with an average rate of absenteeism of 48 percent (UNHCO 2012). Important correlates include work environment, supervision, job satisfaction with different incentives, level of education, location of health facility (remoteness), length of service in the current facility, job stress, and marital status. A 2008 public expenditure tracking study in Zambia, measuring absenteeism on the day of the survey (and not through strict surprise visits), finds 31 percent of doctors, 20 percent of clinical officers, and 14 percent of midwives and other clinical staff to be absent. Somewhat surprising, self-reported absenteeism from a health worker survey was still higher. In general, clinical staff is more absent than administrative staff. The number of self-reported days absent in the previous month was five on average, but showed some variation: six days for rural health centers and eight days for urban ones, while three for hospitals. The main reasons for self-reported absenteeism were taking care of sick relatives (18 percent) and attending another job (9 percent). The study also measures self-reported late arrival during the last month, which was 43 percent overall, 37 percent among staff in rural health centers, and 47 percent among staff in urban health centers.

Explaining Absenteeism

The preceding studies provide a number of useful insights on the correlates of absenteeism. Because these studies are based on cross-sectional data, however, they shed only limited light on the causes of absenteeism. In most studies, key economic variables of interest—such as the wage rate, the contracted hours, monitoring arrangements, and nonlabor income—that are considered important in the conceptual literature on absenteeism presented previously are not included.

Despite fundamental differences in context between high-income and developing countries, especially concerning monitoring, it is interesting to briefly consider the analysis of absenteeism in high-income countries, which often takes a more structural approach. A literature exists to test the predictions in high-income countries of the model presented earlier, although these predictions are more often applied outside the health sector, regularly using cross-sectional data and focusing on the private sector in general.[16] These analyses typically include as right-hand variables the wage rate, contracted working hours, and a proxy for the penalty for absenteeism; they find expected relationships confirmed.[17] Models are often extended with personal and demographic characteristics of the employee and work environment conditions, both of which are found to matter.[18] One study tests whether absence is related to both individual preferences for shirking and group interaction effects, to see whether workers are more likely to shirk if coworkers shirk (see Ichino and Maggi 2000). They find that individual characteristics offer the most explanatory power, but that workers can also get socialized into absenteeism.[19] Leontaridi and Ward (2002) find job stress, which in turn depends on both worker characteristics and worker conditions, to be the most important determinant of absenteeism across 15 Organisation for Economic Co-operation and Development (OECD) countries. One shortcoming of many of the studies is that they do not consistently distinguish between voluntary and involuntary absence (an example of the latter would be absence due to illness).[20] The cross-section data on which the studies rely also do not allow definitive conclusions to be drawn on the causal effect of own wages on absenteeism.

Health Labor Market Analyses in Low- and Middle-Income Countries
http://dx.doi.org/10.1596/978-1-4648-0931-6

Because of the loose connection between existing work on absenteeism of health workers in developing countries with theoretical models used in the preceding literature on absenteeism in high-income countries, Serneels, Lindelow, and Lievens (2008) carried out qualitative preresearch in Ethiopia and Rwanda.[21] A total of 95 health workers and 46 users of health services were interviewed using semistructured group discussions.[22] Starting from the theoretical framework set out earlier, the study identifies a number of additional factors that play a role for absenteeism; these include access to a second job, intrinsic motivation and internalized norms, job mobility, and perceived health risks. The study also confirms that, compared with the cost of detection in high-income country settings, a key distinction for health workers in developing countries is that the expected cost of detection is very low, if not zero. First, there is no penalty when found absent. As also discussed by others, sanctions among civil servants in many developing countries tend to be very weak; and this is also true for countries in Sub-Saharan Africa.[23] Second, monitoring technology is weak. There may be administrative monitoring, but it is unclear how accurate this is and what it means. At the same time, attendance can be ameliorated by improved monitoring.

The benefits of oversight are best illustrated by the results from the study carried out by Duflo, Hanna, and Ryan (2012) for the education sector, where absenteeism for teachers is reduced through advanced monitoring—in their case, a bonus payment determined by daily pictures as proof of presence.[24] The study by Bjorkman and Svensson (2009) show how an intervention where communities are activated to monitor and give feedback to health workers can make absenteeism drop by 13 percentage points. Ongoing work also focuses on the power of incentives to reduce absenteeism, which provides another motivation behind recent efforts to move toward results-based financing in the health sector.

Addressing Absenteeism

The preceding empirical evidence illustrates that absenteeism is widespread among health workers in developing countries. An important but difficult question to answer is whether absenteeism is necessarily bad.

One way to respond is to look at the consequences of absenteeism. Although the negative consequences of absenteeism may seem obvious, there is limited focused research to document this conviction, and the general equilibrium effects are unclear. Attendance is indeed a necessary condition for service delivery, but it does not in itself guarantee the delivery of good health care. Moreover, absenteeism in the public sector may provide health workers with the job security required to engage in other health care jobs in the private sector, which may provide a desirable outcome for society as a whole.

Chapter 7, "Measuring the Performance of Health Workers," provides ample evidence of poor on-the-job performance of health workers. Results from qualitative research illustrate the frustrations that users of health facilities experience, especially with the unpredictability of facility opening hours and the long waiting times. However, since the presence and performance of health workers is only one input into the production of health care, a better understanding is needed to determine whether increased presence alone would lead to better health outcomes. If, for instance, health workers are absent because there is no medicine or functioning refrigeration for medical supplies, then a wider analysis is needed. Goldstein et al. (2013) provide unique evidence documenting how health provider absence can impact health outcomes. The study shows that pregnant women who first visited a clinic when a nurse was present are more likely to test for human immunodeficiency virus (HIV) and deliver in a hospital. Moreover, women with high pretest expectations of being HIV positive are more likely to deliver in a hospital and receive appropriate medication, and are less likely to breastfeed (a mode of HIV transmission) if their visit to the facility coincides with nurse attendance. These results provide strong evidence that health worker presence is likely to lead to improved health outcomes.

More difficult to answer is the question of whether absenteeism can be seen—in some or all settings—as an efficient response to prevailing conditions, leading to positive outcomes at the societywide level. Although observed rates of absenteeism are high and undesirable, tolerating some absenteeism may be a price worth paying to keep health workers in the public sector rather than seeing them move to full-time private sector work or abroad. This may be especially relevant for rural and unattractive areas, where poverty is typically at its deepest. Banerjee, Deaton, and Duflo (2004), focusing on rural Rajasthan in India, argue that the observed levels of absenteeism of nurses are likely to be inefficiently high, especially in the case of small health subcenters. Efficiency, they argue, would require the facility to be open at fixed times so patients know when it is worthwhile to travel to the clinic, and not at unpredictable times, as is observed in the study. For highly skilled health workers such as doctors, the situation may be different because people may know when they are around and where to find them, as also argued by Chaudhury et al. (2006). The latter study provides some evidence in support of this argument, since health workers who serve at their chosen location tend to be less absent—although it cannot be excluded that this is because they are also at better locations. However, in these areas it seems inefficient to have contracts that require full-time presence, as current contracts typically do.

According to Chaudhury et al. (2006), a likely explanation of the inefficient setup lies in the incentive design and political economy of the setting. Health workers, like teachers, represent a well-organized interest group likely to defend acquired benefits, such as permanent employment and relatively good salaries, in the civil service. Patients, on the other hand, are more diffuse. This explains why political efforts to improve health service delivery are weak.[25] At the same time, the defense for a status quo, where health workers are not fired for absenteeism, may create a situation where shirking goes unpunished, which in itself may contribute to a culture of absence (see Basu 2006).

Regarding incentive design, two important insights are gained from the analysis in previous sections. First, theory shows that increasing wages does not necessarily improve attendance. Instead, improved attendance depends on whether the income or the substitution effect dominates—that is, whether leisure is a normal good. Although evidence regarding the effect of own wages on absenteeism is inconclusive, the study of labor supply suggests that a backward-bending labor supply curve cannot be excluded, indicating that wages do not always have a positive effect on labor supply. Descriptive evidence for teachers in developing countries further underlines the low correlation between wages and attendance. A second insight is that improved monitoring (and sanctioning) is a first and necessary step to improve health worker attendance. The question then is: how can this be done?

Despite the possible gridlock from a political economy perspective, one way forward lies in (partially) redesigning existing institutions and incentive schemes. An increasingly popular approach is to include beneficiaries in monitoring. The study by Bjorkman and Svensson (2009) provided an intensive intervention in rural Uganda where information was disseminated to both community members and staff, and different meetings were organized for each group and then together. The study finds very large intervention impacts, including on infant mortality rates.[26] However, the channel through which this type of intervention works is not well understood: is it the provision of information as such or the induction of collective action that brings about the impact? Evidence from education and other sectors indicates that information alone may not have much impact (see Banerjee and Duflo 2006; Olken 2007; Piper and Korda 2010), while collective action is necessary (see Barr et al. 2012). Ongoing work by Nyqvist, de Walque, and Svensson (2014), on the other hand, suggests that collective action without information remains ineffective, implying that information and collective action function as complements when including beneficiaries in the monitoring of service delivery. One possible reason that both information and collective action are needed is given by Banerjee, Duflo, and Deaton (2004), who in their study in rural Rajasthan observe that, despite the high absenteeism, users seem to have relatively high levels of satisfaction, reflecting their apparently low expectations. It seems that for people to believe that things can be changed, both the provision of factual information and the stimulation of collective action are needed. These are important insights for future research in this area.

Lessons for Future Policy Research

The existing evidence suggests that absenteeism among health workers in developing countries is high, with some indications that this may lead to lower health outcomes. However, there are cases where health workers should not be asked to work a full working day. Since health service delivery depends on the presence of health professionals, which remains low, future work should focus on how to improve the accountability of health workers. Increasing payment is often thought to bring a solution, but this may not be effective. Studies in the education sector suggest that teachers who are paid more are, if anything, *more* absent. A change in the structure of pay may be more effective, with part of the earnings dependent on performance. This performance is best measured at the facility level for a number of reasons. The multidimensional nature of health makes it difficult to summarize health outcomes into one compact indicator. Moreover, with some dimensions measured more easily than others, such measures would steer performance in a specific direction. The complementarity of tasks carried out by different health workers is another argument in favor of rewarding performance at the facility level. This approach also provides an opportunity to strengthen facility management where rewards linked to individual performance may weaken it. The effect of performance pay on health worker intrinsic motivation remains unknown so far. Although it is a theoretical possibility, there is no evidence for the studied contexts that intrinsic motivation is eroded by performance pay, but more research is needed.

Current work does suggest that job attributes other than pay also play an important role. These attributes include such facility characteristics as the type, sector, and location of the facility.

A promising way forward to increase attendance lies in improving monitoring. Although ameliorations in technology for automated monitoring can be explored, based on recent experiences in the education sector they are unlikely to provide a final solution.[27] One promising approach is to involve beneficiaries in the monitoring of health services. Currently only limited rigorous evidence is available on the effect of beneficiary monitoring on health outcomes. Combined evidence from the health and education sectors indicates that both activation (collective action) and provision of information are important.

One final direction to investigate is how to reduce the implications of absenteeism. Absenteeism of doctors, for instance, may be difficult to prevent but possible to work around by trying out pragmatic solutions—for example, by requiring doctors' presence only on certain days.

Job Choice: the Role of Sector, Location, and Type of Facility

An understanding of why people choose to be a health worker in either developing or high-income countries is currently limited; more is known about the choice between jobs once the professional training is completed. This section draws from qualitative and quantitative studies using similar designs in Ethiopia, Ghana, and Rwanda implemented by the authors, supplemented with insights from other work. In total, 48 doctors, 125 nurses, and 63 users of health services were interviewed. This qualitative preresearch was followed by quantitative surveys in Ethiopia and Rwanda. A cohort study of 90 medical and 219 nursing students was conducted in Ethiopia, where subjects were interviewed first during their final year of training and a second time three years later, after having entered the labor market. In Rwanda the first wave of a survey of 123 medical and 288 nursing students was conducted, focusing on occupational preferences and expected career paths.[28] The insights generated from these studies are compared and contrasted where possible with those from the scarce literature on job choice among health workers in high-income countries.

A number of issues stand out from the data. First, three dimensions seem to be key to health worker job choice in Sub-Saharan Africa: sector of work (facility ownership), location of work, and type of facility. Second, although remuneration is important, other job attributes also play an essential role. Apart from the three key dimensions, health workers care about access to training and the characteristics of the workplace when they compare different jobs. Third, individual characteristics of health workers matter. For example, health workers with more altruistic motivations are more likely to prefer a job in the not-for-profit sector and in remote areas. These findings correspond closely with insights from a small and growing literature on high-income countries.[29] We discuss each of these three key dimensions for job choice in developing countries (left-hand variables) in turn.

Sector of Work

Health workers can choose among jobs in the public, private for-profit, and not-for-profit sectors. Across Sub-Saharan African countries, the public sector is often the largest. The not-for-profit private sector, which can be active in rural as well as urban areas, can differ substantially in size across countries and often follows public sector rules and pay, although not always; sometimes it provides additional benefits and bonuses. The private for-profit sector is especially active in urban areas and typically offers higher pay but lower job security. Although health workers often combine work across sectors, in this discussion, for clarity, the choice is considered to be mutually exclusive. A consideration of dual job holdings across sectors follows in the section on dual jobs and moonlighting.

The results from comparative qualitative work across Ethiopia, Ghana, and Rwanda indicate that many health workers prefer to work in the private for-profit sector, which typically offers higher salaries and better physical infrastructure. Pay is often per hour and the pace of work tends to be higher, with effort possibly geared toward the more profit-making activities. Job security is typically limited, as is access to training. The public sector offers more job security and more training, but generally pays less. The not-for-profit sector often provides additional benefits, such as housing—health workers frequently live on the premises of the facility—but tends to require a relatively heavy workload. Expectations for performance are high, supervision and workplace norms are stricter in this sector, and facilities are often run by faith-based organizations; in Ghana health workers typically need to be a member of a church in order to get a job in a nongovernmental organization (NGO) facility.

Users across the three countries find that health workers in the public sector put in less effort, which results in long waiting times. At the same time, public sector workers are often perceived to be more competent than those in the private for-profit sector. Private for-profit workers are typically perceived as hard working, with better attitudes toward patients than their colleagues in the public sector. According to patients, more staff is available and waiting times are shorter in private for-profit facilities, but the quality of staff is not superior.

In contrast, the not-for-profit or NGO workers are seen to provide patient-centered care, typically of higher quality, with shorter waiting times and less absenteeism of staff.

Because of the differences in attributes associated with each sector, health professionals often change sector over the course of their careers. Most health workers start in the public sector, often as a way to pay back subsidized training. They then either combine with or switch to the private sector when they advance in their careers. In Rwanda, despite the fact that the public sector is the most important health care employer, only 54 percent of nursing students and 55 percent of medical students expect to work in a public facility in five years, with 40 percent of nursing students and 31 percent of medical students keeping these preferences for the long run. Some of these qualitative insights are tested formally for high-income countries using quantitative analysis. Sæther (2003), in a discrete choice analysis, identifies wages, hours of work, and type of practice as important determinants of sector choice.

Employment Location

The most salient issue is whether a job is in a rural or urban area. Across the world, health workers prefer to work in urban rather than rural areas. This holds true for high-income countries and LMICs alike. These within-country geographical imbalances can be severe, especially in Sub-Saharan Africa; they also matter for the gap in health outcomes between rural and urban areas (Lemiere et al. 2013; Serneels 2014). Geographical imbalances are often discussed in terms of numbers of workers. Although robust evidence allowing for a causal interpretation is scarce, correlation between numbers of health workers and health outcomes is strong (Serneels 2014). This has often been interpreted as evidence that important health gains can be made by increasing the number of health workers in rural areas. However, a clear understanding of the optimal number of staff needed remains limited, and recent evidence indicates that gaps in attendance and quality of care are as important as number of staff.

Ultimately the low numbers of health professionals in rural areas is rooted in the choice of health workers themselves. Although in theory workers can be compensated for unattractive job attributes, in most cases earnings will need to be very high to compensate for the disutility associated with posts in rural areas. Indeed, although rural jobs typically offer extra payment and benefits, these tend to be insufficient to compensate for other drawbacks, which can be severe, as suggested by cross-country qualitative research: professional isolation, limited access to training, poor working conditions characterized by limited access to equipment and infrastructure, low housing quality, and an absence of good schools for the children. Urban areas also tend to provide more opportunities to carry out a second job in the private sector, and salary payments are paid without delay. The lack of supervision from colleagues, together with higher levels of responsibility, may, on the other hand, give more freedom and opportunities to gain clinical experience in rural posts. These results are supported by a growing body of quantitative evidence. Although rigorous studies measuring revealed (rather than stated) preferences and identifying causal effects remain absent, careful descriptive studies, using contingent valuation and discrete choice methods, provide relevant insights.[30]

International migration can also be modeled as a choice between jobs and may be intertwined with sector choice. Pettersson and Serneels (2010) find that international migration of health workers in Rwanda is linked to sector choice with those who prefer to work in an NGO sector—which in Rwanda is dominated by international organizations—and who are also more eager to migrate abroad, suggesting that international NGOs offer a road to international employment.[31] See chapter 6, "Migration of Health Care Professionals from Sub-Saharan Africa," for a more detailed discussion of this topic.

Type of Facility

A final key factor for occupational choice suggested by qualitative research across three countries is the type of facility. At one end of the spectrum is basic primary health care and at the other end specialized hospitals. However, this issue has received limited attention, and no studies analyzing this element of job choice are known to be available.

Explanatory Variables

Having described the main left-hand variables, the chapter now turns to the right-hand side variables that play a role in health workers' job choice. As set out in the theoretical framework, three dominant right-hand side variables can be distinguished in occupational choice models: remuneration, other job attributes, and individual characteristics.

Remuneration

Qualitative research indicates that pecuniary job attributes such as salary, benefits, and allowances play a key role, as expected.[32] Overall, basic remuneration in the health sector is often perceived as too low given the workload and in comparison with other sectors. Allowances and bonuses tend to be associated with jobs in the not-for-profit sector. In many countries, the public sector has tried various incentives schemes that have not been entirely successful to affect health worker behavior. Although these schemes have often been appreciated, health workers are often uncertain about how they can be accessed and to whom they apply.

A number of quantitative studies confirm the crucial importance of pay. Willingness to work in a rural area is strongly influenced by pay among prospective doctors and nurses in Ethiopia and in Malawi (Mangham 2007; Serneels 2014). The Ethiopia study finds that expected wages significantly affect take-up of a rural post, with a simulation showing that salaries would need to increase by 83 percent for doctors and 57 percent for nurses to get 80 percent of needed health workers in rural areas (where 80 percent of the population lives); this would imply an increase in annual health expenditures of 0.9 percent. A discrete choice experiment study focusing on doctors in Ethiopia finds that doubling wages would increase the share of doctors willing to work in rural areas from 7 percent to over 50 percent, while for nurses doubling salaries would increase those willing to work in rural areas from 4 percent to 27 percent (Hanson and Jack 2010). Analysis for Tanzania confirms similar strong effects of increasing salary and hardship allowance, with women less responsive to these financial incentives (Kolstad 2011). Focusing on Vietnam, another survey (Vujicic et al. 2010) finds that increased pay would be the single most powerful incentive to get health workers willing to locate in rural areas. An older study for Indonesia, Chomitz et al. (1998) finds that modest cash incentives can make health workers more likely to work in moderately remote areas, but that staffing of very remote areas would be prohibitively expensive. Across studies, health workers who grew up in remote areas tend to require less compensation to take up a remote position. Analyses of discrete choice experiments with health students in Kenya, Thailand, and South Africa underline the finding that differences across countries play a role, and suggest that financial incentives have more important effects in poorer countries—but only if salary increases are higher than 10 percent, because smaller increases tend to be ineffective in all three countries (Blaauw et al. 2010).

Among benefits, housing consistently appears among the most important. The study of doctors in Ethiopia finds that providing high-quality housing would increase the share of doctors willing to work in rural areas to 27 percent, or the equivalent of a wage bonus of 46 percent (Hanson and Jack 2010). In Tanzania and Malawi housing is also found to be important. Being able to have a second job is another factor that seems to play an important role (Kolstad 2011; Mangham 2007).

Nonpecuniary Job Attributes

With nonpecuniary job attributes, four factors seem to be important in qualitative research across countries (this is largely confirmed by quantitative research, although there are differences across countries). The four factors are workload, career prospects and access to training, availability of medical equipment, and workplace management.

The required hours of work can vary considerably across jobs, as illustrated in the previous section on sector choice. These studies in high-income countries also pay considerable attention to shift work, which has so far remained absent from the analysis in low-income countries.

Having access to training is seen as significant, and the public sector provides the most opportunities for further training and specialization. However, senior management may not select or allocate training opportunities based on professional need, or as part of staff career development. Rural jobs may provide lower access to training, but they can offer thorough first-job experience, which is strongly appreciated by some health workers and employers alike.

Access to professional training and chances for promotion are found to be important among starting health workers in Ethiopia (Serra et al 2010). A study for Tanzania (Kolstad 2011) finds that offering continuing education after some period of service would encourage health workers to work in rural areas, although improving clinical officers' access to upgrade training would not improve their retention in rural areas. A survey in Vietnam (Vujicic et al. 2010) finds that long-term education was a primary factor in making rural posts attractive, although not as important as increased pay. The three-country study comparing Kenya, South Africa, and Thailand (Blaauw et al. 2010) also finds that among nonfinancial incentives, access to training and career development opportunities are particularly relevant. Evidence for Malawi shows that graduate nurses highly valued the opportunity to upgrade their qualifications quickly (Mangham 2007).

The availability of equipment is another factor. One reason that rural service is often unattractive is that facilities in rural areas are generally poorly equipped and health workers serving a long time in rural facilities are perceived as delivering poor-quality care. The Ethiopia study with doctors finds that the quality and availability of equipment and drugs is the nonwage attribute that is most effective in inducing take-up of a rural post, having a result equivalent to a salary increase of 57 percent for men and 69 percent for women.

The study of workplace management in health facilities is just beginning. Recent work on high-income countries suggests that management practices and leadership are important (Bloom et al. 2014); evidence for developing countries, however, remains absent.

Health Worker Characteristics

A final category of variables is health worker characteristics. In the conceptual framework, personal characteristics are typically considered as a residual primarily because they are either seen as proxies for personal preferences, which are left unobserved, or because they proxy the unobserved ability of health workers. Although it has become standard in labor economics to account for unobserved ability—because it may bias estimates of the wage effect on job choice—this remains rare in studies on health workers. The inclusion of individual characteristics as proxy for personal preferences is relevant from a policy perspective when there is strong heterogeneity across groups of workers. Straightforward characteristics of interest are the worker's level of education, gender, and ability.[33]

Other characteristics may be of interest depending on which left-hand variable is being analyzed. For example, when focusing on the choice between rural and urban postings, the rural background of health workers is of interest. Both qualitative and quantitative evidence shows that although the majority of health workers prefer to work in urban areas, those with a rural background are found to be more willing to work in rural areas in Indonesia, Ethiopia, Rwanda, and Thailand, among others. More highly educated health workers, such as doctors, are less willing to work in rural areas (Ethiopia and Uganda), while female health workers are also less willing to work in rural areas (Democratic Republic of Congo and Ethiopia), probably for security- or marriage-related reasons (Dussault and Franceschini 2006). Younger health workers may be more likely to take up a rural post, although their preparedness to work in a rural area may fall rapidly once they enter the labor force, as suggested by evidence from Ethiopia (Serneels et al. 2016). Other factors, such as appreciation for a slower pace of life, may also play a role, as suggested by qualitative evidence, underlining the potential of adverse selection. A recent test of whether less-skilled health workers—as measured by a medical knowledge test—are more likely to work in rural areas finds no evidence for such adverse selection in Ethiopia (Serneels et al. 2016). Exploiting the existence of a lottery for allocating doctors to jobs, however, another study (De Laat and Jack 2010) finds that adverse selection may occur in a different way with lottery participants, who are not able to use their first job as a signal of ability, having flat wage-seniority profiles and higher exit rates.

Emerging evidence from high-income countries also shows the importance of socioemotional skills and personality traits for occupational choice. Using data for Germany, Nieke and Störmer (2010) find that personality traits matter, as measured by the "Big Five" personality characteristics categorized in psychology (extraversion, agreeableness, openness, conscientiousness, and neuroticism), after controlling for workplace features.[34] Skriabikova, Dohmen, and Kriechel (2012) provide evidence that attitudes toward risk are also related to occupational choice in Ukraine. Studying occupational switching behavior, they find that workers who are more willing to take risks change to occupations with larger variation in earnings. Ham, Junankar, and Wells (2009), in a study in Australia, find that personality effects are significant and relatively large and persistent across all occupations, while human capital variables such as education have strong signaling effects, although parental status effects are limited. Personality effects are strong enough to rival education credentials in many instances. Effects also differ between the genders for key variables, with personality traits in females having a relatively larger effect on their occupational outcomes because of the diminished effects of education. Recent work on occupational choice in Germany finds teachers to be more altruistic than other professionals (see Dohmen and Falk 2010).

One issue of special interest now receiving renewed attention is the role of intrinsic motivation, both for performance and for occupational choice. In the health sector, intrinsic motivation has often been argued to be related to altruistic motivations (as in the Hippocratic Oath); this has been measured through surveys as well as experimental games. Quantitative studies for Ethiopia and Rwanda find that a simple question measuring health worker willingness to help the poor is strongly correlated with willingness to work in rural areas, and this is interpreted as evidence for intrinsic motivation (Serra et al 2008; Serneels et al. 2010). Comparing this survey measure with a measure for altruism obtained from an experimental game from a study on Rwanda provides evidence that both are significant predictors for preferring to work in the NGO sector (Serra, Serneels, and Barr 2011). Evidence for Thailand and South Africa also finds a strong relationship between motivation as measured by a game and willingness to work in a rural area (Blaauw et al. 2010). Using panel data for Ethiopia, one study finds that unobserved individual characteristics—proxied by fixed effects obtained from a panel regression—are strongly related to a measure of prosocial motivations, in this case trustworthiness, and are seen as further evidence of the role of intrinsic motivation (Serneels et al. 2016). The latter study also offers a rare empirical investigation of the crowding out of motivation by increased monetary rewards. The study finds evidence suggesting that increased payment may instead induce higher motivation. In Ethiopia motivation is also linked to the school where the health worker was trained, with those trained at an NGO school having higher motivation. This may suggest that either health workers get socialized into motivation or that they self-select at an earlier stage and choose a school that matches their beliefs and motivations. Ongoing work for Zambia using a rigorous impact evaluation confirms a role of intrinsic motivation (Ashraf, Bandiera, and Jack 2012).

Dual Jobs and Moonlighting

Existing evidence from both quantitative and qualitative research suggests that health workers commonly hold dual jobs. A survey of medical doctors working in the public sector in LMICs across Africa, Asia, and Latin America finds that 87 percent had a second job (Macq et al. 2001). Although detailed quantitative evidence remains absent, existing studies suggest multiple motivations, as described in this section.

In high-income countries health workers in the public sector often have nonfinancial motivations to engage in private practice; these include increased autonomy and ability to offer better services, and the ability to spend more time with patients and offer more treatment options (Humphrey and Russell 2004; Svab, Progar, and Progar 2001). In LMICs the motivation is overwhelmingly financial: to raise household income and improve family welfare (Van Lerberghe et al. 2002).

Qualitative findings for Rwanda and Ghana show the key role that additional income from dual practice plays in the appeal of urban jobs (Lievens et al. 2010; Lievens et al. 2011). Being able to work in the private sector (while holding another job in the public sector) was also the most valued job attribute in a discrete choice study in Ethiopia and a major reason health workers are reluctant to work in rural areas (Hanson and Jack 2010).

The underlying reason for dual practice is that the public sector often cannot provide sufficient income to support the health worker and his or her family. Extreme situations occur, as illustrated by a study of doctors in Portuguese-speaking African countries, which found that the average public wage provided sufficient income for seven days a month (Ferrinho et al. 1998), while research for Tanzania finds that earnings may not be enough to provide food for the whole month (Stringhini et al. 2009). Similarly, qualitative research on Ghana finds that assistant nurses see their salary as insufficient to cover basic needs, while doctors see their income from moonlighting as complementing their base salary (Lievens et al. 2011).

The qualitative study for Rwanda confirms that the motivation to work in dual practice is primarily financial. It also underlines potential conflicts of interest when combining jobs, because work hours in the public sector seem to be used "to 'embezzle' patients to private sector practice" (Lievens and Serneels 2006, 47). In some cases doctors seem to adopt strategies of making it difficult for patients in public facilities, for instance by increasing waiting times, to encourage them to visit their private clinic (Lievens and Serneels 2006). This finding is confirmed by a survey in Cameroon, where health workers have argued that "low salaries do not allow one to practice medicine ethically, our morale is down and this encourages malpractice" (Israr et al. 2001, 290).

A cohort study for Ethiopia indicates that dual practice is adopted at an early stage of career, with close to one-fifth of doctors having a secondary job in a private clinic three years out of college, with the primary motivation being to increase earnings (Serra, Serneels, and Barr 2011). The Rwanda qualitative study also finds that dual practice is structurally embedded in the system, because half of the medical students who expect to be working in the public sector five years after graduation expect to have an additional income from dual practice that is close to 50 percent of their base public sector salary (Lievens and Serneels 2006).

As for absenteeism, an important question is whether dual practice is necessarily harmful for health service delivery. One view is that dual practice ensures that staff can afford to continue to work in the public sector while at the same time earning a decent living and building an attractive career. An alternative view is that dual jobs are largely parasitic with private practice eroding the time and quality of public care.

There seems little doubt that unregulated dual practice, as it is often found in low-income countries, can severely dampen the delivery of public health care. It often leads to high absenteeism, as discussed earlier. The combination of two jobs may also be exhausting, leading to decreased efficiency and worse attitudes toward patients, as indicated by health workers themselves (Lievens et al. 2011). Moreover, working hours and effort in the private job seem invariably to be given priority over effort and performance in the public job. A study of Portuguese-speaking African doctors found that most doctors engaging in private practice acknowledged it had a negative impact on quality of public provision (Ferrinho et al. 1998).

But dual practice may also benefit public health care. The Portuguese-speaking doctors in Africa also recognized that dual practice may bring benefits for qualified personnel by allowing them to achieve a higher level of income from within the sector (Ferrinho et al. 1998). It is generally recognized that the most able health workers are also likely to be the most sought after in both the public and private sectors.

Where can applied research help to identify ways forward for dual practice? Empirical studies for Latin America suggest that increasing real wages in the public sector have limited impact on unofficial payments and other illicit practice because the probability of detection is very low (Di Tella and Savedoff 2001). The studies on absenteeism and labor supply also suggest a limited correlation between wage levels and absenteeism or labor supply.

Health Labor Market Analyses in Low- and Middle-Income Countries
http://dx.doi.org/10.1596/978-1-4648-0931-6

The qualitative research for Ethiopia and Rwanda also suggests that both the chances of being caught in the act of dual practice and the ensuing fine are low in the public sector (Serneels, Lindelow, and Lievens 2008). The main way forward, therefore, seems to be to formalize dual work, developing contracts where incentives to have out-of-hours private practice also lead to more effort in the public sector patients (González 2004). This is an area that has so far remained unexplored, and where applied research can provide useful insights. Increased attention for contract design is further discussed in the final section of this chapter.

3. Ways Forward

Most existing studies for developing countries that analyze health worker labor choices are descriptive in nature and provide limited insights on causal relationships.[35] Two valuable exceptions are the Rwanda study on pay for performance (Basinga et al. 2011) and the Zambia study on motivation (Ashraf, Bandiera, and Jack 2012). To contrast the strengths and weaknesses of descriptive and causal analysis, it is useful to compare observational to experimental data.

From Descriptive to Causal Analysis
Descriptive Analysis
The most common way to generate quantitative microdata is through survey methods. The analysis of these data can provide excellent insights, but typically cannot assess causal relationships—although econometric techniques can help address this in some instances, as will be discussed in the next section.

Survey data have both strengths and weaknesses. Surveys are good at measuring a broad range of issues, which produce results representative of a wider population and provide strong opportunities for comparison across settings (jobs, facilities, sectors, countries), especially for straightforward factual information making use of standard questions. Surveys can rely on a rich and long tradition that provides possible examples and templates. The data can provide excellent descriptions of reality and allow testing the strength of relationships. In some instances causal analysis is feasible. Survey data can also generate hypotheses for further work.

The discussions in the previous sections provide ample illustration of how the analysis of survey data can shed light on the behavior of health workers. They can reveal the incidence and scope of labor supply, absenteeism, and occupational choice, as well as describing the relative importance of correlates such as remuneration and other job attributes, in addition to workplace, household, and individual characteristics. This type of analysis creates clear descriptive overviews of who works where, what attributes seem to matter most in a given context, and which individual characteristics stand out. They also provide an insight into the equilibrium career path for health workers under prevailing conditions.

When data over time are available, movements and transitions in the labor market can be observed. A transition matrix showing movements between different positions as well as in and out of the labor force can contribute to a better understanding of the dynamics of the labor market. The data to build such a matrix can be obtained by including recall questions in a cross-section survey or, more reliably, by repeating surveys over time, ideally with the same respondents. Although panel data provide many advantages, insights can also be gained from repeated cross-section surveys using cohort analysis. Of particular interest is the collection of long-term panel data to reveal long-run career paths.

Surveys also have weaknesses: for example, they are often not good at measuring sensitive issues or issues bordering on illegality. The practice of dual jobs can, for instance, be difficult to investigate with general surveys in settings where it is illegal. In these contexts, qualitative techniques may provide an alternative. Surveys also yield measurement error. Although understanding the accuracy of measurement through survey remains limited today, this is receiving increasing attention for survey methods in general, and for measurement of labor issues in particular.[36]

Surveys are at their strongest when they are combined with information on an exogenous event, such as a change in regulation, and when they collect data on both baseline and endline in treatment and control groups. But even with these data, important identification challenges often remain. With respect to labor supply, one concern is whether the reported figures should be taken as proxy for the demand or supply of labor, since they actually reflect the intersection of supply and demand. In the absence of exogenous variation, and perhaps especially in the presence of a large monopsony (the public sector), how to interpret the results obtained from labor supply analysis with survey data often remains unclear.

Causal Analysis

From an analytical and econometric perspective, a frequent weakness of observational data is that they do not allow the identification of an unbiased causal effect because unobserved variables may be important. Panel data can provide some solution because they permit controlling for (or differencing out) individual effects. Combining panel data with changes in the environment that are exogenous to the individual health worker—such as a change in regulation or law—can shed further light and can allow for estimating causal effects of this environmental change when using the appropriate econometric technique. A discussion of the most frequently used techniques—including difference in differences (DID) analysis, instrumental variable (IV) estimation, regression discontinuity design (RDD), and propensity score matching (PSM)—falls outside the scope of this work; see existing work for an in-depth treatment.[37]

Although panel data can provide insights on causal relationships, a more robust approach is to carry out an RCT.[38] RCTs have both strengths and weaknesses, which often remain underappreciated. Even though RCTs now increasingly start from a theory of change, they frequently do not allow the identification of the channel through which change occurs.[39] Another weakness is the problem of generalizability, because RCTs typically estimate a local average treatment effect (LATE) and the results often yield weak external validity. Environmental dependence is seen by some as the major shortcoming of this method. RCTs also say little about general equilibrium effects, or what happens when agents, aware of the treatment, behave strategically. Moreover, the method crucially depends on careful design and implementation, because small deviations may lead to biased results.

RCTs also have many strengths; the most important is the estimation of causal effects for which they allow. Their increased use has brought to the fore the challenges of identification and causal inference in social science. From this perspective, RCTs provide a useful starting point to think about the relationship of interest as well as the method of analysis.

To identify a causal relationship, three questions are key: (a) What is the counterfactual? (b) Can the observed change be attributed to this causal factor? (c) Through what channel did change occur? Thinking in terms of an experiment often helps to address these questions because it makes more explicit what channels are to be tested and what variables need to be controlled for. The following example clarifies this. To identify the causal effect of health worker pay on labor supply, one can consider what experimental setup is needed to study this effect. The RCT would vary wages exogenously for some (the treatment group) but not for others (the control group), and then compare the change in labor supply before and after treatment between these two groups. Classic theory would expect labor supply to go up (as discussed earlier, because leisure is considered to be a normal good). A behavioral approach is more agnostic and argues that the sign of the effect depends on the reference point. Considering this RCT design (without implementing it) underlines a number of key messages, including the need for a control group and for an exogenous variation in wages. It also triggers further thinking on the channel through which this works. This thought exercise also helps when looking for natural experiments that mimic this situation. The Canadian study mentioned earlier (Kantarevic, Kralj, and Weinkauf 2008) provides an example: exploiting a change in the law that is exogenous to the health workers to study the causal effect of changes in pay on labor supply.

Reasoning in terms of an experiment—even if not implemented—clarifies why observational data often cannot provide a good answer to the causal questions: there is no independent variation in the explanatory (right-hand) variable of interest in the earlier example wages. Concerns such as reverse causality, where the explained (left-hand) variable also causes the explanatory (right-hand) variable; or simultaneity, where both the explained (left-hand) and explanatory (right-hand) variables are caused by a third unobserved variable, are not addressed. This is assuming that all key variables are observed—if not, there is an additional omitted variable bias as well.

A number of econometric approaches exist to try and build a counterfactual and, using exogenous variation, to identify the causal relationship, as discussed earlier. Only a few examples use these techniques applied to health worker behavior. Apart from the Canadian study on the effect of a change in regulation of physician remuneration using instrumental variable estimation, another example is the study on health worker job choice in Tanzania using propensity score matching to construct a counterfactual (Kolstad 2010).

The use of RCTs in the study of health worker behavior also remains scarce. The two studies mentioned earlier—by Bjorkman and Svensson (2009) and Basinga et al. (2011)—stand out; they look at the effect of community monitoring and pay for performance on different aspects of health worker behavior, including health worker absenteeism (as well as patient health outcomes), respectively.

Data and Measurement Concerns

A key question facing applied and operational research of health worker behavior is whether additional data need to be collected or data that already exist can be used. Although the decision ultimately depends on the research question, it is clear that existing data that can properly investigate issues of labor supply, absenteeism, and the occupational choice of health workers are severely limited. Given this dearth of data, the emphasis is on self-collected data. A final section discusses in more depth the potential of building more and better administrative data.

Using Existing Data

Two types of existing data can be used for health worker labor analysis: administrative data and data obtained from surveys. Administrative data are often limited to descriptive information that informs policy decisions at a rudimentary level; furthermore, they are available only for the public sector. Administrative data are typically scattered across different ministries, with, for instance, the ministry of health keeping information on issues such as the target number of health workers by occupation, gender, and facility, while payroll information, on the other hand, is typically housed at the ministry of finance. The different data are often difficult to merge at the individual level. Moreover, these data are not collected with a research question in mind and typically are missing information on key dimensions of interest.

Existing survey data suffer from similar shortcomings. Because no dedicated surveys of hospitals and their staff exist (as there are, for instance, for farms or manufacturing firms in many countries), survey data are typically limited to specific data collected by researchers with particular research interests in mind. Combining data across surveys is fraught with difficulties because the measurement of labor supply, earnings, occupation, and so on typically differs across the surveys.

Some good examples do exist of what can be learned from combing data. Fujisawa and Lafortune (2008) provide a good example for OECD countries, presenting a descriptive analysis of the remuneration of doctors in 14 OECD countries. Using data for general practitioners and medical specialists, the study finds large variations across countries in the remuneration levels of general practitioners and even greater variations for specialists, whose earnings have increased more rapidly than for general practitioners in nearly all countries over the past decade.[40]

McCoy et al. (2008) follow a similar approach to generate insights on earnings of health workers in the public sector across four African countries (Burkina Faso, Ghana, Nigeria, and Zambia). They conclude that pay structures and levels of income vary widely across and within countries; they also underline that accurate and complete data are scarce.

Existing national household surveys, such as a labor force survey (LFS) or Living Standards Measurement Survey (LSMS), may also shed light. However, because their aim is to be nationally representative, they typically yield small samples of health workers, leaving limited degrees of freedom to analyze variation within professions. In the case of Ethiopia, for instance, a nationally representative survey of the workforce (an LFS) resulted in a sample of fewer than 200 health workers spread across a range of occupations, making the sample too small to carry out a meaningful analysis. At the same time, interesting basic insights can be gained from these types of data, especially across countries, if the questions are uniform. This is illustrated by the WHO's efforts to combine LFSs across countries, which has resulted in some primary insights regarding the age, gender, and geographical distribution of health workers across professions.[41]

Other creative approaches can be used to gain insights from existing data. Ensor, Serneels, and Lievens (2013) use survey data to assess whether the distribution of health workers across public and private sectors has changed over time. Because demand for health worker labor is derived from the demand for health care, the authors compare patient spending, formally called "private expenditure," from surveys for 39 countries in Sub-Saharan Africa over a five-year period using annual data. Although the results need to be interpreted with care, they suggest that while private sector growth was strong over the studied period, the share of private spending as a proportion of total spending declined, signaling strong public sector growth.[42]

Collecting New Data

When planning to collect new data, surveyors face a number of issues. A decision must be made about whether to conduct surveys only or to implement a full RCT that includes a baseline survey, an intervention, and an endline survey. What group is being researched must also be determined: is it current or prospective health workers, and which professions?

To answer these questions, first the causal relationship of interest must be defined. Thinking in terms of the ideal experiment that would address the research question often helps: what intervention is needed and what change is expected? To answer this requires defining (a) the treatment (that is, the key right-hand variable), such as a change in pay or other job attributes; and (b) the outcome (the left-hand variable), such as labor supply, absenteeism, or occupational choice. A theory of change then sets out how this effect takes place and clarifies the lines along which treatment should be designed heterogeneously, and determines what other variables need to be included in the analysis and are required in the information gathering.

Collecting new data also raises the issue of measurement error. Measurement error of the left-hand variable is discussed first. Whether one opts for RCT or survey, the outcome (left-hand) variable is typically measured through surveys, although in some cases the outcome is determined through direct observation (for example, surprise visits to measure absenteeism). To what extent surveys introduce measurement error and bias estimation results is the subject of a small but growing literature. Although nonrandom measurement error of a continuous left-hand variable is of limited concern because it does not bias estimation results (although it may reduce precision), the worry is bigger with discrete dependent variables such as labor force participation. Here measurement error may bias point estimates (see Hausman 2001; Hausman, Abrevaya, and Scott-Morton 1998). However, in both cases structural estimates of coefficients of left-hand variables of interest may be biased because of particular characteristics of the instruments used. Different surveys may, for instance, use distinct screening questions that occur early in the questionnaire to define labor force participation. These differences may lead to varying categorizations of subjects resulting in different sub-samples on which estimations are carried out, introducing a selection bias.

Another example may occur when respondents systematically differ across survey methods, with certain types of respondents—such as proxy respondents, often the household head—actively or strategically trying to guess the true value of a variable about which they have imperfect information, such as the income or labor supply of their spouse, thereby introducing systematic errors. A recent study of labor statistics and estimates of labor supply in Tanzania, for instance, finds that both the type of questions and the type of respondent affected the resulting labor force participation, labor supply, and occupational categorization (see Bardasi et al. 2011). Follow-up analysis finds that structural estimates, such as returns to education, can also be affected by survey method. In the case of returns to education it is the type of questionnaire used, but not type of respondent, that introduces the bias (see Serneels et al. 2016). These results indicate that care needs to be taken when designing labor supply and occupational choice studies.

Extant studies on absenteeism also provide insights on measurement error. Measuring absenteeism in developing countries typically happens one of two ways: either through spot checks or surprise visits to the facility to verify the presence of the health worker (Chaudhury et al. 2006), or through frequent or semipermanent observations (Banerjee and Duflo 2006). Both methods provide more reliable data than employer- or facility-based registers or self-reported data, which are often used in the general literature on absence from work but are likely to be downward biased.[43] Although the incidence of absenteeism is the most-used measure in studies of health worker absenteeism, more careful measurement using permanent observation can also look at its duration.[44]

Measurement of occupational choice raises specific issues. As mentioned earlier, in the absence of incentive-compatible study designs, two types of methods have been applied to measure job choice: contingent valuation and discrete choice methods. The former distills the precise reservation wage to work in one job versus another, while discrete choice methods concentrate on the trade-off between sets of attributes associated with different jobs. Although each of these approaches has its strengths, they both require a strict implementation method to obtain reliable data.[45]

The concern that measurement error in right-hand side variables may bias estimation is the subject of a richer literature. Shields (2004) and Antonazzo et al. (2003) discuss the standard issues related to the measurement error of wages that are relevant for health workers. A central concern is whether wages might be driven by characteristics that remain unobserved by the researcher (the focus is on "unobserved ability"). This can be addressed with the use of panel data and random allocation of health workers to jobs. Serneels et al. (2016), for instance, focusing on Ethiopia, make use of a job lottery to obtain predicted wages of health workers in alternative occupations. Similar concerns about biased estimates can be raised for both monetary and nonmonetary benefits.

One issue receiving heightened attention is how to measure health worker motivation. Although there is increasing interest in formally testing the role of intrinsic motivation, there are challenges to calibrating this concept. Contemporary work has measured this variably through survey questions (see Serneels et al. 2007; Serneels et al. 2010) and experimental games (see, for instance, Serneels et al. 2016; Serra, Serneels, and Barr 2011). Ashraf, Bandiera, and Jack (2012) compare effort among health workers under different reward schemes using an RCT that compares performance when providing high financial rewards with performance when providing low financial but also social rewards (stars). They interpret the latter as effects of intrinsic motivation. It remains open for debate whether either of these are good measures.

An example of a possible questionnaire for a health worker study that was implemented in Ethiopia is provided by Serneels et al. (2007). More inspiration for LFS can also be obtained from general survey instruments used in LSMS studies; see Grosh and Glewwe (2000).

The preceding discussion focuses on health worker labor supply. A full analysis also considers demand. To obtain information on the demand side, inspiration can be obtained from firm surveys. Asking facilities about the number of vacancies and length of time they have been available would provide new information, for example. Worker-facility matched data in particular would provide new insights.

Building Administrative Data

To address some straightforward questions and inform policy making, there is also an increasing interest in improving administrative records of health workers and their career choices. Distinguishing between the key concepts of interest and the sources of data helps to structure the administrative data.

Among the key concepts needed to understand the labor market is the distinction between supply and demand for labor. A country's supply of health professionals is primarily a function of the number of people choosing that profession and securing a place to be trained. Although the training of health professionals in Sub-Saharan Africa is dominated by the public sector, the number of private schools is on the rise. Data on the aggregate number of students for each profession are often available from the ministry of health, although it typically excludes the private schools, and more detailed information about student career preferences tends to be absent. Information on the aggregate demand of health workers across sectors is even scarcer. Although data on public sector vacancies are mostly available at the central government level, little information is available on the direct recruitment by private facilities, which account for a significant share of jobs in the sector. As a result, much of the existing analysis cannot distinguish between supply and demand and instead focuses on the available number of health workers. This number is typically obtained from the ministry of health, which oversees public facilities and delivers licenses, or from the ministry of finance, which has information on payroll data.

In practice, much of the existing analysis implicitly considers the WHO norm of 2.28 health workers per 1,000 population as a target number (see also endnote 3). These data often focus on the public sector; reliable data for the private sector are typically missing. Combining administrative data in creative ways can improve our understanding. Ensor, Serneels, and Lievens (2013) provide an example. Considering eight countries in Sub-Saharan Africa, they estimate the number of workers active in the private sector by subtracting public staff numbers, typically available from the ministry of health, from the total number of health workers registered with professional bodies. Although these estimates suffer from measurement error,[46] they offer an idea of the orders of magnitude and suggest that, on average, 42 percent of registered doctors work outside the public sector (this percentage varies from 20 percent in Tanzania to 52 percent in South Africa), while 32 percent of registered nurses work outside the public sector.

Although the analysis of administrative data may yield important basic insights, survey data are needed for a more detailed descriptive analysis that can be had by obtaining richer information on the individual health worker and, using panel data, by obtaining information on the same individuals over time.

Topics for Future Research

The last decade has seen a booming interest in the role of human resources for health. The role of health workers has been discussed mostly in terms of their shortages.[47] Recent work is concerned with both the quality and quantity of services. To better understand the behavior of current health workers, this chapter has focused on labor supply issues among health workers using a non-normative analysis.

Starting from labor economic analysis, this chapter set out a framework for analysis to investigate questions related to labor supply, absenteeism, and occupational choice. It then discussed the evidence available for developing countries, as well as the relevant insights from high-income countries. It reviewed two types of analysis that can inform future applied work: descriptive and causal analysis, and discussed data and measurement issues. Starting from what is known today, this conclusion focuses on key research questions in the field of labor supply, absenteeism, and occupational choice of health workers.[48]

A first research question is whether health worker labor supply can be increased and, if so, how. Using classic labor analysis as a natural starting point, the effect of a raise in pay is considered. Evidence from high-income countries suggests that a pay increase does not necessarily lead to an increase in labor supply, and that the labor supply curve may even be bending backwards. Rather than increasing the level of pay, the future seems to lie in linking (part of) pay with performance. The study by Basinga et al. (2011) provides unique evidence from an RCT in Rwanda that performance pay—in this case at the facility level—can affect health worker behavior. Replication and extension of this study in other contexts would generate important insights, in particular when also paying more attention to the behavior response of individual health workers: their labor supply, absenteeism, and job choice.

A second question is how to improve health worker attendance. The framework of analysis described in the first section of the chapter suggests two key variables of interest: payment and monitoring (which includes sanctioning). It remains unclear whether increasing the level of pay will reduce absenteeism; it is possible that this has very little effect. Making pay conditional on attendance is more likely to be effective. Regarding the monitoring of health workers, Bjorkman and Svensson (2009) provide evidence that community monitoring can work when implemented well. Replication and extension of this study would be welcome, in particular when focusing on the channel through which this works.

Third, the occupational choice of health workers is still poorly understood. More research is needed on who becomes a health worker, and on how and why health workers move across jobs.

Two new themes that cut across these three topics are emerging. The first has to do with contracts. This is already implicit in the discussion earlier, and is expected to receive increased attention in the years to come, especially given the potential rise of the private sector. The second theme is concerned with the allocation mechanism by which health workers are matched to posts. This is receiving some attention in high-income countries but remains largely unstudied in developing countries. Each is discussed in turn.

As it stands, *contract design* is largely the focus of theoretical work. Emerging experimental and empirical results indicate that it is important for job choice as well. The current interest in results-based financing is likely to enhance interest in this topic. Two areas where contract choice can play an important role for health workers in developing countries are evident. In the short run, a change in contracts is expected to affect health worker labor choices. In the medium (and long) run, it will also influence the types of individuals sorting into certain jobs. The primary interest from a policy perspective is how performance is improved and the role of remuneration in this process—more specifically, how earnings are linked to performance. The RCT implemented in Rwanda led to a change in contract, providing rigorous evidence that linking pay to performance at the facility level can have important effects on health workers' behavior and improve health outcomes among the population. The earlier quoted study on doctors in Canada also looks at a change in contract: specialist doctors could choose between a traditional fee-for-service contract, where they receive a fee for each service provided, and a mixed remuneration scheme where they receive a per diem amount as well as a reduced fee-for-service (Fortin, Jacquement, and Shaerer 2010). Using a discrete choice approach, the analysis shows that physician effort and type of service are more sensitive to contractual changes than is time spent at work. Evidence from outside the health sector indicates that contracts can have strong effects on the type of workers who (self-) select into specific occupations. Results from recent lab experimental evidence suggest that workers self-select depending on the type of contract and whether pay is linked to effort (see Abeler et al. 2010; Dohmen and Falk 2010). Empirical work on health workers in high-income countries also underlines the role of other contract characteristics, such as whether the job is full time or part time, and whether it includes working in shifts. A further exploration of these and other aspects of contracts—including contract length, implied employment (in)security, and whether the job allows engaging in secondary work—would deepen our understanding.

A second issue that deserves more attention is that of *job allocation*. The models discussed in the conceptual framework at the start of this book all rely on the underlying assumption that jobs are allocated through a market, without much discussion of the characteristics of this market. There seem good reasons to pay little attention to alternative allocation mechanisms, such as job lotteries, which have largely gone out of fashion. The centralized approach does not seem to be as successful in taking individual preferences and abilities into account; it also seems prone to rent seeking when operationalized, even if it appears to deliver equity at first glance. Labor markets, despite their shortcomings, may be more efficient and also more equitable. But it would be interesting to know more about the characteristics of the distinct labor markets, and their regulations, to build a better understanding of what works best.

For example, where the public sector is dominant, the labor market for health workers seems to function more like a monopsony. But there has been little study of how governments allocate jobs to candidates in developing countries. Recent work in high-income countries illustrates the usefulness of such study and how improved allocation can improve market outcomes. Roth and Sotomayor (1990) study the allocation of internships to medical students using two-sided matching models.[49] These models focus on designing an allocation mechanism that optimizes matches between health workers and facilities, maximizing the desired outcome for each party. This is particularly relevant when health workers look for twofold posts, which frequently occurs when one health professional is married to another health professional (as often turns out to be the case). The design of such improved matching mechanisms may be technically demanding, but it can bring substantial improvements to job allocation in the health sector. The increased recognition of health workers' personal preferences also brings attention to selection issues. Who self-selects into certain types of jobs (or even the profession), and whether higher wages would lead to adverse selection of less-motivated health workers, are questions that are gaining in priority on the research and policy agenda. The study of how jobs are best allocated to health workers may enrich our understanding. A concrete example is provided by the study of Ethiopia's job lottery for health workers, which was compulsory until recently. De Laat and Jack (2010), studying outcomes and career paths of doctors in Ethiopia, observe that those who participated had lower levels of professional ability, illustrating how the lottery yielded adverse selection and induced inefficient allocation. A further study of how market design can further improve outcomes would be welcome.

One key issue that should be addressed when pushing this work forward is to select the right study design, including data collection and method of analysis. Summarizing the insights presented in the last section shows three primary types of analysis, linked to three types of data, both within and across countries, that can be used to carry out the preceding research. The least demanding approach is to carry out simple descriptive analysis using administrative data, whether or not combined with survey data. A second approach is to carry out advanced descriptive analysis of survey data. In both cases the key question is what reliable administrative and survey data can be used. A third approach is to conduct causal analysis using advanced econometric analysis of survey data or using the results of the implementation of an RCT. Here it helps to think in terms of designing an experiment: what would the ideal RCT look like? Even if not implemented, this exercise in experiment design may help identify exogenous changes that allow building a counterfactual using advanced econometric analysis.

These elements are intended to serve as an invitation to applied researchers to carry out further research in these areas and, thus, ultimately help to build more informed policy making on human resources for health.

Annex 5A: Cross-Country Data Set

Table 5A.1 Cross-Country Data set

Region	Countries	Total
East Asia and Pacific	Myanmar, Timor-Leste	2
South Asia	India, Maldives, Pakistan, Sri Lanka	4
Middle East and North Africa	Algeria; Djibouti; Egypt, Arab Rep.; Iraq; Morocco; Oman; Tunisia; Yemen, Rep.	8
Europe and Central Asia	Romania	1
Latin America	Brazil, Honduras	2
Sub-Saharan Africa	Burkina Faso; Benin; Burundi; Cameroon; Central African Republic; Chad; Comoros; Congo, Dem. Rep.; Congo, Rep.; Côte d'Ivoire; Equatorial Guinea; Eritrea; Gabon; Gambia, The; Ghana; Guinea; Guinea-Bissau; Liberia; Madagascar; Malawi; Mali; Mauritania; Mauritius; Namibia; Niger; Nigeria; Rwanda; São Tomé and Principe; Sierra Leone; Sudan; Swaziland; Tanzania; Togo; Uganda; Zambia	35

Annex 5B: Equations and Variable Definitions for the Models

Static Labor Supply Model

$$U = u(C, F) \tag{5B.1}$$

$$L = L\ (w, w_s, y, \varepsilon) \tag{5B.2}$$

where
  U = Utility
  F = Free time, leisure, time not working
  C = Consumption
  L = Labor supply; this can refer to labor force participation or hours of work
  w = Wage rate
  w_s = Wage rate of spouse
  y = Other household income that is independent of labor supply, such as transfers or inheritance
  ε = Error term, or unobserved variation due to differences in preference

Absenteeism

$$A = A\ (w, h_c, \pi, P, \varepsilon) \tag{5B.3}$$

where
  A = Absenteeism from work
  w = Wage
  h_c = Contracted number of hours
  C = Cost of detection
  π = Probability of being detected
  P = Penalty when detected

Occupational Choice and Job Choice

$$u^A = u(w^A, O^A, \varepsilon) > u^B = u(w^B, O^B, \varepsilon) \tag{5B.4}$$

$$J = J(w^A, O^A, w^B, O^B, \varepsilon), \tag{5B.5}$$

where
  w^A = Wage in job A; w^B = wage in job B
  O^A = Other job attributes in job A; O^B = other job attributes in job B
  J = A categorical variable with a separate value (1,2,3,...) for each type of job (A,B,C,...)

Dual Job Holding
a. when legally permitted

$$D = D(w^A, O^A, w^B, O^B, w_s, y, \varepsilon) \tag{5B.6}$$

Health Labor Market Analyses in Low- and Middle-Income Countries
http://dx.doi.org/10.1596/978-1-4648-0931-6

b. when illegal

$$D = D(w^A, O^A, w^B, O^B, w_s, y, \pi^A, P^A, \varepsilon) \tag{5B.7}$$

where
  D = Dual job holding
  Others, as above

Notes

1. See WHO Global Health Atlas database at http://apps.who.int/globalatlas/default.asp.

2. The data do not allow for an in-depth economic analysis, since they reveal only that the health workforce is young, gender-balanced, and concentrated in urban areas and in certain occupations, and that this can vary substantially across countries.

3. Indeed, demand for health workers is even harder to investigate than supply because virtually no data are available. Demand for health workers is often considered in normative terms, such as the WHO norm of 2.28 workers per 1,000 population. Although this approach may be useful to press a point, the empirical basis for this norm is unclear. There is currently limited understanding of the optimal or desirable number of health workers required to deliver health care because much of the existing empirical analysis suffers from omitted variable problems and the underlying data suffer from availability and selectivity problems, leading to biased estimates. See Serneels (2014) for further discussion.

4. The substitution effect reflects the fact that a rise in wages changes the proportion of leisure and consumption in function of their relative cost.

5. Other extensions take into account home production, which is especially relevant for individuals (such as housewives) heavily involved in home work, or consider decisions made at the family level (rather than at the individual level) to reflect intrahousehold bargaining. The model here abstracts from search behavior primarily because unemployment tends to be very low among health workers.

6. For general dynamic models that consider (optimal) career paths over time, see overviews provided for instance in Bosworth, Dawkins, and Stromback (1996) and Cahuc, Carcillo, and Zylberberg (2014).

7. Alternatives are to use semiparametric models that are less sensitive to distributional assumptions, such as censored least absolute deviation models. Cragg's (1971) double hurdle model also provides an alternative.

8. It is also possible to consider both hours contracted and hours worked in order to take absenteeism into account (directly or indirectly). This is especially useful in the case of a growing private sector, which allows for more flexible contracted hours.

9. The model includes a penalty function, and later extensions include the presence of a sick-leave plan as an explanatory variable (see Winkler 1980). An alternative approach is offered by efficiency wage models (see Shapiro and Stiglitz 1984). Here absenteeism is seen as an extreme case of shirking and the focus is on unemployment. When unemployment is high, workers are expected to work harder because there is an "army of unemployed" waiting to take their places. Absenteeism is then modeled as a function of wages, the unemployment rate, and the expected cost of detection. Since unemployment tends to be generally low among health workers, this approach is less relevant for our purposes.

10. If reservation wages are observed, the reservation wage can be modeled explicitly, letting k represent the difference in utility derived from job attributes in jobs A and B, and assuming log linear utility, so that $k = ln\left(J_i^B - J_i^A\right)$, job A will be preferred if $w_i^A \mid \varepsilon_i > k + w_i^B \mid \varepsilon_i$, or the corresponding reservation wage to accept job A is $r_i^A = k + w_i^B + \varepsilon_i$.

11. See Lievens, Lindelow, and Serneels (2009) for advice on qualitative research on health workers.

12. One earlier study observes such discontinuity in labor supply function and finds higher responsiveness of labor supply to changes in wages (Phillips 1995).

13. These medians have 90 percent intervals of [0.169, 1.238] and [0.254, 3.338], respectively.

14. Health workers who were on night shift are found to be less likely to be absent when on duty during the day. Because night shifts are often voluntary, this may proxy intrinsic motivation. Alternatively, night shifts may be assigned to health workers who are less powerful, and therefore less able to influence what shift they get, and who also tend to be less absent.

15. The Chaudhury and Hammer study (2003) relies on a survey covering 180 health facilities in Bangladesh. Providers' absence is measured on the basis of unannounced visits made at each facility at 9:30 a.m. and again around 2:30 p.m. Health workers have been accordingly classified as "absent all day," "absent half day," or "present." An obvious limitation of this absence measure—acknowledged by the authors—is that a certain absence rate, say 50 percent, could indicate that 50 percent of providers were absent half day, or that all staff was absent all day.

16. An exception is the study by Kenyon and Dawkins (1989), who use time series data on Australian firms. The few existing works on public sector absenteeism concern the public education sector (see Cloud 2000; Winkler 1980).

17. Allen (1981) also considers work schedule flexibility. Studies that make use of efficiency wage models add a proxy for unemployment rate—generally the worker's perception of the probability of finding a new job. Although this is less interesting for the present context given the low unemployment rate of health workers in developing countries, it can reveal some relevant insights. Ichino and Riphahn (2003, 2004) empirically test the effect of employment protection on absence behavior and Ichino and Riphahn (2004) examine three case studies that provide examples of employment protection and find, as predicted by theory, that workers who are more protected against firing are more likely to be absent from work.

18. Many studies have found the frequency of absence to differ significantly across gender, with female employees generally more absent, most likely because they have different responsibilities in the household, especially in the presence of young children (see, for instance, Bridges and Mumford 2000; Leigh 1983; Paringer 1983). Married men and women are less likely to be absent. The effect of age on absenteeism is uncertain both theoretically and empirically. On the one hand, younger workers are more likely to find a new job in the case of dismissal and give a higher value to the opportunity cost of leisure; this would therefore increase the probability of being absent. On the other hand, older workers are more likely to be absent because of illness. The impact of education on absenteeism is also ambiguous; more-educated workers face more alternative employment opportunities, yet they are more likely to be working within a pleasant work environment and be characterized by good work habits (Drago and Wooden 1992). Allen (1981) considers, for instance, individual perceptions about the

workplace being dangerous or unsafe. Similarly, Ose (2003) includes 20 work environment proxies, 15 of which are health, environment, and safety indicators based on workers' evaluations. The main finding of Ose's study is a confirmation that workplace conditions matter: employees with high degrees of monotonous work, heavy and frequent lifting, and bad work postures, and who are exposed to high levels of noise, are found to be more likely to be "voluntarily" absent (the work distinguishes between illness-related and voluntary absence). Moreover, Drago and Wooden (1992) test the effect of workgroup cohesiveness on the absence decision. Based on answers to various questions related to the degree of job satisfaction and group cohesiveness, they find that workgroup cohesiveness leads to low absence when job satisfaction is high and high absence where job satisfaction is low.

19. Using data on regional absenteeism differentials among employees of the same bank located in branches in northern and southern Italy, Ichino and Maggi (2000) find that "individual backgrounds," which are thought to affect individual preferences, are the most important explanatory factor for absenteeism; workers born in southern Italy seem to be more likely to be absent. Interestingly, the estimates also suggest that shirking increases gradually as one spends more time in the south, possibly because of group interaction effects.

20. The distinction between illness-related and voluntary absence is rarely acknowledged. Bridges and Mumford (2000) underline that different results may be obtained when the total time absent is used instead of incidence of absenteeism. Winkler (1980) tests the labor-leisure model predictions by considering only short-term absence as dependent variable, under the assumption that this kind of absence would be more likely to proxy for voluntary absence, considering only the one-half and one-day absence episodes, and checking for the number of Monday and Friday absences, since these days are less likely to be illness-related. Ose (2003) models short-term and long-term absence, with three days as point of distinction. His analysis leads to different results, with the economic variables influencing only short-term absence, as predicted by theory.

21. This type of exploratory data analysis has an important role as the first stage in research; it is followed by the formulation of theory, testing, and estimation, and then by prediction and policy evaluation (see Mookherjee et al. 2005). In practice, exploratory analysis in economics is typically quantitative in nature, adhering to the bias of the economics discipline toward quantitative methods. For a discussion see also Serneels, Lindelow, and Lievens (2008).

22. About half the health workers (52 percent) were women and about three-quarters (76 percent) had children. Fifty-eight percent were working in the public sector, while 23 percent were working in the private for-profit sector and 19 percent in the private nonprofit sector. Forty-one percent of the users were women, and 87 percent had children. The work in Ethiopia and Rwanda followed a strict methodology to determine the groups, select the participants, carry out the discussions, and record and analyze the data. In each country, eight focus group discussions structured the study in separate sessions with doctors, nurses, health assistants, and users, and covered both urban and rural areas. Each group counted eight participants, who were selected to ensure diversity along a number of dimensions. Individual characteristics that are believed to influence occupational choice or performance levels were also represented in a well-balanced manner among the participants in each focus group. In general, a key to the richness of qualitative data is the fact that only a minimum structure is imposed on the process of collection and analysis, thereby permitting the main messages to emerge freely. Adhering to this practice, the study held semistructured

discussions for which the interview scripts served as checklists only. The discussions lasted approximately two hours and were audio recorded, literally transcribed, and translated. During analysis only a minimum structure was imposed, categorizing the data by theme and comparing the quotes across focus groups using matrices.

23. Chaudhury et al. (2006) illustrate this low risk of penalty in the education sector: their study finds evidence of one case of a teacher being fired for absence in 3,000 head-master interviews in India.

24. Teachers were required to take a daily picture of themselves and their students to qualify for a bonus.

25. If health workers, moreover, are able to escape the consequences of defending their own interests, for instance by using private health care for their own family, this leads to a sustainable equilibrium.

26. The intervention provided both information and strong activation of the community. A report was compiled for each facility containing the findings from the baseline facility survey on utilization and quality of services, as well as a comparison with other health facilities. This report was then disseminated through meetings in each community. Three meetings were held: one with the community of beneficiaries, one with staff, and one interface meeting with the two groups together. The community meetings were organized during two afternoons with 100 participants from the beneficiary community, which were a selection of representatives from different spectra of society (to avoid elite capture), in cooperation with staff from local nongovernmental organizations (NGOs) as facilitators, who used a variety of participatory methods to disseminate the information of the report cards and encourage community members to develop a shared view on how to improve service delivery (including focus groups). The staff meetings were single afternoon sessions with all health staff, contrasting provider information on service delivery with findings from the household survey. In the interface meeting, members chosen in the community meetings and health workers were brought together to discuss suggestions for improvement and the rights and responsibilities of patients and medical staff. This led to a shared action plan (a *community contract*) outlining agreement on what needs to be done, how, when, and by whom; and suggestions for how the community could monitor the agreements. Communities were themselves in charge of further monitoring the provider. After six months, communities and health facilities were revisited.

27. Banerjee, Duflo, and Glennerster (2007) discuss how automated monitoring using punch cards or cameras has been subject to tampering and sabotage, and may also be expensive.

28. See Serneels et al. (2007) and Lievens et al. (2010), respectively.

29. These studies mostly focus on explaining the choice for sector of work, facility, and type of contract, and consider wages as well as other job attributes and individual characteristics as explanatory (right-hand) variables. The most important difference for analysis for developing countries seems to be that the type of contract—including whether the work is shift work or part time—plays a more prominent role in high-income countries. A study of job choice among nurses in Norway finds, for instance, that sector is important, with the wage amount and whether the job involves shift work both playing a role (Di Tommaso, Strøm, and Sæther 2009). An analysis of sector choice among doctors in Norway focuses on the role of wages, hours, and type of practice (Sæther 2003). Andreassen, Di Tommaso, and Strøm (2013) estimate a model where physicians can choose between combinations of sector, hospital or primary care, part- and full-time work (and not working).

30. For an overview see Serneels (2014).

31. Qualitative evidence for Ghana confirms that migration abroad is strongly motivated by financial factors. The poor access to postgraduate training, the lack of a performance-based promotion system, and the absence of a regular pay raise are said to push Ghanaian health workers abroad. Family pressure to take up a well-paid job abroad and send remittances home can also play a role. Recent salary increases seem to have slowed down migration abroad for nurses, but it is unclear what the effect is for doctors.

32. Lievens et al. (2011), researching health workers in Ghana, provide a good overview of pecuniary job attributes as a factor in job choice.

33. These are also the variables that come up in general occupational choice results. See, for instance, Constant and Zimmermann (2003).

34. Across the entire German population, Nieke and Störmer (2010) find, for instance, that manual workers are less extroverted, more conscientious, and less agreeable and open than employees from most other occupational groups.

35. While most studies in high-income countries also typically rely on survey data, there is a wider use of econometric techniques to identify causality.

36. See, for instance, several papers in the 2012 special issue of *Journal of Development Economics* 98 (1).

37. See, for instance, Ravallion (2001) and Gertler et al. (2011).

38. There is discussion in the literature about whether RCTs provide an inherently superior methodology or not—see, for instance, Deaton (2010).

39. For a discussion of RCT design that allows the identification of channels through which change occurs, see Ludwig, Kling, and Mullainathan (2011).

40. Remuneration of general practitioners was found to be between 2 (Finland, Czech Republic) and 3.5 times (United States, Iceland) the average wage in the concerned country, and ranging from 1.5 times to 2 times the average wage in Hungary and the Czech Republic, to 5 to 7 times higher for self-employed specialists in the Netherlands, the United States, and Austria.

41. For details about WHO's efforts in this area, see the Global Health Atlas (database) available at http://apps.who.int/globalatlas/default.asp.

42. The data indicate that although patient spending almost doubled from US$17 to US$30, the proportion spent in the private sector fell from 62 percent in 2001 to 57 percent in 2005. These numbers should be interpreted with care. For example, patient spending reflects out-of-pocket expenditures, and total patient expenditures in the public sector may be covered at least in part by the state.

43. Existing empirical studies on worker absenteeism in general typically employ either firm data on the employees' recorded days of absence during a specified period of time (see Barmby, Orme, and Treble 1991 and Kenyon and Dawkins 1989, among others) or workers' self-assessed information about whether they were absent during a specified period of time. Allen (1981) considers, for instance, a two-week period, whereas Leigh (1983) refers to 10 working days, and Drago and Wooden (1992) ask for respondents' estimation of the number of days they were absent over the previous 12 months. Other researchers classify workers as absent if they report their own absenteeism (Bridges and Mumford 2000). Self-reported absenteeism data are generally accepted to have a potential downward measurement bias due to both the lack of precise memory (especially if the specified period covers several weeks) and workers' aversion to publicly reported absence if it is perceived as a form of shirking, for reasons of shame.

44. See Barmby, Orme, and Treble (1991) and Cloud (2000) for the estimation issues raised by measuring the duration of absenteeism.

45. See Mangham, Hanson, and McPake (2008) and Ryan, Gerard, and Amaya-Amaya (2008) for excellent overviews of both measurement and estimation issues related to discrete choice methods. Serneels et al. (2007) provide an illustration of contingent valuation methods applied to the labor market choice of health workers in Sub-Saharan Africa. For a contemporary discussion of contingent valuation in general, see several papers in the Fall 2012 issue of *Journal of Economic Perspectives*.

46. In one way the figures overestimate the number of active health workers outside the public sector because individuals who are inactive or working abroad are also included, while in another way they underestimate the number of health workers outside the public sector because many combine a job in the public and private sector, and in some extreme cases are permanently absent from their public sector job.

47. As mentioned in endnote 3, this is perhaps best illustrated by the WHO guideline recommending 2.28 health professionals—including doctors, nurses, and midwives—per 1,000 inhabitants to allow the delivery of quality health services.

48. Issues related to the quality of care provided are another promising topic of research, and we refer to chapter 7, "Measuring the Performance of Health Workers," and chapter 8, "Analyzing the Determinants of Health Worker Performance."

49. See Roth's follow-up studies (http://web.stanford.edu/~alroth/) and works with coauthor Niederle (http://web.stanford.edu/~niederle/).

References

Abeler, J., A. Falk, L. Goette, and D. Huffman. 2010. "Reference Points and Effort Provision." *American Economic Review* 101 (2): 470–92.

Alcázar, L., and R. Andrade. 2001. "Induced Demand and Absenteeism in Peruvian Hospitals." In *Diagnosis: Corruption*, edited by R. Di Tella and W. D. Savedoff, 123–62. Washington, DC: Inter-American Development Bank.

Allen, S. G. 1981. "An Empirical Model of Work Attendance." *Review of Economics and Statistics* 63 (1): 77–87.

Andreassen, L., M. L. Di Tommaso, and S. Strøm. 2013. "Do Medical Doctors Respond to Economic Incentives?" *Journal of Health Economics* 32: 392–409.

Antonazzo, E., A. Scott, D. Skatun, and R. F. Elliott. 2003. "The Labour Market for Nursing: A Review of the Labour Supply Literature." *Health Economics* 12 (6): 465–78.

Ashraf, N., O. Bandiera, and K. Jack. 2012. "No Margin, No Mission? A Field Experiment on Incentives for Pro-Social Tasks." Economic Organisation and Public Policy Discussion Papers series, Suntory and Toyota International Centres for Economics and Related Disciplines, LSE.

Askildsen, J. E., B, H. Baltagi, and T. H. Holmås. 2002. "Will Increased Wages Reduce Shortage of Nurses? A Panel Data Analysis of Nurses' Labor Supply." CESifo Working Paper 794, Center for Economic Studies, Munich.

Ault, D. E., and G. L. Rutman. 1994. "On Selecting a Measure of Labour Supply: Evidence From Registered Nurses 1981 and 1989." *Applied Economics* 26 (1994): 851–63.

Baltagi, B. H., E. Bratberg, and T. H. Holmas. 2003. "A Panel Data Study of Physicians' Labor Supply: The Case of Norway." Stein Rokkan Centre for Social Studies Working Paper 3.

Banerjee, A., A. Deaton, and E. Duflo. 2004. "Health Care Delivery in Rural Rajasthan." *Economic and Political Weekly* 39 (9): 944–49.

Banerjee, A., and E. Duflo. 2006. "Addressing Absence." *Journal of Economic Perspectives* 20 (1): 117–32.

Banerjee, A., E. Duflo, and R. Glennerster. 2007. "Putting a Band-Aid on a Corpse: Incentives for Nurses in the Indian Public Health Care System." *Journal of the European Economic Association* 6: 487–500.

Bardasi E., K. Beegle, A. Dillon, and P. Serneels. 2011. "Do Labor Statistics Depend on How and to Whom the Question Was Asked? Results from a Randomized Survey Experiment." *World Bank Economic Review* 25 (3): 418–47.

Barmby, T. A., C. D. Orme, and J. G. Treble. 1991. "Worker Absenteeism: An Analysis Using Microdata." *Economic Journal* 101 (405): 214–29.

Barr, A., F. Mungisha, P. Serneels, and A. Zeitlin. 2012. *Field and Lab Experimental Evidence from Uganda.* Manuscript. https://www.dartmouth.edu/~neudc2012/docs/paper _277.pdf.

Basinga, P., P. J. Gertler, A. Binagwaho, A. L. B. Soucat, J. Sturdy, and C. M. J. Vermeersch. 2011. "Effect on Maternal and Child Health Services in Rwanda of Payment to Primary Health-Care Providers for Performance: An Impact Evaluation." *Lancet* 377 (9775): 1421–28.

Basu, K. 2006, "Teacher Truancy in India: The Role of Culture, Norms and Economic Incentives." CAE Working Paper 06-03. Cornell, NY: Center for Analytical Economics. http://dx.doi.org/10.2139/ssrn.956057.

Besley, T., and M. Ghatak. 2005. "Competition and Incentives with Motivated Agents." *American Economic Review* 95 (3): 616–36.

Bjorkman, M., and J. Svensson. 2009. "Power to the People: Evidence from a Randomized Experiment on Community-Based Monitoring in Uganda." *Quarterly Journal of Economics* 124 (2): 735–69.

Blaauw, D., E. Erasmus, N. Pagaiya, V. Tangcharoensathein, K. Mullei, S. Mudhune, C. Goodman, M. English, and M. Lagarde. 2010. "Policy Interventions That Attract Nurses to Rural Areas: A Multicountry Discrete Choice Experiment." *Bulletin of the World Health Organization* 88 (5): 350–56.

Bloom, N., C. Propper, S. Seiler, and J. Van Reenen. 2014. "The Impact of Competition on Management Quality: Evidence from Public Hospitals." CEP Discussion Paper 983, May 2010 (revised November 2014), Center for Economic Performance, London.

Blundell, R., and T. Macurdy. 1999. "Labor Supply: A Review of Alternative Approaches." In *Handbook of Labor Economics*, vol. 3, edited by O. C. Ashenfelter and D. Card. New York: Elsevier.

Bognanno, M. F., J. S. Hixson, and J. R. Jeffers. 1974. "The Short-Run Supply of Nurse's Time." *Journal of Human Resources* 9 (1): 80–94.

Bosworth, D. L., P. J. Dawkins, and T. Stromback. 1996. *The Economics of the Labour Market.* London: Longman.

Bourguignon, F., M. Fournier, and M. Gurgand. 2007. "Selection Bias Corrections Based on the Multinomial Logit Model: Monte Carlo Comparisons." *Journal of Economic Surveys* 21 (1): 174–205.

Bridges, S., and K. Mumford. 2000. "Absenteeism in the UK: A Comparison across Genders." Discussion Paper in Economics 2000/12, University of York, Helsington, York.

Brock, J. M., K. Leonard, M. C. Masatu, and P. Serneels. 2013. "Health Worker Performance." In *The Labor Market for Health Workers in Africa: A New Look at the Crisis*, edited by A. Soucat, R. M. Scheffler, and T. A. Ghebreyesus, 67–92. Directions in Development. Washington, DC: World Bank.

Brown, S., and J. G. Sessions. 1996. "The Economics of Absence: Theory and Evidence." *Journal of Economic Surveys* 10 (1): 23–53.

Burkett, J. P. 2005. "The Labor Supply of Nurses and Nursing Assistants in the United States." *Eastern Economic Journal* 31 (4): 585–99.

Cahuc P., S. Carcillo, and A. Zylberberg. 2014. *Labor Economics*. 2nd ed. Cambridge, MA: MIT Press.

Camerer C., L. Babcock, G. Loewenstein, and R. Thaler. 1997. "Labor Supply of New York City Cabdrivers: One Day at a Time." *Quarterly Journal of Economics* 112 (2): 407–41.

Charness, G., and P. Kuhn. 2011. "Lab Labor: What Can Labor Economists Learn from the Lab?" In *Handbook of Labor Economics*, vol. 4, edited by O. Ashelfelter and D. Card. Amsterdam: Elsevier North Holland.

Chaudhury, N., and J. S. Hammer. 2003. "Ghost Doctors: Absenteeism in Bangladeshi Health Facilities." Policy Research Working Paper 3065, World Bank, Washington, DC.

Chaudhury, N., J. S. Hammer, M. Kremer, K. Muralidharan, and F. Halsey Rogers. 2006. "Missing in Action: Teacher and Health Worker Absence in Developing Countries." *Journal of Economic Perspective* 20 (1): 91–116.

Cheriyan, G., O. P. Arya, and A. D. Singh. 2010. "Improving Service Delivery through Measuring Rate of Absenteeism in 30 Health Centres in Tonk District of Rajasthan, India." Case Study Note. Jaipur, India: CUTS Centre for Consumer Action, Research and Training (CUTS CART).

Chomitz, K. M., G. Setiadi, A. Azwar, N. Ismail, and Widiyarti. 1998. "What Do Doctors Want? Developing Incentives for Doctors to Serve in Indonesia's Rural and Remote Areas." Policy Research Working Paper 1888, World Bank, Washington, DC.

Cloud, D. L. 2000. "Absenteeism and Endogenous Preferences." North Carolina A&T State University Working Paper in Economics, School of Business and Economics, North Carolina Agricultural and Technical State University, Greensboro, NC.

Constant, A. F., and K. F. Zimmermann. 2003. "Occupational Choice across Generations." IZA Discussion Paper 975, Institute for the Study of Labor (IZA), Bonn, Germany.

Cragg, J. G. 1971. "Some Statistical Models for Limited Dependent Variables with Application to the Demand for Durable Goods." *Econometrica* 39 (5): 829–44.

Crawford, V. P., and J. Meng. 2011. "New York City Cab Drivers' Labor Supply Revisited: Reference-Dependent Preferences with Rational-Expectations Targets for Hours and Income." *American Economic Review* 101 (5): 1912–32.

Crossley, T. F., J. Hurley, and S.-H. Jeon. 2009. "Physician Labour Supply in Canada: A Cohort Analysis." *Health Economics* 18: 437–56.

Das, J., J. Hammer, and K. Leonard. 2008. "The Quality of Medical Advice in Low-Income Countries." *Journal of Economic Perspectives* 22 (2): 93–114.

Deaton, A. 2010. "Instruments, Randomization, and Learning about Development." *Journal of Economic Literature* 48 (2): 424–55.

De Laat, J., and W. Jack. 2010, "Adverse Selection in the Labor Market: Earnings and Exit of High Skilled Ethiopian Physicians." Working paper, Georgetown University, Washington, DC. http://faculty.georgetown.edu/wgj/papers/Delaat-Jack-Adverse-Selection-Oct2010.pdf.

Di Tella, R., and W. Savedoff, eds. 2001. *Diagnosis Corruption: Fraud in Latin America's Public Hospitals*. Washington, DC: Inter-American Development Bank.

Di Tommaso, M. L., S. Strøm, and E. M. Sæther. 2009. "Nurses Wanted: Is the Job Too Harsh or Is the Wage Too Low?" *Journal of Health Economics* 28: 748–57.

Dohmen, T., and A. Falk. 2010. "You Get What You Pay For: Incentives and Selection in the Education System." *Economic Journal* 120 (546): 256–71.

Drago, R., and M. Wooden. 1992. "The Determinants of Labour Absence: Economic Factors and Workgroup Norms across Countries." *Industrial and Labor Relations Review* 45 (4): 764–78.

Duflo, E., R. Hanna, and S. P. Ryan. 2012. "Incentives Work: Getting Teachers to Come to School." *American Economic Review* 102 (4): 1241–78.

Dussault, G., and M. C. Franceschini. 2006. "Not Enough There, Too Many Here: Understanding Geographical Imbalances in the Distribution of the Health Workforce." *Human Resources for Health* 4: 12.

Ensor, T. 2004. "Informal Payment for Health Care in Transition Economies." *Social Science and Medicine* 58 (2): 237–46.

Ensor, T., P. Serneels, and T. Lievens. 2013. "Public and Private Practice of Health Workers." In *The Labor Market for Health Workers in Africa*, edited by Agnes Soucat, Richard M. Scheffler, and T. A. Ghebreyesus, 191–219. Directions in Development Series. Washington, DC: World Bank.

Farber, H. S. 2008. "Reference-Dependent Preferences and Labor Supply: The Case of New York City Taxi Drivers." *American Economic Review* 98 (3): 1069–82.

Ferrinho, P., W. Van Lerberghe, M. R. Julien, E. Fresta, A. Gomes, F. Dias, A. Gonçalves, and B. Bäckström. 1998. "How and Why Public Sector Doctors Engage in Private Practice in Portuguese-Speaking African Countries." *Health Policy and Planning* 13 (3): 332–38.

Fortin, B., N. Jacquement, and B. Shaerer. 2010. *Labour Supply, Work Effort and Contract Choice: Theory and Evidence on Physicians*. Scientific Series. Montreal: Cirano.

Fujisawa, R., and G. Lafortune. 2008. "The Remuneration of General Practitioners and Specialists in 14 OECD Countries: What Are the Factors Influencing Variations across Countries?" Health Working Papers 41, OECD Directorate for Employment, Labour and Social Affairs, Paris.

Gertler, P. J., S. Martinez, P. Premand, L. B. Rawlings, and C. M. J. Vermeersch. 2011. *Impact Evaluation in Practice*. Washington, DC: World Bank.

Goldstein, M., J. Graff Zivin, J. Habyarimana, C. Pop-Eleches, and H. Thirumurthy. 2013. "The Effect of Absenteeism and Clinic Protocol on Health Outcomes: The Case of Mother-to-Child Transmission of HIV in Kenya." *American Economic Journal: Applied Economics* 5 (2): 58–85.

González, P. 2004. "Should Physicians' Dual Practice Be Limited? An Incentive Approach." *Health Economics* 13 (6): 505–24.

Grosh, M., and P. Glewwe. 2000. *Designing Household Survey Questionnaires for Developing Countries: Lessons from 15 Years of the Living Standards Measurement Study*. Vols. 1, 2, and 3. Washington, DC: World Bank.

Ham, R., P. N. Junankar, and R. Wells. 2009. "Occupational Choice, Personality Matters." IZA Discussion Paper 4105, Institute for the Study of Labor (IZA), Bonn, Germany.

Hanel, B., G. Kalb, and A. Scott. 2012. "Nurses' Labour Supply Elasticities: The Importance of Accounting for Extensive Margins." Melbourne Institute Working Paper 9/12, University of Melbourne, Victoria, Australia.

Hanson, K., and W. Jack. 2010. "Incentives Could Induce Ethiopian Doctors and Nurses to Work in Rural Settings." *Health Affairs* 29 (8): 1452–60.

Hausman, J. A. 2001. "Mismeasured Variables in Econometric Analysis: Problems from the Right and Problems from the Left." *Journal of Economic Perspectives* 15 (4): 57–67.

Hausman, J. A., J. Abrevaya, and F. M. Scott-Morton. 1998. "Misclassification of the Dependent Variable in a Discrete Response Setting." *Journal of Econometrics* 87 (2): 239–69.

Humphrey, C., and J. Russell. 2004. "Motivation and Values of Hospital Consultants in South-East England Who Work in the National Health Service and Do Private Practice." *Social Science and Medicine* 59 (6): 1241–50.

Ichino, A., and G. Maggi. 2000. "Work Environment and Individual Background: Explaining Regional Shirking Differentials in a Large Italian Firm." *Quarterly Journal of Economics* 115 (3): 1057–90.

Ichino, A., and R. T. Riphahn. 2003. "The Effect of Employment Protection on Worker Effort: A Comparison of Absenteeism during and after Probation." CEPR Discussion Paper 3847, Centre for Economic Policy Research, London.

———. 2004. "Absenteeism and Employment Protection: Three Case Studies." *Swedish Economic Policy Review* 11: 95–114.

Israr, S. M., O. Razum, V. Ndiforchu, and P. Martiny. 2001. "Coping Strategies of Health Personnel During Economic Crisis: A Case Study from Cameroon." *Tropical Medicine and International Health* 5 (4): 288–92.

Kantarevic, J., B. Kralj, and D. Weinkauf. 2008. "Income Effects and Physician Labour Supply: Evidence from the Threshold System in Ontario." *Canadian Journal of Economics* 41 (4): 1262–84.

Kenyon, P., and P. Dawkins. 1989. "A Time Series Analysis of Labour Absence in Australia." *Review of Economics & Statistics* 71 (2): 232–39.

Killingworth, M., and J. Heckman. 1986. "Female Labor Supply: A Survey." In *Handbook of Labor Economics*, edited by O. Ashenfelter and R. Layard, vol. 1, chapter 2. Amsterdam: Elsevier Science Publishers.

Kolstad, J. R. 2010. "How Does Additional Education Affect Willingness to Work in Rural Remote Areas?" Working Papers in Economics 02/10, University of Bergen, Department of Economics.

———. 2011, "How to Make Rural Jobs More Attractive to Health Workers: Findings from a Discrete Choice Experiment in Tanzania." *Health Economics* 20 (2): 196–211.

Leigh, P. J. 1983. "Sex Differences in Absenteeism." *Industrial Relations* 22 (3): 349–61.

Lemiere, C., C. H. Herbst, C. Dolea, P. Zurn, and A. Soucat. 2013. "Rural-Urban Imbalances of Health Workers in Sub-Saharan Africa." In *The Labor Market for Health Workers in Africa: A New Look at the Crisis*, edited by A. Soucat, R. M. Scheffler, and T. A. Ghebreyesus, 147–68. Directions in Development Series. Washington, DC: World Bank.

Leonard, K. L., P. Serneels, and J. M. Brock. 2013. "Intrinsic Motivation." In *The Labor Market for Health Workers in Africa: A New Look at the Crisis*, edited by A. Soucat, R. M. Scheffler, and T. A. Ghebreyesus, 255–84. Directions in Development. Washington, DC: World Bank.

Leontaridi, R. M., and M. E. Ward. 2002. "Work-Related Stress, Quitting Intentions and Absenteeism." IZA Discussion Paper 493, Institute for the Study of Labor (IZA), Bonn, Germany.

Lievens, T., M. Lindelow, and P. Serneels. 2009. "Understanding Health Workforce Issues: A Selective Guide to the Use of Qualitative Methods." In *Handbook on Monitoring and Evaluation of Human Resources for Health*, edited by M. R. Dal Poz, N. Gupta, E. Quain, and A. L. B. Soucat, 129–46. Geneva: World Health Organization.

Lievens, T., and P. Serneels. 2006. *Synthesis of Focus Group Discussions with Health Workers in Rwanda*. Washington, DC: World Bank.

Lievens, T., P. Serneels, J. D. Butera, and A. Soucat. 2010. "Diversity of Career Preferences in Future Health Workers in Rwanda: Where, Why and for How Much?" World Bank Working Paper No. 189, World Bank, Washington.

Lievens, T., P. Serneels, S. Garabino, P. Quartey, E. Appiah, C. H. Herbst, C. Lemier, A. Soucat, L. Rose, and K. Saleh. 2011. "Creating Incentives to Work in Ghana: Results from a Qualitative Health Worker Study." Health, Nutrition, and Population Discussion Paper, World Bank, Washington, DC.

Link, C. R., and R. F. Settle. 1979. "Labor Supply Responses of Married Professional Nurses: New Evidence." *Journal of Human Resources* 14 (2): 256–66.

Ludwig, J., J. Kling, and S. Mullainathan. 2011. "Mechanism Experiments and Policy Evaluations." *Journal of Economic Perspectives* 25 (3): 17–38.

Macq, J., P. Ferrinho, V. De Brouwere, and W. Van Lerberghe. 2001. "Managing Health Services in Developing Countries: Between Ethics of the Civil Servant and the Need for Moonlighting: Managing and Moonlighting." *Human Resources Health Development* 5 (1–3): 17–24.

Mangham, L. 2007. "Addressing the Human Resource Crisis in Malawi's Health Sector: Employment Preferences of Public Sector Registered Nurses." ESAU Working Paper 18, Overseas Development Institute, London.

Mangham, L., K. Hanson, and B. McPake. 2008. "How to Do (or Not to Do) ... Designing a Discrete Choice Experiment for Application in a Low-Income Country." *Health Policy and Planning* 24 (2): 151–58.

McCoy, D., S. Bennett, S. Witter, B. Pond, B. Baker, J. Gow, S. Chand, T. Ensor, and B. McPake. 2008. "Salaries and Incomes of Health Workers in Sub-Saharan Africa." *Lancet* 371 (9613): 675–81.

Mookherjee, D., A. Banerjee, P. Bardham, K. Basu, and R. Kanbur. 2005. "New Directions in Development Economics: Theory or Empirics?" BREAD Working Paper 106, Bureau for Research and Economic Analysis of Development.

Muralidharan, K., and S. Venkatesh. 2011. "Teacher Performance Pay: Experimental Evidence from India." *Journal of Political Economy* 119 (1): 39–77.

Nieke, P., and S. Störmer. 2010. "Personality as Predictor of Occupational Choice: Empirical Evidence from Germany." Discussion Paper 8/2010, University of Hamburg, Hamburg, Germany.

Nyqvist, M. B., D. de Walque, and J. Svensson. 2014. "Information Is Power: Experimental Evidence on the Long-Run Impact of Community Based Monitoring." Policy Research Working Paper 7015, World Bank, Washington, DC.

Olken, B. A. 2007. "Monitoring Corruption: Evidence from a Field Experiment in Indonesia." *Journal of Political Economy* 115 (2): 200–49.

Ose, S. O. 2003. "Worker Absenteeism and Working Conditions." Working Paper, Norwegian University of Science and Technology, Trondheim, Norway.

Paringer, L. 1983. "Women and Absenteeism: Health or Economics?" *American Economic Review* 73 (2): 123–27.

Penceval, J. 1986. "Labour Supply of Men: A Survey." In *Handbook of Labor Economics*, edited by O. Ashenfelter and R. Layard, vol. 1, chapter 1. Amsterdam: Elsevier.

Pettersson, G., and P. Serneels. 2010. "Future Physicians in Rwanda: Do Academic Ability and Risk Attitude Affect Willingness to Migrate?" Manuscript.

Phillips, V. L. 1995. "Nurses' Labor Supply: Participation, Hours of Work, and Discontinuities in the Supply Function." *Journal of Health Economics* 14 (5): 567–82.

Piper, B., and M. Korda. 2010. *Early Grade Reading Assessment (EGRA) Plus: Liberia*. Program evaluation report prepared for USAID/Liberia. Research Triangle Park, NC: RTI International.

Qin, X., L. Li, and C.-R. Hsieh. 2013. "Too Few Doctors or Too Low Wages? Labor Supply of Health Care Professionals in China." *China Economic Review* 24 (2013): 150–64.

Ravallion, M. 2001. "The Mystery of the Vanishing Benefits: An Introduction to Impact Evaluation." *World Bank Economic Review* 15 (1): 115–40.

Rijckeghem, C. V., and B. Weber. 1997. "Corruption and the Rate of Temptation: Do Low Wages in the Civil Service Cause Corruption?" Working Paper 97/73, International Monetary Fund, Washington, DC.

Roth, A. E., and M. A. O. Sotomayor. 1990. *Two-Sided Matching: A Study in Game-Theoretic Modeling and Analysis*. Econometric Society Monographs. Cambridge, U. K.: Cambridge University Press.

Ryan, M., K. Gerard, and M. Amaya-Amaya, eds. 2008. *Using Discrete Choice to Value Health and Health Care*. Dordrecht, The Netherlands: Springer.

Sæther, E. M. 2003. "A Discrete Choice Analysis of Norwegian Physicians' Labor Supply and Sector Choice." Working Paper 2003:19. Health Economics Research Programme, University of Oslo.

Serneels P. 2014. "Internal Geographical Imbalances: The Role of Human Resources Quality and Quantity." In *Encyclopedia of Health Economics*, vol. 2, edited by Anthony J. Culyer, 91–102. San Diego: Elsevier.

Serneels, P., A. Barr, J. G. Montalvo, and M. Lindelow. 2016. "Public Service in Hardship Destinations: The Role of Wages, Job Attributes and Motivation." Mimeo.

Serneels, P., M. Lindelow, and T. Lievens. 2008. "Qualitative Research to Prepare Quantitative Analysis: Absenteeism Amongst Health Workers in Two African Countries." In *Are you Being Served? New Tools for Measuring Service Delivery*, edited by S. Amin, J. Das, and M. Goldstein, 271– 98. Washington, DC: World Bank.

Serneels, P., J. Montalvo, M. Lindelow, and A. Barr. 2007. "For Public Service or for Money: Understanding Geographical Imbalances in the Health Workforce." *Health Policy and Planning* 22 (3): 128–38.

Serneels, P., J. Montalvo, G. Pettersson, T. Lievens, J. D. Butera, and A. Kidanu. 2010. "Who Wants to Work in a Rural Health Post? The Role of Intrinsic Motivation, Rural Background and Faith Based Institutions in Rwanda and Ethiopia." *Bulletin of the World Health Organization* 88 (2010): 342–49.

Serra, D., P. Serneels, and A. Barr. 2011. "Intrinsic Motivations and the Nonprofit Health Sector." *Personality and Individual Differences* 51 (3): 309–14.

Serra D., P. Serneels, M. Lindelow, and J. G. Montalvo. 2010. "Discovering the Real World – Health Workers' Early Work Experience and Career Preferences in Ethiopia." Working Paper 191, Africa Human Development Series, World Bank, Washington, DC. http://documents.worldbank.org/curated/en/671021468024610941/pdf/555450PUB 0disc1EPI1976923101PUBLIC1.pdf.

Shapiro, C., and J. E. Stiglitz. 1984. "Equilibrium Unemployment as a Worker Discipline Device." *American Economic Review* 74 (3): 433–44.

Shields, M. A. 2004. "Addressing Nurse Shortages: What Can Policy Makers Learn from the Econometric Evidence on Nurse Labor Supply?" *Economic Journal* 114 (November): F464–F498.

Skriabikova, O, T. Dohmen, and B. Kriechel. 2012. "Risk Attitudes and Occupational Choice." http://www.sole-jole.org/12213.pdf.

Soucat, A., R. M. Scheffler, and T. A. Ghebreyesus, eds. 2013. *The Labor Market for Health Workers in Africa: A New Look at the Crisis.* Directions in Development Series. Washington, DC: World Bank.

Stringhini, S., S. Thomas, P. Bidwell, T. Mtui, and A. Mwisongo. 2009. "Understanding Informal Payments in Health Care: Motivation of Health Workers in Tanzania." *Human Resources for Health* 7: 53.

Svab, I., I. V. Progar, and M. Progar. 2001. "Private Practice in Slovenia after the Health Care Reform." *European Journal of Public Health* 11 (4): 407–12.

UNHCO (Uganda National Health Consumers Organisation). 2012. "Prevalence and Factors Associated with Absenteeism of Health Providers from Work in Bushenyi District." UNHCO, Kampala, Uganda. http://siteresources.worldbank.org /EXTHDOFFICE/Resources/5485726-1239047988859/5995659-1270654741693 /10_Session2.2_UNHCO_Uganda.pdf.

Van Lerberghe, W., C. Conceicao, W. Van Damme, and P. Ferrinho. 2002. "When Staff Is Underpaid: Dealing with the Individual Coping Strategies of Health Personnel." *Bulletin of the World Health Organization* 80 (7): 581–84.

Vujicic, M., M. Alfano, B. Shengelia, and S. Witter. 2010. "Attracting Doctors and Medical Students to Rural Vietnam: Insights from a Discrete Choice Experiment." HNP Discussion Paper 58461, World Bank, Washington, DC.

Winkler, D. R. 1980. "The Effects of Sick-Leave Policy on Teacher Absenteeism." *Industrial and Labor Relations Review* 33 (2): 232–40.

Migration of Health Care Professionals from Sub-Saharan Africa: Issues, Data, and Evidence

Çağlar Özden

Introduction

Existing data indicate that over a quarter of the physicians who were trained in Africa are currently living in Organisation for Economic Co-operation and Development (OECD) countries (Arah, Ogbu, and Okeke 2008; Bhargava, Docquier, and Moullan 2011; OECD 2008). Among the recent studies, OECD (2015) presents data that show similar patterns are continuing. In the presence of severe public health challenges, these numbers create serious concerns and stimulate a lively public debate on the impact this has on Africa and the policy implications of African doctors migrating to OECD countries. This chapter provides an overview of the data needs for the proper analysis of determinants of health professional migration and its implications for the origin countries. It then discusses the existing data along with their conclusions and shortcomings. Finally, the chapter provides two examples of this analysis. The first example combines different data sets in innovative ways to identify career paths of African doctors who immigrate to the United States, considering place of birth, training, and professional practice. The second utilizes a detailed survey of Ghanaian physicians to answer some of the most relevant career and migration questions. The main focus of the chapter is on physicians, since this has received the most

This chapter incorporates some of the work done by the author with Erhan Artuc, Michel Beine, Frederic Docquier, David Phillips, Mirwat Sewadeh, Benjamin Siankam (whose work appears under the name A. B. S. Tankwanchi), and Sten Vermund. I am truly grateful to have worked with them and acknowledge their intellectual contributions, without holding them responsible for any of the mistakes. My colleagues at the World Bank—Agnes Soucat, Chris Herbst, and Richard Scheffler—provided me with much appreciated comments and suggestions on this chapter and my earlier work in this area. I am also grateful to Hope Steele for her superb editorial support. The standard disclaimer applies: The findings, conclusions, and views expressed in this chapter are entirely those of the author and should not be attributed to the World Bank, its executive directors, or the countries they represent.

attention in public policy debates and is where most comprehensive and reliable data are available. While many of the data challenges are similar across different health care professions, the complications posed by physician migration and appropriate policy responses might be different. This confirms one of the key messages of the chapter regarding the need for higher-quality and more comprehensive data.

The migration of health care professionals, especially physicians from Sub-Saharan African countries to high-income OECD countries, generates significant attention in the academic literature and the policy debate on human resources in health care. The main concern is that "medical brain drain" potentially undermines the quality and delivery of health care services in the region by siphoning off the critical human capital required. Former World Health Organization (WHO) Director-General Lee Jong-wook captured prevailing sentiment with his remarks that "it takes a considerable investment of time and resources to train health workers" and when they emigrate, "there is loss of hope and years of investment" (WHO 2006).

As a result of these sentiments, the migration of health care professionals across national boundaries has become a critical, controversial, emotional, and difficult subject for all parties involved. It is critical because it involves the transfer of human capital in a key area where there are significant global shortages and imbalances. Lack of access to simple health care services, such as vaccinations or other treatments, at critical points in time or in critical locations will have long-term consequences for both individuals and societies. Long-term economic growth and development rely significantly on the availability of basic health care services.

This issue is also controversial because health care professionals, quite frequently, migrate from developing countries in the South where there are significant human capital and resource shortages to developed countries in the West where there is relative abundance. In the majority of the cases, medical training in developing countries is financed through limited public funds at considerable opportunity costs. The migration of a physician or a nurse is frequently viewed as an implicit subsidy of a rich country by a poor one.

The migration of health care professionals is also an emotional issue. It is more complicated than the movement of a product, a financial asset, or even other highly skilled professionals because health care is frequently associated with basic citizenship rights. The debate is frequently accompanied by images of children in Sub-Saharan Africa who could be saved with simple and cheap interventions if the medication and the health care professionals were simply available at the right place and time. On the other side, references are made to wasteful medical tests and expenditures in the OECD countries simply because they are available and paid for.

Finally, the migration of health care professionals is a difficult issue. A lack of data means that neither the causes nor the impacts of the phenomenon are well established. The debate and the analysis take place behind a relatively thick veil of ignorance, especially for a subject that receives such public attention. In the absence of reliable and detailed data, emotions and controversy dominate the policy agenda.

After reviewing the basic reasons that health care professionals migrate, especially those who train in Africa and then move to the OECD countries, the chapter will focus on more analytical issues. More specifically, it will discuss (a) factors that influence migration patterns, (b) the measurement of these factors, and (c) the data constraints policy makers and researchers face in making evidence-based trade-offs.

The data issues that create such challenges are an especially important topic of this chapter. Without high-quality and comprehensive data from origin and destination countries, the policy debate will not lead to feasible and effective solutions. Thus, the chapter will try to answer what kind of data are needed for a well-informed policy debate that would engage all parties involved—the producers and consumers of health care services in both destination and origin countries as well as the migrant health care professionals themselves. Implementation of efficient and fair public health policies regarding training and employment of health care professionals can take place only with proper and high-quality data. In other words, the modest goal of this chapter is to reduce the level of controversy and emotion in the debate so that fact and analysis gain some ground.

Reasons for Migration

In some ways the question of why people migrate is very easy to answer. People have been moving from one location to another—crossing mountains, rivers, and oceans—for as long as humans have lived in communities. Historical motivations to move—such as more plentiful food, better living conditions, escape from violence and persecution, and natural disasters—exist even today. The world is still full of political refugees and asylum seekers who are willing to take personal risks for basic needs that we take for granted, especially in the West.

When it comes to the migration of health workers or other highly skilled and educated professionals, additional reasons enter the picture. Even though these reasons can be divided into several separate categories to discuss them more easily, they are still closely related to each other. The three main categories are (a) financial motivations, (b) professional development concerns, and (c) personal and family reasons.

Average annual income per capita shows great variation across Africa— from around $400 in the Democratic Republic of Congo to around $36,000 in Equatorial Guinea, $15,000 in Gabon, and $12,000 in South Africa. Yet the fact that all of the 15 countries at the very bottom of the global per capita income rankings (World Bank 2013) are from Sub-Saharan Africa gives an idea of the low income levels in most African countries. Clearly, Equatorial Guinea and Gabon are outliers because of their small populations and natural resource endowments. Furthermore, significant inequality exists within each country where the median income is significantly lower than the mean income.

In every country around the world, incomes of health care professionals are naturally linked to overall income levels. However, in Africa, the incomes of health care professionals tend to be significantly higher than the average incomes because of relative shortages and high returns to education. WHO (2006) estimates that in most countries in Sub-Saharan Africa, the average income of a doctor is around 20–40 times greater than the average income per capita. Still, even at these relative levels, average physician salaries in the region are quite low when compared with those in Organisation for Economic Co-operation and Development countries. For example, in the United States, the average annual income of a physician ranges between $150,000 and $250,000 depending on the specialization (AMA 2012). These stark wage differences range between 4 and 15 times depending on the African and OECD countries used in the comparison, and they provide some of the most powerful pull factors for African doctors who migrate to Western labor markets.

The second most powerful set of factors can be classified under professional advancement opportunities. The first example is the availability of training during and after medical school to acquire, develop, and practice new findings, technologies, and information. This issue is extremely critical for a field such as medicine, where the pace of development and introduction of new medicines, equipment, and other treatment techniques are quite high. Doctors and other professionals need to keep abreast of new developments and have easy access to them to improve their performance and provide better services to their patients. Unfortunately this is quite difficult in most of Africa, where many countries are still without medical schools, advanced specialization programs, or easy access to scientific developments in medicine.

Another advantage often cited by African doctors who have migrated to the West is being part of institutions—universities, hospitals, clinics—and being surrounded by accomplished and motivated colleagues in their new positions. Frequent and close interaction with such colleagues creates knowledge spillovers in high-skill environments, as economics literature has consistently shown. These positive externalities, in turn, increase the level of both productivity and job satisfaction, creating more incentives to migrate.

Another limitation of professional environments in Africa is the financial resource constraints on support staff, equipment, facilities, and medicines. Doctors in Africa are often forced to practice with very limited resources—older equipment, facilities below internationally accepted standards, and inadequate support staff—relative to their counterparts in the West; at the same time, they must deal with heavier and more dangerous health care burdens (Soucat, Scheffler, and Ghebreyesus 2013). The professional and financial environment in many Western countries is structured to increase the effectiveness of the doctors. In addition to impacting their productivity, most African doctors cite the demoralizing effects of these constraints, because they feel helpless (Özden 2012).

The final sets of reasons are personal in nature, as is the case with hundreds of millions of migrants around the world. Doctors want to provide better opportunities for their families, especially for their children. Having lived through difficult environments with limited resources and having achieved relative success, it is natural for parents to want better physical, educational, and financial opportunities for their children. In addition, most migrant professionals send remittances to their extensive families back at home, even at times supporting whole villages. One of the most fascinating findings of the survey of Ghanaian doctors in the West is that they have a large number of nonphysician siblings who also migrated abroad (Özden 2012). Many doctors took advantage of family reunification programs and sponsored their siblings and their families. In short, migration of the doctor was part of a strategy to help the extended family (Özden 2012).

Data Needed to Analyze Health Care Professional Migrations

In other areas of heath economics, education, or public policy, researchers and policy makers have access to vast amounts of data to determine the appropriate costs and benefits of different policies. Unfortunately this is not the case when it comes to analyzing the determinants and consequences of health care professionals' migration, especially from developing to developed countries. This section lists the ideal data sets that a researcher can ask for when performing such analyses. It is clear that such data sets do not exist in reality or would be cost-prohibitive to collect. The section following this one will identify existing data sources that have been used so far or are available and waiting to be tapped. Fortunately, medical professions are among the most tightly regulated ones in almost every country. This makes the collection of certain types of data relatively easy, as described in further detail below. However, because of the nature of the data, collaboration and the cooperation of both the origin and destination countries are needed in the collection process. This, unfortunately, may be problematic in many cases.

Data needs can be divided into several categories that track the career paths of health care professionals: their social environment and education prior to medical school, their medical training, and their professional career; and the health care outcomes in their home communities.

Personal and Demographic Variables

The first data category covers personal and demographic backgrounds of the medical professionals that are especially relevant for the future migration decisions. Family and personal reasons for migration were noted earlier: some of these variables enter this category. The place of birth (or even the region of birth within the home country) and other relevant demographic or family variables are some examples. These data—especially place and year of birth—could be obtained from administrative records. However, the only possible way to collect data for the other variables would be to conduct a detailed survey of the professionals.

Education and Training

The second category covers medical education and training; this includes both formal training at medical or appropriate vocational schools and practical or on-the-job training. This category also includes information related to the specializations chosen and how the education was financed (private versus public) as well as indicators of the quality of training. These data are relatively easier to collect and analyze, especially compared to the other categories, since they would come from the medical school registration records, administrative data collected for licensing requirements, and professional councils.

Professional Career Paths

The third category concerns the career paths that health care professionals pursue *after* they complete their medical training. Data on current and past geographic locations of their practice would be collected in this section. This would be the main source of data for migration because the data set would track when and where the health care professionals moved. In addition to the data on the county of location, the data set would ideally indicate the specific region to which the migrant moved, which would be important when considering large destination countries such as the United States and Canada.

In the career path category, there would be additional data on professional details along with geographic location. For example, it would be useful to know whether the physician is working in a research lab, a full-service hospital, a small clinic, or in private practice. If the data were collected from a survey, questions on professional activities and links—both personal and professional—with the home country could be included.

Ways to Measure the Relative Importance of Migration Determinants

The previous two sections listed the causes of migration and then the data needed at the individual level of the health workers. Listing the causes—whether they are financial, professional, or personal—of the migration of health care professionals is actually the easier part. The more difficult and policy-relevant issue is how to *measure the relative importance* of these factors in determining the migration decision. If this were accomplished, policy makers would be able to determine more easily what policies need to be modified to increase retention in home countries at minimal cost, especially in countries with limited fiscal resources. For example, it would be possible to determine whether an extra dollar spent on equipment, salaries, or advanced medical training is more effective in reducing the likelihood of migration of physicians.

Various methods can measure the relative importance of different motivations, based on the data outlined above. An example is the method employed by Özden (2012) using survey data of Ghanaian doctors both abroad and at home (survey details are discussed later in the chapter in the section "Determinants of Migration: Ghana as a Case Study"). The most basic way to identify determinants of migration is to construct a discrete choice model where the dependent variable is the migration status and the explanatory variables are the personal, academic, and professional categories. The single most important issue is that the migrant doctors are not randomly selected. For example, they might be more academically accomplished, come from specific regions, or already have family members abroad. Thus, it is necessary to collect data on both the migrant and nonmigrant doctors to make the appropriate comparison and construct metrics of the various factors that impact migration decision so they can be used in the estimation.

It is also possible that people who want to migrate abroad choose to become doctors since a medical education might make it easier to obtain residency in an OECD country. A two-stage estimation technique might be used where certain personal or family characteristics (that do not influence the migration decision) are used to determine selection into the medical education and then additional variables are used to estimate their effect on the migration decision.

Ways to Measure the Impact of Migration

The data categories listed previously pertain to the characteristics of individual health care professionals. The next critical data category relates to the impact of migration on the health outcomes, especially in origin countries. These are possibly the most difficult and costly data to collect. The main cost for an origin country when health care professionals migrate is the potential decline in the quality and quantity of the services provided to the public. Disease burdens, life expectancy, prevalence of infectious diseases, and other health indicators are all examples of potential health outcome indicators that can be used in the analysis. To link the immigration of doctors and nurses to declines in health outcomes, it is important to collect such public health information with as much detail and frequency as possible.

Data on health outcomes is collected on a regular basis by governments and other national and international institutions. Their aim is not necessarily to measure the impact of the immigration of health care professionals but rather to keep track of outcome patterns so that appropriate policies can be implemented in a timely and cost-effective manner. There are two ways to collect such data. One is to rely on administrative data collected at the health care facilities or other service delivery points when patients arrive to receive treatment and other services. This option, even though extremely useful, might provide several challenges. The first challenge is that many patients *choose* not to, or are unable to, receive treatment. They might lack the financial resources to pay for what is required of them, they might be living far from an existing facility, or they might decide not to seek treatment at all since the facility does not have the resources for their specific issue or cannot provide adequate services.

Health Labor Market Analyses in Low- and Middle-Income Countries
http://dx.doi.org/10.1596/978-1-4648-0931-6

The second challenge is that the staff at the facility might fail to keep adequate records, or, worse, might have the incentive to falsify records to obtain additional resources and benefits. Finally, the patients might seek health care services through private channels, which might not be fully captured through official administrative data, especially if the private services are provided through informal or small practices. In short, such administrative data can be used for certain outcomes that are collected widely and reliably, such as fertility or mortality, but might not be appropriate for other indicators such as specific disease patterns.

Another option for health data is to conduct a detailed survey of the population, most likely at the household level. The Demographic and Health Surveys (DHS) Program is a prominent example of regularly conducted surveys. They capture more detailed health outcomes relative to administrative data, especially regarding diseases, injuries, and other treatments.

Certain selection problems that arise from patients choosing not to seek treatment through official channels are mitigated by DHS data. Furthermore, certain health outcomes and chronic problems, such as underweight, stunting, or other problems can be directly observed during the survey.

Another advantage of DHS-style household surveys is that additional economic and social variables can be collected at the same time. For example, DHSs include many questions on income, consumption, education, and cultural norms that clearly influence health outcomes, along with available health care service resources such as facilities, medications, and staff. This is very valuable for empirical analysis since all of these additional factors need to be simultaneously controlled for to properly determine their impact on health care service indicators. Administrative data are unlikely to capture these economic, social, and cultural determinants of health care outcomes at the household level in such detail.

The final benefit of surveys is that they can be repeated with the desired frequency, and the same household can be visited to assess the *changes* in health outcomes it experiences over time. Panel data sets are especially important in health outcomes if the goal is to measure the differential impact of a change in policy or any other intervention.

The drawback of surveys is that they are costly and require significant resources. Surveys cannot cover the whole population, so the sample has to properly account for relevant subsamples. Pilots need to be conducted in advance of the actual surveys; questions, especially culturally sensitive ones, need to be designed carefully to elicit truthful responses. Data need to be entered properly and disseminated rapidly. All of these factors increase the cost of conducting a survey, especially in poor developing countries in Africa where access to certain remote areas can be difficult and data collection infrastructure might not be present.

Once the surveys are conducted and data are collected, the next stage would be to match the survey data with the appropriate health resource data that capture facilities, equipment, staff, and available medicines. In other words, detailed data are needed on health care inputs linked to outcomes. An ideal data source would be a census of private, public, and other nonprofit facilities that the World Bank conducted in several African countries. It is important to match the health outcome data (for example, from DHSs) with health resource data (for example, from health care facilities and resource censuses) at the smallest geographic unit possible. If this is done accurately, causation can be established with much more precision. Furthermore, if both the health care outcome and resource data are in panel format, the analysis can better identify causation. The impact on various measures of health outcomes of the decline in the number of physicians as a result of immigration can then be determined through annual changes in both variables while controlling for income, geographic variables, and other exogenous determinants.

Potential sources of reverse causality and endogeneity need special attention. For example, an area might suffer from a high disease burden as a result of external reasons such as climate. In that case, more doctors and other health resources would be expected to be employed in that region as an endogenous response to the disease burden. Under normal circumstances, more resources should lead to lower disease burdens, but this case would find a positive correlation when comparing health outcomes with health inputs across regions. A more sophisticated regression of health outcomes on resources might even statistically confirm that more resources lead to worse health outcomes. Therefore it is important for the analysis to control for external factors—in this example, climate—as well as endogenous policy responses—such as the government sending more doctors to high disease density areas.

Data Availability for Africa

In most cases, the analysis of the impact of migration focuses on the origin developing countries since they are viewed as "losing" their doctors. As mentioned previously, there are two main types of losses. The first type consists of the public financial resources that were spent to train the health workers. The second is the actual human capital that is considered irreplaceable, even if the origin country was somehow compensated for the fiscal cost of training. A decline in human capital levels, especially in socially and economically important sectors such as health care, is a source of serious concern. Even though there is significant level of North-North mobility of highly skilled professionals, these tend to be more balanced. It is the one-way movement from developing countries to the developed that has become the focus of attention in policy debates (Docquier, Lohest, and Marfouk 2007; Docquier and Marfouk 2006).

Among developing countries, those in Sub-Saharan Africa receive even more special attention. Despite the availability of significant amounts of aid from the rest of the world, the health care burden in Africa outweighs the existing delivery capacity and other resources. In terms of every basic health care measure, Africa lags every other region of the world.

Lack of human resources—the absence of doctors, nurses, and other professionals—has been cited as one of the main reasons for failures in the adequate delivery of health care services in many countries of the region. Of course, health care delivery facilities, medical equipment, medicines, and sophisticated logistics network along with appropriate human resources and financing mechanisms are necessary. Doctors without support staff, facilities, and equipment cannot perform miracles. In many cases, it is difficult to convincingly determine where the true constraints lie. There is a lively debate on the issue that is beyond the scope of this chapter, but the next section explores several studies that analyze migration in this context. This section presents the existing data sources on migration of health care professionals.

Emigration Patterns of African Physicians

One of the most widely watched and quoted statistic in comparing the health care systems across the world is physician density. The World Health Organization's (WHO) Global Health Observatory provides detailed time series data and shows that Africa lags the rest of the world significantly in this indicator. For example, physician density (physicians per 10,000 people) was around 0.2 on average in Burundi, Rwanda, Niger, Mozambique, Sierra Leone, and Liberia in 2010. The density in these countries had stayed the same since the 1970s, barely keeping up with the population growth. The same ratio is around 50 times higher in many OECD countries; this is the gap that receives much attention (WHO 2011).

In most OECD countries, through the professional licensing bodies such as the American Medical Association (AMA) in the United States, it is possible to obtain detailed information on the age, place of birth, current location, practice, and specialization areas of physicians, as well as details of their education. More specifically, it is possible to obtain information on when and where (medical school) each degree (medical degree, residency, fellowships, and specializations) was obtained. The same data are generally not publicly available in most African countries. One prominent exception is South Africa, where the Health Professions Council of South Africa collects and provides such data, not only for physicians but also for all other health care professionals. Similar data are likely to be collected in other countries for licensing purposes. However, significant effort is needed to access the microdata for research purposes.

To analyze the effects of migration on the origin countries, the most critical data would cover migrant doctors in OECD destination countries since they attract the largest portion of foreign doctors. There have been quite a few efforts to collect detailed data but they are now outdated and need to be modernized. One of the initial and most prominent attempts was that of Hagopian et al. (2004), who focused only on the migration to the United States. Using the 2002 American Medical Association Physician Masterfile, they identify a total of 5,334 physicians who had graduated from Sub-Saharan Africa–based medical schools and were located in the United States. The key feature of this database was the fact that it identified individual source countries: the leading source countries from Africa were, as expected, Nigeria, South Africa, Ghana, and Ethiopia, in declining order.

Including the physicians in Canada, Hagopian et al. (2004) estimate that close to 10 percent of the physicians from Sub-Saharan Africa were in North America. Mullan (2005) extends this analysis to include registration data from Australia, Canada, and the United Kingdom. Mullan concludes that the Sub-Saharan Africa region had the highest emigration rate when compared with other parts of the world.

The next effort, funded by the World Bank, was that of Bhargava and Docquier (2008), which added yet more OECD destination countries as well as South Africa to the sample. The Bhargava and Docquier database has the number of physicians from 192 origin countries to Austria, Belgium, Denmark, Finland, France, Germany, Ireland, Italy, Norway, New Zealand, Portugal, South Africa, Sweden, and Switzerland in addition to the four English- speaking countries (the United States, the United Kingdom, Canada, and Australia) in the Mullan (2005) database. According to Bhargava and Docquier (2008), Sub-Saharan Africa has the highest ratio of physician emigration in the world: around 25 percent of the physicians trained in the region emigrate (figure 6.1).

In absolute numbers, a small group of countries—generally these also have the largest populations in the region—is the source of the vast majority of migrant physicians in OECD countries because they have the largest supply of physicians.

Figure 6.1 Stock of Immigrant Physicians in OECD Countries as a Percentage of Locally Trained Physicians in Source Region

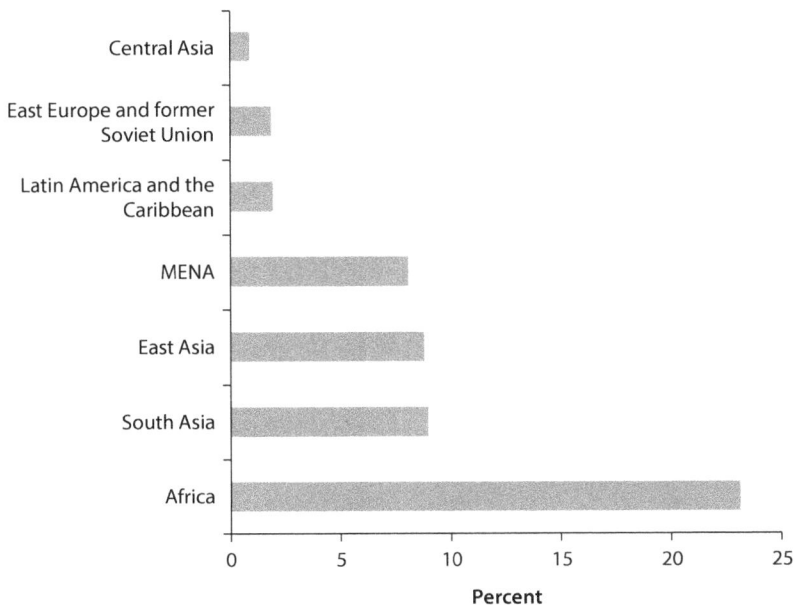

Source: Bhargava and Docquier 2008.
Note: MENA = Middle East and North Africa.

Five countries—South Africa, Nigeria, Sudan, Ghana, and Ethiopia—accounted for more than 87 percent of all African physicians in OECD countries in 2004; South Africa alone accounted for 60 percent of the total stock of migrant physicians from Sub-Saharan Africa in 2004 (Bhargava and Docquier 2008).

These five African countries are not necessarily the ones facing the highest rates of migration as a share of the existing physician stock (Bhargava and Docquier 2008). Most countries with high emigration rates (of over 10 percent) for physicians experienced an increase in migration rates between 1991 and 2004 (figure 6.2). Small countries were most affected. Cape Verde had the highest rate of physician migration in 2004 (55 percent), followed by São Tomé and Principe in 2004 (45 percent) (Bhargava and Docquier 2008).

One of the main strengths of the Bhargava and Docquier data set (2008) is that it is a panel for 1991–2004; it presents the number of doctors trained in each of the 192 origin countries and who are practicing in the 18 destination countries for each year in this time period. This is extremely useful when identifying patterns and correlating other annual data. When the timeline is plotted, the rapid increase in the number of African physicians who migrated to the OECD countries in this short period is evident (figure 6.3). The data indicate that the number of African-trained physicians working in OECD countries increased by 91 percent between 1991 and 2005. The increase in the number of African-trained physicians working in Africa during the same timeframe was comparatively low, at 61 percent. As mentioned earlier, this growth

Figure 6.2 African Countries with the Highest Rates of Physician Emigration, 1991 and 2004

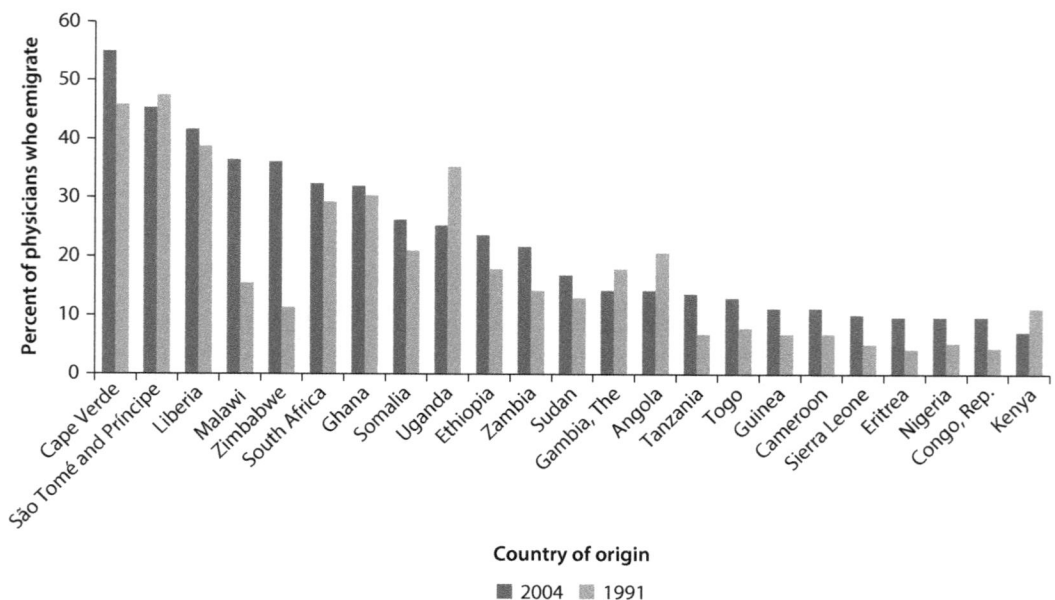

Country of origin

■ 2004   ■ 1991

Source: Bhargava and Docquier 2008.

Figure 6.3 Number of Trained African Physicians in Africa and OECD Countries, 1991–2004

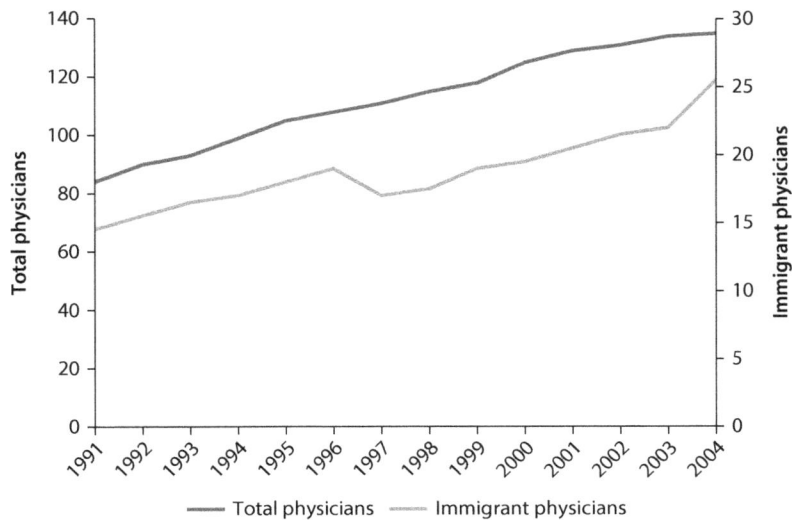

Source: Bhargava and Docquier 2008.

barely managed to keep up with the overall population growth in a large num-ber of the African countries.

Another strength of the Bhargava and Docquier data set (2008) is that it is bilateral in nature, so the main migration corridors can be identified. The United Kingdom, the United States, Canada, and Australia account for more than 85 percent of African physicians in the sample; the United Kingdom alone accounts for 55 percent (figure 6.4). Ireland is the sixth largest destination in terms of number of migrant African physicians among OECD countries.

Most physicians in developing countries are trained in or fluent in English. The practice of medicine requires interaction with other professionals and patients. As a result, English-speaking countries become natural destinations for physicians from developing countries. The principal language still has some influence: France and Belgium, for example, are the dominant destinations for physicians from francophone countries. The fact that the United States receives a significant share of physicians from francophone countries suggests that, in some cases, economic prospects and selective immigration policies can super-sede language and colonial links as determining factors of immigration destina-tion. On the other hand, countries that do not have English or French as a native language have a very hard time attracting immigrant physicians. One final data set that should be mentioned is that of Dumont and Zurn (2007), which is quite similar to Docquier and Bhargava in terms of construction and content, but differs for several destination countries because of differences in data sources.

Figure 6.4 Number of African Physicians Working in Selected OECD Countries, 1991 and 2004

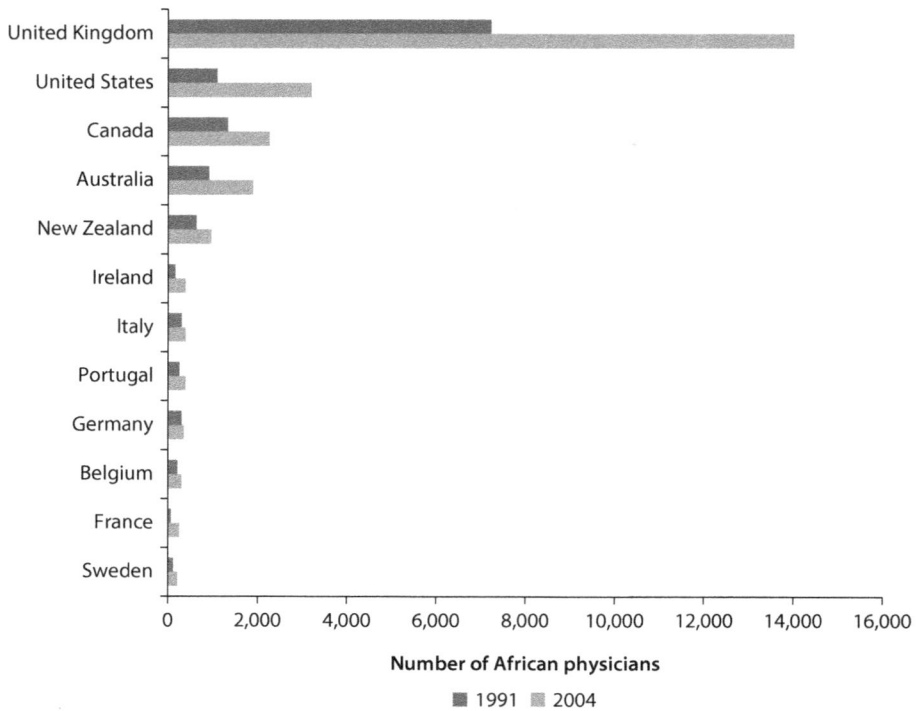

Number of African physicians

■ 1991 ■ 2004

Source: Bhargava and Docquier 2008.
Note: OECD = Organisation for Economic Co-operation and Development.

The Bhargava and Docquier data set (2008) uses the location of training as the key identifying criterion (see also the Hagopian et al. 2004 and Mullan 2005 studies). The drawback of this assumption is that it potentially excludes a large number of African-born physicians who might have been trained outside Africa and are practicing in OECD countries. To address this issue, Clemens and Pettersson (2008) use the country of birth as the identifying criterion whenever possible. In many cases, this distinction does not make a large difference, but there are several cases where it does. For example, the United States reports more African physicians than does the United Kingdom when the criterion is the country of medical education, as seen in Hagopian et al. (2004), Mullan (2005), and Bhargava and Docquier (2008). But when the country of birth is used as the selection criterion, the pattern is reversed, as shown by Clemens and Pettersson (2008). This suggests that many African physicians may have entered the United Kingdom quite young—likely as children or students—and decided to stay and practice there. At the same time, most African migrant physicians come to the United States at much older ages, primarily to work or specialize after completing medical education in their home countries. As a result, the actual emigration of physicians as a transfer of resources from Africa to the United States might be larger.

New Analysis of Place of Birth versus Place of Education

The distinction between place of birth and place of education is a critical issue that deserves further scrutiny, especially in the context of Sub-Saharan Africa. On the one hand, large numbers of African-born physicians are trained outside their home countries or even outside Africa because of the lack or complete absence of adequate capacity in local medical schools. In many of these cases, their respective governments financed their education abroad with the assumption that they would return and practice at home. On the other hand, many other African-born physicians had migrated abroad as children with their parents. They complete their education in their adopted countries with minimal intention or requirement to their countries of birth. Their bonds with Africa are weaker, and it is not appropriate to treat them as African migrant physicians for public health policy purposes (Hagopian et al. 2005). Finally, there is the possibility of a group of physicians who were not born in Africa but were trained there. These might be the children of African immigrants who have the citizenship of their parents' countries and might have wanted to complete their education in Africa. It is also important to identify and separate this group.

To identify the distinctions between these three groups—born and trained in Africa, born in Africa but trained outside, born outside but trained in Africa—Tankwanchi, Özden, and Vermund (2013) conducted a new study. They obtained AMA data lists for all doctors who received their education in medical schools in Africa and all medical graduates who were born in Africa, but trained outside Africa. The records include name, gender, name of the medical school attended and year of graduation, year of birth, birth country, contact information, primary specialty, residency program attended, and date of residency completion. Unfortunately, data on country of birth is incomplete (30 percent) since it is voluntary to provide that information to the AMA. However, medical school information is fully available. So it is possible that the data set will be missing some doctors born in Africa who were trained abroad but did not fill out that portion of the registration sheet.

The AMA data list 17,376 physicians who were born or trained in Africa as of 2011 (Tankwanchi, Özden, and Vermund 2013). Sub-Saharan Africa accounts for slightly over 60 percent of the total (10,819) while North African countries (6,557) account for the remainder. Of the Sub-Saharan African physicians, 7,370 were trained in the region, while the other 3,449 were born in there but trained elsewhere. More specifically, 2,129 were trained in medical schools in the United States, 449 in Europe, 443 in Asia and the Pacific, 254 in the Caribbean, 107 in the Middle East, and 5 in Latin America. Since physicians are required to report where they obtained their training but not their country of birth, these numbers correctly present physicians trained in Sub-Saharan Africa but are likely to underreport those who were born in Sub-Saharan Africa but trained elsewhere in the world.

The details of Tankwanchi, Özden, and Vermund's data (2013) are presented in table 6.1. For example, of the 449 Sub-Saharan African-born doctors trained in Europe, 275 were trained in Western Europe. There are almost as many

Table 6.1　Regions of Training of African Physicians Identified in the 2011 AMA Physician Masterfile

Main regions of training	Number	Percent
IMGs trained in Sub-Saharan Africa (*n* = 7,370)		
West Africa	4,082	37.7
Southern Africa	1,989	18.4
East Africa	1,216	11.2
Central Africa	83	0.8
Born in Sub-Saharan Africa and trained in North America (*n* = 2,191)		
United States	2,126	19.7
Other North America	65	0.6
Born in Sub-Saharan Africa and trained in Europe (*n* = 449)		
Western Europe	275	2.5
Eastern and Central Europe	94	0.9
Other European region	80	0.7
Born in Sub-Saharan Africa and trained in Asia/Pacific (*n* = 443)		
South Asia	420	3.9
Other Asia region	23	0.2
Born in Sub-Saharan Africa and trained in the Caribbean (*n* = 254)		
Dominica	67	0.6
Grenada	60	0.6
Other Caribbean countries	127	1.2
Born in Sub-Saharan Africa and trained in MENA (*n* =107)		
Middle East	79	0.7
North Africa	28	0.3
Born in Sub-Saharan Africa and trained in Central/South America (*n* = 5)	5	0.1
Subtotal	10,819	100
North African Emigrés		
IMGs trained in North Africa	5,544	84.6
Born in North Africa and trained outside Africa	1,011	15.4
Other (unidentified)	2	0.0
Subtotal	6,557	100
Total	17,376	

Source: Tankwanchi, Özden, and Vermund 2013.
Note: AMA = American Medical Association; IMG = international medical graduate; MENA = Middle East and North Africa.

African doctors trained in South Asian countries, mainly in India, as there are trained in Europe. These tend to be sub-Saharan African-born members of the South Asian diaspora whose families migrated over a century ago to ex-British colonies such as Kenya, South Africa, Uganda, Zambia, and Zimbabwe. Because of the continuing bonds that their families maintained and the special privileges granted by South Asian countries, they are able to attend medical school in South Asia and eventually migrate to the United States.

Table 6.2 presents the same data in more detail at the country level for the 12 countries with the highest emigration rates (Tankwanchi, Özden, and Vermund 2013). For example, there are 56 Liberian-born and-trained doctors

Table 6.2 **Top 12 Countries of Emigration Physicians Appearing in the 2011 AMA Physician Masterfile, by Emigration Rate**

Countries with ≥ 20 SSA-IMGs in the 2011 AMAPM	SSA-trained (SSA-IMGs)	SSA-IMGs increase since 2002 (%)	SSA-born US-trained (SSA-USMG)	SSA-born trained outside SSA & U.S.	Total SSA-born trained abroad	Aggregate total of émigrés in U.S.	Physicians reported in emigration country[b]	Migration rate to U.S.[c] (%)	Total of potentially active émigrés (aged ≤ 70)	Potential addition to domestic workforce in case of return (%)
Liberia	56	19.1	96	23	119	175	51	77.4	170	333.3
Tanzania	24	60.0	35	95	130	154	300	33.9	141	47.0
Ghana	721	50.8	404	118	522	1,243	2,033	37.9	1,226	60.3
Ethiopia	531	106.6	240	91	331	862	1,806	32.3	830	46.0
Zambia	81	20.9	82	59	141	222	649	25.5	221	34.1
Kenya	173	86.0	296	394	690	863	4,506	16.1	844	18.7
Uganda	145	9.0	70	126	196	341	3,361	9.2	321	9.6
Zimbabwe	112	49.3	43	9	52	164	2,086	7.3	155	7.4
Nigeria	3,271	51.6	407	139	546	3,817	55,376	6.4	3,763	6.8
Cameroon	63	350.0	66	70	136	199	3,124	6.0	199	6.4
South Africa	1,787	−8.0	178	43	221	2,008	34,829	5.5	1,789	5.1
Sudan	329	282.6	31	43	74	403	11,083	3.5	390	3.5
Other[a]	77	n/a	178	113	291	368	21,666	1.7	328	1.5
Total	**7,370**	**38.2**	**2,126**	**1,323**	**3,449**	**10,819**	**142,165**	**7.1**	**10,377**	**7.3**

Source: Tankwanchi, Özden, and Vermund 2013.

Note: AMAPM = American Medical Association Physician Masterfile; IMG = international medical graduate; SSA = Sub-Saharan African; USMG = United States medical graduates.

a. Sub-Saharan African countries with fewer than 15 SSA-IMGs (Sub-Saharan African international medical graduates) in the 2011 AMAPM.

b. Latest domestic stocks as reported in the *Global Health Observatory Data Repository.*

c. Physician emigration rate = Aggregate total of Sub-Saharan African physicians in the United States/(physician stock in the country of emigration + the aggregate total of Sub-Saharan African physicians in United States)*100.

in the United States. There are 96 Liberian-born but U.S.-trained doctors. Finally, 23 additional doctors were born in Liberia and were trained both outside of Liberia and outside the United States. Thus the total number of Liberian-born doctors is 175, and fewer than one-third of them were trained at home. In total, close to one-third of all Sub-Saharan African physicians in the United States were actually trained outside Africa; the vast majority of them were trained in the United States. South Africa and Nigeria have the lowest number of doctors trained outside their countries in relative terms, because they have large numbers of big medical schools (Tankwanchi, Özden, and Vermund 2013).

The third group mentioned earlier consists of those born outside but trained inside Africa (Tankwanchi, Özden, and Vermund 2013). There are 342 doctors born outside Africa, led by the United States, the United Kingdom, and India. There is also a significant level of mobility within Africa for medical training. Nigeria and South Africa trained many students from other African countries who then migrate to the West, including the United States. Of 752 Nigerian-trained doctors, 26.5 percent (199) reported a birth country other than Nigeria, and 156 out 376 South African–trained doctors (41.5 percent) were born outside of South Africa. This fraction is the highest for Zambia (65.2 percent): the majority of Zambian-trained doctors practicing in the United States were born in India, as mentioned earlier.

In addition to making the distinction between place of birth and of training, Tankwanchi, Özden, and Vermund (2013) also try to identify the age at which migration takes place by looking at the year in which doctors completed their residency, which is a requirement for all foreign-trained doctors who would like to practice in the United States. They find that the latest cohort of doctors are coming to the United States at a younger age and spending less time serving their countries of origin as physicians. Figure 6.5 shows that the cohort that arrived in the 1980s spent, on average, 8.4 years after completing their medical training in their home country before coming to the United States. On the other hand, the latest cohort of arrivals spent only 1.3 years prior to their arrival in the United States. This pattern indicates that the home countries are basically not receiving services from physicians who are choosing to migrate right after the completion of medical school back at home.

This section provides an overview of data collected about migrant physicians from administrative sources of the destination countries. These data need to be extended and supplemented in three dimensions:

- The data need to be updated. The Bhargava and Docquier (2008) data set ends in 2004. More than a decade has passed, and it is important to see how the patterns have changed. Given the rapid evolution observed between 1991 and 2004, it is quite likely that important changes have taken place since 2004. The current, persistent financial crisis and the anti-immigrant sentiment in politics might also have influenced migration patterns.
- The data on the number of migrants must be supplemented with other educational and professional data. As Tankwanchi, Özden, and Vermund (2013) show,

Figure 6.5 Estimated Years of Service in Country of Origin before Emigration, by Graduation Cohort

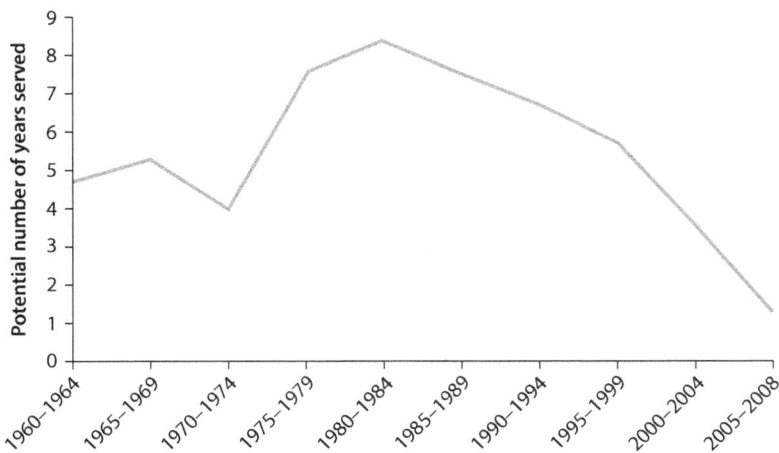

Source: Tankwanchi, Özden, and Vermund 2013.
Note: The data set ends in 2008.

such additional variables can lead to analysis that will answer important and interesting research questions. These data should be collected from other OECD countries and other key destination countries.

- All of the data sets above and their analysis rely on the data collected by the destination OECD countries. This is because of the reliability and availability of high-quality data in these countries. If it were possible to collect complementary data from the origin countries and match these data to the destination country data, many more interesting and relevant policy questions could be addressed.

Determinants of Migration: Ghana as a Case Study

Migration decisions are influenced by many factors that lead an individual or a family to move from one country to another, and it is almost impossible to identify all of them. Low wages, poor working conditions, lack of professional development and career opportunities, and political and ethnic problems are among the main push factors. A World Bank survey of Ghanaian physicians in 2012 in the United Kingdom and the United States aimed to collect detailed information from Ghanaian doctors to identify determinants of their migration decisions and their perceptions (Özden 2012).

Reasons Ghanaian Doctors Emigrate

The exodus of Ghanaian doctors is not recent. In the 1930s a scholarship scheme trained African physicians in the United Kingdom, planting the seeds for the first physician migrations from Ghana. For at least 20 years, medical schools in Ghana included a U.K. study component. By 2004 nearly one of every three Ghanaian doctors worked in an OECD country, mostly the United Kingdom and the United States. Dovlo and Nyonator (1999) estimate that fewer than 40 percent of approximately 500 physicians who graduated from the University of Ghana between 1985 and 1994 remained in the country. More than half of these graduates immigrated to the United Kingdom and about a third to the United States.

Between 1991 and 2004 the number of Ghanaian physicians in OECD countries grew steadily, though at a slower pace than that of physicians in Ghana during the period (figure 6.6) (Özden 2012).

In 2004 the United States was the largest destination for Ghanaian physicians among OECD countries, absorbing 41 percent of all Ghanaian migrant doctors, followed by the United Kingdom with 39 percent. Large numbers of Ghanaian doctors also migrated to Australia and South Africa (Bhargava and Docquier 2008).

The 2012 World Bank survey (Özden 2012) of Ghanaian physicians in the United Kingdom and the United States collected detailed information on the backgrounds of the physicians and their education and careers, especially after they migrated. In addition, the survey asked detailed questions about the physicians' motivations to migrate and their personal, professional, and financial links with Ghana.

Among the interesting findings of the survey (Özden 2012) is that immigrant physicians do not come from a random sample of Ghanaian society. For example, 56 percent of the fathers and 27 percent of the mothers of immigrant physicians have bachelor's or professional degrees, whereas the level of tertiary education in the broader Ghana workforce is only slightly above 3 percent (figure 6.7). Parents' education and social status influence the secondary education of their children, which becomes the main determinant of entry into the highly selective medical schools.

The social and economic gap between the backgrounds of doctors and the rest of Ghanaian society seems to influence most physician career choices and preferences, including those of migration. The top three reasons why the interviewed doctors chose to study medicine include intellectual challenge (36 percent), opportunities to help others (20 percent), and family influence (18 percent). Earning potential, social status, and migration opportunities were listed much lower (Özden 2012).

The World Bank survey (Özden 2012) offers insights not only into the demographic attributes of migrant doctors but also into the factors that affected their decision to migrate. More than 70 percent of Ghanaian migrant doctors cited better training opportunities as one of their top three reasons for leaving home (figure 6.8). Another 42 percent cited better medical practice opportunities as one of their main reasons. Higher salaries (39 percent) and improved family life (45 percent) were also highly ranked. Political stability in Ghana and exposure to new cultures seem to have little effect on migration decisions. Of Ghanaian immigrant doctors, 44 percent practice

Figure 6.6 Number of Ghanaian Physicians at Home and Abroad, 1991–2004

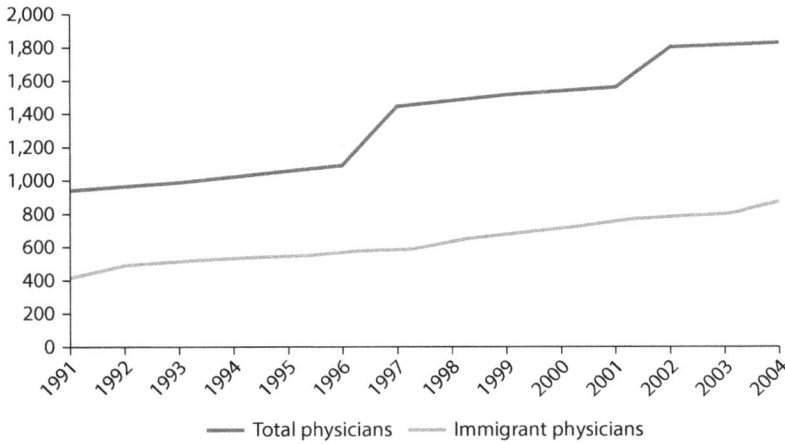

Total physicians   Immigrant physicians

Source: Özden 2012.

Figure 6.7 Education Level of Ghanaian Migrant Physicians' Parents

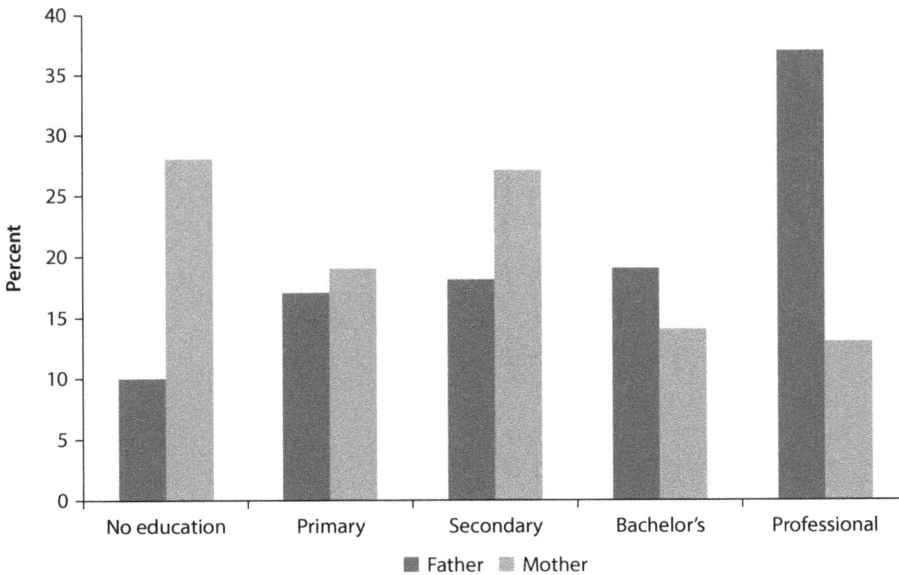

Father   Mother

Source: Özden 2012.

in university and teaching hospitals, which tend to be the leaders in scientific and professional areas. Another 28 percent work in private practice, and 16 percent work in smaller clinics.

The World Bank survey (Özden 2012) asked Ghanaian physicians practicing abroad what policy changes would keep physicians in Ghana. Better health care facilities were the top responses, with 71 percent of respondents saying this strongly influences migration decisions. Higher salaries, free housing or automobiles, improved pensions, and better educational options for the children follow close behind. As expected, physicians strongly oppose the mandatory service requirements advocated by nonphysicians.

The World Bank survey (Özden 2012) asked migrant doctors to compare various aspects of life in Ghana with their new lives in the destination countries (table 6.3). Of the respondents, 41 percent stated that incomes of physicians relative to other professionals in Ghana are satisfactory. Physician satisfaction with absolute income in Ghana was only 17 percent. Close to 90 percent of migrant physicians think both absolute and relative incomes are satisfactory in their new country of residence.

Figure 6.8 Ghanaian Migrant Doctors' Top Reasons for Migration

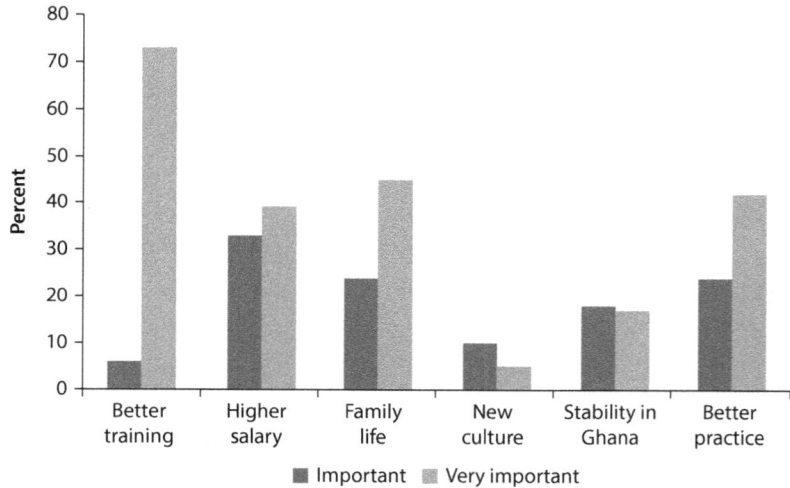

Source: Özden 2012.

Table 6.3 Main Differences between Ghana and Abroad for Ghanaian Migrant Doctors
Percent of respondents

	Ghana			Abroad		
	Bad	Average	Good	Bad	Average	Good
Income relative to other professionals	29	31	41	3	10	86
Overall income	42	41	17	3	8	88
Opportunities for professional development	70	25	5	3	1	96
Incentives to work hard	78	18	4	3	8	89
Respect from community	4	11	85	7	34	58
Making a difference for others	4	13	83	3	24	74

Source: Özden 2012.

The vast majority—more than 70 percent—think professional opportunities and incentives to work are weak in Ghana (table 6.3). By contrast, 96 percent appreciate the professional opportunities available in their new countries, and 89 percent find that incentives to work are strong.

Social issues tend to be in favor of Ghana (table 6.3). More than 80 percent of respondents think doctors receive great respect from the community and they make a big difference in the lives of others in Ghana. In destination countries, only 58 percent feel they receive respect and 74 percent think they make a difference. Although most physicians believe social respect and fulfillment are greater in Ghana, these factors do not outweigh the professional and financial benefits of practicing medicine abroad.

The diaspora externalities—the benefits that the diaspora can generate for the home country—are analyzed in the migration literature. In addition to remittances, diasporas can create crucial links with the rest of the world for trade, finance, and technology transfers. Of surveyed Ghanaian physicians (Özden 2012), 67 percent sent remittances back home in the 12 months preceding the survey. The average remittance was slightly more than $10,000 per year, a relatively low share of the average annual physician income. Given that most doctors are from upper-income families, their remittances are not likely to have a big impact. Families list general expenses (83 percent), weddings or funeral expenses (41 percent), housing (33 percent), and school fees (30 percent) among their top four expenditure categories for remittances.

Remittances are not the only links between migrant doctors and Ghana (figure 6.9). Migrant physicians often return to Ghana for leisure and business travel. Many of them provide advice to medical students considering emigration. Slightly more than 20 percent provided free medical service to Ghanaians abroad and more than 40 percent send medical books and equipment to Ghana. While investments in housing and land in Ghana by physicians abroad are relatively high (70 percent), other business links are minimal. More than 70 percent of respondents explored opportunities to invest in health-related business in Ghana, but only a small minority succeeded in doing so. This gap indicates the problems in overall business climate in Ghana.

The World Bank survey (Özden 2012) asked migrant physicians how many siblings they had and how many were in the same country with them. A large portion of the siblings are also migrants, so physician migration appears to be part of a larger decision-making process with consequences for all family members.

Ghanaian migrant physicians often remain emotionally linked to Ghana. More than 60 percent of survey respondents think they will return to Ghana within the next 10 years. Although a large portion of doctors stay permanently in their destinations, the majority would like eventually to return to Ghana permanently (Özden 2012).

This section highlighted a novel data collection effort based on a survey of Ghanaian doctors in the United States and the United Kingdom (Özden 2012). Participants were asked detailed background questions on their personal characteristics, education, and professional development. They were also asked questions

Figure 6.9 Main Links with Ghana for Ghanaian Migrant Doctors

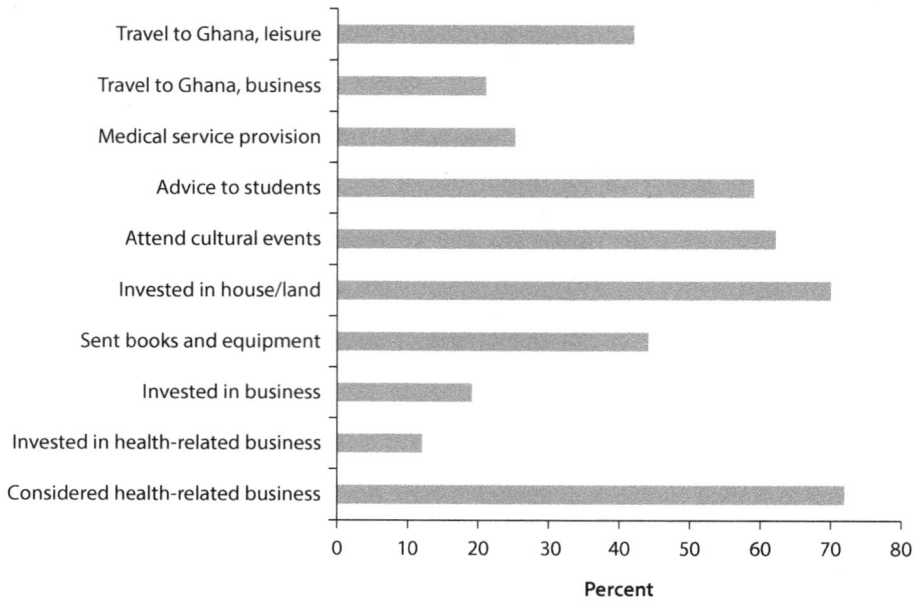

Source: Özden 2012.

that sought to identify the reasons for migrating, personal perceptions on different factors that influence the quality of life in Ghana and abroad, and views on potential policies to be implemented for retention. The goal of the survey is to collect information available from administrative data (from licenses and registration) and personal information that would be useful to answer the questions on the reasons for migration.

Impact of Migration

The last section of this chapter explores ways to determine the impact of emigration on health outcomes in the origin country. This is likely to be the main cost of immigration and is the source of much of the debate on the medical brain drain. As mentioned earlier, the optimal strategy involves matching the health outcomes in a certain geographic area with the data on health care resources available within the same areas. Ideally the health care outcome data should be obtained through household surveys that also ask questions on other variables that impact health outcomes such as income, expenditure, social norms, and so on.

Unfortunately, no such study is known to determine the health care cost of migration. Instead, several studies have been aimed at analyzing the impact of immigration using aggregate, country-level variables. Here is a brief list of these studies, highlighting the main methods and data sources used.

Anand and Bärninghausen (2004) perform a cross-country analysis of maternal mortality, infant mortality, and under-five mortality rates. Their results suggest that the density of human resources for health care is significant in accounting for the three mortality rates tested, with elasticities ranging from −0.39 to −0.17. A later study by the same authors in 2005 using a similar method suggests that health care worker density is correlated with the coverage of three vaccinations: meningococcal vaccine (MCV); diphtheria, pertussis, and tetanus (DPT3); and polio. When the impact of doctors and nurses is assessed separately, Anand and Bärninghausen (2005) find that only nurse density is positively associated with the three vaccinations.

Clemens (2007) tests the hypothesis that decreases in emigration raise the number of domestic health care professionals, increase the mass availability of basic primary care, and improve a range of public health outcomes. His results suggest that Africa's generally low staffing levels and poor public health conditions are the result of factors—such as the segmentation of labor markets for health workers—entirely unrelated to international movements of health professionals. He argues that emigration has increased the production of health workers in Africa. He highlights the various benefits associated with migration, such as remittances.

Bhargava and Docquier (2008) aim to see if the prevalence of human immunodeficiency virus/acquired immune deficiency syndrome (HIV/AIDS) and physician migration are related. Using their database, they construct a panel of physician migration from each country. In addition to using data on HIV/AIDS prevalence rates, they use public health expenditures, physicians' wages, and other economic and demographic variables at the national level in their estimation. They find that lower wages and higher HIV/AIDS prevalence rates are strongly associated with the brain drain of physicians from Sub-Saharan African to OECD countries. In countries in which the HIV/AIDS prevalence rate exceeds 3 percent, a doubling of the medical brain drain rate is associated with a 20 percent increase in adult deaths from AIDS. Their findings underscore the need to improve economic conditions for physicians in order to retain physicians in Sub-Saharan Africa, especially as antiretroviral treatment becomes more widely available.

Bhargava, Docquier, and Moullan (2011) analyze the effect of physician migration on child mortality and vaccination levels using a random effects model. Their more nuanced results indicate that many health indicators improve with higher physician levels when adult literacy levels exceed 55 percent. They demonstrate the importance of the complex links among migration, development, and the overall social and economic environment of the country in question and show that the number of physicians in a country is only one of the inputs into the provision of health services. Stopping their migration, they conclude, would have a positive but small impact on the overall human development indicators they analyze.

Conclusions

This chapter has multiple objectives. The first objective is to present the requirements for the proper identification of the determinants and implications when health care professionals migrate abroad. The data needs can be split into two broad categories. The first category covers data on the health care professionals and would consist of three headings: (a) data on the personal characteristics and backgrounds of the migrants; (b) the education profile of migrants; and (c) the career paths of migrants, including details of migration experiences. These data are used mainly to identify patterns and *determinants* of migration.

The second broad category consists of data on health outcomes and can be used to measure the *impact* of migration. Importantly, as noted earlier, these data should ideally be collected via household surveys to avoid selection problems and to capture other variables that influence health outcomes, such as income, expenditure, social norms, and so on. Once matched with health care inputs at the smallest geographic unit possible, the role of inputs—especially human resources—on outcomes can be identified at the level of suggested association.

The second objective of the chapter is to highlight what has already been accomplished in the academic and policy literature until this point. While describing these studies, special attention is paid to their shortcomings and possible improvements. For example, outdated bilateral migration data need to be updated. Furthermore, there is great value strengthening the ability of origin countries to capture the key information on the emigrant professionals.

Third objective, since this is part of a toolkit volume, is to present examples from two recent projects and highlight the "tools" employed. The first one uses AMA licensing data from the United States to draw a clearer picture of migration patterns of African doctors. More specifically, it aims to distinguish between the locations of birth and of education. A large number of "African" doctors are born in Africa but not trained there. Similarly, there are many others born outside Africa but trained inside Africa. These distinctions are important for designing appropriate policies. The second project is designed around a survey filled out by Ghanaian doctors in the United Kingdom and the United States. In addition to collecting a range of personal and professional variables, the survey asks questions on perceptions and other determinants of migration decisions.

This chapter reviews data and tools needed for answering a range of questions on migration of health care professionals. Needless to say, the chapter is neither exhaustive nor definitive. The conclusions and data will be outdated immediately because more data sources, papers, and research questions appear continuously. But the aim is to provide a glimpse of where the research agenda is headed and where it comes from, and what tools are needed to move forward.

References

AMA (American Medical Association). 2012. *Physician Compensation and Production Survey*. Chicago, IL: AMA.

Anand, S., and T. Bärninghausen. 2004. "Human Resources and Health Outcomes: Cross-Country Econometric Study." *Lancet* 364 (9445): 1603–09.

———. 2005. *Human Resources for Health and Vaccination Coverage in Developing Countries*. Oxford, U.K.: Oxford University Press.

Arah, O. A., U. C. Ogbu, and C. E. Okeke. 2008. "Too Poor to Leave, Too Rich to Stay: Developmental and Global Health Correlates of Physician Migration to the United States, Canada, Australia, and the United Kingdom." *American Journal of Public Health* 98 (1): 148–54.

Bhargava, A., and F. Docquier. 2008. "HIV Pandemic, Medical Brain Drain, and Economic Development in Sub-Saharan Africa." *World Bank Economic Review* 22 (2): 345–66.

Bhargava, A., F. Docquier, and Y. Moullan. 2011. "Modeling the Effects of Physician Migration on Human Development." *Economics and Human Biology* 9 (2): 172–83.

Clemens, M. 2007. "Do Visas Kill? Health Effects of African Health Professional Emigration." Working Paper 114, Center for Global Development, Washington, DC.

Clemens, M., and G. Pettersson, 2008. "New Data on African Health Professionals Abroad." *Human Resources for Health* 6: 1–11.

Docquier, F., and A. Marfouk. 2006. "International Migration by Educational Attainment (1990–2000)." In *International Migration, Remittances and Development*, edited by C. Özden and M. Schiff. New York: Palgrave Macmillan.

Docquier, F., O. Lohest, and A. Marfouk. 2007. "Brain Drain in Developing Countries." *World Bank Economic Review* 21 (2): 193–218.

Dovlo, D., and F. Nyonator 1999. "Migration of Graduates of the University of Ghana Medical School: A Preliminary Rapid Appraisal." *Human Resources for Health Development Journal* 3 (1): 34–37.

Dumont, J. C., and P. Zurn. 2007. "Immigrant Health Workers in OECD Countries in the Broader Context of Highly Skilled Migration." In *International Migration Outlook 2007*, 161–228. Paris: SOPEMI. doi: 10.1787/migr_outlook--2007--5--en.

Hagopian, A., M. J. Thompson, M. Fordyce, K. E. Johnson, and L. G. Hart. 2004. "The Migration of Physicians from Sub-Saharan Africa to the United States of America: Measures of the African Brain Drain." *Human Resources for Health* 2: 17.

Hagopian, A., A. Ofosu, A. Fatsui, R. Biritwum, A. Essel, L. G. Hart, and C. Watts. 2005. "The Flight of Physicians from West Africa: Views of American Physicians and Implications for Policy." *Social Science and Medicine* 61 (8): 1750–60.

Mullan, F. 2005. "The Metrics of the Physician Brain Drain." *New England Journal of Medicine* 353 (17): 1810–18.

OECD (Organisation for Economic Co-operation and Development). 2008. *The Looming Crisis in the Health Workforce: How Can OECD Countries Respond?* Paris: OECD Publishing.

———. 2015. *International Migration Outlook*. Paris: OECD Publishing.

Özden, C. 2012. "Ghanaian Physicians at Home and Abroad: The Pull and the Push Factors." Photocopy. Washington, DC: World Bank.

Soucat, A., R. M. Scheffler, and T. Ghebreyesus. 2013. *The Labor Market for Health Workers in Africa*. Washington, DC: World Bank.

Tankwanchi, A. B. S., C. Özden, and S. Vermund. 2013. "Physician Emigration from Sub-Saharan Africa to the United States: Analysis of the 2011 AMA Physician Masterfile." *PLOS Medicine* 10 (12). doi:10.1371/annotation/64ffd514-00bb-4a5e -9e2e-584763637d14.

WHO (World Health Organization). 2006. *World Health Report*. Geneva: WHO.

———. 2011. *World Health Statistics*. Geneva: WHO.

World Bank. 2013. *The Little Data Book on Africa 2012/13*. Washington, DC: World Bank.

CHAPTER 7

Measuring the Performance of Health Workers

Kenneth Leonard and Ottar Mæstad

Introduction

Health care quality is often analyzed by reference to three types of quality: structural quality, process quality, and outcome quality (Donabedian 1980, 1988). This chapter analyzes the contribution of human resources in health, which may be the single most important input to the health sector in low-income countries (Hongoro and McPake 2004). Indeed human resources for health, shortages of health personnel, and poor health worker performance are among the most pressing problems of health systems in these countries. The shortage of health workers in the health system (structural quality) is addressed elsewhere in this volume, and this chapter focuses on the performance of those health workers who do work in the system. This more directly aligns with process quality—diagnosis, treatment, preventive care, and patient education. The knowledge, experience, skills, and dedication of health workers help to translate other key inputs, such as hospitals and medicines, into health. This chapter discusses ways to measure their performance within this system.

Many tools are available for measuring performance; which is the best will depend on the questions being asked, the comparisons being made (between health workers, health facilities, or health systems), and even the location of the health facilities being studied. In particular, are we doing research on the determinants of quality, measuring quality of care in a pay for quality scheme, measuring quality as part of a continuous quality improvement scheme, or measuring quality as part of an ongoing monitoring exercise? When the most important question is, "Is this facility improving over time?", then the types of measurement that can be useful are different than if the question were, "Which facility is delivering the best quality care?"

Health care is different from most other processes of production, which can make measuring performance difficult. Some of the difficulties discussed in this chapter include (a) the inherent problem of quantitative measurement in skilled professions, (b) the fact that health workers face varying patient populations (case mix), and (c) the fact that scrutiny has an impact on behavior. All recommended tools for measuring performance suffer from shortcomings. Thus, when the goal is to deeply understand the reasons for low-quality care or the possible solutions to low-quality care (discussed in chapter 8, "Analyzing the Determinants of Health Worker Performance"), multiple tools should be used to evaluate performance within the health system. However, when the goal is to determine whether something is improving over time, then individual measures can sometimes be adequate. For example, a measure that does not properly control for case mix is adequate to measure improvements in quality when the case mix is not expected to change. The best approach will always depend on the particular question being asked.

Performance Is Presence, Quality, and Productivity

Three measures of health worker performance are discussed: presence, quality, and productivity. Clearly, health workers must be present in order to provide health care. This means that they must be trained, posted to the facility, and available to patients seeking care. In addition, health workers must provide care of adequate quality to those patients who do come. Finally, health workers should be productive at transforming inputs (including their own time) into outputs: the greater the number of patients a present health worker can help with quality care, the better.

Presence

Presence is an important element of performance: if presence is low, both quality and productivity will be low. If there is no health worker present when a patient arrives, that patient cannot receive any services. If a properly trained health worker is not present, the patient will probably receive inadequate services.

Presence can be measured in different ways. One approach is to measure how many health workers are present out of those who are supposed to be present at a given point in time. Alternatively, presence can refer to whether a health facility is sufficiently staffed so that it can adequately serve potential clients. From a potential client's perspective, the important question in evaluating presence is not whether a particular person on the schedule is actually present, but whether sufficient numbers of qualified health workers are present. A facility may be completely staffed even if scheduled workers are not present, and it is possible for all scheduled health workers to be present and for the facility to be insufficiently staffed. The way to measure presence will depend on the larger questions being asked. In practice, presence is often measured in terms of its opposite—absenteeism—but the concepts are the same.

Quality

There are many definitions of *quality in health care*, but one of the standard definitions is the following: "the degree to which health services for individuals and populations increase the likelihood of desired health outcomes and are consistent with current professional knowledge" (Lohr 1990, 21). This definition underscores the idea that the most important measure of quality is the outcome: are patients as healthy as they could be after visiting a health facility, given the conditions from which they suffer? This is very difficult to measure properly, however. This chapter therefore focuses on measuring the quality inherent in the process of providing health care, in particular whether health workers provide services that are

- *Effective.* Services based on scientific knowledge (adherence to clinical guidelines and protocol)
- *Patient-centered.* Care that is respectful of and responsive to individuals (responsiveness)
- *Timely.* Reduced waiting times

Therefore, the patient experience during and as a result of treatment is as important an element of quality in health care as the medical aspects of the service.

Process quality can be measured either directly or by the types of inputs. These inputs are (a) knowledge, (b) equipment and infrastructure (medicines, diagnostic tools, and so on), and (c) effort on the part of the provider. All three are necessary to produce quality, and measuring quality correctly must properly take all three into account. Many measures of quality do not properly take into account the combination of these three inputs. For example, examining a health worker's credentials provides a measure of knowledge, but since it does not examine available equipment or effort expended by the health worker, it is not a sufficient measure of quality. Examining the infrastructure of a facility and the levels of key medicines is useful, but since these measures do not take into account the knowledge or the effort of the health worker, alone it is insufficient. And measuring the time a health worker spends with his or her patients is a measure of effort, but it does not take into account knowledge or equipment and therefore is not a good measure of quality.

This chapter discusses measures of process quality that focus directly on what health workers do with their patients, comparing actual behavior with professional standards and guidelines. The actual activities of health workers on their patients' behalf is the best measure of process quality because it takes into account the combination of knowledge, equipment (and medicines), and effort.

Productivity

Productivity is a measure of the efficiency of health service provision that focuses on avoiding wasting time and other resources. Productivity is measured as the outputs of a facility relative to the inputs used. A health facility is more productive if it can provide either more outputs with the same level of inputs or the same level of outputs with fewer inputs.

The idea of producing more outputs with fewer inputs is intuitively simple, but the practical reality of measurement is more complicated. All health facilities and health workers produce multiple outputs (outpatient visits and vaccinations, for example), and all health facilities use multiple inputs (health workers' time, vaccination doses, and so on). If health workers produce more of one output by refocusing their efforts away from other outputs, this is not increased productivity but only a shift of priority. Therefore outputs need to be measured so they account for all the activities required of health workers. Thus, to measure productivity, data must be collected on (most of) the outputs of a health facility and (many of) the inputs.

Properly measuring inputs and their value is difficult, but since most inputs are purchased, it is possible to do this given the right information about costs. Where this information is not attainable, for instance because inputs are provided in-kind, it is often possible to compare units (health workers, or facilities of similar size) that have similar costs, even when those costs are unknown. In general, even when costs can be measured properly, it will often be useful to compare facilities with similar cost structures and objectives: comparing a regional referral hospital to a village dispensary will never be easy and is unlikely to be useful since they serve different functions.

An additional difficulty comes from combining outputs to measure the total output provided. In this case, it helps to have facilities that produce similar outputs, but it is still necessary to aggregate them in some way. Since the outputs are not sold at their value, the value of each output may have to be assigned to allow for their aggregation. Thus, for example, two vaccinations may be declared to have the same value as one outpatient visit.

Once a measure of aggregate outputs and inputs has been established, there are several ways to calculate productivity. Three common measures of productivity include total factor productivity, technical efficiency, and scale efficiency. Total factor productivity is a summary measure of productivity that simply compares aggregate outputs to aggregate inputs. Technical efficiency is a measure of a health facility's ability to attain its maximum output given its inputs. A facility that is technically efficient might be able to further increase its output-input ratio (that is, the output produced per unit of input) by changing the size of its operations, but since it may not be an option to change the size of the facility, technical efficiency may be a more appropriate productivity measure than total factor productivity. Scale efficiency is a measure of the degree to which a facility is optimizing its size.

Difficulties Inherent in the Measurement of Performance

This section considers challenges inherent in performance measurement that cannot be easily surmounted, but the impact of which can be minimized. Three major issues are discussed: the professional nature of medicine, the choices of patients in seeking care, and the impact of observation on behavior.

Measuring the performance of a health worker is not the only way to infer quality and in many cases, some of the measures discussed are not necessary to infer deficiencies in quality. For example, measuring verifiable outcomes for specific types of cases (TB cure rates or postnatal readmission rates due to sepsis) may indicate problems with quality at specific facilities. However, these measures will not be adequate to indicate the reasons for low quality.

Health Workers Are Professionals

The two most general ideas underlying professionalism are the belief that certain work is so specialized as to be inaccessible to those lacking the required training and experience, and the belief that it cannot be standardized, rationalized, or ... commodified. (Freidson 2001, 18)

Health workers practice in a field with all the classic traits of a profession. With every patient, they must use their knowledge to decide what to do and apply their skills to do it. The application of knowledge cannot be easily replaced by something like a decision tree or an "if-then" series of computer commands: the health worker must almost always use discretion in deciding what to do. Even two health workers with identical training facing the same patient may make different choices and—in many cases—it would be almost impossible to determine which of the two was better (see box 7.1). The lack of an objective standard of correct practice makes it harder to measure quality of care.

Box 7.1 Two Professionals Evaluating the Same Patient

The following example is drawn from a research project in urban Tanzania (Leonard 2012). A member of the research team (who also practiced medicine in the same area) observed the consultations of another clinician and noticed two patterns that concerned him. First, a few women were sent to have a urine test, despite the fact that none of their symptoms indicated the need for such a test. Second, one man who came to the facility with a skin lesion was prescribed an expensive medicine although less expensive medicines were likely to have been effective. To the observer, both cases indicated supplier-induced demand: unnecessary and expensive treatments.

In subsequent conversations with the researcher and the clinician being observed it became clear that each of these two clinicians practiced in very different settings. To the observed clinician, when people presented who did not appear to have been to a health facility in a long time, it made sense to use tests like the urine test to screen for conditions that were independent of the presenting symptoms. In the case of the skin lesions, the observed clinician assumed that the patient would have already sought and received the simpler (and less expensive) medicines based on the distance that he had traveled to reach the facility. If those medicines had already failed, it would not help the patient to send him home with the wrong medicines again; far better to send him home with something that was more likely to work. The observing clinician, on the other hand, worked in a hospital that was significantly less expensive and whose patients mostly came from within town. Screening a patient for conditions about which she had not complained or trying to save a patient another trip to the hospital were not normal concerns in his daily practice. Thus, two clinicians with very similar training reached different conclusions about the same patient because the environments in which they practiced medicine were so different.

This chapter advocates primarily for the use of checklists that record whether or not a health worker performed certain key tasks. The idea is to create a list of tasks that are clearly positive or negative contributions to process quality. Being polite to a patient, for example, is always a positive feature of a consultation. Similarly, prescribing antidiarrheal medicine to an infant with diarrhea is always a negative feature of a consultation because it masks symptoms but does not deal with dehydration or the underlying infection. The checklist is not a list of all the things a clinician must do, but rather a way of scoring the consultation: better consultations are ones in which clinicians do more good things and fewer bad things. The checklists should be used by peers and therefore require professionally informed evaluation, but they are less susceptible to the subjective judgment of observers. However, compressing a consultation into a checklist will not result in a complete and precise view of process quality. The instruments discussed here each deal with these issues in slightly different ways.

The same concerns about professionalism can be applied to measurements of absenteeism and presence. From the patient's perspective, presence is simple to evaluate: is there someone present to provide health care? The early studies of absenteeism in the health sector (Chaudhury and Hammer 2004; Chaudhury et al. 2006) had an important impact on policy because the aggregate numbers were shockingly poor and there was no easy explanation for these numbers. If 40 percent of facilities are inadequately staffed during a random site visit, clearly something is wrong. However, absenteeism can be the result of health workers visiting a patient in a nearby community because the patient cannot travel, health workers attending workshops that will increase future quality of services, or health workers staying in their nearby house because there were no patients (but still ready to provide services if someone arrives). Hence, without knowing the broader picture, it is not possible to automatically conclude that being technically absent reduces performance. This is even more the case when considering the absenteeism of individual health workers: the absence of an individual health worker on the schedule does not reduce performance if this health worker was replaced by someone equally skilled. Professionals often need to use their judgment in choosing how they work and an objective evaluation of these decisions can be complicated.

Patient Selection and Case Mix
Health facilities and health workers face different types of patients. This makes it more challenging to compare quality and productivity across health facilities. Two different facilities providing the same kinds of services might be visited by patients who differ significantly in income, education, and even how sick they are. These differences are often such factors as the location of the facility, the cost of services, and even the quality of care. These differences are often predictable (the income levels of patients at rural facilities are usually different than those of the patients at urban facilities) but not always, and the differences can make the proper measurement of quality difficult. For example, handing a written prescription to a patient is reasonable care when your patients can read, but is low-quality care when they cannot. Box 7.2 shows how, in a particular area, the quality of care provided by

Box 7.2 Quality of Care and Patient Outcomes

Figure B7.2.1 shows the pattern of quality and outcomes for a sample of health episodes in rural Tanzania. Each individual patient has both a location of first visit (a choice they make) and an outcome (a product of their original condition and the performance of the health workers they saw). The sample is divided into two groups: above and below median quality of care as measured by an objective assessment performed by medical personnel. Choosing to visit a higher-quality facility would be expected to lead to a better outcome. At the same time, however, patients choose facilities based on their own assessment of the needs of their illness. The small differences between the outcomes at the two different types of facilities are exactly the opposite of expectations. Patients who visit low-quality facilities are more likely to be cured and less likely to be not cured or to die. Perversely, the higher rate of good outcomes at low-quality facilities is the product of low performance at that facility because patients with serious illnesses went elsewhere.

Knowing both quality and outcomes demonstrates that quality and outcomes are not easily linked. The main point of the figure is to show that outcomes themselves cannot be used as a measure of performance.

Figure B7.2.1 Outcomes Categorized by the Average Quality of Care at Location of First Visit, Rural Tanzania, 2003

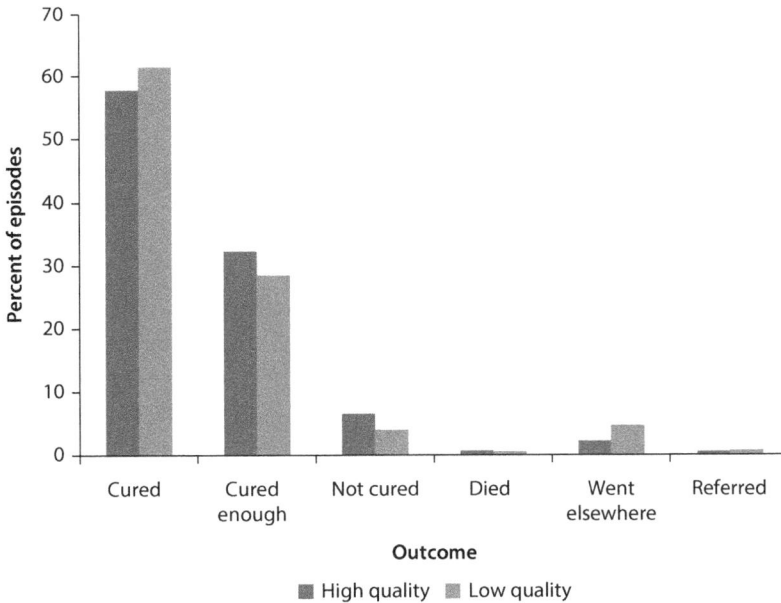

Source: Klemick, Leonard, and Masatu 2009.
Note: The figure shows the outcomes of 1,399 health episodes from a household survey in the rural Arusha region in Tanzania for which the patient has completed treatment matched with the average quality provided at the first facility visited for that illness. Quality is categorized as high quality (above the median) or low quality (below the median) and measured by objective assessment of medical personnel. Outcomes are cured; cured enough (saw marginal improvement); not cured (no improvement); died; went elsewhere (have since sought care at a different facility); and referred (were referred to another facility when they visited the first facility).

facilities attracts patients who are sicker and more likely to experience bad outcomes. This means that comparing outcomes across facilities will be misleading.

Differences in case mix have several implications for performance measurement. First, the measurement and comparison of quality is made more difficult
because the appropriate professional behavior may differ across health workers
and health facilities. Thus, even if health workers do the same jobs, their perfor-
mances might not be equal. If differences in patients are observable to the
researcher, it might be possible to adjust for difference in case mix by ensuring
that quality is compared for similar patient groups. Unobservable differences
may still create problems, though. One way to eliminate this problem is to "create" an artificial patient and investigate how health workers would deal with this
patient. As explained later, there are several ways of doing this, but all methods
have certain drawbacks.

Second, the comparison of productivity is made difficult because some patient
groups require more time and other resources. One health facility may have
served fewer patients per health worker because the patients were sicker and
required more intensive care. Standard productivity measures will not account
for such differences unless the patients are registered as different types of
patients. Thus, the "solution" is more fine-grained categorization of outputs,
reflecting different resources requirements. But there are clearly limits to how far
this strategy can be developed.

Impact of Observation

It is necessary to measure the quality of the process to properly measure quality
overall. This usually requires the observation of health workers while they are
providing services. But being in the presence of a health worker while they perform their tasks can alter their behavior. In many cases, this change does not have
significant consequences, but in others it means that what is actually being measured is not what is set out to be measured.

Being observed is likely to change the behavior of health workers, particularly
when there are underlying standards for quality care. Such effects are commonly
referred to as Hawthorne effects. When health workers know what they are supposed to do, additional scrutiny can lead them to attempt to meet these standards
even when they do not routinely make this attempt.

At least four types of changes are possible. First, if health workers know they
are being observed at the moment they are performing the task, they can improve
their performance. Thus the measured performance will exceed the normal
performance.

It is also possible that health workers will find out they are being observed
after they have performed the activity and will alter their behavior in anticipation of being observed again. In this case, the first observation is an accurate
picture of behavior, but the subsequent ones are measures only of the altered
behavior. This can happen, for example, with repeated attendance checks; health
workers cannot retroactively be present for the first visit, but they can choose to
attend more frequently after the first visit in anticipation of future visits.

A third type of behavior comes when researchers repeatedly observe the activities of health workers without explaining what they are looking for or providing any feedback on what they find. In this case, health workers are likely to change their behavior in the beginning, but return to their normal behavior as time passes. In a sense, they are learning that their behavior does not invoke a response from the observer and therefore they abandon their attempts to change it.

Finally, if performance measurement is based on reported behavior, such as service outputs, patient records, and so on, health workers may be tempted to misreport, leading to inaccurate performance measurement.

Because of the concern that the presence of a research team can alter the behavior being evaluated, the tools discussed here are categorized into two categories: those that are obtrusive and those that are not obtrusive. In the most obvious sense, an obtrusive tool is one in which the health workers know that they are being observed, and an unobtrusive tool is one in which health workers do not ever know that their activities were being examined.

In most cases, an unobtrusive tool is preferred to an obtrusive tool because it is most likely to measure actual behavior. Since this chapter focuses on the real levels of presence, quality, and productivity, unobtrusive tools are preferred. However, as discussed in chapter 8, an obtrusive tool can allow for measurement of such features as the capacity for quality that an unobtrusive tool can not.

Tools for Measuring Performance

This section reviews the tools that can be used to measure presence, quality, and productivity. Some of the tools outlined in this section are useful for only one type of performance, but others are useful in multiple measures of performance.

Record Reviews

Purpose: To measure productivity (and possibly attendance and some aspects of process quality)

Description: Health facilities produce records of various kinds, some of which may be used to measure performance. Health management information systems usually require health workers to report the number of patients served by different types of services. This is the best source of information about outputs, which is required for productivity measurement. Health facilities may also keep administrative records with data on the use of inputs (health workers, drugs, and so on). In some countries, health facilities also keep clinical records that may be used to study the quality of the services. Finally, some facilities may keep records of the attendance of health workers.

Strengths and weaknesses: High-quality records provide large amounts of data at low costs. A one-day visit to a health facility with adequate record keeping could yield one year's worth of data on inputs and outputs. The main problem is that records often are not accurately kept and therefore provide only incomplete information. Records are also relatively easy to falsify, and increased monitoring may exacerbate this problem.

Instruments: The World Bank Impact Evaluation Toolkit[1] contains instructions on how to collect data from administrative records, including interviews with staff members present at the hospital (module 5, item 5.06a, which provides a "Health Facility Field Manual"). One example is the "General Health Management System" (module 4, item 4.09); see also annex 7A, table 7A.1.

Attendance Checks

Purpose: To measure presence and absence at the individual or facility level

Description: Attendance checks usually take place as unannounced visits to health facilities to see who is present. Actual attendance is compared with scheduled attendance to measure the level of presence or absence of staff. Scheduled attendance can be expressed either at the individual level (which health workers were supposed to be at work) or at an aggregate level (how many health workers of a particular type are supposed to be present).

Strengths and weaknesses: Single spot checks may give an inaccurate picture of absenteeism at a particular health facility since absenteeism may vary a lot from day to day. This issue can be addressed by repeated attendance checks, but it is then important to vary the timing of the unannounced visits, since absenteeism may vary systematically by time of the day and day of the week. Repeated attendance checks may, however, alter health worker behavior in anticipation of new checks. A further concern with attendance checks is their poor ability to distinguish between absenteeism that is unproductive and absenteeism that may improve health services (for example, absenteeism to attend training seminars).

Instruments: With attendance checks, the key is to record who is present across a variety of positions (lab technicians, pharmacists, doctors, and so on) and also to record information that would be useful in understanding why health personnel are absent. An example of an instrument that can be used is included in the annex as table 7A.2 (Klemick, Leonard, and Masatu 2009). If the research is tracking the presence of individuals, an instrument that records the names of personnel would be necessary. Note that table 7A.2 requires the data collection team to assess how many staff in a particular position are posted to the facility and how many are scheduled to be present on a particular day.

Patient Exit Interviews

Purpose: To measure quality (satisfaction, responsiveness, and protocol adherence)

Description: Patient exit interviews are conducted at the health facility after patients have received their services. Exit interviews can be used to collect information about various aspects of quality, including patient-centeredness and responsiveness and waiting time as well as certain aspects of clinical quality. Exit interviews yield different answers to the same questions asked at home (see following section on household surveys). By asking specific questions about the activities of health workers, patient exit interviews can generate an approximate measure of the quality of clinical care.

Strengths and weaknesses: Recall bias is likely to be small since the exit interview is conducted shortly after the consultation. If health workers are unaware of the interviews, their behavior will not be affected either, and the exit interviews are likely to provide an accurate measure of actual performance. Thus information about the activities of a health facility is more likely to represent an accurate view of what would happen in the absence of a research team. Such decoupling of health workers from interviews is easier to achieve in large facilities than in small ones with few health workers.

One weakness of this tool is that health workers may perform tasks that the patients are unable to observe and hence unable to report. As with all health care, patients are rarely able to assess the necessity or quality of the activities of health workers. However, the exit interview does not ask if health workers did the right thing, it simply asks if they performed certain activities. The list is based on the expertise of the designed, not the patient. Thus a patient can assess whether a stethoscope was used (provided a common term for such an instrument is used). However, patients cannot assess whether the clinician knows what to listen for. Exit interviews therefore provide a narrower picture of clinical quality than other tools discussed later.

Instruments: The World Bank Impact Evaluation Toolkit[2] contains examples of instruments that can be used to interview patients as they are leaving the facility. Table 7A.3 in annex 7A is an example of an interview sheet drawn from that toolkit. It contains a series of opinion questions about the satisfaction with services provided. Other examples of exit interviews are available, including outpatient services[3] and hospital evaluation, including obstetrics, pediatrics, triage, emergency care, and surgery.[4]

Some questions posed by other researchers include whether the patient would return to that facility for a similar illness in the future (or recommend the facility if others were suffering from a similar condition (Leonard 2011) and whether the patient believes other people are asked to pay bribes at the facility (Lindkvist 2013).

The retrospective consultation review instrument asks patients to recall the activities of the clinician after an outpatient visit.[5] Leonard and Masatu (2006) and Leonard (2008) use this instrument to measure the quality of care provided by clinicians. Leonard and Masatu (2006) show that it is a reasonable (though not perfect) representation of the quality of care by comparing what patients say the clinician did to what medical staff on a research team observed during the same consultation.

In addition to patient satisfaction, the exit interview can be used to assess the costs that patients face when seeking care. Table 7A.4 in annex 7A provides an example of such a sheet drawn from the World Bank Impact Evaluation Toolkit. These questions can help put quality into perspective. If patients have traveled a significant distance and chosen not to visit other closer facilities, they are signaling with their feet what they think about the quality of care available.

Household Surveys

Purpose: To measure quality (satisfaction and responsiveness)

Description: Household surveys are conducted with randomly selected households that live in the catchment area of a particular health facility. They can be used to understand how patients view the services available at a facility even if they do not frequently visit that center because of experienced or perceived low quality. It is possible to search for households in which someone has visited a particular facility recently; in that case the household survey would allow households to give a more balanced opinion of their visit to that facility.

Strengths and weaknesses: Household surveys have the advantage that they include individuals who chose not to visit the health facility being examined. They therefore mitigate some of the problems introduced by case mix among the patients present at the facility. In addition, patients often feel pressure to be positive about health workers when interviewed on-site. Glick (2009) examines the responses given by patients when interviewed at the health facility and when interviewed at home and finds very different responses to the same questions. The general rule is that patients complain about different things right after their visit (they are more likely to complain about waiting times) and are more likely to claim to be satisfied than they are in their responses later when they are at home. The prevailing wisdom is that responses given at home are a better indicator of satisfaction than those given at the facility. The major disadvantage of household surveys is that they are more expensive than exit surveys. The research team must travel out to find households across a variety of locations rather than taking advantage of the presence of patients at the health facility.

Instruments: Examples of highly comprehensive population health surveys can be found in the World Health Organization's (WHO) Responsiveness Surveys and Questionnaires.[6] In a developing country setting, a simpler set of questions is more useful. Tables 7A.5 and 7A.6 in annex 7A are examples of household surveys that examine the decision-making process for seeking care and the experience of care at the facility visit. Key questions include those that seek to understand the severity of the illness before the patient sought care (table 7A.5), and questions about the fees paid and satisfaction with the quality of care sought (table 7A.6).

Mystery Clients and Audit Clients

Purpose: To measure process quality (adherence to clinical guidelines)

Description: The "mystery client" is an expensive but high-quality way to assess the performance of health facilities. Enumerators are trained to present a specific case and take that case to a series of health facilities, recording the performance of staff at the facilities they visit. Although health workers may be informed that a mystery client might visit them, they do not know that the specific person they are seeing is a mystery client. There is no formal distinction between an audit client and a mystery client.

Strengths and weaknesses: The two major advantages to the mystery patient approach are that health workers do not know they are being evaluated, and the patient is exactly the same at every facility (thus controlling for the case mix problem). The two disadvantages are that training the team that acts out the mystery patients is very involved and expensive, and only a limited number of illnesses can be convincingly recreated. The mystery patient cannot suffer from anything that would present physically (pregnancy, fevers, and coughs are ruled out) or that may require a lab test (malaria and infections are ruled out), injected medications, or intrusive examinations. This leaves a small set of illnesses that can be considered. Thus these types of instruments are not applicable to all cases, and in general their expense rules them out for all but the most intensive research cases.

Instruments: Two recent studies that use mystery clients to assess the quality of care in an outpatient setting are Currie, Lin, and Zhang (2010) and Das et al. (2012), although many other studies have used mystery clients to assess such topics as the availability of medicines in pharmacies. Madden et al. (1997) report on the use of mystery clients in a variety of settings (and refer to the clients as "undercover care seekers" and "simulated clients"). Das et al. (2012) focus on adherence to clinician guidelines for a series of different case study patients with a particular focus on the diagnosis given.[7] Currie, Lin, and Zhang (2010) examine the willingness of doctors to avoid antibiotics when the mystery client displays knowledge about appropriate antibiotic use. As such, this study is a perfect example of creating a very specific type of patient who might never report to a particular facility: they can compare a doctor's response to clearly informed patients with the same doctor's response to uninformed patients.

Vignettes and Written Exams
Purpose: To measure competence in following clinical guidelines

Description: Vignettes are case studies of patients designed to elicit the health workers' knowledge of clinician guidelines. They can be administered as written tests or oral tests, or they can be acted out as a role play in which someone pretends to be a patient.

Strengths and weaknesses: Vignettes allow the research team to control for case mix by presenting similar cases to all of the health workers studied. Since every health worker is examined in the same situation, it is easier to compare competence across health workers and facilities. These vignettes can be administered at the health facility. Acted case study vignettes take more time and require a trained enumeration team, whereas written (or oral) exams are relatively easy to administer. You can give a written exam to a room full of nurses at a major

Health Labor Market Analyses in Low- and Middle-Income Countries
http://dx.doi.org/10.1596/978-1-4648-0931-6

hospital; you cannot do the same thing with vignettes. In a developing country setting, written vignettes may be measuring levels of formal education, not competence, and they do not mirror the normal process of examining a patient. Acted case study vignettes work better when health workers come from a variety of educational backgrounds, and they more accurately measure the competence of health workers in a real clinical setting than do exams. However, it is also possible that the acted case study vignettes are so similar to actual practice that performance in the vignettes is partly influenced by how health workers normally behave with actual patients. In this case, something between performance and competence is measured. Appropriate framing of the purpose of the measurement can alleviate this potential bias.

Both acted and written case studies suffer from being artificial. They cannot be used to measure the actual quality of care because they are not representative of what a health worker would do with his or her normal patients. They can, however, be used to measure competence, which is an important aspect of quality because, all other things equal, patients would rather visit a health worker with greater competence.

Instruments: Das and Hammer (2004); Leonard and Masatu (2005); and Barber, Gertler, and Harimurti (2007) have all used acted case study vignettes.[8] The vignettes designed by Das and Hammer are in the World Bank Impact Evaluation Toolkit.[9] Das and Leonard (2007) present an extensive discussion of how to use these instruments and process the data collected. Vignettes for use in hospital services are available in the "Hospital Quality Assessment" section of the Health Systems Strengthening Project in Liberia.[10] Chapter 8 also includes vignettes and their uses in research.

Dresselhaus et al. (2000) and Tiemeier et al. (2002) use written exam vignettes to assess the competence of doctors in particular settings. The advantage of these instruments is that they can be implemented without actors and it may even be possible to have doctors submit their answers by mail or over the Internet. The studies find wide variation across countries and hospitals in the competence of doctors. The instruments used by Dresselhaus et al. (2000) and by Tiemeier et al. (2002) are not known to be publicly available. These vignettes represent what are called *test vignettes* as opposed to the case study vignettes mentioned earlier. The main difference is that the test vignettes are a more accurate representation of the training a health worker has a received (similar to a test in the classroom) and the case study vignettes are believed to be a more accurate representation of what they know how to do in practice.

Direct Observation

Purpose: To measure quality (adherence to clinical guidelines and patient responsiveness)

Description: The direct observation of clinicians uses a checklist based on clinical guidelines and produces a record of the things that health workers actually do that can be compared with a list of the things they are supposed to do.

Strengths and weaknesses: Direct observation is an intensive way to measure the activities of a health worker. Health workers are very likely to change their behavior in such a setting, so the quality of care observed is most likely higher than would have been provided in the absence of the observer (Leonard and Masatu 2006). In addition, direct observation does not control for case mix, meaning that the type of patient may change significantly between health workers and facilities. These factors can be addressed by assessing and adjusting for severity and presenting symptoms but can never be fully surmounted. On the other hand, direct observation is the closest one can get to seeing what the health worker actually does with his or her patients. Since direct observation is performed by medically trained personnel, it is a much better way to assess the appropriateness of care than patient exit interviews (where patients do not know what is appropriate).

Instruments: Leonard and Masatu (2005) developed an instrument for observing the clinical practices of health workers in Tanzania; this has been used in modified form by Leonard and Masatu (2006) and Mæstad, Torsvik, and Aakvik (2010).[11] The first two pages of the four-page instrument are shown in annex 7A, table 7A.7 (part 1 and 2). That survey tracked three main types of symptoms: fever, cough, and diarrhea. These were among the most commonly reported symptoms in the area of the study, and also represented cases where the clinician guidelines were relatively straightforward. A severe case and a nonsevere case should exhibit similar responses from clinicians. On the first page, the enumerator records some of the standard information about the consultation (age and symptoms) and on the second page they begin to record whether the clinician asked a series of important questions (depending on the reported symptoms).

All three studies that have used this instrument report a marked downturn in the adherence to clinician guidelines during the course of observation. Adherence begins to drop after the first six or seven patients and continues to decline after that point. Leonard and Masatu (2006) show that this decrease is directly caused by the Hawthorne effect: the health worker increases effort at the very beginning, but after a while begins to return to normal levels of effort. This outcome suggests that if the research team is passive (does not encourage the health worker) and if team members stay long enough, they will begin to witness a quality of care closer to the normal quality of care. Thus it is suggested that direct observation be of sufficient duration. In addition, the initial high quality of care and the later low quality of care demonstrate different measures of quality: normal quality (late) and scrutinized quality (early). Whereas the lower level is a good measure of normal quality, the earlier scrutinized quality might be a good measure of the capacity of the health worker. Direct observation can also be used at the hospital level.[12]

Indicators

Using the instruments discussed previously, research can develop a set of indicators to describe the performance of health workers (table 7.1).

Table 7.1 Indicators and Possible Tools to Describe Performance of Health Workers

Performance area	Tool						
Indicator	Record reviews	Attendance checks	Exit interviews	Household surveys	Mystery clients	Vignettes and case studies	Direct observation
Absenteeism	Average proportion of staff present	Proportion of staff absent at random visit	—	—	Presence or absence of particular staff or positions on random visit	—	Proportion of staff absent at random visit
Process quality	Adherence to protocol for specific recorded items	—	Adherence to protocol as measured by the retrospective consultation review instrument	—	Adherence to protocol	Adherence to protocol; proportion of cases diagnosed correctly	Adherence to protocol
Competence	—	—	—	—	—	Knowledge of protocol	—
Capacity	Proportion of indicated equipment or medications that are present	—	—	—	—	Proportion of indicated equipment or medications that are present	Proportion of indicated equipment or medications that are present
Satisfaction and responsiveness	—	—	—	General opinion of services available at named facilities	—	—	—
Productivity	Ratio of outputs to inputs	—	—	—	—	—	Adherence to protocol average output

Note: — = not applicable.

Presence

Presence can be measured both at the facility level and at the level of individual health workers.

Presence at the Facility Level

At the facility level, *presence* is the number of health workers actually present divided by the number of health workers that should be present. There are multiple measures of "should" in this case. Klemick, Leonard, and Masatu (2009) compare the number of health workers present to (a) national staffing guidelines, (b) the number of health workers posted to the facility, and (c) the number of health workers scheduled to be on duty at the time of the site visit. In addition, presence can be measured by the qualifications of health worker (doctors versus lab technicians, for example). The first measure of presence turned out not to be very informative since almost no facilities met the national standards, and even the more effective hospitals and health centers were understaffed by this criterion. The second measure demonstrated the difficulty in sending health workers to rural areas and differing institutional job standards: many health workers in the public sector who were posted to rural facilities had never been to their posts, and in many cases people who did work at those facilities had no idea these workers were supposed to be there. The third measure turned out to be more informative about problems at a facility level: the number of health workers present compared to those who were scheduled to be present. At many facilities with low levels of staffing, most health workers were present when they were supposed to be.

Presence at the Health Worker Level

If the goal is to understand why some health workers show up for work and others do not, presence at the individual level needs to be tracked. In such a case, *presence* is the number of times a health worker is present during a site visit compared with the total number of site visits.

Quality

Quality can be measured in several realms. Here the focus is on process quality, competence, and patient satisfaction.

Process Quality

Process quality should be measured in comparison to national guidelines and recorded as a percentage of the items required by the patients' symptoms. Thus process quality varies between 0 percent and 100 percent. The goal is not necessarily to reach 100 percent compliance with guidelines, but rather to increase compliance: any improvement is usually valuable in terms of improving patient outcomes. In practice, compliance varies by patient for the same doctor. Thus, a doctor may comply with 80 percent of the items that should be performed for one patient and only 60 percent for the other. Thus, in most settings, measuring the proportion of clinicians who follow proper protocol would yield a very

Health Labor Market Analyses in Low- and Middle-Income Countries
http://dx.doi.org/10.1596/978-1-4648-0931-6

different view of process quality than the average adherence to protocol. The first number might be close to zero in most settings (and virtually impossible to change) whereas the second might be much higher.

Because adherence to protocol depends on a number of factors other than how well the doctor is doing, it can be important to control for such factors when measuring the quality of a particular doctor. One way to do this is to run a regression where the dependent variable is the proportion of protocol items successfully completed. Independent variables then can include the gender, age, and education of the patient; the severity of the illness (either as assessed by the enumerator or by the patient in an exit interview); and a fixed effect or dummy variable for the particular health worker. This allows the research to control for some of the factors (such as case mix) that might drive quality while still measuring one average score per health worker.

When process quality is measured by exit interviews, there is no need to control for the Hawthorne effect unless the health worker knows that patients will be interviewed, but when process quality is measured by direct observation this can be important. One way to control for the Hawthorne effect is to eliminate the first four or five observations from the data set before calculating the health worker score, as described earlier. If there is no significant difference between the scores from the full data set and the shortened data set, then the concerns were not warranted and the full data set can be used. Most likely the scores will change for some clinicians and not for others.

Scrutinized process quality can be used as a measure of capacity by focusing on the first couple of observations and discarding the later ones. Thus two measures of process quality can be derived from the same underlying process.

Competence

Competence is derived from the adherence to clinician guidelines demonstrated in case study vignettes. Because these are case studies, they do not represent what a health worker normally does with his patients, but they do represent what a health worker knows is necessary (competence). Unlike with direct observation, there is no need to control for case mix or the Hawthorne effect and therefore the average adherence is a useful measure of competence.

Patient Satisfaction with Quality and Responsiveness

The responses of patients to questions about satisfaction can be used to develop measures of overall satisfaction as well as determining satisfaction with particular aspects of care, including quality and responsiveness.

Productivity

Productivity indicators can be determined both by simple calculations of output-input ratios and by sophisticated techniques such as linear programming and regression analysis. The starting point of productivity analysis is usually to produce a measure of aggregate output.

Aggregate Output

Aggregate output (quantity of services) is a measure of the total amount of services provided, usually measured at the health facility level over a period of a year. Data from record reviews will produce the total quantity of each service (vaccinations, outpatient visits, deliveries, and so on). To create a measure of aggregate outputs, it is necessary to assign a value to each output. In other sectors, the value of the output is its price. In the health sector, however, market prices are not quoted, and the value of the output has to be measured differently. The recommended approach will be to use the marginal cost of producing the service. Note that the goal is *not* to have an exact measure of marginal costs, but to have a good measure of the *relative* marginal costs across different services. In practice, it may be difficult to obtain precise measures of the value of each service; therefore an approximation based on the relative use of inputs across services may have to be used.

Measures of aggregate outputs will give an indication of where aggregate workload is high and may be used as a basis for allocating health workers to different facilities.

Productivity

Having produced a measure of aggregate output, a measure of productivity is obtained by dividing aggregate output by the value of the inputs used (staff, equipment, buildings, and so on). If all inputs are purchased in the market, it is easy to measure the total value of inputs. However, when this is not the case (for instance, when inputs are received in-kind), market prices will have to be collected from elsewhere to value the inputs.

Note that productivity is by nature a relative phenomenon: a health facility has high or low productivity only in comparison with other facilities. In productivity analysis, it is therefore crucial to establish a benchmark against which to compare productivity levels. The benchmark is usually the most productive among the facilities. Hence, productivity ranges between 0 and 1.

Total factor productivity is the value of outputs divided by the value of all inputs. In some cases it may be desirable to measure productivity for a single input. For example, *health worker productivity* would be defined as aggregate output divided by the total input of health workers, usually measured by staff costs. In this case, all other costs (buildings, equipment, and so on) will be excluded from the input measurement.

It is not necessarily of great value to compare productivity levels across health facilities that differ substantially in size. If there are economies or diseconomies of scale, the sheer size of the facility will influence whether it is productive or not. Moreover, it is usually not desirable to make all facilities the efficient size, as some facilities serve special functions, such as providing services to small and remote communities. In practice, it may therefore be useful to compare productivity only across facilities of a similar size.

An alternative approach to this challenge is to estimate a production frontier representing the maximum attainable output level at each level of inputs.

This can be done when the productivity analysis involves many facilities. Productivity for each facility can then be measured as the closeness to the production frontier (a number between 0 and 1) at the given level of inputs of the facility. This productivity measure is called *technical efficiency* and may be very useful in the health sector.

There are alternative ways of estimating a production frontier. The dominating methods are data envelopment analysis (linear programming) and stochastic frontier analysis (econometric estimation). For further discussion of these approaches, see Mwisongo and Mæstad (2013).

Conclusions

The three measures of health worker performance presented in this chapter—presence, quality, and productivity—are essential elements of an analysis of the health system of any country. Although these measures are especially difficult to assess in the health care setting, the need for data collection is great. Although, because of the nature of health care, there are multiple complicated difficulties inherent in measuring performance in health care, the multiple tools presented in this chapter point toward a way to evaluate performance within the health system.

Annex 7A: Examples of Tools for Measuring Performance

Table 7A.1 General Health Management Information Systems

	RESPONDENT: HEAD OF THE FACILITY OR BEST INFORMED STAFF MEMBER			
(7.01)	Do you have an estimate of the size of the catchment population that this facility serves, that is, the target, or total population, living in the area served by this facility?	YES 1		
		NO 2 ▶ (7.03)		
(7.02)	How many people is the catchment [POPULATION CATEGORY]?	a. Total population		
		b. Total male population		
		c. Total female population		
		d. Total female population 15–49 years, i.e., women of childbearing age		
		e. Total population <5 years		
		f. Total population <1 year		

Now I would like to see the register that shows the total number of patients attended in this facility in the last completed calendar month.

INTERVIEWER: FOR QUESTIONS (7.03) TO (7.18), RECORD FOR THE LAST COMPLETED CALENDAR MONTH. FOR QUESTIONS (7.04) TO (7.12), IF SOME CATEGORIES CAN'T BE IDENTIFIED FROM REGISTER, RECORD "DON'T KNOW" FOR THESE CATEGORIES.			RECORD RESPONSE
(7.03)	**TOTAL** number of patients		
(7.04)	**TOTAL** number of male patients		
(7.05)	**TOTAL** number of female patients		
(7.06)	**TOTAL** number of pregnant women		
(7.07)	**TOTAL** number of patients under 5		
(7.08)	**TOTAL** number of male patients under 5		
(7.09)	**TOTAL** number of female patients under 5		
(7.10)	**TOTAL** number of patients under 1		
(7.11)	**TOTAL** number of male patients under 1		
(7.12)	**TOTAL** number of female patients under 1		
(7.13)	Monthly Integrated Activity Report	SEEN, FULLY COMPLETED 1	
		SEEN, NOT COMPLETE 2	
		NOT SEEN 3	
(7.14)	Monthly Aggregated Activity Report	SEEN, FULLY COMPLETED 1	
		SEEN, NOT COMPLETE 2	
		NOT SEEN 3	
(7.15)	Facility Status Report	SEEN, FULLY COMPLETED 1	
		SEEN, NOT COMPLETE 2	
		NOT SEEN 3	
(7.16)	Notifiable Disease Report	SEEN, FULLY COMPLETED 1	
		SEEN, NOT COMPLETE 2	
		NOT SEEN 3	
(7.17)	Vaccination/Immunization Coverage Report	SEEN, FULLY COMPLETED 1	
		SEEN, NOT COMPLETE 2	
		NOT SEEN 3	
(7.18)	Family Planning Register	SEEN, FULLY COMPLETED 1	
		SEEN, NOT COMPLETE 2	
		NOT SEEN 3	

Source: World Bank Impact Evaluation Toolkit, http://go.worldbank.org/IT69C5OGL0.

Health Labor Market Analyses in Low- and Middle-Income Countries
http://dx.doi.org/10.1596/978-1-4648-0931-6

Table 7A.2 Attendance Check Data Sheet (Example)

OPD Technical Quality Evaluation

Facility ☐   Date ☐

Enumerator ☐

	Posted #	Present #	Not scheduled #	Present nearby (in village, for example) #	Not present at all, but frequently present #	How frequent presence is verified (see codes)	Not present at all, and rarely present #	Reason for absence (put letter A, B, etc.)
Dispensary								
Clinical officer								
Clinical assistant								
Registered nurse midwife								
Public health nurse								
MCH aide								
Laboratory assistant								
Health center (see above)								
Assistant medical officer								
Pharmaceutical assistant								
Medical attendant								
Hospital (see above)								
Medical officer								
Pharmacist								
Laboratory technician								
Radiographer								
Other								
Other								

To verify frequent presence,
use as many methods as possible:

1) Examine log books
2) Ask other staff
3) Ask key people in village
4) Ask patients who come to visit
5) Other (list) _____

Reasons for Absence:

A)

B)

C)

D)

E)

Source: Based on Klemick, Leonard, and Masatu 2009.
Note: MCH = maternal and child health; OPD = outpatient department.

Table 7A.3 Patient Exit Interview (Satisfaction, Example)

(4)	Patient satisfaction						RECORD RESPONSE
(4.01)	What was the **most important** reason you chose this health facility today instead of a different source of care? INTERVIEWER: DO NOT READ OPTIONS ALOUD. ONLY ONE ANSWER IS ALLOWED.	LOCATION CLOSE TO HOME			01			
		LOW COST			02			
		TRUST IN PROVIDERS / HIGH-QUALITY CARE			03			
		AVAILABILITY OF DRUGS			04			
		AVAILABILITY OF FEMALE PROVIDER			05			
		RECOMMENDATION OR REFERRAL			06			
		OTHER, SPECIFY:			96			
(4.02)	What was the **next most important** reason you chose this health facility today instead of a different source of care, if there is any other reason? INTERVIEWER: DO NOT READ OPTIONS ALOUD. ONLY ONE ANSWER IS ALLOWED.	NO OTHER REASON			01			
		LOCATION CLOSE TO HOME			02			
		LOW COST			03			
		TRUST IN PROVIDERS / HIGH-QUALITY CARE			04			
		AVAILABILITY OF DRUGS			05			
		AVAILABILITY OF FEMALE PROVIDER			06			
		RECOMMENDATION OR REFERRAL			07			
		OTHER, SPECIFY:			96			

I'm going to read you a series of statements regarding this health facility. Please tell me if you agree, neither agree nor disagree, or disagree with each statement. Some statements may not apply to your situation. Please let me know if a statement does not apply to you.

INTERVIEWER: READ EACH STATEMENT TO THE RESPONDENT AND RECORD THE RESPONSE CODE FOR EACH QUESTION. PLEASE SHOW AND ASK TO PICK OUT THE COLORED AND NUMBERED CARDS WITH RESPONSE CODES

		Agree	Neither agree nor disagree	Disagree	Not applicable	RECORD RESPONSE	
(4.03)	It is convenient to travel from your house to the health facility.	1	2	3	4		
(4.04)	The health facility is clean.	1	2	3	4		
(4.05)	The health staff are courteous and respectful.	1	2	3	4		
(4.06)	The health workers did a good job of explaining your condition.	1	2	3	4		
(4.07)	It is easy to get medicine that health workers prescribe.	1	2	3	4		
(4.08)	The registration fees of this visit to the health facility were reasonable.	1	2	3	4		
(4.09)	The lab fees of this visit to the health facility were reasonable.	1	2	3	4		
(4.10)	The medication fees of this visit to the health facility were reasonable.	1	2	3	4		
(4.11)	The transport fees for this visit to the health facility were reasonable.	1	2	3	4		

table continues next page

Table 7A.3 Patient Exit Interview (Satisfaction, Example) *(continued)*

		Agree	Neither agree nor disagree	Disagree	Not applicable	RECORD RESPONSE	
(4.12)	The amount of time you spent waiting to be seen by a health worker was reasonable.	1	2	3	4		
(4.13)	You had enough privacy during your visit.	1	2	3	4		
(4.14)	The health worker spent a sufficient amount of time with you.	1	2	3	4		
(4.15)	The hours the facility is open are adequate to meet your needs.	1	2	3	4		
(4.16)	The overall quality of services provided was satisfactory.	1	2	3	4		

Source: World Bank Impact Evaluation Toolkit, http://go.worldbank.org/IT69C5OGL0.

Table 7A.4 Patient Exit Interview (Travel and Expenditure, Example)

(3)	Patient travel and expenditure					RECORD RESPONSE
(3.01)	How far is your household from this health facility?	KILOMETERS				
(3.02)	How long did it take you to reach this health facility from home today, <u>one way</u> in minutes?	MINUTES				
(3.03)	What was your primary mode of transportation today? (One way)	By foot	01	►	(3.05)	
		Bicycle	02			
		Animal	03			
		Private car	04			
		Public car/bus including cab	05			
		Private motorcycle	06			
		Taxi moto	07			
		Other (Specify:_____)	96			
(3.04)	How much did it cost in Currency for you to travel to the health facility today, one way?	CURRENCY				
(3.05)	How long did you wait in the health facility before being seen in consultation by the health worker?	MINUTES				
(3.06)	Do you think the time you spent waiting was too long?	YES	1			
		NO	2			
(3.07)	How long did you spend with the doctor or nurse during the consultation?	MINUTES				
(3.08)	Did you have to pay a registration, consultation, or doctor's fee?	YES	1			
		NO	2	►	(3.10)	

table continues next page

Table 7A.4 Patient Exit Interview (Travel and Expenditure, Example) *(continued)*

(3.09)	How much did you pay for this in Currency?	CURRENCY				
(3.10)	Was a laboratory test done?	YES	1			
		NO	2	►	(3.12)	
(3.11)	How much was paid in Currency for this?	CURRENCY				
(3.12)	Was an ultrasound done?	YES	1			
		NO	2	►	(3.14)	
(3.13)	How much was paid in Currency for this?	CURRENCY				
(3.14)	Were medicines dispensed to you today?	YES	1			
		NO	2	►	(3.16)	
(3.15)	How much was paid in Currency for this?	CURRENCY				
(3.16)	How much was spent in total in Currency at the facility for this visit, not including transportation costs?	CURRENCY	IF ZERO	►	(3.18)	
(3.17)	Where did the money come from that was used to pay for health care today? INTERVIEWER: DO NOT READ OPTIONS ALOUD, BUT FOR EACH OPTION RECORD "1" IF MENTIONED, "2" IF NOT MENTIONED. YOU MAY PROBE WITHOUT USING SPECIFIC ANSWERS (E.G., "ANYTHING ELSE?") MENTIONED.......1 NOT MENTIONED..2	a. SAVINGS OR REGULAR HOUSEHOLD BUDGET				
		b. HEALTH INSURANCE				
		c. SELLING HOUSEHOLD POSSESSIONS				
		d. MORTGAGING OR SELLING LAND OR REAL ESTATE				
		e. FROM A FRIEND OR RELATIVE				
		f. FROM SOMEONE OTHER THAN FAMILY AND FRIENDS				
		g. OTHER, SPECIFY:				
(3.18)	Are you currently covered under a health insurance scheme?	YES	1			
		NO	2	►	(4.01)	
(3.19)	What type of health insurance is this? Is it public, private, or both?	Public	01			
		Private	02			
		Both	03			
(3.20)	In the last 12 months, how many months have you been enrolled in the insurance scheme that covers you now?	MONTHS. MAXIMUM 12.				

Source: World Bank Impact Evaluation Toolkit, http://go.worldbank.org/IT69C5OGL0.

Table 7A.5 Household Survey Questionnaire on Decision Making (Example)

Page 3	Survey on Choice and the Perception of Quality		Folio		
	Individual illness episode data (decision)	Interviewer	Date		

Patient NAME				
Episode number			Respondent Name	

What were the first complaints that NAME experienced (not the diagnosis)?

Which of these complaints made NAME decide to seek assistance?

HEAD		LIMB		GENITALS AND SKIN		CHILDREN	
01	headache	15	general injury	29	urethral discharge	43	slow growth
02	fever	16	broken bone/fracture	30	urinary complaints	44	convulsions
03	running nose	17	deep cut	31	blood in urine	45	epilepsy
04	cough	18	pain in extremities	32	skin lesions	46	worms (seen)
05	sore throat	19	swelling in extremities	33	genital lesions	47	
06	eye problems	20	accident/trauma	34	rash	48	
07	ear problems	21	head (eye) injury	35	abscess	49	
STOMACH		**GENERAL**		**HEALING**		**WOMEN**	
08	loss of appetite	22	chest pain	36	protection	50	irregular menses
09	vomiting	23	coughing up blood	37	charm	51	blood loss
10	diarrhea	24	short of breath	38	poisoning	52	antenatal checkup
11	constipation	25	lower back pain	39	infertility	53	abortion
12	abdominal pain	26	general weakness/ malaise	40	impotence	54	miscarriage
13	distended abdomen	27	weight loss	41		55	
14	stomachache	28	high blood pressure	42		56	

If they give the diagnosis put the name here		
How many days was the patient sick before that person sought help?		
If the patient was bedridden, for how many days?		

Could the patient perform the following tasks before he or she was sick (B), and then during (S)?

For adult males ask:

Walk 1 hour with cattle to grazing	B | S	Hold a cow for treatment or bleeding	B | S

For adult females ask:

Go 20 minutes walk and carry water	B | S	Cook food for family	B | S

For all adult patients ask:

Bathe themselves	B | S	Work in Shamba	B | S

For all patients over 5 ask:

Eat with good appetite	B | S	Walk 20 minutes	B | S

For all patients under 5 ask:

Eat with good appetite	B | S	Play appropriately	B | S

In your opinion how severe was the illness? *(read these aloud)*

1 we thought he/she might die   2 very severe   3 severe   4 mild   5 almost nothing

Where did you **first** go for **medical** help?

put name of person, or facility and location (if necessary)

What was the result of the visit to this provider?

1	died	4	went to another provider	
2	cured	5	returned home (without cure)	
3	well enough	6	referred	7 still under treatment

Remind them that people can change their opinions about which places are good and which are not good. Maybe they used to think one was very good and now they don't. Maybe they used to think one was bad and now they think it is good.

Would you return if you suffered from the same condition?		
If no, why not?		

Source: Based on Klemick, Leonard, and Masatu 2009.

Table 7A.6 Household Survey Questionnaire, Health-Seeking Experience (Example)

Page 4 B	Survey on Choice and the Perception of Quality		
Treatment of episode (visit)		Interviewer	Date
Name of sick person			
Episode number	Visit number		
1	Was there a consultation?		
	If no, go to question number 7.		
2	At this location what was the title of the person you consulted with? *Write out title.*		
	Put the title they give (doctor, nurse, etc.).		
3	Did you pay for consultation?		*If no, skip to question 7.*
4	How did you pay?		1. Cash 2. In kind 3. Both
5	How much was given in kind?		
6	What was given in kind?		
7	Were drugs prescribed?		*If no, skip to question number 12.*
8	How much did you pay for the drugs you received?		*Put 0 if they were free.*
9	Did you get all of the drugs there?		*If yes, skip to question 12.*
10	If not, why not?		
	1. Not available 2. Too expensive 3. I have my own supply 4. I prefer to buy drugs elsewhere		
11	Where did you get the additional drugs?		
12	Did you travel or walk to the facility?		*If no, skip to 16.*
13	How did you travel to this facility or person?		
	1. On foot 2. Public transport 3. Donkey 4. Private car 5. Carried		
14	How much did you pay?	*Put 0 if they walked or used private car.*	
15	How long did it take you to get there?		
16	How many other people traveled with you? *Put additional number.*		
17	What was the amount of other costs incurred (in food, lodging etc.)?		
18	Were you admitted to the hospital?		
19	How did you get the money for these things? (multiple possible)		
1	No money needed		Borrowed from:
2	Personal savings	6 Elder	9 Village lender
3	Family savings	7 Friend	10 Care provider
4	Gift from extended family	8 Extended family	11 Social group
5	Sold animal		
20	If you borrowed, how much did you borrow? *Put zero if didn't borrow.*		
21	What was the result of the visit to this provider?		
1	Died	4 Went to another provider	
2	Cured	5 Returned home (without cure)	
3	Well enough	6 Referred	7 Still under treatment
22	Were you satisfied with your visit to this provider?		
	1 Fully 2 Mostly 3 Not particularly 4 Very dissatisfied		
23	Was the experience 1 better, 2 worse, or 3 the same as you expected?		
24	Did you give an appreciation or money after you learned the outcome?		
	Cash	In kind	
25	Before, during, or after this visit, did you seek medical care from anyone else?		
	If they say before or during, fill this page again and put visit number 2; If they say after, put the name of the facility.		

Source: Based on Klemick, Leonard, and Masatu 2009.

Table 7A.7 Direct Observation Checklist

OPD Technical Quality Evaluation				Consultation observation		Page 1
	Facility	☐	Enumerator ☐	Doctor ☐		
				Observation ☐	☐	
	Patient number	☐				
	Time at start of consultation	☐			☐	
Greeting, Receiving		**Does the health worker:**				
1.1	Welcome the patient?			☐	☐	
1.2	Greet the patient?			☐		
1.3	Look at the patient while he or she is talking?			☐		
1.4	Does the patient have a chair to sit on?			☐		
	Is this consultation a re-attendance?					
	Follow-up ☐		More medication	☐	☐	
History Taking			**If not, go to list of symptoms.**			
	Does the health worker ask:					
2.1	If there is any improvement since the last visit?			☐	☐	
	If there is significant improvement,					
	check this box and end the survey		☐		☐	
		Condition/diagnosis	☐		☐	
2.2	If completed the treatment given on the first visit?			☐	☐	
Symptoms						
	Fever	☐				
	Cough	☐	Patient age:			
	Diarrhea	☐	Under 5	☐	☐	
	Genital discharge, ulcers,	☐	Child	☐		
	or sores, scrotal or inguinal swelling,		Adult	☐		
	lower abdominal pain in females					
	Skin rash	☐	Headache	☐		
	Eye problems	☐	Backache	☐		
	Ear problems	☐			☐	
	Abdominal pain	☐			☐	
	Accident/wound/burn	☐	Other	☐☐☐	☐	
	Vomiting	☐	Other	☐☐☐	☐	
	Does the health worker ask:					
2.3	Duration of primary symptom?			☐	☐	
2.4	Probe regarding symptoms if patient was brief?			☐ NA	☐	
2.5	If there are other associated symptoms?			☐	☐	
2.6	Duration of other symptoms?			☐ NA	☐	
2.7	If received treatment elsewhere or taken medicines?			☐	☐	

Table 7A.7 Direct Observation Checklist *(continued)*

OPD Technical Quality Evaluation		Consultation observation	Page 2
History Taking (continued)			
Fever	Check if this is a primary or significant symptom		
3.1	Pattern (periodicity) of fever		
3.2	Presence of chills, sweats		
3.3	Presence of cough, sore throat, pain during swallowing		
3.4	Presence of diarrhea or vomiting		
3.5	Presence of convulsions	NA	
Cough	Check if this is a primary or significant symptom		
3.6	The duration of cough		
3.7	Sputum production or dry cough	NA	
3.8	Presnce of blood in sputum	NA	
3.9	Presence of chest pain	NA	
3.10	Presence of difficulty in breathing		
3.11	If child is under 5, history of vaccinations	NA	
3.12	Presence of fever		
Diarrhea	Check if this is a primary or significant symptom		
3.13	Frequency of stools		
3.14	Consistency of stools		
3.15	Presence of blood and/or mucus in stools		
3.16	Presence of vomiting		
3.17	Presence of fever		
STD symptoms	Check if this is a primary or significant symptom		
3.18	Type of discharge, or how ulcer started		
3.19	Presence of pain or itching		
3.20	Presence of fever		
3.21	Pain on urination		
3.22	History of recent sexual contact		
3.23	Any previous exposure to STDs		
3.24	Any treatment given to sexual partners	NA	
General			
3.25	Take history according to symptoms?		
	Note any significant faults in investigation here:		

Source: Based on Klemick, Leonard, and Masatu 2009.
Note: NA = not applicable; OPD = outpatient department; STDs: sexually transmitted diseases.

Notes

1. See the World Bank Impact Evaluation Toolkit, http://go.worldbank.org/IT69C5OGL0.

2. See the World Bank Impact Evaluation Toolkit, http://go.worldbank.org/IT69C5OGL0.

3. For outpatient services, see www.kleonard.umd.edu/healthsurveys#healthseeking.

4. For hospital evaluation, see https://sites.google.com/site/hfqualityassessment/home/hpa.

5. A version of the retrospective consultation review instrument is available at www.kleonard.umd.edu/healthsurveys#rcr.

6. See WHO Responsiveness Surveys and Questionnaires, available at http://www.who.int/responsiveness/surveys/en/.

7. The instruments and training manuals for that study are available from Health & Education in India at www.healthandeducationinindia.org (a site that requires free registration).

8. The vignettes designed by Leonard and Masatu are available at www.kleonard.umd.edu/healthsurveys.

9. See also the World Bank Impact Evaluation Toolkit, available at http://go.worldbank.org/VEX5C8U5M0.

10. See the Hospital Quality Assessment section of the Health Systems Strengthening Project in Liberia, available at https://sites.google.com/site/hfqualityassessment/home/hpa.

11. The instruments are described in detail at www.kleonard.umd.edu/healthsurveys.

12. Instruments that measure process quality in emergency, obstetrics, and surgery are available at https://sites.google.com/site/hfqualityassessment/home/hpa.

References

Barber, S. L., P. J. Gertler, and P. Harimurti. 2007. "Differences in Access to High-Quality Outpatient Care in Indonesia." *Health Affairs* 26 (3): 352–66.

Chaudhury, N., J. Hammer, M. Kremer, K. Muralidharan, and F. H. Rogers. 2006. "Missing in Action: Teacher and Health Worker Absence in Developing Countries." *Journal of Economic Perspectives* 20 (1): 91–116.

Chaudhury, N., and J. S. Hammer. 2004. "Ghost Doctors: Absenteeism in Bangladeshi Health Facilities." *World Bank Economic Review* 18 (3): 423–41.

Currie, J., W. Lin, and W. Zhang. 2010. "Patient Knowledge and Antibiotic Abuse: Evidence from an Audit Study in China." NBER Working Paper 16602, National Bureau of Economic Research, Cambridge, MA.

Das, J., and J. Hammer. 2004. "Strained Mercy: The Quality of Medical Care in Delhi." *Economic and Political Weekly* 39 (9): 951–61.

Das, J., A. Holla, V. Das, M. Mohanan, D. Tabak, and B. Chan. 2012. "In Urban and Rural India, a Standardized Patient Study Showed Low Levels of Provider Training and Huge Quality Gaps." *Health Affairs* 31 (12): 2774–84.

Das, J., and K. L. Leonard. 2007. "Use of Vignettes to Measure the Quality of Health Care." In *Are You Being Served? New Tools for Measuring Service Delivery*, edited by A. Samia, J. Das, and M. Goldstein. Washington, DC: World Bank.

Donabedian, A. 1980. *The Definition of Quality and Approaches to Its Assessment.* Ann Arbor, MI: Health Administration Press.

———. 1988. "The Quality of Care: How Can It Be Assessed?" *JAMA* 121 (11): 1145–50.

Dresselhaus, T. R., J. W. Peabody, M. Lee, M. M. Wang, and J. Luck. 2000. "Measuring Compliance with Preventive Care Guidelines: Standardized Patients, Clinical Vignettes, and the Medical Record." *Journal of General Internal Medicine* 15 (11): 782–88.

Freidson, E. 2001. *Professionalism: The Third Logic*. Chicago, IL: University of Chicago Press.

Glick, P. 2009. "How Reliable Are Surveys of Client Satisfaction with Healthcare Services? Evidence from Matched Facility and Household Data in Madagascar." *Social Science and Medicine* 2 (68): 368–79.

Hongoro, C., and B. McPake. 2004. "How to Bridge the Gap in Human Resources for Health." *Lancet* 364 (9443): 1451–56.

Klemick, H., K. Leonard, and M. Masatu. 2009. "Defining Access to Health Care: Evidence on the Importance of Quality and Distance in Rural Tanzania." *American Journal of Agricultural Economics* 91 (2): 347–58.

Leonard, K. L. 2008. "Is Patient Satisfaction Sensitive to Changes in the Quality of Care? An Exploitation of the Hawthorne Effect." *Journal of Health Economics* 27 (2): 444–59.

———. 2011. *Improving Health Outcomes by Choosing Better Doctors: Evidence of Social Learning about Doctor Quality from Rural Tanzania*. Technical Report, University of Maryland.

———. 2012. Personal observation, Tanzania.

Leonard, K. L., and M. C. Masatu. 2005. "The Use of Direct Clinician Observation and Vignettes for Health Services Quality Evaluation in Developing Countries." *Social Science and Medicine* 61 (9): 1944–51.

———. 2006. "Outpatient Process Quality Evaluation and the Hawthorne Effect." *Social Science and Medicine* 63 (9): 2330–40.

Lindkvist, I. 2013. "Informal Payments and Health Worker Effort: A Quantitative Study from Tanzania." *Health Economics* 22 (10): 1250–71.

Lohr, K., ed. 1990. *Medicare: A Strategy for Quality Assurance*. Vol. 1 of *Committee to Design a Strategy for Quality Review and Assurance in Medicare*. Washington, DC: National Academy Press.

Madden, J. M., J. D. Quick, D. Ross-Degnan, and K. K. Kafle. 1997. "Undercover Careseekers: Simulated Clients in the Study of Health Provider Behavior in Developing Countries." *Social Science and Medicine* 45 (10): 1465–82.

Mæstad, O., G. Torsvik, and A. Aakvik. 2010. "Overworked? On the Relationship between Workload and Health Worker Performance." *Journal of Health Economics* 29 (5): 686–98.

Mwisongo, A., and O. Mæstad. 2013. "Productivity of Health Workers: Tanzania." In *The Labor Market for Health Workers in Africa: A New Look at the Crisis*, edited by A. Soucat, R. M. Scheffler, and T. A. Ghebreyesus. Washington, DC: World Bank.

Tiemeier, H., W. J. de Vries, M. van het Loo, J. P. Kahan, N. Klazinga, R. Grol, and H. Rigter. 2002. "Guideline Adherence Rates and Interprofessional Variation in a Vignette Study of Depression." *Quality & Safety in Health Care* 11 (3): 214–18.

World Bank. n.d. *Impact Evaluation Toolkit*. World Bank, Washington, DC. http://go.worldbank.org/IT69C5OGL0.

CHAPTER 8

Analyzing the Determinants of Health Worker Performance

Kenneth Leonard and Ottar Mæstad

Indicators for Analyzing the Determinants of Performance

The previous chapter focused on the ways to measure performance of health workers, specifically presence, process quality, and productivity. For policy making, however, it is not particularly useful just to know that there is a performance shortfall unless the underlying cause is identified and unless it is determined whether or not something can potentially be done about the problem.

This chapter looks at tools that allow the determinants of performance to be understood, with the aim of better understanding how to improve performance. Frameworks that can be used to decompose and analyze performance shortfalls are developed, and a set of indicators that can be used to shed light on the magnitude of various sources of performance shortfalls is presented. This analysis will provide guidance to how to close the performance shortfalls observed.

Note that process quality, productivity, and presence are closely interlinked. Low presence can cause low productivity (because fewer patients are being served) or low process quality (because health workers may be more time-constrained when they see patients). High process quality can lead to more time spent per patient and thereby low productivity—at least insofar as productivity does not capture the quality of the services. The relationship may also be the opposite: high process quality may cause increased demand for services, which may lead to higher productivity if there was slack capacity at the outset. Hence explanations of one type of performance shortfall may also contribute to understanding shortfalls in other domains. This chapter will focus on the determinants of process quality and productivity. Presence will be discussed insofar it affects productivity.

Ways of Understanding Process Quality Shortfalls

To determine how best to improve performance and the ramifications of different types of shortfalls, this section begins by considering the reasons that process quality can fall short.

Three-Gap Model of Quality of Care

The inputs of knowledge, equipment (including everything from X-ray machines to medicines, buildings, and electricity), and effort are all required to produce performance in the health system, but it is not always clear which element is missing or inadequate when performance is low. To help organize an overview of the role of each input into performance, the three-gap model of process quality (or simply "quality") is described here. Each health worker can be described by the measurable triplet of competence, capacity, and performance. *Competence* measures knowledge of health care processes and the skills employed in utilizing this knowledge. It is the result of training (including initial training, on-the-job training, and continuing education) and experience, and determines what the health worker knows how to do. *Capacity* measures the health worker's ability to use his or her knowledge in the current workplace and is a function of health facility and health system structure, particularly access to equipment, infrastructure, and consumables. Health workers who are highly competent are likely to have greater capacity if they are posted to a referral hospital than if they are posted to a rural clinic. *Performance* is the measure of what a health worker does with his or her normal patients, and is the result of effort, which is not directly observed. Capacity is a function of competence combined with the input of equipment; performance is a function of capacity combined with the input of effort. Although management practices are traditionally considered as part of structural quality, in this chapter the management is an input into motivation and therefore impacts *performance*, not *capacity*.

Figure 8.1 graphs these three measures of care (competence, capacity, and performance) as well as the target level of performance (Bawo, Leonard, and Mohammed 2015). The three gaps defined by these four levels are the *know gap*, the *know-can gap*, and the *can-do gap*. Performance originates with knowledge, education, and skills as measured by competence (C), shown on the vertical axis extending below the origin: increases in competence are shown by points closer to the bottom of the figure (further from the origin). Capacity (K) comes from competence taking into account the infrastructure, equipment, and medicines necessary to appropriately use training, education, and skill, shown on the horizontal axis to the right of the origin. Finally, performance comes from taking capacity and combining it with effort, shown on the vertical axis above the origin: health workers must choose to use their knowledge and equipment in order to perform.

An important feature of this model is that performance is limited by capacity and capacity is limited by competence: a health worker cannot do better than he or she knows how to do, for example. This is shown in the graph by the capacity and performance "barriers." In the transformation from competence to capacity and again from capacity to performance, the capacity barrier and performance barrier are taken into account, shown as 45-degree lines from the origin in the lower right and upper right quadrants of the figure. These barriers reflect the fact that better equipment cannot produce capacity beyond the level of competence,

Figure 8.1 Three-Gap Framework

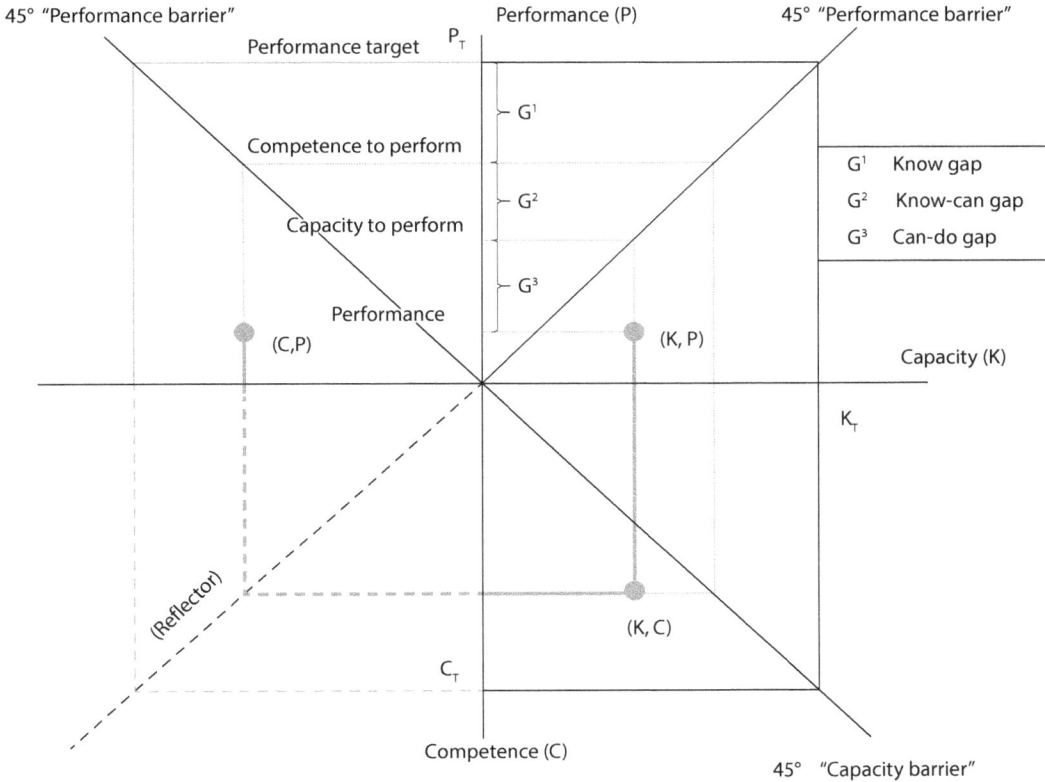

Source: Bawo, Leonard, and Mohammed 2015.

and greater effort cannot produce performance beyond the level of capacity. In other words, competence limits capacity and capacity limits performance.

Target competence is the level required to perform according to the target level of performance, marked in figure 8.1 as C_T. In the ideal world, any health worker with target competence would also have target capacity K_T: if health workers had all the equipment and medicines to work according to their training, capacity and competence would be the same. In addition, this capacity (K_T) would ideally translate directly into targeted performance, P_T.

The idea of the three-gap framework is that in the real world not all health workers have target competence, competence does not always translate into capacity, and capacity does not always translate into performance. In addition to this ideal triplet (C_T, K_T, P_T), figure 8.1 shows an example of another possible triplet (C, K, P). In this case, competence (C) is lower than targeted performance and, because some equipment or medicine are not available, this particular health worker has capacity (K), which is lower than his competence. This is shown by the pair (K,C) in the lower right quadrant and that (K,C) to the left of the capacity barrier. Furthermore, because effort is not ideal, the health worker does not fully transform capacity into performance (P), as shown by the pair (K,P) in the upper right quadrant. Thus, performance is significantly below target performance. The shortfall can be divided into three gaps:

- *Know gap.* The difference (G^1) between targeted performance and the competence to perform
- *Know-do gap.* The difference (G^2) between competence and capacity
- *Can-do gap.* The difference (G^3) between capacity and performance

A slightly simplified two-gap framework is also examined. It is possible to reduce the three gaps down to two gaps; this is also shown in figure 8.1. By using the lower left quadrant as a "reflector," competence can be measured on the horizontal axis going to the left from the origin. The competence performance pair is shown in the upper right quadrant as (C,P). In such a case, the know-do gap—which is also the sum of the know-can and can-do gaps—can be measured.

The three gaps constitute a way to think about individual health workers. For example, a health worker with a significant know gap has insufficient training, a health worker with a large know-can gap has insufficient access to equipment and materials, and a health worker with a large can-do gap has insufficient motivation. The presence of only one gap indicates an obvious place to begin understanding determinants of low quality. For example, a health worker with low levels of training (a large know gap), but who translates all the available knowledge into capacity and performance, would gain from a focus on increasing knowledge. Similarly, a health worker with high levels of knowledge and capacity but low performance (a large can-do gap) would benefit from a focus on motivation.

In addition, the relationship between knowledge, competence, and performance can reveal problems with larger groups of health workers. For example, figure 8.2 shows data from a sample of health workers in Tanzania, with each health worker's competence and performance represented by a single dot on the graph (Leonard, Masatu, and Vialou 2007, discussing data from 2003). This graph is a representation of an example of the upper left quadrant of figure 8.1 (with the x axis flipped). Significant variance in competence is evident in this sample (which may come from either a know gap or a know-can gap). However, examining the relationship between competence and performance is revealing. The dashed line, which shows the average relationship between competence and performance, indicates that increasing the competence of the average health worker would result in almost no change in performance, whereas addressing the motivation (effort) of the average health worker might lead to a significant improvement in performance. Thus, for this sample, addressing motivation is more important than addressing training. It may be true that once addressing motivation has been achieved, training would lead to greater gains, but addressing training without addressing motivation does not result in important changes.

Figure 8.2 Empirical Evidence of the Know-Do Gap

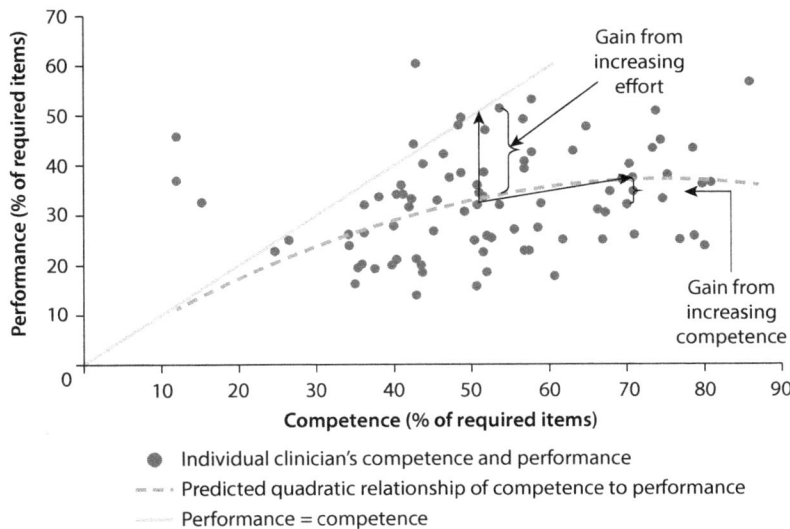

Sources: Data from Leonard, Masatu, and Vialou 2007; Leonard and Masatu 2010.
Note: The data show the measured competence and performance of a sample of clinicians, measured as the percentage of items required by national protocol for the patients' presenting symptoms. If clinicians followed their training, every data point would be near the 45-degree line, where competence is equal to performance. The dashed line shows the estimated relationship for the whole sample.

To the extent that the know-do gap is a significant portion of the performance shortfall of particular health workers or facilities, it is important to understand why effort levels are low. Many authors have addressed the variation in quality—some explicitly looking at the gaps outlined earlier and others addressing the elements within the gaps directly. Das and Hammer (2007) and Leonard, Masatu, and Vialou (2007) examine the variation in the can-do gap across different institutions, showing that the can-do gap is much larger in the public sector than it is in the private or charitable sectors. Whereas Das and Hammer (2007) examine the difference between public and private, Leonard Masatu, and Vialou (2007) show that the gap is related to the degree of decentralization: facilities that are more decentralized in management have smaller can-do gaps than facilities with centralized decision making. Das and Sohnesen (2007) consider the variation in quality across types of patients, looking for evidence of discrimination (which they do not find). Leonard and Masatu (2007) and Das and Gertler (2007) look at variation in quality (and the can-do gap) across rural and urban divides across five different countries. Mæstad, Torsvik, and Aakvik (2010) examine the link between caseload and quality directly and find no evidence that a high caseload can reduce the capacity of a health worker to provide quality. Brock, Lange, and Leonard (2016) and Leonard and Masatu (2010) examine the link between altruism and professionalism and quality and find that prosocial tendencies in health workers decrease the can-do gap and improve the quality of care provided.

Health Labor Market Analyses in Low- and Middle-Income Countries
http://dx.doi.org/10.1596/978-1-4648-0931-6

These studies show that it can be useful to establish that low effort is driven in part by features of the health workers' environment that are not related to access to medicines or caseload. When low effort causes low quality, it suggests a strong role for incentives that increase quality: the push for performance-based financing is driven in part by the recognition that effort is at least as important a factor as training in providing care. Basinga et al. (2011) show that in Rwanda, without additional training, funding that incentivizes effort has a greater impact on quantity and quality than funding that allows facilities to improve capacity.

Ways of Measuring the Three Gaps

To better understand the determinants of process quality it is important to measure these gaps, which can be done by measuring the triplet of competence, capacity, and quality. This section reviews some of the methods discussed in the previous chapter and introduces some new ways to measure these health worker characteristics. All three measurements focus on the activities of health workers: Do they know what they should do? Do they have the capacity to do it? Do they do it? What is missing from all three is the skill with which practitioners perform each activity. Two health workers may both know that they should be listening to a patient's heart, but one may have significantly more experience and therefore skill, allowing him to provide higher-quality care. Despite this shortcoming, the measures provide significantly greater understanding about a health worker than his or her credentials, for example.

Note that effort is a particularly fundamental factor for quality. There will always be a need for effort to put new opportunities out into practice. When the can-do gap is small (effort is high), new knowledge might be more quickly translated into practice, but if the gap is large, fixing other gaps may not be as useful, as shown in figure 8.2. Thus, even if the can-do gap is small relative to the other gaps, it does not imply that performance necessarily will increase by increasing knowledge and capacity.

Competence

To assess the competence (knowledge) of health workers, the use of either written test vignettes or case study vignettes discussed in the previous chapter is recommended. Both types test knowledge, although the case study vignette is preferred for outpatient consultation because it tests competence of health workers in practice, not just their knowledge of underlying medical concepts. To measure competence with a case study vignette it is important to instruct the health workers to demonstrate the actions they would take if they had the proper tools and medicines, without concern for whether those tools and medicines are actually available. They should also be informed that the test is a knowledge test, and not a test of how they would do a consultation in practice. To make the measures of competence and quality as comparable as possible, the vignettes should examine cases similar to those the health worker might see in practice. Furthermore, the scoring system used to grade the vignettes should be relatively easy to translate into the score sheet used for direct observation, so that the grading rubric remains the same even if the setting and instructions are different.

Capacity

The capacity of health workers can be assessed using case study vignettes, encouraged direct observation, or early stages of direct observation. The idea is to measure the quality of care provided by a health worker in her actual setting (with the normal knowledge and equipment), but when she is providing extraordinary levels of effort. Thus what is measured is the best they can do with their existing medicine and equipment.

Written case study vignettes do not allow the capacity of health workers to be measured. Case study vignettes, on the other hand, can sometimes be used to measure capacity. First, because they mimic actual cases, they can be scored by the same metric as actual cases. However, because it is not always clear whether health workers feel limited by the equipment or medicines available at their location, the health worker should be instructed to demonstrate the actions he would take using only the tools and resources currently available at the facility. Any actions that the health workers say they would take should be validated by being able to demonstrate that the equipment or materials are available at the facility. In this way, a case study vignette would measure the capacity, or the best that a health worker could do given the existing equipment.

It is also possible to use encouraged direct observation to measure the capacity for quality. In encouraged direct observation, the observer deliberately attempts to increase the quality of care by framing the research in such a way that expectations of high effort are clear. In the same way that most people want to demonstrate their best abilities on a test, the proper setting can encourage health workers to demonstrate their fullest capacity. It is possible to use the maximum quality of care provided over a large set of patients (the case in which the clinician demonstrates the highest capacity for quality). This follows from the assumption that sometimes a patient's case is so severe that the health worker will respond by exerting extra effort, even if he or she is not encouraged or observed. However, this number is likely to be a lower bound on the capacity for quality if the health worker is providing low levels of effort for all of his or her patients.

One of the factors that limit the capacity of most health workers is the amount of time available to do the job. If health workers have a very heavy caseload, their capacity for quality is constrained by this factor: they may not have the time to expend the proper amount of effort. Using an artificial setting such as the case study vignette will not capture this particular constraint, since the health worker can give his or her full attention to the case study. Using direct observation or encouraged observation may do a better job of capturing this constraint, especially if the observation takes place over a lengthy period—long enough for the constraint to force the health worker to speed up (if that is necessary).

Health Labor Market Analyses in Low- and Middle-Income Countries
http://dx.doi.org/10.1596/978-1-4648-0931-6

Unfortunately, it can be difficult to tell whether health workers are decreasing the amount of time they spend with patients because they are no longer trying to show their full capacity or because they have reached the limit of their time. Thus caseload is a constraint that is difficult to capture in this form of measurement. If caseload is expected to be a problem, more attention should be paid directly to this.

Ways of Measuring Capacity and Competence with Similar Instruments

One way to observe the difference between *know* and *can* is to alter the instructions for the same case study patients. In other words, have the health worker demonstrate the actions he would undertake with only the resources currently at his disposal and then ask him to explain what he would do differently if he had all necessary resources at his disposal. The differences between the activities of a health worker in this context help to directly reveal potential problems with equipment and materials.

Table 8.1 gives a shortened version of a vignette used to measure the capacity and competence of health workers to manage newborn asphyxia, drawn from the Liberia Hospital evaluation instruments.[1] This vignette could be administered under two different sets of instructions:

1. Describe all the actions you would take to resuscitate the baby while it is not breathing using the equipment and medication that is available to you now.
2. Describe all the actions you would take to resuscitate the baby while it is not breathing using any equipment or materials that you know how to use.

The column asking the enumerator to verify the presence of equipment is necessary in the first example to verify that it *is possible* to manage the case using existing equipment.

Quality

The best indicator for measuring the quality of care (performance) in this setting is the process quality indicator such as direct observation or mystery clients, as discussed in chapter 7, expressed as a proportion of the maximum possible quality. In the examples used above, drawn from data collected in Tanzania (Leonard and Masatu 2006), adherence to protocol—the percentage of items required by protocol that are actually provided—is examined. This can be measured with passive direct observation after the Hawthorne effect stage or with retrospective consultation review. As discussed in the previous chapter, the presence of a research team watching the activities of health workers causes an artificial increase in effort (the Hawthorne effect), such that a health worker is approaching his or her capacity for care. However, after some time has passed, health workers return to something approaching their normal level of effort.

Table 8.1 Vignette to Measure Competence and Capacity

Checklist for management of newborn asphyxia

RECORD TIME OF BEGINNING OF THE SIMULATION (HH:MM)   __ __: __ __AM/PM

THE FOLLOWING QUESTIONS CORRESPOND TO A CLINICAL CASE SCENARIO THAT THE HEALTH WORKER COULD EXPECT TO OBSERVE IN THE CLINIC. READ THE CASE SCENARIOS AND QUESTIONS EXACTLY AS THEY ARE WRITTEN. DO NOT READ THE OPTIONS OF ANSWERS. FOR CERTAIN QUESTIONS, MULTIPLE ANSWERS ARE POSSIBLE; IN THIS CASE, CIRCLE ALL ANSWERS GIVEN BY THE HEALTH WORKER. AFTER THE HEALTH WORKER HAS FINISHED ANSWERING THE QUESTION, ASK "ANYTHING ELSE?" IF ADDITIONAL ANSWERS ARE GIVEN AT THAT TIME, MAKE DUE RECORD OF THEM ON THE SURVEY FORM. BE CAREFUL TO FOLLOW THE SKIPS AS THEY ARE MARKED.

DO NOT READ OPTIONS ALOUD. FOR EACH OPTION, NOTE WHETHER THE HEALTH WORKER MENTIONED THIS ACTION OR NOT.

Scenario: Mrs. Farida had a prolonged second stage of labor. Her baby developed fetal distress and was delivered by vacuum extraction. He is limp and does not breathe spontaneously at birth.

Question	Yes	No	Verify present/ not present
Observer: Describe all the actions you would take to resuscitate the baby while it is not breathing.			
A. Keep the baby warm.	1	0	—
B. Clamp and cut the cord if necessary.	1	0	1
			0
C. Transfer the baby to a dry, clean, and warm surface.	1	0	—
D. Inform the mother that the baby has difficulty initiating breathing and that you will help the baby to breathe.	1	0	—
E. Keep the baby wrapped (and under a radiant heater if possible).	1	0	1
			0
F. Open the airway.	1	0	—
G. Position the head so it is slightly extended.	1	0	—
H. Suction first the mouth and then the nose.	1	0	1
			0
I. Repeat suction if necessary.	1	0	—
J. Ventilate the baby.	1	0	1
			0
K. Place mask to cover chin, mouth, and nose (to form seal).	1	0	1
			0
L. Squeeze the bag 2 or 3 times and look if the chest is rising.	1	0	—
RECORD TIME OF END OF THE SIMULATION (HH:MM) __ __: __ __AM/PM			

GO BACK TO EACH ITEM IN THE SIMULATION THAT REQUIRES A PIECE OF EQUIPMENT OR A MEDICATION AND VERIFY THAT THE EQUIPMENT OR MEDICATION IS PRESENT USING THE COLUMN MARKED "VERIFY."

Source: Liberia Hospital evaluation instruments.
Note: HH = hour; MM = minute; — = not applicable.

Ways of Understanding Productivity Shortfalls

Low productivity means that output is low for the current level of input, or that the use of inputs is high for the current level of output. These two ways of describing low productivity mirror each other, but it is useful to use both in analyzing the reasons for low productivity in the health sector.

As described in chapter 7, low productivity can in some cases be caused by the high quality of services: the high use of inputs can be the result of the health facility investing in proper equipment and securing the proper supply of drugs and supplies. Therefore, as long as the output measures do not properly reflect the quality of the service, it is not necessarily useful to lump together all inputs in measuring productivity. For the purpose of this toolkit, therefore, analyzing productivity as health worker productivity—that is, aggregate output divided by the costs of health workers—is recommended.

Three-Factor Model of Health Worker Productivity

The output of health services is determined directly by the number of patients seeking care, and *demand for health services* is therefore a crucial determinant of productivity. The other major factor determining productivity is supply-side efficiency, which can be decomposed into efficiency of the organization of service provision (*organizational inefficiency*) and the *level of effort* that health workers put into providing services. This section focuses on the following three factors that determine productivity:

- Organizational efficiency
- Health worker effort
- Service demand

Note that this framework is similar to the three-gap model of process quality in that it focuses both on enabling factors (*organizational efficiency* here and *competence* and *capacity* in the three-gap model) and on the importance of health worker effort as crucial for high performance. It differs from the three-gap model in that it points to factors external to the health sector (service demand) as a determinant of performance. These three factors may be interlinked in various ways.

Organizational Efficiency

Organizational inefficiency arises when the service is organized in ways that make health workers spend more time than necessary to provide a certain service output. Organizational bottlenecks, poor logistics, and so on can have such effects. For example, organizational inefficiency can arise when health workers are busy at all times but spend much of their time on unproductive activities (walking from one place to another, filling out forms, and so on). In such a case, each health worker can serve fewer patients and either more health workers are required or fewer services are provided. Inefficient service provision can lead to increased waiting time, which may reduce demand and thereby output levels: organizational inefficiency may be interlinked with low demand.

Health Worker Effort

Health worker effort is obviously crucial for productivity. Low effort may, for instance, involve spending more time than necessary per task (time inefficiency).

In this case, more health workers are needed to serve a given number of patients. Alternatively, spending more time than necessary may increase waiting times, which may reduce productivity through lower demand.

Low effort can also take the form of low presence at work (high absenteeism). This can reduce productivity because the facility may have to be closed, more health workers may have to be recruited to cope with the situation, or waiting times may increase so that fewer patients come.

There is considerable evidence that health workers do not always perform to their capacity when it comes to process quality. Although there is not a similar pool of evidence when it comes to spending more time than necessary per task, it is likely that some of the same motivational factors that lead to low process quality may also cause such time inefficiency.

Service Demand

When fewer patients are seeking care, productivity will decrease. This can lead to health workers spending considerable amounts of their time waiting for patients. This reduction in productivity can obviously also be explained by saying that the reduction in demand was not followed by a corresponding reduction in staffing. So why can it still be useful to focus explicitly on the demand side when analyzing productivity?

One widely acknowledged reason is that many health services currently are underutilized, a situation that partly has to do with the quality of the services provided or with high formal or informal payments. The appropriate policy response to low demand may therefore be to increase efforts to attract more patients rather than to reduce staffing. Another reason is that populations in many low-income countries are geographically quite dispersed. To provide minimum access to services, some facilities may then have to be located in areas with fewer potential patients who live nearby, causing low productivity. Reducing inputs in such cases might imply closing the facility, which may not be a desirable option.

Tools to Uncover Reasons for Low Productivity

To devise an appropriate policy response to issues of low productivity, it is essential to first determine the reasons for that low productivity. This section presents some tools that can be used to identify the determinants of low productivity.

Low Demand

The aggregate service output divided by the catchment population of one health facility compared to other facilities may be a good indicator of relative levels of demand. If this indicator is low, the next step is to try to figure out the underlying reasons. A household survey may be useful in this regard, since it may shed light on issues such as perceived quality, service costs (formal and informal payments), transport distances, and so on. These different reasons for low demand should lead to quite different policy responses. Note that although transport costs are often regarded as being outside the control of the health facility, it might be

Health Labor Market Analyses in Low- and Middle-Income Countries
http://dx.doi.org/10.1596/978-1-4648-0931-6

possible to provide more outreach services that would partly overcome such reasons for low demand. However, a household survey in the context of productivity analysis may be prohibitively expensive, since it would be necessary to sample a number of households for each facility to make meaningful comparisons across facilities.

The catchment population by itself is also a potentially useful indicator to capture low demand. In sparsely populated areas, health facilities may, by default, have a low catchment population as an attempt to provide a meaningful service to all people, including those in sparsely populated areas. When productivity is low because of low catchment population, the goal should not necessarily be to reduce inputs to increase productivity, since this could imply closing the service altogether.

Note that indicators utilizing catchment populations may work better at lower levels of the health system than at the referral level. For referral facilities, catchment populations include the catchment population of lower-level facilities, which usually makes them difficult to compare.

Organizational Inefficiency

Time and motion studies can be used to identify whether an organization is inefficient. Such studies were originally developed to study the time used and number of motions for particular work tasks along assembly lines, with the aim of increasing productivity and reducing worker fatigue. Using such an approach as a basis for management has been heavily criticized, and it clearly has limited applicability in the health sector. However, as a way to identify slack capacity, it may still be useful.

A time and motion study is simple to undertake but resource demanding. Typically particular health workers are followed over an extended period of time (from a day up to a week) while noting at frequent intervals what they do. The purpose is to identify whether time is spent unnecessarily on unproductive activities (waiting, moving from one place to the other, and so on).

Study costs can be reduced by increasing the intervals between observations, since the surveyor may then be able to follow several workers simultaneously. For instance, if activities performed are recorded every sixth minute, the surveyor may be able to follow three health workers, recording activities for one of the workers every second minute.

One of the problems of time and motion studies is that workers may become more "productive" simply by being observed (the Hawthorne effect). This is not necessarily a serious problem, though, because if all workers are changing their productivity proportionately (admittedly, this is a huge if), it may still be possible to make unbiased comparisons across workers and health facilities, and over time.

Low Effort

Low effort in the context of productivity analysis can take two different forms: absence from work and the slow execution of tasks. How to measure absenteeism is discussed in chapter 5. Time and motion studies can be used to identify the time used for specific tasks. However, spending more time per task is not necessarily a sign of low effort. For many services, spending more time could instead be the result of providing better-quality services. It is therefore meaningful to measure effort by time spent only for highly standardized services. Vaccination could be one candidate.

Ways of Analyzing Motivation Shortfalls

Clearly the motivation of health workers is essential to quality. Simply knowing that motivation is low does not, however, help determine how to fix it—ordering people to be motivated is not generally known as an effective tool for improving motivation. Instead the reasons for the low motivation must be addressed. Two strategies for examining reasons for low motivation are outlined in this section.

The first strategy comprises laboratory experiments that can be used to analyze different types of health workers. These experiments can be designed to help understand the underlying or core motivation of health workers. The second type of instrument is the motivation survey in which health workers are asked, essentially, what motivates or demotivates them. A third category (which is well covered elsewhere in this book) is the discrete choice surveys where health workers make choices between types of jobs, revealing what is important to them.

Laboratory Experiments

Economic laboratory experiments (lab experiments) attempt to measure the characteristics of individuals or groups by presenting participants with decisions that have real-world consequences, almost always monetary rewards and losses. Frequently these experiments are referred to as "games" by economists, although this is a poor choice of words. Ideally the lab experiment combines the best qualities of a survey and the real world. Decisions made in a lab experiment have real and immediate consequences, unlike survey questions about hypothetical choices or opinions. Moreover, with careful design, the experimenter can get a measure of the preferences of participants that would be very difficult to infer from observing real-world decisions. The two biggest problems with lab experiments are that participants either do not understand the instructions and therefore the consequences of the decisions they are making or the participants feel that they are supposed to be making one particular decision. This means that simple experiments are really the best: the easier it is to explain the decision, the more likely the participant will understand and the less likely the instructions will lead the participant to a particular choice.

One experiment that has been used previously with health workers is the "dictator game." The dictator experiment is poorly named because it measures how generous or fair the participant is to strangers. The reason for the label "dictator" is that the experiment allows one person in a pair to be the dictator: this person chooses how much money each person will receive. This experiment can be used with health workers to see what they do when they can dictate the outcomes that someone else receives, a situation that bears some resemblance to the doctor-patient relationship. Of course, the dictator game is not the same thing as a consultation because there is no interaction between the dictator (doctor) and recipient (patient), but the experiment isolates the "power" portion of the exchange: the doctor makes decisions on the behalf of the patients.

In this experiment, the dictator is given a sum of money and told that he is paired with another individual. He does not know that person and that person does not know him, nor will the identity of either ever be revealed. The only task for the dictator is to allocate the total sum of money between him- or herself and the other person in the pair. True to the term "dictator," the recipient has no choice but to accept what is given. In the purest form of this game, the roles of dictator and recipient are randomly assigned within every pair; thus the dictator knows that only luck puts him or her in the role of determining the outcome, with the power to decide how much money each person should get. Because the recipient never does anything in this game (but must exist for the game to be valid) it is a waste to use health workers as recipients. Thus it makes more sense to have two rooms of people in which all the people in one room are dictators and all the people in the other room are recipients. The recipients can be drawn from the local population, and the experimenter can observe the actions of every health worker in the study.

In most studies with the dictator game, the most common choice for dictators is to keep all of the money. There is no economic reason to give any money away to a stranger you will never see again. The second most common choice is to divide the money in half. Brock, Lange, and Leonard (2016) find that about a third of health workers in their study gave half of the money to the recipient, and that those health workers who chose this allocation provided higher-quality care than all other health workers. They found that there were no significant differences in the allocations of public, charitable, and private sector clinicians. Interestingly, the amount of money given to the partner is not correlated with quality: those who gave just a little are not better than those who gave nothing, and the few participants who give more than half are not better than those who give just half. It seems the key choice is that of choosing fairness, not the choice of deciding how much to give. Thus, current evidence suggests that this experiment yields one useful piece of information: whether the doctor is fair or not fair.

The measure of fairness should be correlated with altruism, but it would be a mistake to say that such a simple experiment can measure altruism. It seems that an altruistic person would be fair (and would give at least half of their tokens away), but there are many other reasons to be fair beyond altruism.

The dictator game can be used to generate measures at the individual level because each participant makes decisions only over his or her own pair. However, the standard setting should involve multiple pairs, in order to maintain the anonymity of pairs: if there is only one dictator and one recipient, there is no anonymity.

Motivation Surveys

Very few studies link motivation to job place environments in developing country health care settings. However, many studies look at the job satisfaction or motivation of health workers, some of which are directly informative of the low levels of performance. For example, Chandler et al. (2009) look at the determinants of low levels of motivation for lower-cadre health workers in Tanzania and find that low salary levels may be one of the most important determinants of low motivation. However, it must be assumed that low levels of motivation is the same thing as low levels of performance, and this link is not established in the paper: there are no measures of performance included. Franco et al. (2004) provide an example of a common research theme in human resources for health research: they show that in three countries, there are strong links between personality types and high levels of motivation. However, in that paper, and all others known in the field, there are no objective measures of performance. Franco et al. (2004) show that certain types of health workers are more likely to say that they are committed to their organization and that they are timely in showing up for work. However, if all the measures in the survey are self-reported, what can be learned from this? It is possible that certain types of doctors believe they are committed, but they may be very different from the types of doctors who actually show up on time and do their jobs to the best of their abilities.

The good news is that as more studies carefully examine performance in the workplace, significantly more about the link between motivation and performance will become evident. Mbindyo et al. (2009) investigate various tools for investigating motivation in a low-resource setting (Kenya). They conclude that a short list of simple questions can provide significant information on the motivation of health workers across a wide variety of settings. Prytherch et al. (2012) test similar instruments and come to a similar conclusion: complexity and nuance are not useful in such surveys. Out of a list of 23 statements (table 8.2), they suggest a reduced list of nine questions in three domains (marked by a plus sign in table 8.2): organizational commitment, job satisfaction, and conscientiousness.

Mbindyo et al. (2009) conclude that the simplified list of questions and resulting domains are useful in explaining performance proxies such as (self-assessed) satisfaction, general motivation, burnout, quality, absenteeism, and turnover.

Recommendations

The three-factor model is designed to highlight weak links in the transmission of structural and human capital inputs to outcomes. Is a particular facility performing poorly because it has insufficient numbers of qualified health workers (low competence and a significant know gap), because these health workers have insufficient access to the tools they need (low capacity and a significant know-can gap), or because the existing health workers are

Table 8.2 Job Satisfaction and Motivation

	Category	Statement	Organizational commitment	Job satisfaction	Conscientiousness
1	General motivation	These days, I feel motivated to work as hard as I can		+	
2		I only do this job so that I get paid at the end of the month *			
3		I do this job as it provides long-term security for me *			
4	Burnout	I feel emotionally drained at the end of every day *			
5		Sometimes when I get up in the morning, I dread having to face another day at work *			
6	Job satisfaction	Overall, I am very satisfied with my job		+	
7		I am not satisfied with my colleagues in my ward *			
8		I am satisfied with my supervisor			
9	Intrinsic job satisfaction	I am satisfied with the opportunity to use my abilities in my job		+	
10		I am satisfied that I accomplish something worthwhile in this job			
11		I do not think that my work in the hospital is valuable these days *			
12	Organizational commitment	I am proud to be working for this hospital	+		
13		I find that my values and this hospital's values are very similar			
14		I am glad that I work for this facility rather than other facilities in the country	+		
15		I feel very little commitment to this hospital *			
16		This hospital really inspires me to do my very best on the job	+		
17	Conscientiousness	I cannot be relied on by my colleagues at work *			
18		I always complete my tasks efficiently and correctly			+
19		I am a hard worker			+
20		I do things that need doing without being asked or told			
21	Timeliness and attendance	I am punctual about coming to work			+
22		I am often absent from work *			
23		It is not a problem if I sometimes come late to work *			

Source: Prytherch et al. 2012.
Note: The plus sign (+) signifies a way to reduce the list of 23 statements to nine questions in three domains: organizational commitment, job satisfaction, and conscientiousness. The asterisk indicates questions for which the positive sense is reversed, for instance, stating that "These days, I feel motived to work as hard as I can" has a positive connotation, but stating "I am not satisfied with my colleagues in my ward" has a negative meaning.

insufficiently motivated to use their knowledge and resources (low performance and a significant can-do gap)? These measures are not simply academic, however: they highlight the ways in which quality can be improved. Is the first priority better trained health workers, better equipped facilities, or improved management practices?

Once the shortfall has been identified, additional analysis remains to find potential solutions to the problem. Based on the existing literature, the following tentative recommendations are advanced. First, where the can-do gap is identified as an important shortfall in a significant number of health workers in a system, collect data using a simplified motivational survey that can be tied to actual levels of performance. Then, using regression analysis, look for association between the quality of care provided and the three domains: organizational commitment, job satisfaction, and conscientiousness. Where statistically significant associations are observed, they suggest sources of low motivation.

The question then is how to determine the source of this low motivation. For this, an analysis of the results from a facility-level survey—such as the one recommended in the World Bank Impact Evaluation Toolkit—should be used.[2]

Notes

1. See Liberia Hospital, "Liberia Hospital Evaluation Instruments," sites.google.com/site /hfqualityassessment.
2. See the World Bank Impact Evaluation Toolkit, http://go.worldbank.org/IT69 C5OGL0.

References

Basinga, P., P. J. Gertler, S. Agnes, and J. Sturdy. 2011. "Effect on Maternal and Child Health Services in Rwanda of Payment to Primary Health-Care Providers for Performance: An Impact Evaluation." *Lancet* 377 (9775): 1421–28.

Bawo, L., K. L. Leonard, and R. Mohammed. 2015. "Protocol for the Evaluation of a Quality-Based Pay for Performance Scheme in Liberia." *Implementation Science* 10 (9).

Brock, J. M., A. Lange, and K. L. Leonard. 2016. "Generosity and Prosocial Behavior in Health Care Provision: Evidence from the Laboratory and Field." *Journal of Human Resources* 51 (1).

Chandler, C. I., S. Chonya, F. Mtei, H. Reyburn, and C. J. Whitty. 2009. "Motivation, Money and Respect: A Mixed-Method Study of Tanzanian Non-Physician Clinicians." *Social Science and Medicine* 68 (11): 2078–88.

Das, J., and P. Gertler. 2007. "Variations in Practice Quality in Five Low-Income Countries: A Conceptual Overview." *Health Affairs* 26 (3): 296–309.

Das, J., and J. Hammer. 2007. "Location, Location, Location: Residence, Wealth and the Quality of Medical Care in Delhi, India." *Health Affairs* 26 (3): 338–51.

Das, J., and T. P. Sohnesen. 2007. "Variations in Doctor Effort: Evidence from Paraguay." *Health Affairs* 26 (3): 324–37.

Franco, L. M., S. Bennett, R. Kanfer, and P. Stubblebine. 2004. "Determinants and Consequences of Health Worker Motivation in Hospitals in Jordan and Georgia." *Social Science and Medicine* 58 (2): 343–55.

Leonard, K. L., and M. C. Masatu. 2006. "Outpatient Process Quality Evaluation and the Hawthorne Effect." *Social Science and Medicine* 63 (9): 2330–40.

———. 2007. "Variation in the Quality of Care Accessible to Rural Communities in Tanzania." *Health Affairs* 26 (3): 380–92.

———. 2010. "Professionalism and the Know-Do Gap: Exploring Intrinsic Motivation among Health Workers in Tanzania." *Health Economics* 19 (12): 1461–77.

Leonard, K. L., M. C. Masatu, and A. Vialou.2007. "Getting Doctors to Do Their Best: The Roles of Ability and Motivation in Health Care." *Journal of Human Resources* 42 (3): 682–700.

Liberia Hospital. N.d. "Liberia Hospital Evaluation Instruments." sites.google.com/site /hfqualityassessment.

Mæstad, O., G.Torsvik, and A. Aakvik. 2010. "Overworked? On the Relationship between Workload and Health Worker Performance." *Journal of Health Economics* 29 (5): 686–98.

Mbindyo, P. M., D. Blaauw, L. Gilson, and M. English. 2009. "Developing a Tool to Measure Health Worker Motivation in District Hospitals in Kenya." *Human Resources for Health* 7 (1): 40.

Prytherch, H., M. Leshabari, C. Wiskow, G. Aninanya, D. Kakoko, M. Kagoné, J. Burghardt, G. Kynast-Wolf, M. Marx, and R. Sauerborn. 2012. "The Challenges of Developing an Instrument to Assess Health Provider Motivation at Primary Care Level in Rural Burkina Faso, Ghana and Tanzania." *Global Health Action* 5 (0).

World Bank. N.d. Impact Evaluation Toolkit. World Bank Washington, DC. http://go .worldbank.org/IT69C5OGL0.

CHAPTER 9

Measuring and Analyzing Salaries and Incentives

Wanda Jaskiewicz, Christophe Lemiere, David Phillips,
Joanne Spetz, and Eric Keuffel

Health Workers' Actual Income

In low-income countries (LICs), health workers in the public sector receive income from various streams of revenue. Some of these revenue streams are official ones, paid by their primary employer (that is, the government); these include a base salary, although—as noted by McCoy et al. (2008)—this component is usually relatively small. The base salary is always supplemented by various cash or in-kind benefits, such as rural allowances or a share of the user fees charged by the facility in which the health worker is employed. But growing evidence indicates that unofficial incomes are a significant source of revenue, and they sometimes account for the majority of the total income of health workers. Compensation is an important factor that significantly contributes to individual utility and motivates participation and effort from health workers, but it is not the only incentive. Status, time (nonwork leisure time) and intrinsic motivation are other factors to consider, but are not the focus of this chapter. This chapter provides an overview of the different types of compensation and details the various instruments and survey techniques that can be used to assess their levels.

Official Income Sources

The four main types of official income[1] are (a) base salaries, (b) cash allowances (for example, allowances for working in rural or remote areas), (c) in-kind benefits (accommodation, vehicles, and so on), and (d) share of user fees.

Adequacy of Official Incomes

Compensation offered to health workers should be compared to one or more benchmarks to determine whether it is adequate. If health care jobs do not offer sufficient compensation to allow health workers to support themselves and their families, then the health worker supply is likely to be diminished because these workers will seek other employment that will provide better earnings.

http://dx.doi.org/10.1596/978-1-4648-0931-6

Figure 9.1 Common Forms of Individual Incentives and Compensation for Public Sector Health Workers in Low-Income Countries

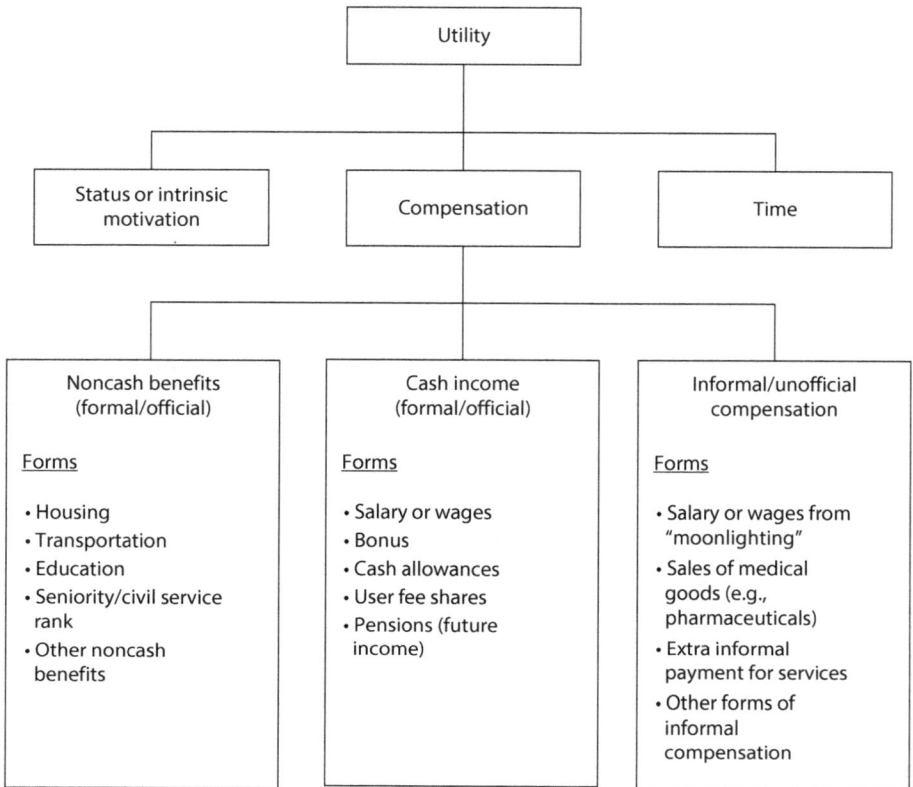

In the government sector, a first—and essential—benchmark is the *income earned by comparable health workers (those who have the same education and experience) in the private sector.* Data on the income earned through moonlighting strongly suggest that government health workers strive to earn moonlighting income so that their total income (official income plus moonlighting income) will match the income of private health workers.[2] For instance, a recent survey in Cambodia found that "total public sector income for experienced doctors and specialists (including incentives and dual practice) is essentially equal to private sector compensation" (World Bank 2013). Similar patterns have been observed in several other LICs. Having some estimates of income earned by private health workers is therefore essential for assessing the adequacy of government compensation levels.

This private sector income benchmark has an important implication. It is likely that health workers do not want to work in rural areas not only because the cost of living there can be higher,[3] but also because the opportunities for dual practice (that is, the chance to earn additional income by moonlighting) are much scarcer. Indeed, it appears that the fewer opportunities health workers have to establish a dual practice, the more likely they are to accept employment in a rural area. Indeed, a large number of studies (for example, Lemiere et al. 2013; Soucat, Scheffler, and Ghebreyesus 2013) find that nurses, midwives, and young doctors were more prone to move to a rural area than experienced doctors (especially specialists). In some countries, such as the Lao People's Democratic Republic, the greater likelihood of rural entry by young cohorts may be a result of either rural service mandates for new health workers or other inducements, such as offers of accelerated civil service status or other noncash incentives (Jaskiewicz et al. 2012; Keuffel et al. 2013). There seems to be an almost perfect negative correlation between the ability to have a dual practice and the willingness to work in a rural area. Consequently it is likely that, to be effective, a rural allowance will have to be set at a level that at least makes up for the foregone dual practice income.

Although other benchmarks are less important, they still deserve some attention. In the public sector, health workers also compare their official incomes to those of their colleagues, with the expectation that a worker with more experience, a higher level of education, or a wider scope of responsibility will earn more. This benchmark suggests the concept of *salary compression*. There is indeed salary compression when salaries are not well differentiated across experience (that is, seniority), education, and responsibility level. This is unfortunately a frequent situation in many LICs. For instance, in Zambia, McCoy et al. (2008) report that the wage ratio between the most qualified and the least qualified health workers fell from 19 to 1 in 1970 to 7 to 1 in 1983. A similar wage compression ratio (between 7 to 1 and 6 to 1) is found in a 2011 study in Nigeria (Akwataghibe et al. 2013). This wage compression phenomenon is explained by the policies triggered by the so-called structural adjustments—the various budget austerity policies implemented by LIC governments in the 1980s and supported by the International Monetary Fund and the World Bank. However, more analysis is needed to definitely attribute wage compression to these policies because, although LIC governments usually froze civil servants' wages and promotions in the 1970s and 1980s, they also introduced various incentives and benefits that may reduce total (official) incomes' compression.[4]

Importance of Assessing Marginal Costs and Benefits

Health workers not only decide whether and where to work in a health job but also decide how much to work. This decision is based on their assessment of the marginal benefit of additional hours of work versus the marginal cost of work, meaning that the value of working one additional hour must be greater than the opportunity cost of that additional hour of work.[5] The opportunity cost can include the personal value of time with family or enjoying leisure pursuits; income that could have been earned from an alternative second job; or any other activity. In general, as the amount of time spent working increases, the compensation for work is less likely to be greater than the opportunity cost of that time. To increase labor supply, it might be less expensive to try to increase the number of people working than to increase the hours that each person works (although it would be important to factor in the additional training costs to supply more workers, particularly if there is a current shortage of health workers) (Preker, Keuffel, and Tuckman 2009). An assessment of the likely marginal benefits versus the marginal cost of work for the health workforce should be part of the overall assessment of whether compensation is adequate.

Health Workers' Perceptions of Compensation Levels

Health workers in many developing countries generally perceive their salaries in the government sector to be low and list remuneration as a particularly demotivating factor in their jobs (Willis-Shattuck et al. 2008). A study of Ugandan health workers demonstrates that only 11 percent of those surveyed felt their salary package was fair (Hagopian et al. 2009). Another study carried out in Uganda among government and faith-based, private not-for-profit health workers finds that the majority believed their pay was insufficient for their family's needs, although about 25 percent more government health workers (89 percent) were dissatisfied with their compensation than the private not-for-profit health workers (65.7 percent) (Ogrodnick et al. 2011). The results from a study of Tanzanian nonphysician clinicians illustrate the need to satisfy salary requirements (Chandler et al. 2009).

As these and many other studies show, a strong correlation is often evident between remuneration and job satisfaction of health workers (Delobelle et al. 2011; Hayes, Bonner, and Pryor 2010). Because job satisfaction is often linked to motivation, retention, and quality of service provision, understanding health workers' perceptions of their salaries, benefits, and other incentives should be an essential component of any survey of health worker compensation. Where compensation and incentive policies cannot be adjusted, efforts should be made to increase nonmonetary factors, which are equally, if not more, important (Mathauer and Imhoff 2006). An unsatisfactory work environment can exacerbate dissatisfaction with compensation; for example, in the Russian Federation, nurses do not have the respect or autonomy that is associated with professional satisfaction; when combined with low salaries, this has led many Russian nurses to seek other work (Difazio, Lang, and Boykova 2004).

When looking at geographic maldistribution and the need to increase health worker recruitment and retention in rural and remote areas, the issue of compensation becomes even more pressing. Recent studies have highlighted the importance of providing an appropriate salary to attract health workers to underserved areas (Bärnighausen and Bloom 2009; McCoy et al. 2008; Rockers et al. 2012; Willis-Shattuck et al. 2008). Salary, however, is only one of many factors that health workers consider when making choices about where to work (Blaauw et al. 2010; Dambisya 2007; Kruk et al. 2010; Rockers et al. 2013). A discrete choice experiment (DCE) can assist in identifying health workers' motivational preferences and determining appropriate incentive packages that will attract and retain health workers in rural and underserved areas.

Health workers in the public sector may have set beliefs about how much they make in comparison to others with similar jobs in other health care settings, such as the private not-for-profit sector (which includes faith-based and other nongovernmental organizations [NGOs]) and the private for-profit sector. Although they may not know exactly how much others make, they may have a reasonably strong signal regarding incomes and other desirable benefits or incentives across sectors. They may also compare their compensation with civil servants outside health care who have similar years of education and training, level of job complexity, and job importance, and thus feel they should be earning the same or higher levels of pay. Information on health worker perceptions about the adequacy of pay relative to other sectors is important not only because it speaks to job satisfaction but also because variances in salary and benefits can result in internal migration between the public and private (both not-for-profit and for-profit) health sectors. As a result, when measuring and analyzing salaries and incentives, it is recommended that questions on health worker perceptions of compensatory comparisons between sectors be included in any study on compensation. Workers' responses will help determine both whether any notions are misconceived and can be adjusted and, if their perceptions are accurate, what financial or nonfinancial incentive policies can be implemented to make switching out of public sector employment less attractive.

Regularity of Official Incomes

In addition to the basic issue of the adequacy of base salary, the process related to salary payment and incentives can negatively affect health worker motivation. The majority of health workers from faith-based health facilities surveyed in Uganda, for example, state that late salary payment was a key contributor to their dissatisfaction in the workplace (Ogrodnick et al. 2011). When health workers do not receive their salaries and incentives in a timely and consistent manner, their generally low levels of pay become an even more critical issue because they are not likely to have large savings reserves on which to rely while they wait for payment to be made. Deussom et al. find that "[i]n some countries, a health worker's first paycheck may take up to six months to process, which could incentivize the health worker to take on other jobs to cover living expenses in the meantime" (2012, 3).

Some payment processes may be so inefficient that they not only lead to an individual's dissatisfaction but also to a reduction in health workforce productivity, because health workers need to make numerous trips to the bank to check on receipt of salary payment. One study finds that "[i]neffective payroll mechanisms force health workers to travel long distances to receive their paychecks" (Deussom et al. 2012, 3). A productivity study in Zanzibar finds that the time health workers spent in collecting their salary from a central facility, such as a district hospital, increased their time away from their work in the clinic (Hassett 2009).

Health Labor Market Analyses in Low- and Middle-Income Countries
http://dx.doi.org/10.1596/978-1-4648-0931-6

Another important point beyond the actual salary amount received as compensation for working in rural and remote areas is the consistent management of the payment of the retention incentives. An effective human resource management system should have clear indicators of which health workers should receive the rural incentive packages and any corresponding percentages for allowances that may apply based on the ruralness of their location. Likewise, when a health worker changes employment from a remote or rural area to an urban or peri-urban area, implementation of any rural incentive scheme should cease or be adjusted to match the reduced percentage of benefits as designated for the area. Unfortunately this is not always the case: poor tracking and management systems can lead to ineffective policies for compensating staff working in rural and remote areas as well as demotivation among health workers.

For these reasons, when surveying health workers regarding their compensation it is important to include questions regarding the management of the payment of salaries and incentives to determine whether any improvements may be needed.

Unofficial Incomes of Health Workers and Their Side Effects

From the literature, four main types of unofficial incomes for health workers can be identified:

- Per diem payments
- Revenue from moonlighting
- Income from sale of medical products and drug pilfering
- Informal payments

Per Diem Payments

Per diems, or travel and training allowances,[6] consist of money received for attending training sessions (organized by the government or by donors). Per diems are intended to pay for the travel, accommodation, and food costs incurred by participants. However, per diems are usually paid as a lump sum, which allows participants to make a small profit. Note that per diem income is legal income.

Although quantitative data on per diems remain scarce, it is clear that this compensation can be a very significant source of income for health workers. The revenue from this income stream is sometimes measured in general surveys on the earnings of health workers (see, for instance, McCoy et al. 2008), though the results may show, as for example in Ghana and Burkina Faso, that per diems are a rather small portion—usually less than 10 percent—of total revenues. Studies that focus explicitly on per diems, however, provide a very different picture. For instance, Ensor, Chapman, and Barro (2006) find that per diem revenue in Burkina Faso exceeds the salaries of health workers. Similarly, Kanakin, Kessou, and Koutchikap (2008) find that in Benin, per diems could account for the equivalent of six months of salary. In Tanzania, a civil servant going on a four-day workshop can earn the equivalent of a month's salary (Jansen 2009). A five-day overseas trip easily doubles a health worker's monthly salary (Søreide, Tostensen, and Skage 2012).

There are numerous negative side effects associated with per diems accounting for a large portion of income. The first and most obvious problem is that it creates a powerful incentive to attend training sessions instead of working with patients. In other words, per diems lead to increased absenteeism of clinical staff. For instance, in Mali, it was found that regional health staff members spend 34 percent of their total working time in income-generating workshops and supervision missions supported by international agencies. For chief medical officers, this is 48 percent of their time (El Abassi and Van Lerberghe 1995 unpublished data, cited in Ferrinho et al. 2004b and Macq et al. 2001).

A more subtle consequence is that per diems strengthen the discretionary power of supervisors and reinforce the culture of corruption, clientelism, and bad governance in health facilities. With per diems, training sessions are viewed more as income-generating activities than as opportunities to improve knowledge and skills. To attend a training session, every health worker must obtain the approval of his or her supervisor. Needless to say, many supervisors attend the training sessions themselves, ask for a percentage of the per diems earned by their subordinates, or select the health workers they like rather than the ones who most need training (Jansen 2009; Policy Forum 2009; Vian 2009). As mentioned by Soreide, Tostensen, and Skage (2012), this is a way of "buying loyalty." A consequence is that "per diems do not even go to the front line staff. In Tanzania, indicative of many allowances being remunerative rather than duty enhancing is the observation that while the majority (approximately 70 percent) of civil servants work as teachers and nurses in front line service delivery activities, the bulk of allowances (70 percent) accrues to the 30 percent of civil servants working at Central Government" (Policy Forum 2009, 3).

Per diems are also very costly. An estimate from Tanzania (reported by Chêne 2009) finds that, for the entire government, per diems account for about $400 million. This huge amount could be used for more effective objectives. Similarly, in Malawi, "as a proportion of salaries the payment of allowances in general accounted for 29 percent, while travel-related allowances specifically accounted for 21.9 percent of salaries" (Soreide, Tostensen, and Skage 2012, 41).

Finally, per diems may undermine the intrinsic motivation of health workers (Ridde 2010). When per diems are often paid, it is difficult to ask health workers to carry out normal tasks (for instance, vaccinations) without paying them a per diem or a "top-up."

Revenue from Moonlighting

Moonlighting consists in having a second job. Having a second job can be legal (as in Nigeria or Central African Republic) or not (as in many other countries). It is usually a clinical job, but it can also be as teacher or consultant, or even a job outside the health sector, such as in agriculture.

The little data available strongly suggest that moonlighting is highly prevalent in Africa, at least among doctors. For instance, in a small sample of

Portuguese-speaking doctors (mostly from Angola and Guinea-Bissau), Ferrinho et al. (1998) find that 68 percent of urban doctors (and 53 percent of rural ones) report having a second job. On average, they indicate that the income from this second job accounts for about 58 percent of their total income (65 percent for urban doctors). With a sample of health workers from various African countries, Roenen et al. (1997) find even higher estimates, with private jobs generating from 4 times to 10 times more money than the official salary. With an even wider sample, Macq and Van Lerberghe (2000, 176) estimate that second jobs generate "an income that is 2.4 times the civil servant salary for the same amount of time." The phenomenon of holding a second job has also been documented as common among nurses in Latin America (Malvarez and Agudelo 2005) and Asia (Ding and Tian 2008).

Income from Sale of Medical Products and Drug Pilfering

In some health systems, it is customary and legal for physicians to sell medical supplies and pharmaceuticals. Policies that endorse legal sale of complementary medicines may require additional regulation to limit incentives to sell unnecessary products, but also are another potential source of alternative private income that can help relieve pressure on public sources to fully fund physicians—particularly as pharmaceutical spending shares tend to be a proportionately larger share of total health expenditures in LICs.

Drug pilfering is common as well, but this unofficial revenue stream is poorly understood. The term *drug pilfering* encompasses all practices involving the theft and sale of drugs from health facilities. The few studies on drug pilfering (Ferrinho et al. 2004a; McPake et al. 2000; van der Geest 1982) clearly confirm that the practice is widespread. McPake et al. (2000) carry out the only study striving to estimate the amount of revenue earned through drug pilfering. With an astute combination of various survey techniques, they find that, after moonlighting, drug pilfering is the most important source of unofficial revenues. On average, drug pilfering revenues are several times higher than base salaries.

Informal Payments

Here *informal payments* is understood in a rather narrow sense.[7] Informal payments are payments made in excess of official fees to public sector health workers for a service delivered within a public sector facility. Consequently, as used here the term excludes both drug pilfering (which is not a service) and moonlighting (which does not happen in a public sector facility). Unfortunately, many researchers have used a broad (and sometimes rather vague) definition of illegal payments, which usually includes drug pilfering and moonlighting, thus making it difficult to differentiate the extent of income specifically from informal payments or gifts asked of patients.

A recent study in Nigeria provides a nice illustration of the prevalence of informal payments and an effective methodology to assess the degree of informal payment. Onwujekwe et al. (2010) have triangulated the costs, revenues, and provider profit margin of malaria care using (a) a household survey, (b) a patient exit survey, and (c) a provider survey. As presented by the authors,

> The findings show that the average expenditure to treat malaria from the consumers' perspectives was very similar at $6.30 and $6.40 from exit poll and household survey respectively.... However, they differed significantly from the prices from the providers' perspectives, which was only $2.20 per treatment for malaria. The magnitude of possible informal payment ranged from $4.10 to $4.20 per episode of malaria and was highest in public hospitals (Onwujekwe et al. 2010, 77).

As the preceding example reflects, physicians possess significant market power to extract additional profits from patients from the sale of either services or complementary products. Policy makers should focus on (a) to what extent this capacity should be regulated, limited, or eliminated and (b) the optimal mechanisms that can be used to regulate the additional income streams from either goods or services.

Methods for Measuring Official Income

Although in some cultures the concept of salaries and open discussion about them can be somewhat sensitive, the overall sensitivity of measuring the official incomes of health workers may depend on the context. For example, surveying government health workers regarding the salary and incentives they receive is often less problematic because public sector employees are paid according to established civil service scales and identified benefits or incentives (housing, transport, hardship allowance, and so on). Private sector health workers may be somewhat more reticent in revealing their earnings, especially if they also work in the public sector (see "Methods for Measuring Unofficial Income" for suggestions of sensitive survey techniques). Furthermore, for-profit organizations may not permit researchers to survey their employees to avoid revealing business practices in a competitive private sector environment. Similarly, but probably for different reasons, access to health workers in the not-for-profit private sector (that is, faith-based organizations and other health care NGOs) to measure their income levels may vary depending on the organization's relationship with the government, any harmonization of pay scales or receipt of salary subsidies from the government, and the competitiveness of the environment.[8] Methods for obtaining information about official incomes include surveying health workers directly and using administrative data from government agencies.

Ways of Surveying Health Workers Directly

A number of survey tools have been used to ask health workers direct questions about the salaries and incentives they receive. Most are study-specific and the questionnaires are not usually widely shared because they are not generally included in the technical reports and journal articles describing the results of compensation studies. Possible questions, along with their specific wording, are provided in this chapter, by type of information sought. If used, they should be adapted to the specific context and research questions. The sample questions throughout this chapter are excerpted or adapted from a health worker compensation survey questionnaire drafted by the World Bank and the global United States Agency for International Development projects Health Systems 20/20 (led by Abt Associates) and Capacity*Plus* (led by IntraHealth International) and the Health Worker Incentives Survey (HWIS), Module 4, Tool 5 of the *Impact Toolkit: A Guide and Tools for Maternal Mortality Programme Assessment.*

Many of the questions are quite straightforward. It may be more appropriate to ask questions about the specific monetary value of wages, benefits, and incentives in one-on-one interviews with a health worker. Other questions regarding health worker perceptions of the adequacy of compensation, human resource management practices in relation to payment, and other such general areas may be acceptable for focus group discussion. Note that these questions were embedded within a broader quantitative or qualitative questionnaire with numerous questions on other factors related to compensation in the health sector.

Salary

Information on a health worker's specific salary can be measured by asking the respondent directly in a one-on-one interview what salary amount she or he receives, as well as how it correlates with the government's pay scale. Various questions to elicit this information include the following:

1. In which salary level of the government pay scale are you now?
2. What is your current gross salary per month?
3. How much do you earn each month in basic salary from your official job?
4. Has your salary changed over the past two years? If so, how much has it changed?
5. What has been the average yearly percent increase in your overall compensation, including salary, allowances, and bonuses, over the last two to three years?

It may also be useful to add other questions that establish a health worker's seniority and level of qualification or additional degrees, as well as years in service, to determine whether the salary figure and level correlate.

Benefits and Incentives

To obtain information on the official benefits and incentives, again direct questions can be asked of health workers in one-on-one interviews (table 9.1). It is helpful to read aloud all the response options to capture all possible incentives since, in a free-form question, respondents may not recall all the benefits they receive or may not consider them benefits per se. The response options should be adapted to the local context. Because some health workers may not know the exact value amounts of benefits and incentives they receive in addition to their base salary, it may also be useful to request to see their

Table 9.1 Sample Survey Question to Determine Benefits and Incentives

Do you receive any of the following benefits or incentives? [*Read options aloud*]

a. Full housing	☐Yes	☐No	_____ bedrooms
b. Housing allowance	☐Yes	☐No	_____ [local currency] per month
c. Vehicle	☐Yes	☐No	
d. Transport allowance	☐Yes	☐No	_____ [local currency] per month
e. Medical coverage	☐Yes	☐No	
f. Medical allowance	☐Yes	☐No	_____ [local currency] per month
g. Tuition support	☐Yes	☐No	_____ [local currency] per semester
h. Leave with pay	☐Yes	☐No	_____ Days per year
i. Paid sick leave	☐Yes	☐No	_____ Days per year
j. Paid education leave	☐Yes	☐No	_____ Days per year
k. Rural hardship	☐Yes	☐No	_____ [local currency] per month
l. Additional duty hours	☐Yes	☐No	_____ [local currency] per month allowance
m. Lunch allowance	☐Yes	☐No	_____ [local currency] per month
n. Other (specify: _____)	☐Yes	_____ [local currency] per _____ (time period)	
o. Other (specify: _____)	☐Yes	_____ [local currency] per _____ (time period)	

Source: Drafted by Capacity*Plus*, Health Systems 20/20, and World Bank.

pay stub or obtain a list of the included benefits by health facility, province, position, cadre, or grade, depending on what basis any benefits or incentives may differ.

The sample question in table 9.1 provides an extensive list of possible benefits and incentives that can be adapted to reflect the available options provided by the employer.

Salary Payment Process

Not only is the value of compensation received important but also the way the process of salary and incentive payment is handled is critical. The following series of questions can help assess whether payments are timely, consistent, and as convenient as possible:

1. Do you always receive your salary on time?
2. [*If no*] How frequently do you receive your salary late?
3. When your salary is late, on average how late is it?
4. Where do you typically receive your salary?
5. Do you sometimes have to go to the capital or elsewhere to resolve a salary issue?
6. [*If yes*] On average, how many days per year are you away from your work to resolve these salary issues?

Performance-Based Incentives

Increasing numbers of countries are implementing results-based financing or performance-based incentive approaches to increase performance, productivity,

Health Labor Market Analyses in Low- and Middle-Income Countries
http://dx.doi.org/10.1596/978-1-4648-0931-6

and quality of health service provision. To assess earnings from this type of arrangement, the following questions can be used:

1. Can you earn a financial bonus from your facility based on performance (at the individual, team, or facility level)?
2. On average, how much do you earn in performance-based incentives?
3. Does your financial bonus depend on the number of patients you treat?
4. Does your financial bonus depend on the quality of services you provide?

User Fees

In some countries a portion of the fees that users pay to access health services may be used to provide incentives to health workers in the facility. The following questions may be helpful in obtaining further information on how this practice adds to a health worker's compensation:

1. Do you receive a share of user fees collected by the facility?
2. On average, how much do you earn from user fees per month?
3. Is approval required from an authority to receive a portion of user fees?
4. How is money from user fees allocated among the workers at the facility? Everyone receives the same amount
   - Allocation is based on individual salaries or salary scales
   - Allocation is based on job title/seniority
   - Other (*Specify:* _____)

Determining Appropriate Incentive Packages for Rural Recruitment and Retention

To determine the most appropriate combinations of incentives to attract and retain health workers in rural and other underserved areas of a country, it can be useful to conduct a DCE. This survey research methodology measures the strength of health workers' motivational preferences and trade-offs related to different job characteristics that can influence the decision to take up rural postings.

Two recent resources to guide users in conducting a DCE:

- *How to Conduct a Discrete Choice Experiment for Health Workforce Recruitment and Retention in Remote and Rural Areas: A User Guide with Case Studies*, developed by WHO, the World Bank, and Capacity*Plus*.[9]
- *Rapid Retention Survey Toolkit: Designing Evidence-Based Incentives for Health Workers*, developed by Capacity*Plus*.[10]

A companion resource to the DCE is the iHRIS Retain software program, developed by Capacity*Plus* and WHO.[11] The open source software provides a step-by-step tool to assist users to cost the incentive packages resulting from a DCE, as well as other recruitment and retention strategies.

Perceptions of the Adequacy of Compensation

Inevitably, in any survey or even conversation on compensation, health workers will naturally share their feelings and perceptions of whether they feel their pay is adequate and fair. It is thus useful to embed focused questions and allow for more in-depth qualitative questioning to better understand health workers' views about their salaries and benefits and how they correlate with similar jobs in other sectors.

To assess health worker perceptions of the adequacy of their compensation, the following questions can be used:

1. How satisfied are you with the overall compensation you receive, including salary, allowances, and bonuses, for your work at this facility?
2. How much do you think you SHOULD receive as monthly compensation, including salary, allowances, and bonuses, for your work at this facility?

Another way to assess adequacy of compensation is through a better understanding of how health workers' household income compares to household expenditures. It may also be helpful to look at how health workers view their overall economic status within their general community; the following questions can be used:

1. How much do you earn as a proportion of the total income of your household?
2. What was your total household expenditure last month? *(This can be broken down to obtain values by category—for example, food, rent, education, or transport.)*
3. What would you estimate to be the economic status of your household compared to others in your community?
   - Among the highest
   - Above average
   - Average
   - Below average
   - Among the lowest

To determine how health workers in the public sector feel their compensation compares to earnings in other health sectors (that is, private not-for-profit and private for-profit), consider applying the following question. (Such information can be useful to determine if public health workers have misconceptions of the adequacy of their own earnings compared with their opinion—correct or incorrect—of what those working in the private sector actually earn.)

1. If you had a similar job in a different setting, how much do you think you COULD earn? Please estimate what you think your total monthly

Health Labor Market Analyses in Low- and Middle-Income Countries
http://dx.doi.org/10.1596/978-1-4648-0931-6

compensation would be, including salary, allowances, and bonuses, if you worked in a facility managed by the following organizations:
- Faith-based organization _____ [local currency]
- NGO (not faith-based) _____ [local currency]
- Private for-profit _____ [local currency]

Perceptions of the Fairness of Compensation

Another issue to explore with health workers is their perception of fair compensation. "A system of fair pay is important for maintenance of morale and quality and for reduction of attrition," as McCoy et al. (2008, 680) note. In a study of public sector and faith-based facility health workers in Uganda, almost half of both types of respondents (45.1 percent and 42.1 percent, respectively) feel that they do not receive fair compensation compared with others performing similar work (Ogrodnick et al. 2011).[12]

Sample qualitative questions that can be used to help determine perceptions of fairness:

1. How fair do you think your current compensation package is? Why?
2. How would you define the concept of fair compensation? What does " fair" mean to you?
3. What should you be able to afford with a fair level of compensation?
4. Which nonhealth government professionals do you think compare to your position in terms of education level and other job requirements, and why?
5. Do you consider the compensation levels received by you and the nonhealth government professionals you mentioned to be mostly the same?
6. [If no] which of the mentioned cadres compensation levels are not the same and why?

Ways of Using Administrative Data from Government Agencies

Most government agencies collect a variety of data that can be used to measure the earnings of health workers and other workers. Some of these data sources are not intended to be used to assess compensation, but may nevertheless be suited to some types of analyses. Some of the types of data that can be accessed include:

- *Payroll data from agencies that directly employ health workers.* In many countries, one or more government agencies are the primary employers of health workers. In some cases, these agencies compensate health workers using a shared pay structure, but in other cases each agency has a unique compensation system. Local government agencies, such as provincial health authorities, also may have their own compensation systems. Data from these agencies are usually available to measure and analyze compensation. These will naturally reflect wage data primarily and other forms of compensation may not be accessible via these systems.

- *Income tax data.* National and local governments often enact an income tax to generate revenue to fund government programs. Workers must thus report their income to the government as part of fulfilling their tax payment obligation. It is rare for a government agency to grant access to individual-level data from these tax payment records, but in some cases the tax-collecting agency might aggregate data by occupation or region to support the analysis of health worker earnings.

- *Payroll tax data.* Some countries require that employers pay taxes to support general government programs or specific programs such as national pensions, unemployment insurance, or disability insurance. If such taxes are collected, they are usually accompanied by detailed reports on the earnings of workers for each employer. These reports often can be tabulated by industry and sometimes by occupation. As with income tax data, it is rare for individual-level data to be released, but some government agencies will collaborate to support the analysis of compensation patterns.

- *Census data.* Many nations conduct a census of the population on a regular schedule, often every 5 to 10 years. Census surveys may include questions about employment and earnings; sometimes these types of questions are distributed to a subset of the population rather than all census respondents.

- *Population surveys.* National and local governments sometimes conduct surveys of samples of their populations. These surveys can focus on a variety of issues and often include questions about employment and earnings. These surveys may have complex sampling schemes, and care must be taken to apply appropriate statistical methods to ensure the data represent the full population.

- *Occupation surveys.* Surveys can focus on people who have been trained in a specific occupation. These surveys often use a sample drawn from licensing or graduation records. Some agencies routinely survey all licensed professionals, asking a few selected questions; such data might include compensation information. Other agencies conduct surveys of a sample subset, selecting a subset of those licensed or educated in a particular occupation; such surveys are often more comprehensive and usually include information about wages and benefits from employment.

Methods for Measuring Unofficial Income

Revenue derived from unofficial sources such as moonlighting, pilfering and selling drugs, and charging additional user fees may compose a large fraction of health workers' total income. Because of the unofficial nature of these sources, health workers may have an incentive to underreport such income. Additional tools may therefore be needed to properly measure the unofficial income of health workers. This section discusses five different measurement methods and their relative advantages and disadvantages: direct health worker surveys, sensitive survey techniques, patient surveys, administrative records, and direct observation.

Direct Health Worker Surveys

Direct questioning is the simplest way to measure income from unofficial sources. Some examples of possible questions from which researchers can choose[13] are presented by unofficial income type:

Per Diem Payments
1. Do you receive per diems for participating in trainings, workshops, or other events?
2. *[If yes]* On average, how much do you earn per year through per diems?
3. *[If yes]* How many days per year, on average, do you receive per diem?

Moonlighting
1. Do you earn income from a private practice?
2. *[If yes]* How much money do you earn per month, on average, from this private practice?
3. Do you carry out any other activities outside your official job to generate income (for example, nonmedical activities, such as trading or farming)?
4. *[If yes]* How much do you earn from these income-generating activities, on average, in a month?
5. In addition to your role at this facility, do you conduct paid work elsewhere or collect income from any other activities or businesses?
6. *[If yes]* What types of additional earning opportunities do you engage in?
   - Private practice, part-time after normal working hours
   - Private practice, part-time during working hours
   - Private practice, on-call service
   - Private not-for-profit facility, after normal working hours
   - Private not-for-profit facility, during working hours
   - Private not-for-profit facility, on-call service
   - Nonclinical business, such as agriculture, trade, or other income-generating activities
   - Other *(Specify)*:_____
7. On average, how many hours per week do you spend working on these additional earning arrangements?
8. How much do you earn, on average, per month from these additional arrangements?
9. Of the total monthly earnings you receive from all sources, what percentage comes from these additional arrangements?

10. What are the primary reasons that you engage in the additional income earning activities?
    - Compensation for work at this facility is not adequate
    - To improve professional skills and abilities
    - To pay for additional goods or services for my family
    - To increase personal savings
    - Other (*Specify*):_____

Sale of Medicines and Drug Pilfering[14]

1. Do you sometimes sell your own drugs directly to your patients?
2. *[If yes]* How do you obtain these drugs?
3. *[If yes]* On average, how much do you earn per month by selling these drugs?

Informal Payments

1. Do you usually receive gifts from patients? Gifts may include food, clothes, animals, and so on.
2. *[If yes]* Please list any gifts received during the previous month.
3. *[If yes]* What is the estimated value of these gifts in your view?[14]

Such questions measure health workers' self-reported participation in unofficial income-generating activities and can be tailored to include not only moonlighting but also selling drugs, charging illegal user fees, and so on. Focus group discussions may ask similar qualitative questions (see, for example, Garbarino et al. 2007). However, in both surveys and focus groups health workers may be reticent to report participation in disallowed activities candidly, so direct questioning will probably lead to inaccurate results. Indirect questions, which ask health workers about others rather than themselves, may also be used to get a general estimate or sense of the trends in unofficial income generation. For example:

1. What forms of additional earning opportunities do you think are most common among your cadre?
2. What percentage of your cadre do you think have additional earning arrangements?
3. What percentage, of their monthly income (from all sources), would you estimate comes from these additional earning arrangements?
4. Do you know colleagues who earn money by selling drugs?
5. *[If yes]* How much do you think they earn selling drugs per month on average?[15]

Sensitive Survey Techniques

Because direct questioning can elicit unreliable results, sensitive survey techniques have been developed to encourage candid answers even when respondents may be reluctant to answer a direct question honestly because

Health Labor Market Analyses in Low- and Middle-Income Countries
http://dx.doi.org/10.1596/978-1-4648-0931-6

of its sensitive nature. Various techniques exist, although they all pursue two goals:

- To obscure the respondent's true answer from being known, even by the interviewer
- To allow the calculation of participation in the sensitive activity *in the aggregate*

Randomized Response Technique

The *randomized response technique* (RRT) was introduced by Warner (1965). This method obscures individual responses via randomness. For instance, consider the instructions from Akwataghibe (2012):

1. After reading each statement, toss a coin. Do not show the result to me.
2. If you get heads, tick the YES box irrespective of what your actual answer is.
3. If you get tails, answer the question honestly by ticking YES or NO.

Then respondents are presented with a series of statements. One example is, "I make more money from my supplementary sources (for example, private practice) than from my salary." The method obscures an individual's true answer to the statement. If the respondent checks "Yes" it is because either that respondent earns outside income or because the coin toss showed "Heads." The interviewer does not know which of these precipitated the "Yes" response, thus providing assurance of confidentiality even beyond the standard interviewer's promise. Although the individual's response is obscured, the researcher can still calculate aggregate participation in the activity at the aggregate level using simple probability calculations. The details of this calculation are provided in box 9.1. It can be shown that:

$$\Pr[Statement\ True] = 2 * \Pr[Yes] - 1 \text{ where Pr is Probability.} \quad (9.1)$$

Inserting the fraction of those surveyed who respond "yes" into equation 9.1 will calculate the fraction of the population for whom the sensitive statement is true. In the preceding example, this would provide the fraction of health workers who earn more income from private practice than from their official salary.

Box 9.1 Randomized Response Technique Calculations

If respondents follow the directions correctly, it must be true that:

$$\Pr[Yes] = \Pr[Heads] + \Pr[Tails] * \Pr[Statement\ True]$$

If the probability of "heads" is ½, rearranging will show that:

$$\Pr[Statement\ True] = 2 * \Pr[Yes] - 1$$

In its standard use, the technique in equation 9.1 represents an improvement over direct questioning to the extent that respondents are willing to respond to the RRT question more candidly than to a direct question. In a meta-analysis, Lensvelt-Mulders et al. (2005) find that RRT increases candid responses to questions about sensitive behavior. However, this original use of RRT does have some drawbacks.

First, implementation can be difficult. Instructions with multiple stages can be difficult to follow, leading to respondent errors. Second, recent studies indicate that respondents are probably still quite reticent when asked sensitive questions using RRT. Azfar and Murrell (2009) use statistically unlikely answer patterns to estimate that at least 35 percent of respondents to a corruption survey do not respond honestly, even when using RRT. Similarly, Akwataghibe et al. (2013) argue that the responses of 58 percent of health workers in their survey were unlikely to have responded candidly.[16]

RRT can still be useful in the following instances, though. As shown in Azfar and Murrell (2009), RRT can be used to identify reticent respondents by looking for statistically unlikely responses. For instance, an individual following the randomized response directions closely will be very unlikely to answer "no" to every question in a series of 10 questions. Even if they participate in none of these activities, they should occasionally flip heads and thus answer "yes."

Following Azfar and Murrell (2009), it is then possible to identify individuals whose responses indicate that they are reticent—for instance, those who answer 9 or more out of 10 questions as "no." These individuals can then be excluded when analyzing responses to questions posed in the direct survey. Akwataghibe et al. (2013) provide an example of this in the context of two Nigerian states.

Item Count Technique

An alternative to RRT is the *item count technique* (ICT), which is also referred to as *unmatched count technique* or *list randomization*.[17] This method obscures individual response by asking the subject to respond to a list of questions all at once. As with RRT, the ICT method provides individual-level confidentiality while maintaining the ability to calculate participation in sensitive behaviors for the whole sample. The details of ICT are not further discussed here. Chapter 10 discusses the detailed application of the ICT method in a health worker survey in Liberia.

ICT is used in many fields outside the health sector and has been shown to encourage candid responses on a number of issues. For instance, Karlan and Zinman (2012) find that ICT leads to higher measured rates of the misuse of microfinance loans. Similarly, Holbrook and Krosnick (2010) find that ICT leads to less overreporting of socially encouraged voting behavior. Additionally, surveyors often find that ICT is easier to implement in practice than other sensitive techniques, such as RRT (Droitcour et al. 1991).

To date, ICT has not seen extensive use in measuring unofficial incomes of health workers. The only known completed applications of this method to the health field are those of Lemiere and Juquois (2010), who apply ICT to the question of hours in private practice; and Phillips (2012), who apply ICT to drug pilfering, private practice, and informal side payments in Liberia, as described in chapter 10. These two studies provide examples of how to apply ICT to the context of human resources in health; however, they also highlight the heavy data requirements of the technique. A small sample size prevents Lemiere and Juquois (2010) from reaching strong conclusions. Chapter 10 suggests that ICT requires a significant time commitment on the part of those being surveyed, and that pairing ICT with other lengthy survey components can lead to uncertain results.

Technical Considerations for Sensitive Survey Techniques

A few technical considerations should be kept in mind when designing a survey that includes an ICT or RRT component.[18] First, both methods introduce greater uncertainty into survey estimates. Of course, any survey conducted on a sample of a greater population includes some uncertainty introduced by its estimates of population parameters. Introducing either random variation (RRT) or two survey forms (ICT) generates even greater variation. As a result, the sample size necessary to obtain a similar statistical power will increase. For RRT, the sample size should increase by a ratio of $\frac{1+p}{p}$, where p is the fraction of the population that participates in the sensitive activity. Thus, if the entire population participates in the activity, then the sample size should be $\left(\frac{1+1}{1} = 2\right)$, or 2 times larger.

For rare activities, this is particularly important. For RRT, if 20 percent of the population is suspected of participating in the sensitive activity, the sample should be 6 times larger to produce statistical accuracy.[19] For ICT, too, sample sizes must increase. Details of this, and other considerations to be taken into account in implementing ICT, are discussed in detail in chapter 10.

Patient Surveys

Interviewing patients instead of providers can sometimes circumvent reticence on the part of health workers to directly report informal income. In general, patients may be less reticent about reporting prohibited activities that they observe, such as informal payments, than health workers would be about reporting their own prohibited activity. The main limitation of this approach is that patients probably have limited information on health worker behavior. They may be able to report on the effects of health workers' activities (for example, drugs that are not available and clinics that are unstaffed); however, they will often have less information on the activities themselves (for example, pilfering drugs and moonlighting). For activities that patients do observe, though, surveys of patients can be a useful complement to service provider reports.

Patient reports usually come from two sources: general household surveys and specialized patient exit surveys. Lewis (2007) provides a useful example of how this information can be used to measure informal fees charged by health workers.

She draws mainly on existing household surveys based on the Living Standards Measurement Survey (LSMS).[20] Individuals who have recently visited a clinic are asked whether they were required to make any informal payment; this information can be used to assess the prevalence of such practices. Aside from using existing data, researchers can design household surveys for a particular question. For instance, Kruk et al. (2008) report on a household survey of women in western Tanzania who had given birth in the past five years. They used these data to study informal payments charged for delivery at a health facility, which was legally required to be free. Focusing on a particular region or on the catchment area of a particular facility can allow the researcher to link household survey results to a particular policy or facility. Patient exit surveys can be used for a similar purpose. In this case, rather than sampling from local households, the researcher intercepts patients exiting the facility and interviews them about the visit they just experienced. Lindelow, Reinikka, and Svensson (2003) provide one example in which patients were interviewed regarding informal payments, the availability of drugs, and the quality of care.

Administrative Records

Survey data can also be complemented by other forms of data. In particular, existing administrative data can be used to track informal sources of income. This method can be particularly useful when estimating income from selling pilfered drugs or income from informal payments. For instance, drugs may disappear when health workers prescribe drugs to patients but do not actually disburse them, or when prescriptions are assigned to nonexistent "ghost" patients. McPake et al. (2000) use administrative records of patient visits and prescriptions from 10 Ugandan health facilities to measure the extent to which missing drug stocks cannot be accounted for. Information from administrative records can be particularly powerful when combined with other data. For example, McPake et al. (2000) compare responses from a patient exit survey to administrative records of drug prescriptions to determine the extent to which drugs that disappear from facility stocks are prescribed but not disbursed to patients. One standardized use of this type of methodology is the Public Expenditure Tracking Survey (PETS) tool described in Reinikka and Svensson (2003). In general, the PETS method targets administrative data that are most likely to be reported accurately and then follows the flow of resources through the system, accounting for leakages along the way.[21]

Direct Observation

Finally, data from surveys and existing administrative sources can be complemented by direct observation. This source of information can be the most reliable because it moves beyond the concern that survey responses and administrative records may not be candid. This reliability represents a major advantage of including some direct observation component in an assessment of unofficial income. On the other hand, direct observation can be costly to implement and may cause health workers to alter prohibited behavior while in the presence of an observer.

In addition to the techniques described above, McPake et al. (2000) use direct observation. For instance, observers directly verified the medications that patients carried with them as they left the facility; this process was completed for a period of one month in an effort to outlast any tendency health workers would have to alter their behavior during observation. These observations then complemented data gained from existing records and surveys. Direct observation can also be a useful way to measure the effects of health workers' alternative work arrangements. For instance, Chaudhury et al. (2006) use surprise spot checks to measure the attendance rate of health workers, finding absentee rates of up to 35 percent. Das, Hammer, and Leonard (2008) report on a series of studies that measure quality of care by comparing direct observations of health workers' clinical actions to best practices. Although this method is potentially costly, direct observation can provide solid evidence that complements standard survey evidence.

Conclusions

This chapter has examined types of official and unofficial income in low-income country (LIC) health care settings and reviewed the reasons that unofficial revenue streams are a growing proportion of the income of the health workers in these countries. Health workers in many LICs feel that official income packages offered by employers are not adequate or fair; furthermore, the public compensation packages are often not sufficient to live on—so health workers often use unofficial incomes, such as per diems, moonlighting, and drug pilfering, to subsidize the inadequate package.

However, to establish effective compensation policies and practices that can help improve the availability, distribution, motivation, and performance of public health workers, accurate data are crucial. Measuring the various types of official and unofficial income, assessing them against different benchmarks, and understanding health workers' perceptions of their compensation will enable policy makers to make evidence-based decisions. The techniques and methods presented in this chapter can help obtain reliable and accurate income-related data, which would go a long way toward enabling an effective way forward for policy makers.

Notes

1. Note that pensions might also be considered a type of official form of compensation, which adds to future income.
2. In theory, the health worker seeks to mirror utility, not necessarily the compensation, that they receive via dual employment. From the policy makers' perspective, this means that instating programs that contribute to utility need not require additional

wages or salary to add incentive to remain in the "public" system. Also if there is greater certainty related to the public sector income, individuals may trade off risk (in a private role in which compensation is higher but more uncertain, if, for example, it is tied to utilization) for lower income (e.g., a public sector role with a guaranteed salary).

3. For the individual settled in a rural area, the cost of living (housing, food) may not be higher (although transportation costs will be). But usually this individual will also have to pay for another house in an urban area, where his or her children and spouse will stay because schooling and job opportunities are much scarcer in rural areas.

4. The burden of salary freeze appears to have fallen more heavily on physicians (otherwise the lower cadre health workers would have seen their incomes decline proportionally and ratios would have been unaffected).

5. Naturally if workers are paid on the basis of utilization or hourly then the trade-offs are more explicit with respect to time investment. If the worker receives a fixed annual salary (independent of hours or utilization) this trade-off becomes less explicit, although individuals may still seek to limit public sector work if attractive private sector opportunities exist.

6. Another type of per diem is the "sitting allowance" (an allowance is paid for every attended meeting). Most of the points in this discussion are equally valid for sitting allowances.

7. This chapter uses the term *informal payments* rather than *illegal payments* simply because these payments may, in some (rare and questionable) cases, not be illegal.

8. Not-for-profit organizations also do not necessarily act substantially differently from for-profit organizations. Both have to remain financially viable and, in competing for revenues from medical services, run their operations in manners similar to those of for-profit private enterprises.

9. See http://documents.worldbank.org/curated/en/586321468156869931/How-to -conduct-a-discrete-choice-experiment-for-health-workforce-recruitment-and -retention-in-remote-and-rural-areas-a-user-guide-with-case-studies

10. See http://www.capacityplus.org/rapid-retention-survey-toolkit.

11. To access iHRIS Retain, see http://retain.ihris.org/retain/.

12. In theory, surveys could also query the degree to which health workers feel the income paid to their colleagues working in separate cadres (e.g., nurses could comment on physician pay and vice versa). This may offer a more nuanced and objective view on the fairness of compensation for policy makers.

13. The questions in this section are also excerpted or Adapted from the health worker compensation survey questionnaire drafted by the World Bank, Health Systems 20/20, Capacity*Plus*, and the HWIS *Immpact Toolkit: A Guide and Tools for Maternal Mortality Programme Assessment Module 4, Tool 5*.

14. The questions on sale of medicines and drug pilfering were added to the compensation survey questionnaire drafted by the World Bank, Health Systems 20/20, and Capacity*Plus* and are excerpted from a tool used in the study described in Akwataghibe 2012 and Akwataghibe et al. 2013. The estimate of the respondent can also be checked with more objective data sources (e.g., pricing data) to estimate the value of declared gifts.

15. Questions 4 and 5 relate to endnote 14.

16. To improve objectivity the RRT could ask other health workers about the behaviors of their colleagues (either within cadre or in other cadres) and the share who exhibit these behaviors. While this may yield more honest answers, the lack of certainty about other individuals' behaviors (which may be well hidden) can introduce bias (likely downward).

17. See Droitcour et al. (1991) and Karlan and Zinman (2012) for greater details about this technique.

18. For more in-depth discussion of these techniques, see Droitcour et al. (1991) and Karlan and Zinman (2012).

19. For the researcher aiming to estimate sample size prior to conducting a full survey, the sample size can be very wide depending on prevalence. One option to help inform the sample size calculation is an initial pilot to generate an initial reasonable prevalence estimate.

20. Information about implementing an LSMS or similar household survey can be found at http://go.worldbank.org/B9VEQWV3Z0.

21. Greater detail about implementing a Public Expenditure Tracking Survey can be found at http://go.worldbank.org/84C1RUHTD0.

References

Akwataghibe, N. 2012. *Assessing Human Resources for Health Revenues & Accountability in Nigeria, Final Report*. Report from the Royal Tropical Institute, Amsterdam.

Akwataghibe, N., D. Samaranayake, C. Lemiere, and M. Dieleman. 2013. "Assessing Health Workers' Revenues and Coping Strategies in Nigeria: A Mixed-Methods Study." *BMC Health Services Research* 13: 387.

Azfar, O., and P. Murrell. 2009. "Identifying Reticent Respondents: Assessing the Quality of Survey Data on Corruption and Values." *Economic Development and Cultural Change* 57 (2).

Bärnighausen, T., and D. E. Bloom. 2009. "Financial Incentives for Return of Service in Underserved Areas: A Systematic Review." *BMC Health Services Research* 9: 86.

Blaauw, D., E. Erasmus, N. Pagaiya, V. Tangcharoensathein, K. Mullei, S. Mudhune, C. Goodman, M. English, and M. Lagarde. 2010. "Policy Interventions That Attract Nurses to Rural Areas: A Multicountry Discrete Choice Experiment." *Bulletin of the World Health Organization* 88: 350–56.

Chandler, C.I., S. Chonya, F. Mtei, H. Reyburn, and C. J. Whitty. 2009. "Motivation, Money and Respect: A Mixed-Method Study of Tanzanian Non-Physician Clinicians." *Social Science Medicine* 68: 2078–88.

Chaudhury, N., J. Hammer, M. Kremer, K. Muralidharan, and F. H. Rogers. 2006. "Missing in Action: Teacher and Health Worker Absence in Developing Countries." *Journal of Economic Perspectives* 20 (1).

Chêne, M. 2009. "Low Salaries, the Culture of Per Diems and Corruption." *U4 Expert Answer.* Transparency International. www.u4.no/helpdesk/helpdesk/query.cfm?id=220.

Dambisya, Y. 2007. "A Review of Non-Financial Incentives for Health Worker Retention in East and Southern Africa." Regional Network for Equity in Health in Southern Africa (EQUINET), Discussion Paper 44, Harare, Zimbabwe.

Das, J., J. Hammer, and K. Leonard. 2008. "The Quality of Medical Advice in Low-Income Countries." *Journal of Economic Perspectives* 22 (2): 93–114.

Delobelle, P., J. L. Rawlinson, S. Ntuli, I. Malatsi, R. Decock, and A. M. Depoorter. 2011. "Job Satisfaction and Turnover Intent of Primary Healthcare Nurses in Rural South Africa: A Questionnaire Survey." *Journal of Advanced Nursing* 67 (2): 371–83.

Deussom, R., W. Jaskiewicz, S. Dwyer, and K. Tulenko. 2012. "Holding Health Workers Accountable: Governance Approaches to Reducing Absenteeism." Capacity*Plus* Technical Brief, IntraHealth, Washington, DC.

Difazio, R., D. Lang, and M. Boykova. 2004. "Nursing in Russia: A 'Travelogue.'" *Journal of Pediatric Nursing* 19 (2): 150–56.

Ding, Y., and J. Tian. 2008. *Annual Review of HRH Situation in Asia-Pacific Region, 2006–2007.* Beijing: Health Human Resources Development Center, Ministry of Health.

Droitcour, J., R. A. Caspar, M. L. Hubbard, T. L. Parsley, W. Visscher, and T. M. Ezzati. 1991. "The Item Count Technique as a Method of Indirect Questioning: A Review of Its Development and a Case Study Application." In *Measurement Errors in Surveys*, edited by P. B. Beimer, R. M. Groves, L. E. Lyberg, N. A. Mathiowetz, and S. Sudman, 185–210. Hoboken, NJ: John Wiley & Sons.

Ensor, T., G. Chapman, and M. Barro. 2006. "Paying and Motivating CSPS Staff in Burkina Faso: Evidence from Two Districts." *Initiative for Maternal Mortality Programme Assessment*, University of Aberdeen, Aberdeen, Scotland.

Ferrinho, P., M. C. Omar, M. de Jesus Fernandes, P. Blaise, A. M. Bugalho, and W. Van Lerberghe. 2004a. "Pilfering for Survival: How Health Workers Use Access to Drugs as a Coping Strategy." *Human Resources for Health* 2: 4.

Ferrinho, P., W. Van Lerberghe, I. Fronteira, F. Hipólito, and A. Biscaia. 2004b. "Dual Practice in the Health Sector: Review of the Evidence." *Human Resources for Health* 2: 14.

Ferrinho, P., W. Van Lerberghe, M. R. Julien, E. Fresta, A. Gomes, F. Dias, A. Gonçalves, and B. Bäcklström. 1998. "How and Why Public Sector Doctors Engage in Private Practice in Portuguese-Speaking African Countries." *Health Policy and Planning* 13 (3): 332–38.

Garbarino, S., T. Lievens, P. Quartey, and P. Serneels. 2007. *Ghana Qualitative Health Worker Study: Draft Report of Preliminary Descriptive Findings.* Unpublished report. Oxford, U.K.: Oxford Policy Management.

Hagopian, A., A. Zuyderduin, N. Kyobutungi, and F. Yumkella. 2009. "Job Satisfaction and Morale in the Ugandan Health Workforce." *Health Affairs* 28 (5): 863–75.

Hassett, P. 2009. *Zanzibar Health Worker Productivity Study: Final Report.* Unpublished. Chapel Hill, NC: Capacity Project.

Hayes, B., A. Bonner, and J. Pryor. 2010. "Factors Contributing to Nurse Job Satisfaction in the Acute Hospital Setting: A Review of Recent Literature." *Journal of Nursing Management* 18 (7): 804–14.

Holbrook, A. L., and J. A. Krosnick. 2010. "Social Desirability in Voter Turnout Reports: Tests Using the Item Count Technique." *Public Opinion Quarterly* 74 (1): 37–67.

Health Worker Incentives Survey (HWIS). 2007. Module 4, Tool 5. Version 2.0. *Impact Toolkit: A Guide and Tools for Maternal Mortality Programme Assessment.* Aberdeen, U.K: University of Aberdeen. https://www.abdn.ac.uk/iahs/content-images/hwis.pdf.

Jansen, E. G. 2009. "Does Aid Work? Reflections on a Natural Resources Programme in Tanzania." *Chr. Michelsen Institute* 4 (2).

Jaskiewicz, W, O. Phathammmavong, P. Vangkonevilay, C. Paphassarang, I. T. Phachanh, and L. Wurts. 2012. *Toward Development of a Rural Retention Strategy in Lao People's Democratic Republic: Understanding Health Worker Preferences.* Washington, DC: CapacityPlus.

Kanakin, J., L. Kessou, and O. Koutchikap. 2008. *Etude sur la gouvernance dans le secteur de la santé: cas de la zone sanitaire d'Abomey-Calavi So-Ava au Benin*. Washington, DC: World Bank.

Karlan, D., and J. Zinman. 2012. "List Randomization for Sensitive Behavior: An Application for Measuring Use of Loan Proceeds." *Journal of Development Economics* 98 (1): 71–5.

Keuffel, E., W. Jaskiewicz, C. Paphassarang, and K. Tulenko. 2013. "Net Costs of Health Worker Rural Incentive Packages: An Example from the Lao People's Democratic Republic." *Medical Care* 51 (11): 985–91.

Kruk, M. E., J. C. Johnson, M. Gyakobo, P. Agyei-Baffour, K. Asabir, S. R. Kotha, J. Kwansah, E. Nakua, R. C. Snow, and M. Dzodzomenyo. 2010. "Rural Practice Preferences among Medical Students in Ghana: A Discrete Choice Experiment." *Bulletin of the World Health Organization* 88 (5): 333–41.

Kruk, M. E., G. Mbaruku, P. C. Rockers, and S. Galea. 2008. "User Fee Exemptions Are Not Enough: Out-Of-Pocket Payments for 'Free' Delivery Services in Rural Tanzania." *Tropical Medicine and International Health* 13 (12): 1442–51.

Lemiere, C., C. H. Herbst, C. Dolea, P. Zurn, and A. Soucat. 2013. "Rural-Urban Imbalance of Health Workers in Sub-Saharan Africa." In *The Labor Market for Health Workers in Africa: A New Look at the Crisis*, edited by A. Soucat, R. M. Scheffler, and T. A. Ghebreyesus, 147–68. Washington, DC: World Bank.

Lemiere, C. and M. Juquois. 2010. "Are You Moonlighting? Using an Item Count Technique to Measure the Prevalence of Dual Job Practice in the Health Sector: A Case Study from Benin." Presentation published by Health Systems for Outcomes Program. http://www.hrhresourcecenter.org/node/4041.

Lensvelt-Mulders, G. J. L. M., J. H. Joop, P. G. M. van der Heijden, and C. J. M. Maas. 2005. "Meta-Analysis of Randomized Response Research: Thirty-Five Years of Validation." *Sociological Methods and Research* 33 (February): 319–48.

Lewis, M. 2007. "Informal Payments and the Financing of Health Care in Developing and Transition Countries." *Health Affairs* 26 (4): 984–97.

Lindelow, M., R. Reinikka, and J. Svensson. 2003. "Health Care on the Frontline: Survey Evidence on Public and Private Providers in Uganda." Africa Region Human Development Working Paper 38, World Bank, Washington, DC.

Macq, J., P. Ferrinho, V. De Brouwere, and W. Van Lergergyhe. 2001. "Managing Health Services in Developing Countries: Between the Ethics of the Civil Servant and the Need for Moonlighting: Managing and Moonlighting." *Human Resources for Health Development Journal* 5 (1–3): 17–24.

Macq, J., and W. Van Lerberghe. 2000. "Managing Health Services in Developing Countries: Moonlighting to Serve the Public?" In *Providing Health Care under Adverse Conditions: Health Personnel Performance & Individual Coping Strategies*, edited by P. Ferrinho and W. Van Lerberghe, 171–80. Studies in Health Services Organisation & Policy, 16. Antwerp: ITG Press.

Malvarez, S. M., and M. C. C. Agudelo. 2005. "Overview of the Nursing Workforce in Latin America." Series Human Resources Development 39, Pan American Health Organization, Washington, DC.

Mathauer, I., and I. Imhoff. 2006. "Health Worker Motivation in Africa: The Role of Non-Financial Incentives and Human Resource Management Tools." *Human Resources for Health* 4: 24.

McCoy, D., S. Bennett, S. Witter, B. Pond, B. Baker, J. Gow, S. Chand, T. Ensor, and B. McPake. 2008. "Salaries and Incomes of Health Workers in Sub-Saharan Africa." *Lancet* 371 (9613): 675–81.

McPake, B., D. Asiimwe, F. Mwesigye, M. Ofumbi, P. Streefland, and A. Turinde. 2000. "Coping Strategies of Health Workers in Uganda." In *Providing Health Care under Adverse Conditions: Health Personnel Performance & Individual Coping Strategies*, edited by P. Ferrinho and W. Van Lerberghe, 131–50. Studies in Health Services Organisation & Policy, 16. Antwerp: ITG Press.

Ogrodnick, A., I. Ron, P. Kiwanuka-Mukiibi, and D. Altman. 2011. *Understanding Intrinsic Motivation and Performance Factors for Public Sector and Faith-Based Facility Health Workers in Uganda*. Health Systems 20/20 Brief. Bethesda, MD: USAID.

Onwujekwe, O., N. Dike, B. Uzochukwu, and O. Ezeoke. 2010. "Informal Payments for Healthcare: Differences in Expenditures from Consumers and Providers Perspectives for Treatment of Malaria in Nigeria." *Health Policy* 96 (1): 72–79.

Phillips, D. 2012. *Income Sources of Liberian Health Workers*. Report for Liberia Ministry of Health and Social Welfare and World Bank Africa Technical Health Unit.

Preker, A. S., E. Keuffel, and H. Tuckman. 2009. "Addressing Unfunded Training Mandates in Hospitals: Engaging the Private Sector in Low- and Middle-Income Countries." *World Hospitals and Health Services* 46 (3): 12–15.

Policy Forum. 2009. *Reforming Allowances: A Win-Win Approach to Improved Service Delivery, Higher Salaries for Civil Servants and Saving Money*. Policy Brief 9.09. Dar es Salaam, Tanzania: Policy Forum.

Reinikka, R., and J. Svensson. 2003. "Survey Techniques to Measure and Explain Corruption." Policy Research Working Paper 3071, World Bank, Washington, DC.

Ridde, V. 2010. "Per Diems Undermine Health Interventions, Systems and Research in Africa: Burying Our Heads in the Sand." *Tropical Medicine and International Health*, Editorial, July 28. doi: 10.1111/j.1365-3156.2010.02607.x.

Rockers, P. C., W. Jaskiewicz, M. E. Kruk, O. Phathammavong, P. Vangkonevilay, C. Paphassarang, I. T. Phachanh, L. Wurts, and K. Tulenko. 2013. "Differences in Preferences for Rural Job Postings between Nursing Students and Practicing Nurses: Evidence from a Discrete Choice Experiment in Lao People's Democratic Republic." *Human Resources for Health* 11 (22).

Rockers, P. C., W. Jaskiewicz, L. Wurts, M. E. Kruk, G. S. Mgomella, F. Ntalazi, and K. Tulenko. 2012. "Preferences for Working in Rural Clinics among Trainee Health Professionals in Uganda: A Discrete Choice Experiment." *BMC Health Services Research* 12: 212.

Roenen, C., P. Ferrinho, M. Van Dormael, M. C. Conceicao, and W. Van Lerberghe. 1997. "How African Doctors Make Ends Meet: An Exploration." *Tropical Medicine and International Health* 2 (2): 127–35.

Søreide, T., A. Tostensen, and I. A. Skage. 2012. *Hunting for Per Diem. The Uses and Abuses of Travel Compensation in Three Developing Countries*. Report 2/2012 Study, Oslo: Norad Evaluation Department.

Soucat, A., R. M. Scheffler, and T. A. Ghebreyesus, eds. 2013. *The Labor Market for Health Workers in Africa: A New Look at the Crisis*. Washington, DC: World Bank.

van der Geest, S. 1982. "The Efficiency of Inefficiency: Medicine Distribution in South Cameroon." *Social Science and Medicine* 16 (24): 2145–53.

Vian, T. 2009. "Benefits and Drawbacks of Per Diems: Do Allowances Distort Good Governance in the Health Sector?" U4 Brief 29. CMI, Anti-Corruption Resource Centre, Bergen, Norway.

Warner, S. L. 1965. "Randomized Response: A Survey Technique for Eliminating Evasive Answer Bias." *Journal of the American Statistical Association* 60: 63–69.

Willis-Shattuck, M., P. Bidwell, S. Thomas, L. Wyness, D. Blaauw, and P. Ditlopo. 2008. "Motivation and Retention of Health Workers in Developing Countries: A Systematic Review." *BMC Health Services Research* 8: 247.

World Bank. 2013. *A Review of Cambodian Public Health Professionals' Earnings Composition, Motivation and Human Resource Practices*. Unpublished report. May 20.

Survey Techniques to Capture Sensitive Information from Health Workers: An Example of Their Application in Liberia

David Phillips, Christopher H. Herbst, and Yah M. Zolia

Introduction

The generation of informal income by health workers is a common occurrence in many health labor markets and determines revenue generation and labor market dynamics. Measuring or capturing the participation of health workers in selling pilfered drugs, moonlighting, and charging informal payments (when services are officially free of charge) to gain income can be difficult. Reporting one's own participation in prohibited activities often carries a large risk. As a result, surveys of health workers using simple, direct questions are likely to understate the prevalence of drug pilfering, moonlighting, and charging informal payments. Patient interviews may avoid some of these issues, but patients may hesitate to challenge the behavior of health workers.

This chapter provides an overview of an application of sensitive survey techniques to capture sensitive information about informal income generation activity from health workers in Liberia. As discussed in chapter 9, sensitive survey techniques have been developed to encourage candid answers even when respondents may be reluctant to answer a direct question honestly. This chapter describes the as-yet unpublished application and results of a Liberia Ministry of Health survey conducted with support from the World Bank in July and August 2012, which experimented with an approach to measure the prevalence among health workers in Liberia's public hospitals of selling pilfered drugs, moonlighting during regular business hours, and charging informal payments.

This example of a practical application of sensitive survey techniques on health workers is meant to provide a more in-depth understanding of these methods for anyone considering their use.

The chapter will show that while the application of sensitive survey techniques holds great potential to obtain information otherwise not accessible, the findings from Liberia are also qualified by some methodological concerns. Quality checks in the survey indicate that respondents did not always closely follow survey directions. Because of the length and cognitive difficulty of the survey, responses to the sensitive surveying module at the end of the survey are likely to have included a large amount of measurement error. Given the nature of the techniques discussed in this chapter, measurement error moreover likely led to underestimates of the prevalence of sensitive activities. As a result, the estimates obtained through the application of sensitive survey techniques in Liberia are most likely too low to be accurate, although this cannot be stated with certainty. Overall, the experience with using sensitive survey techniques in Liberia reveals both strengths and weaknesses of this approach in practice, all of which should be taken into consideration when replicating similar techniques elsewhere.

Sensitive Survey Techniques

The goal of the exercise in Liberia, carried out in 2012, was to measure not only the official income of Liberian health workers gained through regular salary, standard incentives, and benefits, but also the income gained through informal means including activities that are (at least sometimes) discouraged or banned. These unofficial revenue streams include selling pilfered drugs to patients, moonlighting for a private practice during regular business hours, and charging informal fees for otherwise free services.

As indicated in chapter 9, a large class of survey techniques has been developed to address situations in which respondents hesitate to respond candidly. In general, all of these tools rely on the same mechanism. Survey questions are designed to obscure the individual's answer about the sensitive question (for example, selling pilfered drugs to patients) while still allowing the researcher to calculate the extent of the activity in the population. This method was pioneered by Warner (1965), who implemented it as a randomized response whereby the individual's response is altered randomly by a coin flip, spinner, or other randomization device. This technique has also been used simply to identify reticent respondents through statistically unlikely answers (Azfar and Murrell 2009).

In Liberia, two specific sensitive survey techniques were used that follow in the tradition of Warner's randomized response: the first is the item count technique (ICT), or list randomization technique; the second is the aggregated response/sum randomization technique. Their design and application are summarized below.

Item Count Technique

The technique referred to as "item count" (Droitcour et al. 1991) or "list randomization" (Karlan and Zinman 2012) obscures an individual's answer to a sensitive question by including it in a list of other statements. Then respondents are asked only to respond *how many* of the statements are true without identifying *which* statements are true. For instance, one question in the survey of Liberian health workers asked the following:

2.1.a. Please count the number of statements that are true about you and write this number in the blank:

1. My mother was born between January and June.
2. I have 2 or more brothers and sisters.
3. I am originally from this city.
4. I earn income from a private practice during normal working hours.
   Number of true statements:_____

In question 2.1a, statements 1, 2, and 3 are nonsensitive statements regarding basic demographic information. The final statement is a sensitive question asking whether the individual participates in moonlighting. Although the respondent may hesitate to respond to the fourth statement if asked directly, the item count provides an opportunity to answer candidly while maintaining plausible deniability about participating in the activity. As discussed in more detail later in the chapter, the first three statements must be chosen carefully to provide this deniability. For instance, if all statements are likely to be true or all are likely to be false, then many respondents should answer *4* or *0*, which provide no cover for the respondent.

Although the individual's answer is hidden among the other statements, the researcher can still estimate participation in the given activity *over the whole sample* by asking two different forms of the question above. In the Liberian health worker survey, half of the sample were asked the above question 2.1.a. Meanwhile, the other half were asked the same question but with the sensitive statement omitted (2.1b):

2.1.b. Please count the number of statements that are true about you and write this number in the blank:

1. My mother was born between January and June.
2. I have 2 or more brothers and sisters.
3. I am originally from this city.
   Number of true statements:_____

Individual health workers were randomly assigned to the two different versions of the survey. As a result, the truth of statements 1, 2, and 3 will be, on average, identical. Thus participation in the sensitive activity can be estimated by calculating the difference in the average number of true statements across the two groups.

Formally, define Y_i as the response of individual i to the item count question and let X_{ij} denote whether statement j is true for person i (equation 10.1). Using item count, we do not observe X_{ij} but we do observe Y_i. Then, if survey respondents follow the item count directions, it will be true that:

$$Y_i = \begin{cases} X_{i1} + X_{i2} + X_{i3} + X_{i4} & \textit{if form } A \\ X_{i1} + X_{i2} + X_{i3} & \textit{if form } B \end{cases} \tag{10.1}$$

Then, it must be true that

$$E[Y_i|A] - E[Y_i|B] = E[X_{i1} + X_{i2} + X_{i3}|A] + E[X_{i4}|A] -$$
$$E[X_{i1} + X_{i2} + X_{i3}|B] = E[X_{i4}] \tag{10.2}$$

where $E[.]$ indicates an expected value. In equation 10.2, the far left expression simply measures the difference in the average number of true statements for form A versus form B. The final equality follows from the fact that the survey form of A or B is set independent from individual characteristics. In this case, the difference in averages measures the far right expression, which is the probability that the fourth statement is true. More simply:

$$\Pr[\textit{statement } 4 \textit{ is True}] = \textit{Average True form } A -$$
$$\textit{Average True form } B \tag{10.3}$$

Equation 10.3 demonstrates that, provided that respondents follow the survey instructions, the difference in the sample mean for form A and the sample mean for form B is a consistent estimator of the proportion of the sample for whom the sensitive statement is true.

This ICT, or list randomization technique, has been used in many settings to avoid underreporting sensitive behaviors. Karlan and Zinman (2012) find that respondents are more likely to report misuse of microfinance loans when asked through item count rather than through direct questions. Alternatively, Holbrook and Krosnick (2010) find that using item count leads to lower reported participation in socially desirable behavior (for example, voting). In the closest existing application, Lemiere and Juquois (2010) apply the technique to health worker moonlighting in Benin. In general, researchers find that using item count questions leads to more candid responses and thus less biased estimates of the prevalence of sensitive behavior. However, this does come at some cost. Obscuring a direct answer with responses to unrelated questions generates additional sampling error. Although the two groups' participation in the nonsensitive activities will be similar in expectation, in finite samples this leads to greater uncertainty. Furthermore, sensitive survey techniques can add to the cognitive load of surveys—that is, respondents may tire as a result of added time—leading to respondent confusion or low attention to survey instructions (see Droitcour et al. 1991; Karlan and Zinman 2012). To test for this final concern, the survey of health workers in Liberia included a placebo item count question, described below, to test the validity of the item count in this context.

Aggregated Response (Sum Randomization)

In addition to the more standard item count method, this survey of Liberian health workers also included questions using aggregated response (or sum randomization). The logic behind aggregated response is similar to that of item count: the individual's response is obscured while asking two slightly differing questions to calculate population-level statistics. The main difference between these methods is that, while ICTs are limited to simple true-false statements, aggregated response techniques can incorporate any quantitative variable. In this method, respondents are asked (explicitly or implicitly) to add together two variables and report only the sum. In the Liberia health worker survey, half of the sample were asked the following question:

2.8.a. Do you earn any income from your own private practice either outside your facility's regular working hours or during your facility's regular working hours?

☐ Yes   ☐ No (If No, skip to section 3)

2.8.b. In total, how many hours in the past month did you devote to private practice, both during and after regular working hours?

_____ hours

Meanwhile, the other half of the sample were asked a slightly different version:

3.7.a. Do you earn any income from private practice outside of your facility's regular hours? Include only income earned outside of your facility's hours and not income earned during your facility's working hours.

☐ Yes   ☐ No (If No, skip to 3.10.a.)

3.7.b. How many hours in the past month did you devote to private practice outside of your facility's regular hours?

_____ hours

For this set of questions from the Liberia health worker survey, the sensitive behavior of interest is moonlighting during regular hours, which is prohibited in these facilities. The first version of the question asks the health worker to report hours in private practice both outside business hours (nonsensitive) and private practice during business hours (sensitive). Meanwhile, the second version excludes private practice during business hours. Thus, the variables are defined as shown in equations 10.4–10.6:

$$Z_{i1} = Hours\ of\ private\ practice\ during\ business\ hours \qquad (10.4)$$

Health Labor Market Analyses in Low- and Middle-Income Countries
http://dx.doi.org/10.1596/978-1-4648-0931-6

$$Z_{i2} = Hours \ of \ private \ practice \ outside \ business \ hours \qquad (10.5)$$

$$Y_i = \begin{cases} Z_{i1} + Z_{i2} \ if \ form \ A \\ Z_{i2} \ if \ form \ B \end{cases} \qquad (10.6)$$

As with the ICT, the individual's participation in the illicit activity is obscured, but participation in the sensitive activity can be estimated across the whole sample as a difference in means because:

$$E[Y_i|A] - E[Y_i|B] = E[Z_{i1}|A] + E[Z_{i2}|A] - $$
$$E[Z_{i2}|B] = E[Z_{i1}|A] = E[Z_{i1}] \qquad (10.7)$$

Once again, this method provides a better opportunity for eliciting candid responses while also allowing the researcher to estimate participation in the sensitive activity in the aggregate. This method also retains the disadvantages of the ICT because it introduces greater sampling variation into the estimates and requires greater attention to detail from the respondent. Unlike item count, the aggregated response allows for calculating the *extent* of participation (hours spent moonlighting, amount of income from selling drugs, and so on) rather than only a "yes" or "no" for participation in the activity. This ability to calculate in greater detail was the main reason for including aggregated response questions, because these (in principle) allow the researcher to estimate *how much* income is earned from prohibited activities.

Application of Sensitive Survey Techniques in Liberia

The 2012 Liberia health worker survey that included the sensitive survey techniques covered the counties of Bomi, Bong, Grand Bassa, Montserrado, and Nimba. These counties were chosen to balance surveying costs and because they are representative of the whole country. This necessarily implies that counties near Monrovia were oversampled. However, the results were considered close to representative for all hospitals in the country because most public hospitals are near Monrovia, and the survey intentionally included rural counties (for example, Nimba) when feasible. All public hospitals within each covered county were included in the sample. Other facilities were not included. Within each covered facility, health workers were sampled randomly from the Ministry of Health's staff rosters. Individuals who were not present or who were unavailable because of work demands were replaced from a randomly selected group of alternates. The random selection of survey respondents ensures that the results were representative of all health workers rather than simply those made available by facility managers. Sampling probabilities were stratified by cadre; all available physicians were included in the sample because of their extremely small numbers. A total of 247 health workers were interviewed.

Each health worker completed demographic background information, an income questionnaire including both direct and sensitive survey questions, and a discrete choice experiment on motivation. Individuals were randomly assigned to one of two different versions of the income module to facilitate the item count and aggregated response analysis. Table 10.1 summarizes the demographic characteristics of the entire sample and for each of the three cadres surveyed.

In total, 18 doctors, 135 nurses, and 94 midwives were interviewed (table 10.1). Eighty-five percent of the sample is female, though this is mainly driven by the nurses and midwives. Only 17 percent of physicians are female. Most health workers were relatively young, with an average age under 40. Doctors, though, tended to be older with an average age of 46 while nurses were younger, averaging 35 years of age. Just over half of the sample was married or living with a partner, and the average household had over seven people in it. Most health workers (65 percent) perceived their economic status to be average or better than those around them, though this was far truer for physicians (94 percent) and nurses (68 percent) than midwives (54 percent). Most health workers were relatively new to the profession, with an average work experience of 6.9 years, half of which were spent in their current facility. Finally, nurses and midwives stated that they worked around 50 hours per week while physicians stated that they work, on average, 96 hours per week.

Table 10.1 Demographic Characteristics of Liberian Health Worker Respondents, 2012

Characteristic	All average	Doctors	Nurses	Midwives	Form A	Form B	p-value of difference
Female	0.85	0.17	0.83	1.00	0.88	0.82	0.18
Age	38	46	35	40	37	39	0.13
Doctor	0.07	1.00	0	0	0.07	0.07	0.96
Nurse	0.55	0	1.00	0	0.54	0.55	0.86
Midwife	0.38	0	0	1.00	0.39	0.38	0.88
Urban	0.40	0.39	0.33	0.51	0.40	0.41	0.92
Married/resident partner	0.57	0.78	0.49	0.65	0.57	0.57	0.93
Number of children	3.0	3.6	2.5	3.7	2.8	3.3	0.11
Household size	7.4	6.8	7.2	7.9	7.1	7.7	0.17
Perceived economic status average or better	0.65	0.94	0.68	0.54	0.66	0.63	0.60
Years at current facility	3.4	3.4	2.8	4.3	3.3	3.5	0.71
Years of professional experience	6.9	9.5	5.1	8.9	6.7	7.0	0.78
Hours of work per week	51	96	47	48	51	51	0.86
Total number	247	18	135	94	122	125	—

Note: Form A and form B refer to the two randomly assigned survey instruments that use different lists for the item count technique and aggregated response questions. P-values test the null hypothesis that there is no difference in the characteristic between responses to Form A versus form B; — = not applicable.

Health Labor Market Analyses in Low- and Middle-Income Countries
http://dx.doi.org/10.1596/978-1-4648-0931-6

Testing Validity of Item Count and Aggregate Response Methods

The final three columns of table 10.1 demonstrate one element of the validity of the item count and aggregated response methods. These methods rely on the fact that the group receiving form A and the group receiving form B are, on average, identical. This must be true in order for the nonsensitive item count statements to cancel out. It is thus useful to check whether the two groups differ on observable demographic dimensions. Of the final three columns, the first two summarize demographic information for those receiving form A and those receiving form B. As can be seen, the two groups are similar. The final column presents a formal test of this hypothesis, showing the p-values for a test of whether the mean values in the two columns are different. For each variable, a null hypothesis of no difference between groups receiving the two forms cannot be rejected. They appear to be similar.

Results

This section presents the results of the analysis of the data obtained from the 2012 survey of Liberian health workers. It looks first at regular or base salary and benefits and then considers the findings from the two different methods used to collect the data: responses to direct survey questions and responses to item count and aggregated response techniques. The survey first requested direct responses and then followed with aggregated response questions.

Regular Salary and Benefits

Table 10.2 summarizes responses of health workers regarding their pay and benefits. All figures are listed as monthly values, and although health workers often receive some parts of their salaries in U.S. dollars and some in Liberian dollars, all figures have been converted to U.S. dollar equivalents at the summer 2012 rate of US$0.0138 per Liberian dollar. The average total pay in the sample was $365 per month. Doctors received $1,561 per month, while nurses and midwives earned $277 and $256, respectively. Total pay was split between regular salary, which makes up about 45 percent of total pay, and a salary top-up referred to as an "incentive," which provides the other half. Incentives are particularly important for physicians. According to the data, total pay increased from 2010 to 2011, rising from $333 to $365 per month. Still, health workers argued that they are underpaid, reporting that their desired pay was more than double the current value, a ratio that is roughly constant across all three cadres.

Aside from salary and incentives, health workers may also receive in-kind benefits. The most common benefit was free medical care, which 68 percent of all respondents reported that they received. Physicians also commonly received free housing; 61 percent of the physicians in the sample received this benefit.

Health Labor Market Analyses in Low- and Middle-Income Countries
http://dx.doi.org/10.1596/978-1-4648-0931-6

Table 10.2 Regular Monthly Compensation and Benefits of Liberian Health Worker Respondents, 2010–12

US$, 2012 exchange rate

Monthly compensation and benefits	All average	Doctors	Nurses	Midwives
Current total pay (US$)	365	1,561	277	256
Regular salary	166	436	144	146
Incentive	190	1,125	129	99
Total pay 2011	333	1,479	241	217
Total pay 2010	256	1,241	170	164
Desired pay	843	3,889	658	524
Housing provided (% workers)	21	61	20	15
Number of rooms	1.3	2.3	1.1	1.0
Vehicle access (% workers)	20	22	21	19
Transport allowance (% workers)	4	11	4	4
Medical benefits (% workers)	68	56	70	67
Tuition support (% workers)	2	6	2	0
Paid education leave (% workers)	5	22	5	2
Rural hardship pay (% workers)	16	6	19	13
Performance bonus (% workers)	7	11	7	8
Trainings/per diem (US$)	148	1,097	62	90

Source: 2012 Liberia Health Workers Survey.

Other benefits are less common, although over 10 percent of staff received access to a vehicle; likewise for rural hardship pay. Finally, as in many LIC settings, health workers can supplement their income significantly through paid trainings and per diems. In Liberia, health workers appeared to add $148 per month on average through this channel, which is just under 41 percent of total pay from official channels.

Sensitive Behaviors: Direct Responses

The survey focused on three activities: moonlighting; selling pilfered drugs; and illegal, informal payments or fees. Table 10.3 provides a first pass at estimating, through simple direct response questions, the extent to which health workers engaged in sensitive behaviors. For the questions in this table, health workers were simply asked directly to report their participation in these activities. As can be seen, health workers reported little involvement. Exactly zero people admitted to the barred practice of selling drugs to patients, and only 3 percent reported moonlighting during business hours. A few respondents (13 percent) reported charging informal payments; however, the amounts charged were quite small. The average health worker reported earning only $1 per month from this activity. Even examining only those health workers who charged any fees, this is still only $7 per month. In sum, health workers reported almost no participation in these three activities when asked directly.

Health Labor Market Analyses in Low- and Middle-Income Countries
http://dx.doi.org/10.1596/978-1-4648-0931-6

Table 10.3 Results from Direct Responses of Liberian Health Workers
US$, 2012 exchange rate

	All (average)	Doctors	Nurses	Midwives
Sells drugs (%)	0	0	0	0
Average income, per month	0	0	0	0
Informal payments (%)	13	12	12	15
Average income, per month	1	1	1	1
Private practice during business hours (%)	3	0	2	4
Average hours per month	1.4	0	1.5	1.4
Average income, per month	9	0	5	16

Source: 2012 Liberia Health Workers Survey.

Sensitive Behaviors: Item Count and Aggregated Response

The results for direct responses could indicate limited involvement in prohibited income-generating activities, or they could simply show that respondents are reticent to report their participation, even when anonymity is guaranteed by the surveyor. It is impossible to tell from these data. The item count and aggregated response techniques provide an opportunity to distinguish between these two explanations by seeing whether measured participation in these activities rises when respondents are given stronger guarantees that no one will know their individual answers.

Table 10.4 reports the results of both the item count and aggregated response questions. The first panel describes the results of the item count. For each activity, the results are displayed in four columns. The first column displays the average response of individuals given the question that includes the sensitive behavior (for example, question 2.1.a). This represents the average number of true statements out of four (three nonsensitive and one sensitive). The second column displays this average response for the list of three nonsensitive statements that excludes the sensitive behavior. The third column reports the difference, which estimates the fractions of the sample participating in the behavior. Finally, the last column presents the p-value for a test of whether that difference is statistically different from zero.

The first row of table 10.4 generates some concern about the item count results. To determine whether respondents were following the item count instructions, a "dummy" question, for which the answer is previously known, is included. Rather than adding a sensitive statement to the list of three nonsensitive statements, this question adds the statement "I am at least 25 years old." Earlier, in the demographic background section of the survey, less than 1 percent of the sample reported an age lower than 25. Thus any individual facing this statement should almost always add 1 to the item count total in the first column. Since this question is not included in the other form of the survey, those in the second column should not add 1. As a result, the difference between the two forms should be 0.99. However, the difference is actually zero

Table 10.4 Results from Sensitive Survey Responses of Liberian Health Workers
US$, 2012 exchange rate

Sensitive behavior	Including sensitive behavior	Excluding sensitive behavior	Difference (attributed to sensitive behavior)	p-value
Item count				
At least 25 years of age	0.98	0.98	0.00	1.00
			(0.11)	
Any income from selling drugs	1.60	1.63	−0.03	0.78
			(0.10)	
Any income from informal payments (Version 1)	1.27	1.26	0.02	0.86
			(0.10)	
Any income from informal payments (Version 2)	1.07	1.10	0.02	0.83
			(0.10)	
Any private practice during business hours	1.61	1.45	0.17*	0.09
			(0.10)	
Aggregated response				
Amount of income from selling drugs per month	43	21	23	0.56
			(40)	
Amount of income from informal payments per month	1.42	1.28	0.14	0.76
			(0.47)	
Amount of income from private practice during business hours per month	15	34	−19	0.49
			(28)	
Number of hours of private practice during business hours per month	15	5	10	0.40
			(12)	

Source: 2012 Liberia Health Workers Survey.
Note: Sensitive behaviors refer to the behavior listed on only one form for the item count and aggregated response questions. Values in parentheses are standard errors.
Significance level: * = 10 percent.

(and statistically different from 0.99) in the data. This indicates that members of the sample did not follow the item count directions for this question. Given the nonsensitive nature of the statement regarding age, it seems unlikely that reticence leads to this result. Instead, reports from the survey team indicate that respondent fatigue led to careless answers. Given the randomization of who receives form A and form B, zero difference is exactly what would be expected if respondents were answering with large but random measurement error. As a result of this measurement error, any estimates of participation in sensitive behavior derived from the sensitive surveying data will be underestimates. This concern should be taken into account when interpreting the item count and sum randomization results.

With that caveat in mind, consider the remaining item count questions (table 10.4). The question for selling drugs indicated little participation. The average response when presented with a list including the sensitive item is 1.60 true statements. When the sensitive item is omitted, the average is 1.63 true statements. The difference is −0.03. Thus, taken at face value, the results suggest limited participation in drug selling. Similar results are obtained for income from requiring informal payments, in which this method estimates that only 2 percent of health workers require informal payments. This finding does not depend on whether the sensitive item is assigned to form A or form B. Finally, the item count does show some evidence that health workers participated in private practice. The item count results indicate that 17 percent of health workers completed private practice during business hours. This result is statistically different from zero at the 10 percent significance level. It includes a large amount of uncertainty but provides some evidence of participation in moonlighting.

The aggregated response results tell a similar story (table 10.4). Respondent error probably affects these items as well, causing them to be biased toward zero. Again, however, the results suggest that private practice during business hours was more common than direct responses by health workers would indicate. The final row of table 10.4 shows that the average respondent spent 15 hours on private practice per month. Those asked only about private practice outside business hours reported only 5 hours of work. Thus the aggregated response method implies that the average health worker spent 10 hours per month moonlighting during regular business hours. Because of the increased uncertainty introduced by sensitive surveying, this estimate is not significantly different from zero. Furthermore, a greater number of hours does not translate necessarily into greater income from private practice (the second to last row), although this finding is mainly the result of one large outlier. The aggregated response provides some evidence of income gained through selling stolen drugs, however, with monthly income from this activity estimated at $23. Finally, income from informal payments was nearly zero and is estimated with considerable certainty.

Conclusions and Considerations

In both surveys and focus groups, health workers may be reticent to report participation in disallowed activities candidly, so direct questioning will probably lead to inaccurate results. Sensitive survey techniques—such as item count and sum randomization techniques—have been developed to encourage candid answers even when respondents may be reluctant to answer a direct question honestly. These tools need to be carefully designed and applied, however, to generate useful information. A few design questions must be kept in mind when creating ICT surveys, in particular. These include:

- When choosing the "nonsensitive options," the fraction of the population for whom these statements are true should be neither zero nor 1. If this is not the case—if the fraction of the population for whom these statements are true is either zero or 1—no confidentiality is added by this option.
- There is a trade-off between precision of the estimates and confidentiality. To provide the most confidentiality, nonsensitive questions should be true for half of the population. However, the precision of the estimates is best

when the nonsensitive statements have a prevalence near zero or 1. In practice, some balance needs to be struck between these two goals.

- The two survey forms *must be randomly assigned within the sample.* The validity of ICT relies on the groups receiving the two forms of the same question to be, on average, identical. If they are not, then the answers to the nonsensitive questions do not "wash out." Randomizing the forms achieves this important goal.
- When using sensitive surveying techniques, research teams should pay special attention to survey length, the potential for respondent fatigue, and providing clear instructions on how to complete these more complex questions.
- It can be useful to add a "dummy" question where the omitted item is one with a known prevalence. For instance, if half of health workers are known to be female, a statement about gender could be the omitted item. This allows the researcher to check survey results after receiving data to see if respondents are following the ICT instructions.

The experience with using sensitive survey techniques in Liberia has revealed that overall, respondent error is likely to lead all of the item count and aggregated response estimates to be biased toward zero. Even so, some interesting findings are evident. There is some indication that a significant fraction of health workers participated in private practice during business hours and spent around 10 hours per month on such practice. This provides some evidence that the direct response of only 3 percent underestimates the prevalence of this activity. On the other hand, the direct responses of health workers, item count estimates, and aggregate response estimates all agree that informal payments were less common. Although the data cannot confirm whether this was the actual case or the result of a combination of respondent fatigue and reticence, all of the available evidence points in the same direction. Finally, the results for participation in selling drugs were inconsistent. Exactly zero health workers directly reported selling drugs, and the item count results gave a similar answer. However, aggregated response results indicate that income gained from selling stolen drugs could be significant.

Altogether, the application of sensitive survey tools in Liberia provides some useful though qualified evidence of income-generating activities by health workers. Limitations in data quality prevent strong answers, and indicate that the results derived from these techniques should not be the sole basis for policy decisions. However, when carefully designed and applied, and when combined with other information (including, for example, patient exit surveys) sensitive survey techniques hold the potential to obtain information on illicit income-generation activities otherwise difficult to capture.

References

Azfar, O. and P. Murrell. 2009. "Identifying Reticent Respondents: Assessing the Quality of Survey Data on Corruption and Values." *Economic Development and Cultural Change* 57 (2): 387–411.

Droitcour, J., R. Caspar, M. Hubbard, and T. Ezzati. 1991. "The Item Count Technique as a Method of Indirect Questioning: A Review of Its Development and a Case Study Application." In *Measurement Errors in Surveys*, edited by P. B. Beimer, R. M. Groves, L. E. Lyberg, N. A. Mathiowetz, and S. Sudman, 185–211. Hoboken, NJ: John Wiley & Sons.

Holbrook, A. and J. Krosnick. 2010. "Social Desirability in Voter Turnout Reports: Tests Using the Item Count Technique." *Public Opinion Quarterly* 74 (1): 37–67.

Karlan, D. and J. Zinman. 2012. "List Randomization for Sensitive Behavior: An Application for Measuring Use of Loan Proceeds." *Journal of Development Economics* 98 (1): 71–75.

Lemiere, C. and M. Juquois. 2010. "Are You Moonlighting? Using an Item Count Technique to Measure the Prevalence of Dual Job Practice in the Health Sector: A Case Study from Benin." Presentation published by Health Systems for Outcomes Program. http://www.hrhresourcecenter.org/node/4041.

Warner, S. L. 1965. "Randomized Response: A Survey Technique for Eliminating Evasive Answer Bias." *Journal of the American Statistical Association* 60: 63–69.

Environmental Benefits Statement

The World Bank Group is committed to reducing its environmental footprint. In support of this commitment, we leverage electronic publishing options and print-on-demand technology, which is located in regional hubs worldwide. Together, these initiatives enable print runs to be lowered and shipping distances decreased, resulting in reduced paper consumption, chemical use, greenhouse gas emissions, and waste.

We follow the recommended standards for paper use set by the Green Press Initiative. The majority of our books are printed on Forest Stewardship Council (FSC)–certified paper, with nearly all containing 50–100 percent recycled content. The recycled fiber in our book paper is either unbleached or bleached using totally chlorine-free (TCF), processed chlorine–free (PCF), or enhanced elemental chlorine–free (EECF) processes.

More information about the Bank's environmental philosophy can be found at http://www.worldbank.org/corporateresponsibility.

green press
INITIATIVE

www.ingramcontent.com/pod-product-compliance
Lightning Source LLC
Chambersburg PA
CBHW080415270326
41929CB00018B/3031